D0553700

THE LOVE

SIMON & SCHUSTER

OF FRIENDS

An Anthology of
Gay and Lesbian Letters
to Friends and Lovers

EDITED BY *Constance Jones*

WITH RESEARCH BY VAL CLARK

SIMON & SCHUSTER
Rockefeller Center
1230 Avenue of the Americas
New York, NY 10020

10 9 8 7 6 5 4 3 2 1

Library of Congress Cataloging-in-Publication Data

The love of friends: an anthology of gay and lesbian
    letters to friends and lovers / edited by Constance
    Jones; with research by Val Clark.
        p.   cm.
    Includes index.
    1. Gay men — Correspondence.   2. Lesbians —
Correspondence.   3. Love letters.   I. Jones,
Constance, 1961–   .
HQ76.25.A76   1997
305.9'0664 — dc21   97-2116   CIP
ISBN 0-684-81409-9

To Heather Lewis,
for rocking my world;

and

In memory of Martha Blumberg,
for saving my life

ACKNOWLEDGMENTS

Many thanks to Malaga Baldi, Marilyn Abraham and Carlo de Vito for making this project a reality and to Sarah Pinckney for seeing it through its ups and downs. Thanks also to Louise Quayle for introducing me to Val Clark and to the many librarians and archivists who produced assistance along the way. For less tangible but truly essential support my gratitude extends to Meredith Carr, Lauren Gorman, Joan Beard and Abigail Topousis. And finally, a sigh of relief goes to Jackie Kohler, just because.

Val Clark extends her sincere thanks to Gene Sirotof and the Dorset Colony House in Dorset, Vermont, as well as to the entire gracious staff of the Tabard Inn in Washington, D.C. Her thanks go as well to Ulli Stephan for her friendship, support and hospitality in Munich and Berlin; to friend and correspondent Irene Schleicher; to mentor and humanist Tony Kushner; and to Mary Ellen Russell for her boundless, extraordinary and life-affirming help and guidance.

CONTENTS

PREFACE

Virginia Woolf, one of history's great correspondents, called letter writing "the humane art, which owes its origins to the love of friends." Written in private for an audience of one, the best letters perfect that humane art, ennobling a creative act like no other. The confidential aspect of letter writing has made it an especially fertile medium for gay and lesbian relationships, which for so much of history have been banished to the hidden corners of human experience. Unfolding as they do outside the traditional bonds of marriage and family, gay and lesbian relationships — like the art of letter writing — are founded solely on the love of friends. Correspondence between gay people can thus offer a singularly engrossing, revealing, and valuable perspective on their lives and worlds.

Letters address many categories of subject matter. They may voice the friendship or passion between correspondents or deliver gossip about friends. They may include lofty discussions of literature, politics, science or art, or they may explore the spiritual or philosophical identity of the writer. Fan letters declare admiration from afar, while journal or travelogue letters send news and information. Other letters may ask for assistance, offer advice, or express sympathy. Solemn or humorous, straightforward or quirky, brief or epic, letters can take many forms.

The letters of gay and lesbian correspondents have much in common with those of heterosexual correspondents but often put a slightly different spin on things. Particularly before the mid-twentieth century, they may have been written in code or may have contained cryptic references to mysterious details that could not be made explicit for fear of compromising writer or recipient. Sometimes they deal with gay subject matter directly, addressing the fears, challenges and joys of being gay in a straight world. Or they may make no mention at all of sexuality, the concerns of the correspondents lying elsewhere.

The letters in this volume span history from Sappho to John Cheever, with about equal space given to men and women. Given the realities
of history, in which literacy and postal service were long restricted, the
correspondents are all men and women of learning, by default hailing
from the upper classes of the modern Western world. This fact, combined
with the concentration of educated gays and lesbians in the creative
disciplines, yields a fairly specialized pool of material from which to
choose. It also, unfortunately, results in an almost entirely white authorship. Yet even within these confines the quantity of available correspondence is enormous. To give the anthology focus and continuity, most
letters were selected from the literary realm, with a smattering from
other people linked to that community — visual artists, actors, intellectu-
als, and so forth.

Not surprisingly, virtually all the letter writers can be located somewhere within a single, vast web of connections. Through blood relation,
friendship, social circle or creative influence, each correspondent can be
directly or indirectly associated with at least some and sometimes most
of the others. A thrilling sense of heritage emerges, joining the many
fragments of gay literary history into a fluid, dynamic whole. To flesh
out the picture, both sides of a correspondence are included wherever
possible. This not only makes the letters easier to read, but sheds considerable light on the varied nature of gay and lesbian relationships between
friends, lovers, colleagues and relatives.

The produce of literary minds, the letters in this volume also expli-
cate the writers' lives. They reveal the influences at work in the creative
process and trace the development of authors' careers. Some exemplify
the literary style of the writer, others reveal its early form or foreshadow
its ripening. A few include samples of the author's work — extracts from
poems or stories — or creations meant for private consumption only. In
some letters, friends describe works in progress or float ideas for possible
future works. And many of the letters offer praise, criticism, support or
advice from one writer to another. This collection thus offers as much
information about the literary community as it does about the gay community.

For the most part, the letters are allowed to speak for themselves.
When possible they appear in their entirety, accompanied only by brief
introductory notes and minimal editorial commentary. Grand passions,
rarefied thinking and celebrity glamour mingle with the mundane details
of everyday life — social arrangements, illness, travel plans and the like.
The overall effect is a multidimensional picture of real people, complete
with their oddities and failings. Products of their times and breeding,
the letter writers sometimes verbalize homophobic, racist, sexist and

otherwise bigoted attitudes that seem offensive today. Again, including this kind of material magnifies the humanity of the correspondents and adds depth to their history by telling the not always pleasant truth about them.

Organized in a loosely chronological format, the letters are occasionally grouped without regard to dates. When social or professional relationships seem more significant, as with Oscar Wilde's circle or with the Bloomsbury group, time takes a backseat to community. Read in the order presented, the letters slowly give form to the writers, to those they write about and to the recipients. Many letters contain references to people mentioned in the letters of others, or to people whose own letters appear elsewhere in the book. These connections build on one another to produce vivid snapshots or complex portraits of the many individuals whose names surface in these pages.

This volume encompasses a tiny portion of the gay and lesbian correspondence currently available. In the final analysis their selection is entirely subjective, meant to provide but a glimpse into the lives of a relatively few distinguished gays and lesbians. Nevertheless, there is a great deal to be discovered and enjoyed in these pages, a wide variety of writing that will amaze, amuse, provoke and fascinate. Together or separately, these letters record a rich and remarkable slice of the gay experience.

Sappho

Recognized in her own time and down through history as one of the most brilliant lyric poets of ancient Greece, Sappho was also an avid letter writer. On the island of Lesbos she taught poetry, music and dance to the daughters of wealthy families, referring to her students as *hetairai,* that is, intimate companions or courtesans. Few of Sappho's writings survive today, but those that do clearly reflect her passion for women. The following love letter to Anactoria is one example.

Sappho to Anactoria

[Mid-Seventh Century B.C.E.]

Some say that the fairest thing upon the dark earth is a host of footsoldiers, and others again a fleet of ships, but for me it is my beloved. And it is easy to make anyone understand this.

When Helen saw the most beautiful of mortals, she chose for best that one, the destroyer of all the house of Troy, and thought not much of children or dear parent but was led astray by love to bestow her heart far off for woman is ever easy to lead astray when she thinks of no account what is near and dear.

Even so, Anactoria, you do not remember, it seems, when she is with you, one the gentle sound of whose footfall I would rather hear and the brightness of whose shining face I would rather see than all the chariots and mail-clad footmen of Lydia.

I know that in this world humans cannot have the best yet to pray for a part of what was once shared is better than to forget it.

Darius/Alexander the Great

Born in Macedonia in 356 B.C.E. and educated by Aristotle, Alexander assumed the throne of Greece before his twentieth birthday. His reign was marked by the conquest of large tracts of Europe, Asia and Africa, achieved by a military acumen still admired today. The young conqueror zealously partook of all the pleasures ancient Greece had to offer, gay and otherwise, before dying at the age of thirty-three. The following exchange with Darius III, ruler of Cyprus, whom he set out to vanquish on the battlefield, captures the audacity of the leader of the known world.

Darius to Alexander

[334 B.C.E.]

From the capital of the kings of the world: As long as the sun shines on the head of Iskander [Alexander] the robber, etc., etc., let him know that the King of Heaven has bestowed on me the dominion of the earth, and that the Almighty has granted to me the surface of the four quarters. Providence has also eminently distinguished me with glory, exaltation, majesty, and with multitudes of devoted champions and confederates.

A report has reached us that you have gathered to yourself numbers of thieves and reprobates, the multitude of whom has so elated your imagination that you propose through their co-operation to procure the crown and throne, lay waste our kingdom, and destroy our land and people.

Such crude resolves are perfectly consistent with the infatuation of the men of Room. It now behooves you, on reading the contents of this epistle, to return instantly from the place to which you have advanced. As to this criminal movement which has proceeded from you, be under no alarm from our majesty and correction, as you are not yet ranked among the number of those who merit our vengeance and punishment. Behold! I send you a coffer full of gold, and an assload of sesame, to give you by these two objects an idea of the extent of my wealth and powers. I also send you a scourge and a ball: the latter, that you may amuse yourself with a diversion suitable to your age; the former, to serve for your chastisement.

Alexander to Darius

[334 B.C.E.]

From Zu-Ul-Kurnain [Alexander], to him who pretends to be king of kings; that the very hosts of Heaven stand in awe of him; and that the inhabitants of the world are by him enlightened! How then can it be worthy of such a person to be afraid of a contemptible foe like Iskander?

Does not Dárá [Darius] know that the High and Mighty Lord gives power and dominion to whomever He wills? And also, whenever a feeble mortal regards himself as a God, and conqueror over the hosts of Heaven, beyond doubt the indignation of the Almighty brings down ruin on his kingdom?

How can the person doomed to death and corruption be a God, he from whom his kingdom is taken away and who leaves the enjoyment of the world to others?

Lo! I have resolved to meet you in battle, and therefore march towards your realms. I profess myself the weak and humble servant of God, to whom I address my prayers and look for victory and triumph, and whom I adore.

Along with the letter in which you make a display of your great power you have sent me a scourge, a ball, a coffer filled with gold, and an assload of sesame; all of which I refer to good fortune and regard as auspicious signs. The scourge portends that I shall be the instrument of your castigation and become your ruler, preceptor, and director. The ball indicates that the surface of the earth and the circumference of the globe shall be under my lieutenants. The coffer of gold, which is part of your treasure, denotes that your riches shall soon be transferred to me. And as to the sesame, although the grains are many in number, it is however soft to the touch and of all kinds of food the least noxious and disagreeable.

In return I send you a kaffis of mustard seed, that you may taste and acknowledge the bitterness of my victory. And whereas through presumption you have exalted yourself, and have become proud through the grandeur of your kingdom, and pretend to be a Divinity on earth, and have even raised to the heavens this standard *I truly am your supreme lord;* and although by the enumeration of your numbers, preparations, and might you have endeavored to alarm me; yet I confidently trust in the interposition of Divine Providence, that it will please the Almighty to make thy boasting attended by the reproach of mankind; and that in the same proportion as you have magnified yourself, He may bring on you humiliation and grant me victory over you. My trust and reliance are in the Lord. And so farewell.

Marcus Aurelius

One of ancient Rome's kinder, gentler emperors, Marcus Aurelius ruled from 161 to 180 C.E. He was also a leading Stoic philosopher and the author of *Meditations*, a discussion of the moral issues confronting ordinary people. Although married, he made no secret of his homosexuality, which early in life centered around his teacher, the famous orator Marcus Cornelius Fronto. When he was twenty-four, Marcus Aurelius wrote the following letter to the forty-year-old Fronto.

Marcus Aurelius to Fronto

[144–45]

Hail, my sweetest of masters.

We are well. I slept somewhat late owing to my slight cold, which seems now to have subsided. So from five A.M. till 9, I spent the time partly in reading some of Cato's *Agriculture,* partly in writing not quite such wretched stuff, by heavens, as yesterday. Then, after paying my respects to my father, I relieved my throat, I will not say by gargling—though the word *gargarisso* is, I believe, found in Novius and elsewhere—but by swallowing honey water as far as the gullet and ejecting it again. After easing my throat I went off to my father and attended him at a sacrifice. Then we went to luncheon. What do you think I ate? A wee bit of bread, though I saw others devouring beans, onions, and herrings full of roe. We then worked hard at grape-gathering, and had a good sweat, and were merry and, as the poet says, "still left some clusters hanging high as gleanings of the vintage." After six o'clock we came home.

I did but little work and that to no purpose. Then I had a long chat with my little mother as she sat on the bed. My talk was this: "What do you think my Fronto is now doing?" Then she: "And what do you think my Gratia is doing?" Then I: "And what do you think our little sparrow, the wee Gratia, is doing?" Whilst we were chattering in this way and disputing which of us two loved the one or other of you two the better, the gong sounded, an intimation that my father had gone to his bath. So we had supper after we had bathed in the oil-press room; I do not mean bathed in the oil-press room, but when we had bathed, had supper there, and we enjoyed hearing the yokels chaffing one another. After coming back, before I turn over and snore, I get my task done and give my dearest of masters an account of the day's doings, and if I could miss him more, I would not grudge wasting away a little more. Farewell, my Fronto, wherever you are, most honey-sweet, my love, my delight. How is it between you and me? I love you and you are away.

Leonardo da Vinci

The prototypical Renaissance man, Leonardo was a master of both science and art. The writer, painter, biologist and inventor rose to prominence in the Florence of the Medici. But at the age of thirty he fled the increasingly decadent city for Milan, ruled by Ludovico Sforza. He immediately applied for a job with the duke, detailing his qualifications in a 1482 letter.

Leonardo da Vinci to Ludovico Sforza

[1482]

Having, most illustrious lord, seen and considered the experiments of all those who pose as masters in the art of inventing instruments of war, and finding that their inventions differ in no way from those in common use, I am emboldened, without prejudice to anyone, to solicit an appointment of acquainting your Excellency with certain of my secrets.

1. I can construct bridges which are very light and strong and very portable, with which to pursue and defeat the enemy; and others more solid, which resist fire or assault, yet are easily removed and placed in position; and I can also burn and destroy those of the enemy.

2. In case of a siege I can cut off water from the trenches and make pontoons and scaling ladders and other similar contrivances.

3. If by reason of the elevation or the strength of its position a place cannot be bombarded, I can demolish every fortress if its foundations have not been set on stone.

4. I can also make a kind of cannon which is light and easy of transport, with which to hurl small stones like hail, and of which the smoke causes great terror to the enemy, so that they suffer heavy loss and confusion.

5. I can noiselessly construct to any prescribed point subterranean passages either straight or winding, passing if necessary underneath trenches or a river.

6. I can make armoured wagons carrying artillery, which shall break through the most serried ranks of the enemy, and so open a safe passage for his infantry.

7. If occasion should arise, I can construct cannon and mortars and light ordnance in shape both ornamental and useful and different from those in common use.

8. When it is impossible to use cannon I can supply in their stead catapults, mangonels, *trabocchi,* and other instruments of admirable efficiency not in general use — In short, as the occasion requires I can supply infinite means of attack and defense.

9. And if the fight should take place upon the sea I can construct many engines most suitable either for attack or defense and ships which can resist the fire of the heaviest cannon, and powders or weapons.

10. In time of peace, I believe that I can give you as complete satisfaction as anyone else in the construction of buildings both public and private, and in conducting water from one place to another.

I can further execute sculpture in marble, bronze or clay, also in painting I can do as much as anyone else, whoever he may be.

Moreover, I would undertake the commission of the bronze horse, which shall endue with immortal glory and eternal honour the auspicious memory of your father and of the illustrious house of Sforza.

And if any of the aforesaid things should seem to anyone impossible or impracticable, I offer myself as ready to make trial of them in your park or in whatever place shall please your Excellency, to whom I commend myself with all possible humility.

Michelangelo Buonarroti

Creator of some of the world's finest sculptures in stone, Michelangelo has been dubbed the founder of the Renaissance, but like other artists of his time he had perpetually to struggle for the support of patrons. At the age of fifteen he entered the court of Lorenzo de' Medici; he susbsequently moved between Bologna, Florence and Rome to accept commissions from the aristocracy and the church. In 1505 Pope Julius II summoned Michelangelo to Rome to work on the lavish tomb he wanted built for himself. Political bickering disillusioned the artist, who soon left. In 1506 the pope commanded him to return, but Michelangelo refused, unless he was guaranteed certain working conditions. He outlined his demands in a letter to one of the papal architects.

Michelangelo Buonarroti to Giuliano da San Gallo

Florence, May 2, 1506

Maestro Giuliano, Architect to the Pope

Giuliano, I learn from a letter sent by you that the Pope was angry at my departure, that he is willing to place the money at my disposal and to carry out what was agreed upon between us; also, that I am to come back and fear nothing.

As far as my departure is concerned, the truth is that on Holy Saturday I heard the Pope, speaking at table with a jeweler and the Master of the Ceremonies, say that he did not want to spend another *baiocco* on stones, whether small or large, which surprised me very much. However, before I set out I asked him for some of the money required for the continuance of my work. His Holiness replied that I was to come back again on Monday: and I went on Monday, and on Tuesday, and on Wednesday, and on Thursday—as his Holiness saw. At last, on the Friday morning, I was turned out, that is to say, I was driven away: and the person who turned me away said he knew who I was, but that such were his orders. Thereupon, having heard those words on the Saturday and seeing them afterwards put into execution, I lost all hope. But this alone was not the whole reason of my departure. There was also another cause, but I do not wish to write about it; enough that it made me think that, if I were to remain in Rome, my own tomb would be prepared before that of the Pope. This is the reason for my sudden departure.

Now you write to me on behalf of the Pope, and in similar manner you will read this letter to the Pope. Give His Holiness to understand ... that if he really wishes to have this tomb erected it would be well for him not to vex me as to where the work is to be done, provided that within the agreed period of five years it be erected in St. Peter's, on the site he shall choose, and that it be a beautiful work, as I have promised: for I am persuaded that it will be a work without equal in all the world if it be carried out.

If His Holiness wishes to proceed, let him deposit the said money here in Florence with a person whose name I will communicate to you. . . . With regard to the aforesaid money and work, I will bind myself in any way His Holiness may direct, and I will furnish whatever security here in Florence he may require. Let it be what it may, I will give him full security, even though it be the whole of Florence. There is yet one thing I have to add: it is this, that the said work could not possibly be done for the price in Rome, but it could be done here because of the many conveniences which are available, such as could not be had in Rome. . . . I beg of you to let me have an answer, and quickly. I have nothing further to add.

Your *Michelangelo*,
Sculptor, in Florence

Étienne de La Boétie

For four years in sixteenth-century France, Michel de Montaigne and Étienne de La Boétie shared an intense friendship, cut short by La Boétie's death in 1563. A politician and influential essayist, Montaigne considered his relationship with La Boétie, a jurist and writer, the most important in his life.

Some years after his friend's death, Montaigne wrote wistfully of their aborted correspondence, "Letter writing . . . is a kind of work in which my friends think I have some ability. And I would have preferred to adopt this form to publish my sallies, if I had had someone to talk to. I needed what I once had, a certain relationship to lead me on, sustain me, and raise me up. . . . I would have been more attentive and confident, with a strong friend to address, than I am now, when I consider the various tastes of the whole public. And if I am not mistaken, I would have been more successful."

For his part, La Boétie extolled the virtues of that "certain relationship" in a 1560 letter to Montaigne, excerpted here.

Étienne de La Boétie to Michel de Montaigne

[1560]

But a love little more than a year old has joined us, and yet it has left nothing undone to attain the highest point of love. Perhaps this is by chance; but it is sacrilegious to speak so, and there is no sage, however morose, who, when he knows us both, and our interests and ways, would inquire into the years our bond has lasted and would not gladly applaud so great a love. There is no reason to fear that our descendants, if only the fates permit, will begrudge placing our names among those of famous friends.

You have been bound to me, Montaigne, both by the power of nature and by virtue, which is the sweet allurement of love.... No power is more effective in bringing men together and kindling in them a beautiful love.

Francis Bacon

An eminent philosopher and essayist, Sir Francis Bacon was also an ambitious political schemer devoted to his own pleasure and advancement. He was a close advisor of Queen Elizabeth, amply paid for doing her dirty work, and a high official under James I, but he lived far beyond his means and accumulated large debts. Charged in 1611 with accepting bribes, Bacon was confined to the Tower of London. There he put his monumental skills as a writer to work, composing a letter that appealed to the king for lenience. Whether James I received the letter is unknown, but Bacon was released after four days.

Sir Francis Bacon to King James I

[1611]

May it please your most excellent Majesty,

In the midst of my misery, which is rather assuaged by remembrance than by hope, my chiefest worldly comfort is to think, That . . . I was evermore so happy as to have my poor services graciously accepted by your Majesty. . . . For as I have often said to your Majesty, I was towards you but as a bucket, and a cistern; to draw forth and conserve; whereas yourself was the fountain. Unto this Comfort of nineteen years' prosperity, there succeeded a comfort even in my greatest adversity, somewhat of the same nature; which is, That in those offences wherewith I was charged, there was not any one that had special relation to your Majesty. . . . I have an assured belief that there is in your Majesty's own princely thoughts a great deal of serenity and clearness towards me your Majesty's now prostrate and cast down servant. . . .

And indeed, if it may please your Majesty, this theme of my misery is so plentiful, as it need not be coupled with any thing else. I have been somebody by your Majesty's singular and undeserved favour; even the prime officer of your kingdom. Your Majesty's arm hath been over mine in council, when you presided at the table; so near I was: I have borne your Majesty's image in metal; much more in heart; I was never in nineteen years' service chidden by your Majesty. . . . But why should I speak of these things which are now vanished? but only the better to express my downfall.

For now it is thus with me: I am a year and a half old in misery: though I must ever acknowledge your Majesty's grace and mercy, for I do not think it possible, that any one that you once loved should be totally miserable. Mine own means, through mine own improvidence, are poor and weak, little better than my father left me. . . .

. . . I have (most gracious Sovereign) faith enough for a miracle, and much more for a grace, that your Majesty will not suffer your poor creature to be utterly defaced, nor blot the name quite out of your book, upon which your sacred hand hath been so oft for new ornaments and additions.

Unto this degree of compassion, I hope God above (of whose mercies towards me, both in my prosperity and my adversity, I have had great testimonies and pledges, though mine own manifold and wretched unthankfulness might have averted them) will dispose your princely heart, already prepared to all piety. . . . I most humbly beseech your

Majesty to give me leave to conclude with those words which Necessity speaketh: Help me (dear sovereign lord and master) and pity me so far, as I that have borne a bag be not now in my age forced in effect to bear a wallet; nor I that desire to live to study, may not study to live. . . . God of heaven ever bless, preserve, and prosper your Majesty.

Your Majesty's poor ancient servant and beadsman,

Fr. St. Alban

Queen Christina

Ascending the Swedish throne at the age of eighteen, Queen Christina drained the royal coffers with extravagant living, refused to marry and rejected the traditional Lutheranism of her country. She abdicated at twenty-seven, declaring her intention to convert to Roman Catholicism. Dressed in male attire and calling herself Count Dohna, she headed south to France, where she scandalized the men but made a hit among the ladies. Christina settled in Rome and became a patron of the arts, stirring up the local scene with her brash and imperious behavior until she died at sixty-two. In a letter to Pierre Chanut, the French ambassador to Sweden, she explained her decision to abdicate.

Queen Christina to Pierre Chanut

Westeras, February 28, 1654

I have told you before the reasons which have obliged me to persist in my design of abdicating. You know that this fancy has lasted long with me, and it is only after having pondered on it for eight years that I have determined to carry it out. It is at least five since I informed you of my purpose, and I then saw that it was only your sincere regard and the interest you took in my fortunes that compelled you to oppose me, in spite of the reasons you could not condemn, however keenly you set yourself to dissuade me. It pleased me to see that you found nothing in the thought that was unworthy of me. You know what I told you on this matter, the last time I had the satisfaction of conversing with you about it. In so long a course of time nothing has happened to alter me.

I have determined all my actions with reference to this end, and have brought them to this final point, without hesitating now that I am ready to finish my part, and go behind the curtain. I care not as to the *Plaudite*. I know that the scenes I have played in could not have been composed according to the ordinary dramatic laws. With difficulty will any strong, masculine, or vigorous touches therein please. I leave it to every man to judge it according to his lights: I can deprive no one of his liberty herein, nor would I even if I could.

I know that there are few who will pass a favorable criticism on it, and I am convinced that you will be of those few. The rest are ignorant of my reasons and my humor, since I have never declared myself to anyone except you, and one other friend, whose soul is great and elevated enough to judge it as you do. *Sufficit unus, sufficit nullus*. I despise the rest, and should do honor to any one of the herd whom I should find ridiculous enough to amuse myself with.

Those who consider this action in the light of common everyday maxims will doubtless condemn it, but I will never take the trouble to make my apology to them. And in the fullness of the leisure which I am preparing for myself, I shall never be idle enough to remember them. I shall pass it in examining my past life and correcting my errors without either astonishment or repentance. What pleasure shall I not find in recollecting that I have joyfully done good to humanity, and punished those that deserved punishment. I shall find consolation in never having made any person guilty who was not so already, and even in having spared those who were.

I have placed the welfare of the State above all other considerations, I have sacrificed all cheerfully to its interests, and have nothing to reproach myself with in its administration. I have possessed without pride, and resign without difficulty. After all this, do not fear for me. I am in safety, and my good is not in Fortune's power: I am happy, whatever occurs:

> *Sum tamen, O superi, felix: nullique potestas*
> *Hoc auferre Deo.*

Aye, I am so, more than anyone, and will always be: I have no fear of that Providence of which you speak to me. *Omnia sunt propitia*. Let Providence take it upon itself to settle my fortunes, and I will submit with that respect and resignation which I owe to its decrees: let it leave the direction of my conduct to myself, and I will employ any such faculties as have been granted to me in making myself happy. And I shall be so as long as I am persuaded that I have nothing to fear from God or man. I shall employ all the rest of my life in familiarizing myself with these thoughts, in fortifying my soul, and observing from the haven the troubles of those who are tossed about in life by the storms that one suffers therein, for want of having applied their minds to these meditations.

Am I not to be envied in my present condition? Beyond doubt I should find many enviers if my happiness were known. You love me, however, well enough not to envy me, and I deserve it, since I am honest enough to admit that I have got some of these sentiments from you; I learned them in conversations with you, and I hope to cultivate them some day with you during my leisure. I am certain that you cannot break your word, and will not cease in these altered circumstances to remain my friend, since I am abandoning nothing that is worthy of your regard. I will, in whatever condition I may be found, preserve my friendship for you; and you will see that no changes will ever be able to alter the views in which I glory.

You know all this, and you are doubtless of opinion that the best pledge I can give you of myself is to tell you that I will always be

Christina

Richard West/Thomas Gray/Thomas Ashton

The eighteenth-century English historian and poet Thomas Gray attracted a circle of educated, literary and queer friends, who exchanged letters with him and with each other. An immensely learned man with a command of numerous languages and disciplines from painting to botany to metaphysics, Gray composed letters of lyrical grace and dry humor. From 1739 to 1741 he made the grand tour of Europe with Horace Walpole, documenting the trip in missives to Dr. Thomas Wharton and a friend named Thomas Ashton. In turn, Richard West sent Gray news from home and also maintained a comically intimate correspondence with Ashton. Gray would later write one of his more distinguished poems, "Sonnet on the Death of Mr. Richard West," in his honor. After Gray returned to England he corresponded with John Chute, a noted man of letters who lived in Florence with the diplomat Horace Mann. All the correspondence is peppered with references to classical poetry and mythology.

Thomas Gray to Thomas Ashton

*Paris — Hotel de
Luxembourg, Rue
des petits Augustins
April 21, N. S.* [1739]

Dear Ashton,

You and West have made us happy to night in a heap of letters, & we are resolvd to repay you twofold: Our English perhaps may not be the best in the World, but we have the Comfort to know that it is at least as good as our French. So to begin. Paris is a huge round City, divided by the Seine, a very near relation (if we may judge by the resemblance) of your old acquaintance, that ancient river, the river Cam. along it on either side runs a key of perhaps as handsome buildings, as any in the World. the view down which on either hand from the Pont Neuf is the charming'st sight imaginable. There are infinite Swarms of inhabitants and more Coaches than Men. The Women in general dressd in Sacs, flat Hoops of 5 yards wide nosegays of artificial flowers on one shoulder, and faces dyed in Scarlet up to the Eyes. The Men in bags, roll-upps, Muffs & Solitaires. Our Mornings have been mostly taken up in Seeing Sights: few Hotels or Churches have escaped us, where there is anything remarkable as to building, Pictures or Statues.

Mr Conway is as usual, the Companion of our travels, who, till we came, had not seen anything at all; for it is not the fashion here to have Curiosity. We had at first arrival an inundation of Visits pouring in upon us, for all the English are acquainted, and herd much together & it is no easy Matter to disengage oneself from them, so that one sees but little of the French themselves. To be introduced to the People of high quality, it is absolutely necessary to be Master of the Language, for it is not to be imagined that they will take pains to understand anybody, or to correct a stranger's blunders. Another thing is, there is not a House where they do'nt play, nor is any one at all acceptable, unless they do so too, a professed Gamester being the most advantageous character a Man can have at Paris. The Abbés indeed & men of learning are a People of easy access enough, but few English that travel have knowledge enough to take any great pleasure in this Company, at least our present lot of travellers have not. We are, I think to remain here no longer than Ld Conway stays, & then set out for Rheims, there to reside a Month or two, & then to return hither again & very often little hankerings break out, so that I am not sure, we shall not come back to-morrow.

We are exceedingly unsettled & irresolute, do'nt know our own Minds for two Moments together, profess an utter aversion for all manner of fatigue, grumble, are ill-natured & try to bring ourselves to a State of perfect Apathy in which [we] are so far advanced, as to declare we have no notion of caring for any mortal breathing but ourselves. In short I think the greatest *evil* could have happen'd to us, is our liberty, for we are not at all capable to determine our own actions.

My dear Ashton, I am ever

Yours sincerely
T: G:

Thomas Ashton to Richard West

London. Aug. 25. 1739.

Friend,

The kind Message thou didst leave with my servant John raised my Appetite of seeing thee to a very great Pitch, in so much that my bowells did yearn, yea verily I did hunger & thirst for thy Company many days. I would have devoured thy Sayings, & would have hung upon thy Mouth, as an infant hangs on the Nipple of the breast. I would have suckd in thy words, as the warm new Milk, but thou hast defrauded my Soul, & withdrawn thyself unkindly from me.

The exhortation I gave thee was good, tho' clothd in the language of the Profane. Feel thy Soul with such food, and truly thou wilt be fat & well liking.

Our friend Whitfield is too hard for Edmund Gibson. Perhaps thou hast seen his Answer it is wrote in the meek Spirit of Satyr, in all the humility of religious Sneer. I doubt the Spirit of Truth had no hand in the Controversy.

Our friends on the other side of the Water salute thee, but they complain as much of the want of thy letters as I do of the want of thyself.

Fare thee well.

Richard West to Thomas Gray

Temple, Sep. 28. 1739.

If wishes could turn to realities, I would fling-down my law books, and
sup with you to-night: But, alas! here I am doomed to fix, while you are
fluttering from city to city, and enjoying all the pleasures which a gay
climate can afford. It is out of the power of my heart to envy your good
fortune, yet I cannot help indulging a few natural desires; as for example,
to take a walk with you on the banks of the Rhône, and to be climbing
up mount Fourviere:

> *Iam mens praetrepidans avet vagari:*
> *Iam laeti studio pedes vigescunt.*

However, so long as I am not deprived of your correspondence, so long
shall I always find some pleasure in being at home. And, setting all vain
curiosity aside, when the fit is over, and my reason begins to come to herself, I have several other powerful motives which might easily cure me of
my restless inclinations. Amongst these, my mother's ill state of health is
not the least, which was the reason of our going to Tunbridge; so that you
cannot expect much description or amusement from thence. Nor indeed is
there much room for either; for all diversions there may be reduced to two
articles, gaming and going to church. They were pleased to publish certain
Tunbrigiana this season; but such ana! I believe there were never so many
vile little verses put together before. So much for Tunbridge. London af-
fords me as little to say. What! So huge a town as London? Yes, consider
only how I live in that town. I never go into the gay or high world, and
consequently receive nothing from thence to brighten my imagination. The
busy world I leave to the busy; and am resolved never to talk politics till I
can act at the same time. To tell old stories, or prate of old books, seems a
little musty; and toujours chapon bouilli, won't do. However, for want of
better fare, take another little mouthful of my poetry.

> *O meæ jucunda comes quietis!*
> *Quæ fere ægrotum solita es levare*
> *Pectus, et sensim, ah! nimis ingruentes*
>   *Fallere curas:*

> *Quid canes? quanto Lyra dic furore*
> *Gesties quando hac reducem sodalem*
> *Glauciam gaudere simul videbis*
>   *Meque sub umbra?*

Thomas Gray to Thomas Wharton

[March 1740]

Proposals for printing by Subscription, in

THIS LARGE
LETTER

The Travels of T:G:GENT: which will consist of the following Particulars.

CHAP:1:

The author arrives at Dover; his conversation with the Mayor of that Corporation; sets out in the Pacquet-Boat, grows very sick; the Author spews, a very minute account of all the circumstances thereof: his arrival at Calais; how the inhabitants of that country speak French, & are said to be all Papishes; the author's reflexions thereupon.

2

How they feed him with Soupe, & what Soupe is. how he meets with a Capucin; & what a Capucin is. how they shut him up in a Post-Chaise, & send him to Paris; he goes wondring along dureing 6 days; & how there are Trees, & Houses just as in England. arrives at Paris without knowing it.

3

Full account of the river Seine, & of the various animals & plants its borders produce. Description of the little Creature called an Abbé, its parts, & their uses; with the reasons, why they will not live in England, & the methods, that have been used to propagate them there. a Cut of the Inside of a Nunnery; it's Structure, wonderfully adapted to the use of the animals, that inhabit it: a short account of them, how they propagate without the help of a Male, & how they eat up their own young ones, like Cats, and Rabbets. supposed to have both Sexes in themselves, like a Snail. Dissection of a Dutchess with Copper-Plates, very curious.

4

Goes to the Opera; grand Orchestra of Humstrums, Bagpipes, Saltboxes, Taburs, & Pipes. Anatomy of a French Ear, shewing the formation of it to be entirely different from that of an English one, & that Sounds have a directly contrary effect upon one & the other. Farinelli at Paris said to have a fine manner, but no voice. Grand Ballet, in which there is no seeing the dance for Petticoats. Old Women with flowers, & jewels stuck in the Curls of their grey hair; Red-heel'd Shoes & Roll-ups innumerable, Hoops, & Paniers immeasurable, Paint unspeakable. Tables, wherein is calculated with the utmost exactness, the several Degrees of Red, now in use, from the riseing blush of an Advocate's Wife to the flameing Crimson of a Princess of the blood; done by a Limner in great Vogue.

5

The Author takes unto him a Taylour. his Character. how he covers him with Silk, & Fringe, & widens his figure with buckram a yard on each side; Wastcoat, & Breeches so strait, he can neither breath, nor walk. how the Barber curls him en Bequille, & a la negligee, & ties a vast Solitaire about his Neck; how the Milliner lengthens his ruffles to his finger's ends, & sticks his two arms into a Muff. how he cannot stir, & How they cut him in proportion to his Clothes.

6

He is carried to Versailles; despised it infinitely. a dissertation upon Taste. goes to an Installation in the Chappel-royal. enter the King, & 50 Fiddlers Solus. Kettle-Drums, & Trumpets, Queens, & Dauphins, Princesses, & Cardinals, Incense, & the Mass. Old Knights, makeing Curtsies; Holy-Ghosts, & Fiery-tongues.

7

Goes into the Country to Rheims in Champagne, stays there 3 Months, what he did there (he must beg the reader's pardon, but) he has really forgot.

8

Proceeds to Lyons. Vastness of the City. Can't see the Streets for houses. how rich it is, & how much it stinks. Poem upon the Confluence of the Rhone, & the Saome, by a friend of the Author's; very pretty!

9

Makes a journey into Savoy, & in his way visits the Grande Chartreuse; he is set astride upon a Mule's back, & begins to climb up the Mountain. Rocks & Torrents beneath; Pinetrees, & Snows above; horrours, & terrours on all sides. the Author dies of the Fright.

10

He goes to Geneva. his mortal antipathy to a Presbyterian, & the cure for it. returns to Lyons, gets a surfeit with eating Ortolans, & Lampreys; is advised to go into Italy for the benefit of the air. . . .

11

Sets out the latter end of November to cross the Alps. he is devoured by a Wolf, & how it is to be devoured by a Wolf. the 7th day he comes to the foot of Mount Cenis. how he is wrap'd up in Bear Skins, & Bever-Skins, Boots on his legs, Caps on his head, Muffs on his hands, & Taffety over his eyes; he is placed on a Bier, & is carried to heaven by the savages blindfold. how he lights among a certain fat nation, call'd Clouds; how they are always in a Sweat, & never speak, but they fart. how they flock about him, & think him very odd for not doing so too. he falls flump into Italy.

12

Arrives at Turin; goes to Genoa, & from thence to Placentia; crosses the River Trebia: the Ghost of Hannibal appears to him; & what it, & he, say upon the occasion. locked out of Parma in a cold winter's night: the author by an ingenious stratagem gains admittance. despised that City, & proceeds thro' Reggio to Modena. how the Duke & Dutchess lye over their own Stables, & go every night to a vile Italian Comedy. despised the, & it; & proceeds to Bologna.

13

Enters into the Dominions of the Pope o' Rome. meets the Devil, & what he says on the occasion. very publick, & scandalous doings between the Vines & the Elm-trees, & how the Olive-trees are shock'd thereupon. Author longs for Bologna-Sausages, & Hams; & how he grows as fat as a Hog.

14

Observations on Antiquities. the Author proves, that Bologna was the ancient Tarantum; that the Battle of Salamis, contrary to the vulgar opinion, was fought by Land, & that not far from Ravenna, that the Romans were a Colony of the Jews, & that Eneas was the same with Ehud.

15

Arrival at Florence. is of opinion, that the Venus of Medicis is a modern performance, & that a very indifferent one, & much inferiour to the K: Charles at Chareing-Cross. Account of the City, & Manners of the Inhabitants. a learned Dissertation on the true Situation of Gomorrah. . . .

And here will end the first part of these instructive & entertaining Voyages. the Subscribers are to pay 20 Guineas; 10 down, & the remainder upon delivery of the book. N:B: A few are printed on the softest Royal Brown Paper for the use of the Curious. . . .

My Dear, dear Wharton

(Which is a dear more than I give any body else. it is very odd to begin with a Parenthesis, but) You may think me a Beast, for not haveing sooner wrote to you, & to be sure a Beast I am. now when one owns it, I don't see what you have left to say. I take this opportunity to inform you (an opportunity I have had every week this twelvemonth) that I am arrived safe at Calais, & am at present at Florence, a city in Italy in I don't know how many degrees N: latitude. under the Line I am sure it is not, for I am at this instant expireing with Cold. You must know, that not being certain what circumstances of my History would particularly suit your curiosity, & knowing that all I had to say to you would overflow the narrow limits of many a good quire of Paper, I have taken this method of laying before you the contents, that you may pitch upon what you please, & give me your orders accordingly to expatiate thereupon: for I conclude you will write to me; won't you? oh! yes, when you know, that in a week I set out for Rome, & that the Pope is dead, & that I shall be (I should say, God willing; & if nothing extraordinary intervene; & if I'm alive, & well; & in all human probability) at the Coronation of a new one. now as you have no other correspondent there, & as if you do not, I certainly shall not write again (observe my impudence) I take it to be your interest to send me a vast letter, full of all sorts of News, & Bawdy, & Politics, & such other ingredients, as to you shall seem convenient with all decent expedition. only do not be too severe upon the Pretender; &, if you like my Style, pray say so. this is a la Francoise; & if you think it a little too foolish, & impertinent; you shall be treated alla Toscana with a thousand Signoria Illustrissima's. in the mean time I have the honour to remain

> Your loving Frind tell Deth. *T: Gray*
> Florence. March 12. N:S:

P:S: This is a l'Angloise. I don't know where you are; if at Cambridge, pray let me know all how, & about it; and if my old friends Thompson, or Clark fall in your way, say I am extremely theirs. but if you are in town, I entreat you to make my best Compliments to Mrs. Wharton. Adieu, Yours Sincerely a second time.

Richard West to Thomas Gray

Bond-street, June 5, 1740

I lived at the Temple till I was sick of it: I have just left it, and find myself as much a lawyer as I was when I was in it. It is certain, at least, I may study the law here as well as I could there. My being in chambers did not signify to me a pinch of snuff. They tell me my father was a lawyer, and, as you know, eminent in the profession; and such a circumstance must be of advantage to me. My uncle too makes some figure in West-minster-hall; and there's another advantage: then my grandfather's name would get me many friends. Is it not strange that a young fellow, that might enter the world with so many advantages, will not know his own interest? &c. &c. What shall I say in answer to all this? For money, I neither dote upon it nor despise it; it is a necessary stuff enough. For ambition, I do not want that neither; but it is not to sit upon a bench. In short, is it not a disagreeable thing to force one's inclination, especially when one's young? not to mention that one ought to have the strength of a Hercules to go through our common law; which I am afraid, I have not. Well! but then, say they, if one profession does not suit you, you may choose another more to your inclination. Now I protest I do not yet know my own inclination, and I believe, if that was to be my direction, I should never fix at all. There is no going by a weathercock. I could say much more upon this subject; but there is no talking tête-à-tête cross the Alps. Oh the folly of young men, that never know their own interest! they never grow wise till they are ruined! and then nobody pities them, nor helps them. Dear Gray! consider me in the condition of one that has lived these two years without any person that he can speak freely to. I know it is very seldom that people trouble themselves with the senti-ments of those they converse with; so that they can chat about trifles, they never care whether your heart aches or no. Are you one of these? I think not. But what right have I to ask you this question? Have we known one another enough, that I should expect or demand sincerity from you? Yes, Gray, I hope we have; and I have not quite such a mean opinion of myself, as to think I do not deserve it. But, signor, is it not time for me to ask something about your future intentions abroad? Where do you propose going next? an in Apuliam? nam illo si adveneris, tanquam Ulysses, cognosces tuorum neminem. Vale. So Cicero prophesies in the end of one of his letters — and there I end.

Yours &c.

Thomas Gray to John Chute

Cambridge, Sunday [October ? 1746]

Lustrissimo

It is doubtless highly reasonable that two young foreigners come into so distant a country to acquaint themselves with strange things, should have some time allowed them to take a view of the King (God bless him) and the ministry & the theatres, and Westminster Abbey and the Lyons and such other curiosities of the capital city. You civilly call them dissipations, but to me they appear employments of a very serious nature, as they enlarge the mind, give a just insight into the nature & genius of a people, keep the Spirits in an agreeable agitation, and (like the true artificial spirit of lavender) amazingly fortify and corroborate the whole nervous system: but as all things sooner or later must pass away, and there is a certain period when by the rules of proportion one is to grow weary of everything, I may hope at length a season will arrive when you will be tired of forgetting me. 'Tis true you have a long journey to make first, a vast series of sights to pass through — let me see, you are at Lady Brown's already; I have set a time when I may say 'Oh he is now got to the waxwork in Fleet Street; there is nothing more but Cupids Paradise and the Hermaphrodite from Guinea & the original Basilisk dragon & the buffalo from Babylon & the new Chimpanzee & then I. have a care, you had best, that I come in my Turn; you know in whose Hands I have deposited my little Interests. I shall infallibly appeal to my *best invisible* Friend in the country.

I am glad Castalio has justified himself & me to You. he seem'd to me more made for Tenderness than Horrour & (I have courage again to insist upon it) might make a better Player than any now on the Stage. I have not alone received (thank you) but almost got thro' Louis Onze. 'tis very well, methinks, but nothing particular. what occasioned his expurgation at Paris, I imagine, were certain Strokes in Defence of the Gallican Church & its Liberties — a little contempt cast upon the Popes, and something here & there on the Conduct of great Princes. there are a few Instances of Malice against our Nation, that are very foolish.

My Companion, whom you salute is (much to my sorrow) only so now and then. He lives 20 miles off at Nurse, and is not so meagre as when you first knew him, but of a reasonable Plumposity. He shall not fail being here to do the Honours, when you make your publick Entry. Heigh ho! when will that be, chi sa? but mi lusigna il dolce sogno! I love Mr Whithed and wish him all Happiness. Farewell, my dear Sir

I am, ever yours,

T. G.

Commend me kindly to Mr Walpole.

Horace Walpole

Noted as one of the greatest letter writers of all time, Horace Walpole, earl of Orford, intended his correspondence to serve as a historical document for generations to come. He carefully recorded his impressions of the people, places, events and ideas he encountered, sending letters to his many friends, including the politicians George Montagu and Horace Mann. Walpole's missives provide a contemporary's uniquely valuable outlook on eighteenth-century English society, on the American Revolution (then taking place) and on the famous writer and critic Samuel Johnson.

Horace Walpole to George Montagu

Houghton, March 25, 1761.

Here I am at Houghton! and alone! in this spot, where (except two hours last month) I have not been in sixteen years! Think, what a crowd of reflections! No, Gray, and forty church-yards, could not furnish so many; nay, I know one must feel them with greater indifference than I possess, to have patience to put them into verse. Here I am, probably for the last time of my life, though not for the last time: every clock that strikes tells me I am an hour nearer to yonder church — that church, into which I have not yet had courage to enter, where lies that mother on whom I doated, and who doated on me! There are the two rival mistresses of Houghton, neither of whom ever wished to enjoy it! There, too, lies he, who founded its greatness, to contribute to whose fall Europe was embroiled; there he sleeps in quiet and dignity, while his friend and his foe, rather his false ally and real enemy, Newcastle and Bath, are exhausting the dregs of their pitiful lives in squabbles and pamphlets.

The surprise the pictures gave me is again renewed; accustomed for many years to see nothing but wretched daubs and varnished copies at auctions, I look at these as enchantment. My own description of them seems poor; but shall I tell you truly, the majesty of Italian ideas almost sinks before the warm nature of Flemish colouring. Alas! don't I grow old? My young imagination was fired with Guido's ideas; must they be plump and prominent as Abishag to warm me now? Doth great youth feel with poetic limbs, as well as see with poetic eyes? In one respect, I am very young, I cannot satiate myself with looking: an incident contributed to make me feel this more strongly. A party arrived, just as I did, to see the house, a man and three women in riding dresses, and they rode post through the apartments, I could not hurry before them fast enough; they were not so long in seeing for the first time, as I could have been in one room, to examine what I knew by heart. I remember formerly being often diverted with this kind of *seers;* they come, ask what such a room is called, in which sir Robert lay, write it down, admire a lobster or a cabbage in a marketpiece, dispute whether the last room was green or purple, and then hurry to the inn for fear the fish should be over-dressed. How different my sensations! not a picture here but recalls a history; not one, but I remember in Downing-street or Chelsea, where queens and crowds admired them, though seeing them as little as these travellers!

When I had drank tea, I strolled into the garden; they told me it was now called the *pleasure-ground*. What a dissonant idea of pleasure! those groves, those *allées,* where I have passed so many charming moments are now stripped up or overgrown — many fond paths I could not unravel, though with a very exact clew in my memory: I met two gamekeepers, and a thousand hares! In the days when all my soul was tuned to pleasure and vivacity (and you will think, perhaps, it is far from being out of tune yet), I hated Houghton and its solitude; yet I loved this garden, as now, with many regrets, I love Houghton; Houghton, I know not what to call it, a monument of grandeur or ruin! How I have wished this evening for lord Bute! how I could preach to him! For myself, I do not want to be preached to; I have long considered how every Balbec must wait for the chance of a Mr. Wood. The servants wanted to lay me in the great apartment — what, to make me pass my night as I have done my evening. It were like proposing to Margaret Roper to be a duchess in the court that cut off her father's head, and imagining it would please her. I have chosen to sit in my father's little dressing-room, and am now by his scrutoire, where, in the height of his fortune, he used to receive the accounts of his farmers and deceive himself, or us, with the thoughts of his economy. How wise a man at once, and how weak! For what has he built Houghton? for his grandson to annihilate, or for his son to mourn over. If lord Burleigh could rise and view his representative driving the Hatfield stage, he would feel as I feel now. Poor little Strawberry! at least it will not be stripped to pieces by a descendant! You will find all these fine meditations dictated by pride, not by philosophy. Pray consider through how many mediums philosophy must pass, before it is purified —

"how often must it weep, how often burn!"

My mind was extremely prepared for all this gloom by parting with Mr. Conway yesterday morning; moral reflections or common-places are the livery one likes to wear, when one has just had a real misfortune. He is going to Germany: I was glad to dress myself up in transitory Houghton, in lieu of very sensible concern. To-morrow I shall be distracted with thoughts, at least images, of very different complexion. I go to Lynn, and am to be elected on Friday. I shall return hither on Saturday, again alone, to expect Burleighides on Sunday, whom I left at Newmarket. I must once in my life see him on his grandfather's throne.

Epping, Monday night, thirty first. — No, I have not seen him; he loitered on the road, and I was kept at Lynn till yesterday morning. It is plain I never knew for how many trades I was formed, when at this time of day I can begin electioneering, and succeed in my new vocation. Think of me, the subject of a mob, who was scarce ever before in a mob, addressing them in the town-hall, riding at the head of two thousand people through such a town as Lynn, dining with above two hundred of them amid bumpers, huzzas, songs, and tobacco, and finishing with country dancing at a ball and sixpenny whisk! I have borne it all cheerfully; nay, have sat hours in *conversation,* the thing upon earth that I hate; have been to hear misses play on the harpsichord, and to see an alderman's copies of Rubens and Carlo Marat. Yet to do the folks justice, they are sensible, and reasonable, and civilized; their very language is polished since I lived among them. I attribute this to their more frequent intercourse with the world and the capital, by the help of good roads and post-chaises, which, if they have abridged the king's dominions, have at least tamed his subjects. Well, how comfortable it will be tomorrow, to see my parroquet, to play at loo, and not be obliged to talk seriously! The Heraclitus of the beginning of this letter will be overjoyed on finishing it to sign himself your old friend,

Democritus.

P.S. — I forgot to tell you that my ancient aunt Hammond came over to Lynn to se me; not from any affection, but curiosity. The first thing she said to me, though we have not met these sixteen years, was, "Child, you have done a thing to-day that your father never did in all his life; you sat as they carried you, he always stood the whole time." "Madam" said I, "when I am placed in a chair, I conclude I am to sit in it; besides, as I cannot imitate my father in great things, I am not at all ambitious of mimicking him in little ones." I am sure she proposes to tell her remarks to my uncle Horace's ghost the instant they meet.

Horace Walpole to George Montagu

Arlington-street, Nov. 20, 1763.

You are in the wrong; believe me you are in the wrong to stay in the country; London never was so entertaining since it had a steeple or a madhouse. Cowards fight duels; secretaries of state turn methodists on the Tuseday, and are expelled the play-house for blasphemy on Friday. I am not turned methodist, but patriot, and what is more extraordinary, am not going to have a place. What is more wonderful still, lord Hardwicke has made two of his sons resign their employments. I know my letter sounds as enigmatic as Merlin's almanack: but *my* events have really happened. I had almost persuaded myself like you to quit the world; thank my stars I did not. Why I have done nothing but laugh since last Sunday; though on Tuesday I was one of a hundred and eleven, who were outvoted by three hundred; no laughing matter generally to a *true* patriot, whether he thinks his country undone or himself. Nay, I am still more absurd; even for my dear country's sake I cannot bring myself to connect with lord Hardwicke, or the duke of Newcastle, though they are in the minority — an unprecedented case, not to love everybody one despises, when they are of the same side. On the contrary, I fear I resemble a fond woman, and dote on the *dear betrayer.* In short, and to write something that you can understand, you know I have long had a partiality for your cousin Sandwich, who has out-Sandwiched himself. He has impeached Wilkes for a blasphemous poem, and has been expelled for blasphemy himself by the beefsteak club at Covent-garden. Wilkes has been shot by Martin, and instead of being burnt at an *auto da fé,* as the bishop of Gloucester intended, is reverenced as a saint by the mob, and, if he dies, I suppose, the people will squint themselves into convulsions at his tomb, in honour of his memory. Now is not this better than feeding one's birds and one's bantams, poring one's eyes out over old histories, not half so extraordinary as the present, or ambling to squire Bencow's on one's padnag, and playing at cribbage with one's brother John and one's parson? Prithee come to town, and let us put off taking the veil for another year: besides, by this time twelvemonth we are sure the world will be a year older in wickedness, and we shall have more matter for meditation. One would not leave it methinks till it comes to the worst, and that time cannot be many months off. In the meantime, I have bespoken a dagger, in case the circumstance should grow so classic as to make it becoming to kill oneself; however, though disposed to quit the world, as I have no mind to leave it entirely, I shall put off my death to the last minute, and do nothing rashly, till I see Mr. Pitt and lord Temple place themselves in their curule chairs in St. James's-market, and resign their throats to the victors. I am determined to see them dead first, lest they should play me a trick, and be hobbling to Buckingham-house, while I am shivering and waiting for them on the banks of Lethe. Adieu!

Yours, *Horatius.*

Horace Walpole to Reverend William Cole

Arlington Street, April 27, 1773.

I had not time this morning to answer your letter by Mr Essex, but I gave him the card you desired. You know, I hope, how happy I am to obey any orders of yours.

In the paper I showed you in answer to Masters, you saw I was apprised of Rastel's *Chronicle,* but pray do not mention my knowing of it, because I draw so much from it, that I lie in wait, hoping that Milles or Masters or some of their fools will produce it against me, and then I shall have another word to say to them which they do not expect, since they think Rastel makes for them.

Mr. Gough wants to be introduced to me! Indeed! I would see him, as he has been mid-wife to Masters; but he is so dull that he would only be troublesome — and besides, you know I shun authors, and would never have been one myself, if it obliged me to keep such bad company. They are always in earnest, and think their profession serious, and will dwell upon trifles, and reverence learning. I laugh at all these things, and write only to laugh at them and divert myself. None of us are authors of any consequence, and it is the most ridiculous of all vanities to be vain of being *mediocre.* A page in a great author humbles me to the dust, and the conversation of those that are not superior to myself reminds me of what will be thought of myself. I blush to flatter them; or to be flattered by them; and should dread letters being published some time or other, in which they would relate our interviews, and we should appear like those puny conceited witlings in Shenstone's and Hughes's correspondence, who give themselves airs from being in possession of the soil of Parnassus for the time being; as peers are proud because they enjoy the estates of great men who went before them. Mr. Gough is very welcome to see Strawberry-hill, or I would help him to any scraps in my possession that would assist his publications, though he is one of those industrious who are only re-burying the dead — but I cannot be acquainted with him; it is contrary to my system and my humour; and besides I know nothing of barrows and Danish entrenchments, and Saxon barbarisms and Phœnician characters — in short, I know nothing of those ages that knew nothing — then how should I be of use to modern literati? All the Scotch metaphysicians have sent me their works. I did not read one of them, because I do not understand what is not understood by those that write about it; and I did not get acquainted with one of the writers. I should like to be intimate with Mr. Anstey, even though he wrote *Lord Buckhorse,* or with the author of the *Heroic Epistle* — I have no thirst to know the rest of my contemporaries, from the absurd bombast of Dr. Johnson down to the silly Dr. Goldsmith, though the latter changeling has had bright gleams of parts, and the former had sense, till he changed it for words, and sold it for a pension. Don't think me scornful. Recollect that I have seen Pope, and lived with Gray. Adieu!

Horace Walpole to Horace Mann

Strawberry Hill, April 3, 1777

I have nothing very new to tell you on public affairs, especially as I can know nothing more than you see in the papers. It is my opinion that the King's affairs are in a very bad position in America. I do not say that his armies may not gain advantages again; though I believe there has been as much design as cowardice in the behaviour of the provincials, who seem to have been apprised that protraction of the war would be more certainly advantageous to them than heroism. Washington, the dictator, has shown himself both a Fabius and a Camillus. His march through our lines is allowed to have been a prodigy of generalship. In one word, I look upon a great part of America as lost to this country! It is not less deplorable, that, between art and contention, such an inveteracy has been sown between the two countries as will probably outlast even the war! Supposing this unnatural enmity should not soon involve us in other wars, which would be extraordinary indeed, what a difference, in a future war with France and Spain, to have the Colonies in the opposite scale, instead of being in ours! What politicians are those who have preferred the empty name of *sovereignty* to that of *alliance,* and forced subsidies to the golden ocean of commerce!

Alas! the trade of America is not all we shall lose! The ocean of commerce wafted us wealth at the return of regular tides: but we had acquired an empire too, in whose plains the beggars we sent out as labourers could reap sacks of gold in three or four harvests; and who with their sickles and reaping-hooks have robbed and cut the throats of those who sowed the grain. These rapacious foragers have fallen together by the ears; and our Indian affairs, I suppose, will soon be in as desperate a state as our American. Lord Pigot [Governor of Madras] has been treacherously and violently imprisoned, and the Company here has voted his restoration. I know nothing of the merits of the cause on either side: I dare to say both are very blameable. I look only to the consequences, which I do not doubt will precipitate the loss of our acquisitions there; the title to which I never admired, and the possession of which I always regarded as a transitory vision. If we could keep it, we should certainly plunder it, till the expense of maintaining would overbalance the returns; and, though it has rendered a little more than the holy city of Jerusalem, I look on such distant conquests as more destructive than beneficial; and, whether we are martyrs or banditti, whether we fight for the holy sepulchre or for lacks of rupees, I detest invasions of quiet kingdoms, both for their sakes and for our own; and it is happy for the former, that the latter are never permanently benefited.

Though I have been drawn away from your letter by the subject of it and by political reflections, I must not forget to thank you for your solicitude and advice about my health: but pray be assured that I am sufficiently attentive to it, and never stay long here in wet weather, which experience has told me is prejudicial. I am sorry for it, but I know London agrees with me better than the country. The latter suits my age and inclination; but my health is a more cogent reason, and governs me. I know my own constitution exactly, and have formed my way of life accordingly. No weather, nothing gives me cold; because, for these nine and thirty years, I have hardened myself so, by braving all weathers and taking no precautions against cold, that the extremest and most sudden changes do not affect me in that respect. Yet damp, without giving me cold, affects my nerves; and, the moment I feel it, I go to town. I am certainly better since my last fit of gout than ever I was after one: in short, perfectly well; that is, well enough for my age.

In one word, I am very weak, but have no complaint; and as my constitution, frame, and health require no exercise, nothing but fatigue affects me: and therefore you, and all who are so good as to interest themselves about me and give advice, must excuse me if I take none. I am preached to about taking no care against catching cold, and am told I shall one day or other be caught — possibly: but I must die of something; and why should not what has done to sixty, be right? My regimen and practice have been formed on experience and success. Perhaps a practice that has suited the weakest of frames, would kill a Hercules. God forbid I should recommend it; for I never saw another human being that would not have died of my darings, especially in the gout. Yet I have always found benefit; because my nature is so feverish, that everything cold, inwardly or outwardly, suits me. Cold air and water are my specifics, and I shall die when I am not master enough of myself to employ them; or rather, as I said this winter, on comparing the iron texture of my inside with the debility of my outside, "I believe I shall have nothing but my inside left!" *Therefore*, my dear Sir, my regard for you will last as long as there is an atom of me remaining.

Horace Walpole to Mary Berry

Berkeley Square, May 26, 1791

I am rich in letters from you: I received that by Lord Elgin's courier first, as you expected, and its elder the next day. You tell me mine entertain you; *tant mieux*. It is my wish, but my wonder; for I live so little in the world, that I do not know the present generation by sight: for, though I pass by them in the streets, the hats with valences, the folds above the chin of the ladies, and the dirty shirts and shaggy hair of the young men, who have levelled nobility almost as much as the nobility in France have, have confounded all individuality. Besides, if I did go to public places and assemblies, which my going to roost earlier prevents, the bats and owls do not begin to fly abroad till far in the night, when they begin to see and be seen.

However, one of the empresses of fashion, the Duchess of Gordon, uses fifteen or sixteen hours of her four-and-twenty. I heard her journal of last Monday. She first went to Handel's music in the Abbey; she then clambered over the benches, and went to Hastings's trial in the Hall; after dinner, to the play; then to Lady Lucan's assembly; after that to Ranelagh, and returned to Mrs. Hobart's faro-table; gave a ball herself in the evening of that morning, into which she must have got a good way; and set out for Scotland the next day. Hercules could not have achieved a quarter of her labours in the same space of time. What will the Great Duke think of our Amazons, if he has letters opened, as the Emperor was wont! One of our Camillas, but in a freer style, I hear, he saw (I fancy, just before your arrival); and he must have wondered at the familiarity of the Dame, and the nincompoophood of her Prince. Sir William Hamilton is arrived — his Nymph of the Attitudes was too prudish to visit the rambling peeress.

The rest of my letter must be literary; for we have no news. Boswell's book is gossiping; but, having numbers of proper names, would be more readable, at least by me, were it reduced from two volumes to one: but there are woful longueurs, both about his hero and himself, the *fidus Achates*; about whom one has not the smallest curiosity. But I wrong the original Achates: one is satisfied with his fidelity in keeping his master's secrets and weaknesses, which modern led-captains betray for their patron's glory and to hurt their own enemies; which Boswell has done shamefully, particularly against Mrs. Piozzi, and Mrs. Montagu, and Bishop Percy. Dr. Blagden says justly, that it is a new kind of libel, by which you may abuse anybody, by saying some dead person said so and so of somebody alive. Often, indeed, Johnson made the most brutal speeches to living persons; for though he was good-natured at bottom, he was very ill-natured at top. He loved to dispute to show his superiority. If his opponents were weak, he told them they were fools; if they vanquished them, he was scurrilous — to nobody more than to Boswell himself, who was contemptible for flattering him so grossly, and for enduring the coarse things he was continually vomiting on Boswell's own country, Scotland. I expected, amongst the excommunicated, to find myself, but am very gently treated. I never would be in the least acquainted with Johnson; or, as Boswell calls it, I had not a just value for him; which the biographer imputes to my resentment for the Doctor's putting bad arguments (purposely, out of Jacobitism,) into the speeches which he wrote fifty years ago for my father, in the 'Gentleman's Magazine'; which I did not read then, or ever knew Johnson wrote till Johnson died, nor have looked at since. Johnson's blind Toryism and known brutality kept me aloof; nor did I ever exchange a syllable with him: nay, I do not think I ever was in a room with him six times in my days. Boswell came to me, said Dr. Johnson was writing the 'Lives of the Poets,' and wished I would give him anecdotes of Mr. Gray. I said, very coldly, I had given what I knew to Mr. Mason. Boswell hummed and hawed, and then dropped, "I suppose you know Dr. Johnson does not admire Mr. Gray." Putting as much contempt as I could into my look and tone, I said, "Dr. Johnson don't! — humph!" — and with that monosyllable ended our interview. After the Doctor's death, Burke, Sir Joshua Reynolds, and Boswell sent an ambling circular-letter to me, begging subscriptions for a Monument for him — the two last, I think, impertinently; as they could not but know my opinion, and could not suppose I would contribute to a Monument for one who had endeavoured, poor soul! to degrade my friend's superlative poetry. I would not deign to write an answer; but sent down word by my footman, as I would have done to parish officers with a brief, that I would not subscribe. In the two new volumes Johnson says, and very probably did, or is made to say, that Gray's poetry is *dull,* and that he was a *dull* man! The same oracle dislikes Prior, Swift, and Fielding. If an elephant could write a book, perhaps one that had read a great deal would say, that an Arabian horse is a very clumsy ungraceful animal. Pass to a better chapter!

Burke has published another pamphlet against the French Revolution, in which he attacks it still more grievously. The beginning is very good; but it is not equal, nor quite so injudicious as parts of its predecessor; is far less brilliant, as well as much shorter: but, were it ever so long, his mind overflows with such a torrent of images, that he cannot be tedious. His invective against Rousseau is admirable, just, and new. Voltaire he passes almost contemptuously. I wish he had dissected Mirabeau too; and I grieve that he has omitted the violation of the consciences of the clergy, nor stigmatised those universal plunderers, the National Assembly, who gorge themselves with eighteen livres a day; which to many of them would, three years ago, have been astonishing opulence.

When you return, I shall lend you three volumes in quarto of another work, with which you will be delighted. They are state-letters in the reigns of Henry the Eighth, Mary, Elizabeth, and James; being the correspondence of the Talbot and Howard families, given by a Duke of Norfolk to the Heralds' Office; where they have lain for a century neglected, buried under dust, and unknown, till discovered by a Mr. Lodge, a genealogist, who, to gratify his passion, procured to be made a Poursuivant. Oh! how curious they are! Henry seizes an Alderman who refused to contribute to a benevolence; sends him to the army on the Borders; orders him to be exposed in the front line; and if that does not do, to be treated with the utmost rigour of military discipline. His daughter Bess is not less a Tudor. The mean, unworthy treatment of the Queen of Scots is striking; and you will find how Elizabeth's jealousy of her crown and her avarice were at war, and how the more ignoble passion predominated. But the most amusing passage is one in a private letter, as it paints the awe of children for their parents a *little* differently from modern habitudes. Mr. Talbot, second son of the Earl of Shrewsbury, was a member of the House of Commons, and was married. He writes to the Earl his father, and tells him, that a young woman of a very good character has been recommended to him for chambermaid to his wife, and if his Lordship does not disapprove of it, he will hire her. There are many letters of news, that are very entertaining too — but it is nine o'clock, and I must go to Lady Cecilia's.

Eleanor Butler

In 1778 Eleanor Butler and Sarah Ponsonby ran away from their proper Irish families and moved into a cottage in the Welsh village of Llangollen. They immersed themselves in intellectual pursuits and came to be known as the Ladies of Llangollen, admired by Wordsworth, Darwin and other notables of their time. But as women of a certain class they had no way to make a living, so they struggled to make due with the meager £100 a year they received from relatives none too happy about their domestic arrangement. When Butler's wealthy mother died she left nothing to her daughter except a tiny allowance. To make matters worse, Butler's sister-in-law Lady Ormonde proved reluctant to release even those funds. Butler was forced to send the following letter in order to collect the money that was rightfully hers.

Eleanor Butler to Lady Ormonde

[1794]

Dear Lady Ormonde,

Your silence to the recent application I troubled you with the first of this month (an instance of disregard to yourself and me for which I was totally unprepared) will influence my abridging (much as is possible) the present intrusion on your attention.

Last Thursday's post brought a Duplicate of the Will accompanied by your promise of letting me know 'when' I may be permitted to draw for the One Hundred Pounds my Mother had the goodness to bequeath me. In Seven Weeks from the Event which added so considerably to your already Princely Resources could nothing be afforded except a promise of future information when I might apply for such a sum?

I shall only lead your Observation to the evident, the unmerited cruelty of this treatment! It may indeed be pronounced so unexampled, that with difficulty will it obtain belief. Equally incredible must it appear that my remonstrance to *Your Friendship* and my *Brother's justice* experienced no other return than a *Silent* Contempt. But now (impelled by many powerful motives, independent of my own particular interests) I once more conjure you to bestow even a momentary consideration on the *Moderate Object* of that remonstrance, and the claims I have upon those to whom it was addressed. Let me also remind you that though for near sixteen Years the constant Inhabitant of 'so remote a dwelling' yet when the Title of Ormande is pronounced at St James this ensuing Birthday the recollections of a Daughter and Sister of that House will consequently be awakened to the minds of some distinguished Characters in the circle, many of whom, as your Ladyship cannot be ignorant, I have the happiness to count in the list of acquaintance and not a few in that of my *real* friends. If the eyes of these persons should unanimously turn towards you on your first introduction to their majesties, let it be I entreat with that degree of approbation which it shall prove my immediate business to convince them you are entitled to from all who feel an interest in my welfare, if by obtaining me the slender addition of One hundred a year you at once fulfill my utmost ambition and Secure to yourself my liveliest Gratitude. I have only one additional favour to solicit, it is the Obligation of not being kept in a state of painful suspense, but that whatever may be your determination, you will without delay communicate it to, dear Lady Ormonde.

Your Most faithful and most Obedient Humble Servant,

Eleanor Butler

George Gordon, Lord Byron

Though the quality of his poetry is still disputed, there is no doubt that George Gordon, Lord Byron's work was the most influential of the nineteenth century. It assumed significance beyond its literary merits because of Byron's celebrity as a man of prodigious vigor, decadent tastes and iconoclastic beliefs. He abused his wife until she left him, a year after they married, taking with her their month-old daughter, Ada. Byron then wandered the globe drinking too much, having numerous affairs with men and women and fathering at least one illegitimate child. In colorful letters to various friends he described his adventures and his life as a poet. His communiqués are often laced with humor: In his June 1818 letter to John Cam Hobhouse, for instance, he announces his own demise in the voice of William Fletcher, his loyal manservant.

Lord Byron to Henry Drury

Salsette frigate, May 3, 1810

My dear Drury:

When I left England, nearly a year ago, you requested me to write to you — I will do so. I have crossed Portugal, traversed the south of Spain, visited Sardinia, Sicily, Malta, and thence passed into Turkey, where I am still wandering. I first landed in Albania, the ancient Epirus, where we penetrated as far as Mount Tomarit — excellently treated by the chief Ali Pacha, — and, after journeying through Illyria, Chaonia, etc., crossed the Gulf of Actium, with a guard of fifty Albanians, and passed the Achelous in our route through Acarnania and Ætolia. We stopped a short time in the Morea, crossed the Gulf of Lepanto, and landed at the foot of Parnassus; — saw all that Delphi retains, and so on to Thebes and Athens, at which last we remained ten weeks.

His Majesty's ship, *Pylades*, brought us to Smyrna; but not before we had topographised Attica, including, of course, Marathon and the Sunian promontory. From Smyrna to the Troad (which we visited when at anchor, for a fortnight, off the tomb of Antilochus) was our next stage; and now we are in the Dardanelles, waiting for a wind to proceed to Constantinople.

This morning I swam from *Sestos* to *Abydos*. The immediate distance is not above a mile, but the current renders it hazardous; — so much so that I doubt whether Leander's conjugal affection must not have been a little chilled in his passage to Paradise. I attempted it a week ago, and failed, — owing to the north wind, and the wonderful rapidity of the tide, — though I have been from my childhood a strong swimmer. But, this morning being calmer, I succeeded, and crossed the "broad Hellespont" in an hour and ten minutes.

Well, my dear sir, I have left my home, and seen part of Africa and Asia, and a tolerable portion of Europe. I have been with generals and admirals, princes and pashas, governors and ungovernables, — but I have not time or paper to expatiate. I wish to let you know that I live with a friendly remembrance of you, and a hope to meet you again; and if I do this as shortly as possible, attribute it to any thing but forgetfulness.

Greece, ancient and modern, you know too well to require description. Albania, indeed, I have seen more of than any Englishman (except a Mr. Leake), for it is a country rarely visited, from the savage character of the natives, though abounding in more natural beauties than the classical regions of Greece, — which, however, are still eminently beautiful, particularly Delphi and Cape Colonna in Attica. Yet these are nothing to parts of Illyria and Epirus, where places without a name, and rivers not laid down in maps, may, one day, when more known, be justly esteemed superior subject, for the pencil and the pen, to the dry ditch of the Ilissus and the bogs of Bœotia.

The Troad is a fine field for conjecture and snipeshooting, and a good sportsman and an ingenious scholar may exercise their feet and faculties to great advantage upon the spot; — or, if they prefer riding, lose their way (as I did) in a cursed quagmire of the Scamander, who wriggles about as if the Dardan virgins still offered their wonted tribute. The only vestige of Troy, or her destroyers, are the barrows supposed to contain the carcasses of Achilles, Antilochus, Ajax, etc.; — but Mount Ida is still in high feather, though the shepherds are now-a-days not much like Ganymede. But why should I say more of these things? are they not written in the *Boke of Gell?* and has not Hobhouse got a journal? I keep none, as I have renounced scribbling.

I see not much difference between ourselves and the Turks, save that we have and they have none — that they have long dresses, and we short, and that we talk much, and they little. They are sensible people. Ali Pacha told me he was sure I was a man of rank, because I had *small ears* and *hands*, and *curling hair.* By the by, I speak the Romaic, or modern Greek, tolerably. It does not differ from the ancient dialects so much as you would conceive; but the pronunciation is diametrically opposite. Of verse, except in rhyme, they have no idea.

I like the Greeks, who are plausible rascals, — with all the Turkish vices, without their courage. However, some are brave, and all are beautiful, very much resembling the busts of Alcibiades; — the women not quite so handsome. I can swear in Turkish; but, except one horrible oath, and "pimp," and "bread," and "water," I have got no great vocabulary in that language. They are extremely polite to strangers of any rank, properly protected; and as I have two servants and two soldiers, we got on with great *éclat.* We have been occasionally in danger of thieves, and once of shipwreck, — but always escaped.

Of Spain I sent some account to our Hodgson, but have subsequently written to no one, save notes to relations and lawyers, to keep them out of my premises. I mean to give up all connection, on my return, with many of my best friends — as I supposed them — and to snarl all my life. But I hope to have one good-humoured laugh with you, and to embrace Dwyer, and pledge Hodgson, before I commence cynicism.

Tell Dr. Butler I am now writing with the gold pen he gave me before I left England, which is the reason my scrawl is more unintelligible than usual. I have been at Athens, and seen plenty of these reeds for scribbling, some of which he refused to bestow upon me, because topographic Gell had brought them from Attica. But I will not describe, — no — you must be satisfied with simple detail till my return, and then we will unfold the floodgates of colloquy. I am in a thirty-six gun frigate, going up to fetch Bob Adair from Constantinople, who will have the honour to carry this letter.

And so Hobhouse's *boke* is out, with some sentimental sing-song of my own to fill up, — and how does it take, eh? and where the devil is the second edition of my Satire, with additions? and my name on the title page? and more lines tagged to the end, with a new exordium and what not, hot from my anvil before I cleared the Channel? The Mediterranean and the Atlantic roll between me and criticism; and the thunders of the Hyperborean Review are deafened by the roar of the Hellespont.

Remember me to Claridge, if not translated to college, and present to Hodgson assurances of my high consideration. Now, you will ask, what shall I do next? and I answer, I do not know. I may return in a few months, but I have intents and projects after visiting Constantinople. — Hobhouse, however, will probably be back in September.

On the 2d of July we have left Albion one year — *oblitus neorum obliviscendus et illis.* I was sick of my own country, and not much prepossessed in favour of any other; but I "drag on my chain" without "lengthening it at each remove." I am like the Jolly Miller, caring for nobody, and not cared for. All countries are much the same in my eyes. I smoke, and stare at mountains, and twirl my mustachios very independently. I miss no comforts, and the musquitoes that rack the morbid frame of H. have, luckily for me, little effect on mine, because I live more temperately.

I omitted Ephesus in my catalogue, which I visited during my sojourn at Smyrna; but the Temple has almost perished, and St. Paul need not trouble himself to epistolise the present brood of Ephesians, who have converted a large church built entirely of marble into a mosque, and I don't know that the edifice looks the worse for it.

My paper is full, and my ink ebbing—good afternoon! If you address me at Malta, the letter will be forwarded wherever I may be. H. greets you; he pines for his poetry,—at least, some tidings of it. I almost forgot to tell you that I am dying for love of three Greek girls at Athens, sisters. I lived in the same house. Teresa, Mariana, and Katinka, are the names of these divinities,—all of them under fifteen.

Your *ταπεινοτατος δουλος,*
Byron

Lord Byron to John Cam Hobhouse

Venice, June, 1818

Sir:

With great grief I inform you of the death of my late dear Master, my Lord, who died this morning at ten of the Clock of a rapid decline and slow fever, caused by anxiety, sea-bathing, women, and riding in the Sun against my advice.

He is a dreadful loss to every body, mostly to me, who have lost a master and a place—also, I hope you, Sir, will give me a charakter.

I saved in his service as you know several hundred pounds. God knows how, for I don't, nor my late master neither; and if my wage was not always paid to the day, still it was or is to be paid sometime and somehow. You, Sir, who are his executioner won't see a poor Servant wronged of his little all.

My dear Master had several phisicians and a Priest: he died a Papish, but is to be buried among the Jews in the Jewish burying ground; for my part I don't see why—he could not abide them when living nor any other people, hating whores who asked him for money.

He suffered his illness with great patience, except that when in extremity he twice damned his friends and said they were selfish rascals —you, Sir, particularly and Mr. Kinnaird, who had never answered his letters nor complied with his repeated requests. He also said he hoped that your new tragedy would be damned—God forgive him—I hope that my master won't be damned like the tragedy.

His nine whores are already provided for, and the other servants; but what is to become of me? I have got his Cloathes and Carriages, and Cash, and everything; but the Consul quite against law has clapt his seal and taken an inventory and swears that *he* must account to my Lord's heirs — who they are, I don't know — but they ought to consider poor Servants and above all his Vally de Sham.

My Lord never grudged me perquisites — my wage was the least I got by him; and if I did keep the Countess (she is, or ought to be, a Countess, although she is upon the town) Marietta Monetta Piretta, after passing my word to you and my Lord that I would not never no more — still he was an indulgent master, and only said I was a damned fool, and swore and forgot it again. What could I do? she said as how she should die, or kill herself if I did not go with her, and so I did — and kept her out of my Lord's washing and ironing — and nobody can deny that, although the charge was high, the linen was well got up.

Hope you are well, Sir — am, with tears in my eyes,

Yours faithfoolly to command,
Wm. Fletcher

P.S. — If you know any Gentleman in want of a Wally — hope for a charakter. I saw your late Swiss Servant in the Galleys at Leghorn for robbing an Inn — he produced your recommendation at his trial.

Lord Byron to John Murray

Venice, April 6, 1819.

I mean to write my best work in Italian, and it will take me nine years more thoroughly to master the Language; and then, if my fancy exist, and I exist too, I will try what I *can* do *really*. As to the estimation of the English which you talk of, let them calculate what it is worth before they insult me with their insolent condescension.

I have not written for their pleasure. If they are pleased, it is that they choose to be so; I have never flattered their opinions, nor their pride; nor will I. Neither will I make "Ladies" books: *al diletlar le femine e la plebe.* I have written from the fulness of my mind, from passion, from impulse, from many motives, but not for their "sweet voices."

I know the precise worth of popular applause, for few scribblers have had more of it; and if I chose to swerve into their paths, I could retain it, or resume it. But I neither love ye nor fear ye; and though I buy with ye, and sell with ye, and talk with ye, I will neither eat with ye, drink with ye, nor pray with ye. They made me, without my search, a species of popular idol; they, without reason or judgment, beyond the caprice of their good pleasure, threw down the image from its pedestal; it was not broken with the fall, and they would, it seems, again replace it, — but they shall not.

Lord Byron to John Murray

Bologna, August 24, 1819.

Keep the *anonymous*, in any case: it helps what fun there may be. But if the matter grow serious about "Don Juan," and you feel *yourself* in a scrape, or *me* either, *own that I am the author.* I will never *shrink*; and if *you* do, I can always answer you in the question of Guatimozin to his minister — each being on his own coals.

I wish that I had been in better spirits; but I am out of sorts, out of nerves, and now and then (I begin to fear) out of my senses. All this Italy has done for me, and not England: I defy all you, and your climate to boot, to make me mad. But if ever I do really become a bedlamite, and wear a strait waistcoat, let me be brought back among you: your people will then be proper company.

I assure you what I here say and feel has nothing to do with England, either in a literary or personal point of view. All my present pleasures or plagues are as Italian as the opera. And, after all, they are but trifles; for all this arises from my "Dama's" being in the country for three days (at Capofiume). But as I could never live but for one human being at a time (and, I assure you, *that one* has never been *myself*, as you may know by the consequences, for the *selfish* are successful in life), I feel alone and unhappy.

I have sent for my daughter from Venice, and I ride daily, and walk in a garden, under a purple canopy of grapes, and sit by a fountain, and talk with the gardener of his tools, which seem greater than Adam's, and with his wife, and with his son's wife, who is the youngest of the party, and, I think, talks best of the three. Then I revisit the Campo Stanto, and my old friend, the sexton, has two — but *one* the prettiest daughter imaginable; and I amuse myself with contrasting her beautiful and innocent face of fifteen with the skulls with which he has peopled several cells, and particularly with that of one skull, dated 1766, which was once covered (the tradition goes) by the most lovely features of Bologna — noble and rich. When I look at these, and at this girl — when I think of what *they were,* and what she must be — why, then, my dear Murray, I won't shock you by saying what I think. It is little matter what becomes of us "bearded men," but I don't like the notion of a beautiful woman's lasting less than a beautiful tree — than her own picture — her own shadow, which won't change so to the sun as her face to the mirror. I must leave off, for my head aches consumedly. I have never been quite well since the night of the representation of Alfieri's *Mirra* a fortnight ago.

Yours ever.

Lord Byron to John Murray

Ravenna, 9bre 19, 1820.

What you said of the late Charles Skinner Matthews has set me to my recollections; but I have not been able to turn up anything which would do for the proposed Memoir of his brother — even if he had previously done enough during his life to sanction the production of anecdotes so merely personal. He was, however, a very extraordinary man, and would have been a great one. No one ever succeeded in a more surpassing degree than he did as far as he went. He was indolent, too; but whenever he stripped, he overthrew all antagonists. His conquests will be found registered at Cambridge, particularly his *Downing* one, which was hotly and highly contested, and yet easily *won.* Hobhouse was his most intimate friend, and can tell you more of him than any man. William Bankes also a great deal. I myself recollect more of his oddities than of his academical qualities, for we lived most together at a very idle period of *my* life. When I went up to Trinity, in 1805, at the age of seventeen and a-half, I was miserable and untoward to a degree. I was wretched at leaving Harrow, to which I had become attached during the last two years of my stay there; wretched at going to Cambridge instead of Oxford (there were no rooms vacant at Christ-church); wretched from some private domestic circumstances of different kinds, and consequently about as unsocial as a wolf taken from the troop. So that, although I knew Matthews, and met him often *then* at Bankes's (who was my collegiate pastor, and master, and patron), and at Rhodes's, Milnes's, Price's, Dick's, Macnamara's, Farrell's, Galley Knights's, and others of that *set* of contemporaries, yet I was neither intimate with him nor with any one else, except my old schoolfellow, Edward Long (with whom I used to pass the day in riding and swimming), and William Bankes, who was good-naturedly tolerant of my ferocities.

It was not till 1807, after I had been upwards of a year away from Cambridge, to which I had returned again to *reside* for my degree, that I became one of Matthews's familiars, by means of Hobhouse, who, after hating me for two years, because I wore a *white hat* and a *grey* coat, and rode a *grey* horse (as he says himself), took me into his good graces because I had written some poetry. I had always lived a good deal, and got drunk occasionally, in their company — but now we became really friends in a morning. Matthews, however, was not at this period resident in College. I met *him* chiefly in London, and at uncertain periods at Cambridge. Hobhouse, in the meantime, did great things: he founded the Cambridge "Whig Club" (which he seems to have forgotten), and the "Amicable Society," which was dissolved in consequence of the members constantly quarrelling, and made himself very popular with "us youth," and no less formidable to all tutors, professors, and heads of Colleges.

Matthews and I, meeting in London, and elsewhere, became great cronies. He was not good-tempered — nor am I — but with a little tact his temper was manageable, and I thought him so superior a man, that I was willing to sacrifice something to his humours, which were often, at the same time, amusing and provoking. What became of his *papers* (and he certainly had many), at the time of his death, was never known. I mention this by the way, fearing to skip it over, and *as* he *wrote* remarkably well, both in Latin and English. We went down to Newstead together, where I had got a famous cellar, and *Monks'* dresses from a masquerade warehouse. We were a company of some seven or eight, with an occasional neighbour or so for visitors, and used to sit up late in our friars' dresses, drinking burgundy, claret, champagne, and what not, out of the *skull-cup,* and all sorts of glasses, and buffooning all round the house, in our conventual garments. Matthews always denominated me "the Abbot," and never called me by any other name in his good humours, to the day of his death. The harmony of these our symposia was somewhat interrupted, a few days after our assembling, by Matthews's threatening to throw Hobhouse out of a *window,* in consequence of I know not what commerce of jokes ending in this epigram. Hobhouse came to me and said, that "his respect and regard for me as host would not permit him to call out any of my guests, and that he should go to town next morning." He did. It was in vain that I represented to him that the window was not high and that the turf under it was particularly soft. Away he went.

Matthews and myself had travelled down from London together, talking all the way incessantly upon one single topic. When we got to Loughborough, I know not what chasm had made us diverge for a moment to some other subject, at which he was indignant. "Come," said he, "don't let us break through — let us go on as we began, to our journey's end;" and so he continued, and was as entertaining as ever to the very end. He had previously occupied, during my year's absence from Cambridge, my rooms in Trinity, with the furniture; and Jones, the tutor, in his odd way, had said, on putting him in, "Mr. Matthews, I recommend to your attention not to damage any of the movables, for Lord Byron, sir, is a young man of *tumultuous passions.*" Matthews was delighted with this; and whenever anybody came to visit him, begged them to handle the very door with caution; and used to repeat Jones's admonition in his tone and manner. There was a large mirror in the room, on which he remarked, "that he thought his friends were grown uncommonly assiduous in coming to *see him,* but he soon discovered that they only came to *see themselves.*" Jones's phrase of *"tumultuous passions,"* and the whole scene, had put him into such good humour, that I verily believe that I owed to it a portion of his good graces.

When at Newstead, somebody by accident rubbed against one of his white silk stockings, one day before dinner; of course the gentleman apologised. "Sir," answered Matthews, "it may be all very well for you, who have a great many silk stockings, to dirty other people's; but to me, who have only this *one pair,* which I have put on in honour of the Abbot here, no apology can compensate for such carelessness; besides, the expense of washing." He had the same sort of droll, sardonic way about everything. A wild Irishman, named Farrell, one evening beginning to say something at a large supper at Cambridge, Matthews roared out "Silence!" and then, pointing to Farrell, cried out, in the words of the oracle, *"Orson is endowed with reason."* You may easily suppose that Orson lost what reason he had acquired, on hearing this compliment. When Hobhouse published his volume of poems, the *Miscellany* (which Matthews *would* call the *"Miss-sell-any"*), all that could be drawn from him was that the preface was "extremely like *Walsh.*" Hobhouse thought this at first a compliment; but we never could make out what it was, for all we know of *Walsh* is his Ode to King William, and Pope's epithet of *"knowing Walsh."* When the Newstead party broke up for London, Hobhouse and Matthews, who were the greatest friends possible, agreed, for a whim, to *walk together* to town. They quarrelled by the way, and actually walked the latter half of their journey, occasionally passing and repassing, without speaking. When Matthews had got to Highgate, he had spent all his money but threepence halfpenny, and determined to spend that also in a pint of beer, which I believe he was drinking before a public house as Hobhouse passed him (still without speaking) for the last time on their route. They were reconciled in London again.

One of Matthews's passions was "the Fancy;" and he sparred uncommonly well. But he always got beaten in rows, or combats with the bare fist. In swimming, too, he swam well; but with *effort* and *labour,* and *too high* out of the water; so that Scrope Davies and myself, of whom he was therein somewhat emulous, always told him that he would be drowned if ever he came to a difficult pass in the water. He was so; but surely Scrope and myself would have been most heartily glad that

> *"the Dean had lived,*
> *And our predicton proved a lie."*

His head was uncommonly handsome, very like what *Pope's* was in his youth.

His voice, and laugh, and features are strongly resembled by his brother Henry's, if Henry be *he* of *King's College.* His passion for boxing was so great, that he actually wanted me to match him with Dogherty (whom I had backed and made the match for against Tom Belcher), and I saw them spar together at my own lodgings with the gloves on. As he was bent upon it, I would have backed Dogherty to please him, but the match went off. It was of course to have been a private fight, in a private room.

On one occasion, being too late to go home and dress, he was equipped by a friend (Mr. Baillie, I believe), in a magnificently fashionable and somewhat exaggerated shirt and neckcloth. He proceeded to the Opera, and took his station in Fop's Alley. During the interval between the opera and the ballet, an acquaintance took his station by him and saluted him: "Come round," said Matthews, "come round." — "Why should I come round?" said the other; "you have only to turn your head — I am close to you." — "That is exactly what I cannot do," said Matthews; "don't you see the state I am in?" pointing to his buckram shirt collar and inflexible cravat, — and there he stood with his head always in the same perpendicular position during the whole spectacle.

One evening, after dining together, as we were going to the Opera, I happened to have a spare Opera ticket (as subscriber to a box), and presented it to Matthews, "Now, sir," said he to Hobhouse afterwards, "this I call *courteous* in the Abbot — another man would never have thought that I might do better with half a guinea than throw it to a door-keeper; — but here is a man not only asks me to dinner, but gives oddities, for no man was more liberal, or more honourable in all his doings and dealings, than Matthews. He gave Hobhouse and me, before we set out for Constantinople, a most splendid entertainment, to which we did ample justice. One of his fancies was dining at all sorts of out-of-the-way places. Somebody popped upon him in I know not what coffee-house in the Strand — and what do you think was the attraction? Why, that he paid a shilling (I think) to *dine with his hat on.* This he called his *"hat* house" and used to boast of the comfort of being covered at meal-times.

When Sir Henry Smith was expelled from Cambridge for a row with a tradesman named "Hiron," Matthews solaced himself with shouting under Hiron's windows every evening,

> *Ah me! what perils do environ*
> *The man who meddles with hot Hiron.*

He was also of that band of profane scoffers who under the auspices of ——, used to rouse Lort Mansel (late Bishop of Bristol) from his slumbers in the lodge of Trinity; and when he appeared at the window foaming with wrath, and crying out, "I know you, gentlemen, I know you!" were wont to reply, "We beseech thee to hear us, good *Lort*" — "Good *Lort* deliver us!" (Lort was his Christian name.) As he was very free in his speculations upon all kinds of subjects, although by no means either dissolute or intemperate in his conduct, and as I was no less independent, our conversation and correspondence used to alarm our friend Hobhouse to a considerable degree.

You must be almost tired of my packets, which will have cost a mint of postage.

Salute Gifford and all my friends,

Yours, etc.

Lord Byron to Lady Byron.

Pisa, November 17, 1821.

I have to acknowledge the receipt of "Ada's hair" which is very soft and pretty, and nearly as dark already as mine was at twelve years old, if I may judge from what I recollect of some in Augusta's possession, taken at that age. But it don't curl, — perhaps from its being let grow.

I also thank you for the inscription of the date and name, and I will tell you why: — I believe that they are the only two or three words of your handwriting in my possession. For your letters I returned; and except the two words, or rather the one word, "Household" written twice in an old account book, I have no other. I burnt your last note, for two reasons: — firstly, it was written in a style not very agreeable; and, secondly, I wished to take your word without documents, which are the worldly resources of suspicious people.

I suppose that this note will reach you somewhere about Ada's birthday — the 10th of December, I believe. She will then be six, so that in about twelve more I shall have some chance of meeting her — perhaps sooner, if I am obliged to go to England by business or otherwise. Recollect however, one thing, either in distance or nearness: — every day which keeps us asunder should, after so long a period, rather soften our mutual feelings, which must always have one rallying-point as long as our child exists, which I presume we both hope will be long after either of her parents.

The time which has elapsed since the separation has been considerably more than the whole brief period of our union, and the not much longer one of our prior acquaintance. We both made a bitter mistake; but now it is over, and irrevocably so. For, at thirty-three on my part, and a few years less on yours, though it is no very extended period of life, still it is one when the habits and thought are generally so formed as to admit of no modification; and as we could not agree when younger, we should with difficulty do so now.

I saw all this, because I own to you, that, notwithstanding everything, I considered our re-union as not impossible for more than a year after the separation; — but then I gave up the hope entirely and forever. But this very impossibility of re-union seems to me at least a reason why, on all the few points of discussion which can arise between us, we should preserve the courtesies of life, and as much of its kindness as people who are never to meet may preserve perhaps more easily than nearer connexions. For my own part, I am violent, but not malignant; for only fresh provocations can awaken my resentments. To you, who are colder and more concentrated, I would just hint that you may sometimes mistake the depth of a cold anger for dignity, and a worse feeling for duty. I assure you that I bear you *now* (whatever I may have done) no resentment whatever. Remember, that *if you have injured me in aught* this forgiveness is something; and that, if I *have injured you,* it is something more still, if it be true, as the moralists say, that the most offending are the least forgiving.

Whether the offence has been solely on my side, or reciprocal, or on yours chiefly, I have ceased to reflect upon any but two things — viz., that you are the mother of my child, and that we shall never meet again. I think if you also consider the two corresponding points with reference to myself, it will be better for all three.

Yours ever,
Noel Byron.

Heinrich Heine

The difficult life of a Jew in nineteenth-century Germany probably molded this poet and critic's extremely unpleasant personality. Insecure and often shunned, Heine harbored a deep misanthropy even while going to great lengths to attract the attention of fellow university and law school students. When Lord Byron's popularity peaked, Heine affected Byronic dress and mannerisms, claimed to be a cousin of the poet and attempted to acquire a reputation for womanizing. But his caustic cynicism and querulous arrogance put off most acquaintances and made publishers balk. Still, Heine harbored genuine talent and sincere passions, which developed into a crush on Johann von Goethe, Germany's leading man of letters. Heine wrote two heated notes to the author, hoping to make his acquaintance, but in this as in so many other things he was doomed to disappointment.

Heinrich Heine to Johann von Goethe

[1821]

I might have a hundred reasons for sending Your Excellency my poems. But I shall give only one: I love you. I believe this is a sufficient reason. My efforts in poetry are, I know, of little worth; yet it may be that here and there will be found passages which reveal what I may in time be capable of producing. For a long time my mind was divided as to what is poetry. I was told: 'Ask Schlegel.' He said to me: 'Read Goethe.' This I have done in all reverence. And if in the course of time I shall produce something worth while, then I shall know to whom I am indebted for it. I kiss your blessed hand which has shown me, and the entire German folk, the way to Heaven.

Heinrich Heine to Johann von Goethe

[1824]

Your Excellency — I beg you to grant me the happiness of being in your presence for a few moments. I shall not trouble you much. I shall only kiss your hand and depart. My name is H. Heine; I am a Rhinelander. . . . I, too, am a poet, and three years ago I took the liberty of sending you my 'Poems,' and a year and a half ago my 'Tragedies,' together with a 'Lyrical Intermezzo.' I am ill, and three weeks ago I journeyed to the Harz Mountains for my health; and as I stood on the Brocken I was seized by a desire to make a pilgrimage to Weimar to pay my respects to Goethe. In the literal sense of the world have I made a pilgrmage hither: that is, on foot and in rags. And now I await the granting of my prayer. . . .

Margaret Fuller

American reformer and critic Margaret Fuller, author of the classic *Woman in the Nineteenth Century*, possessed a mind and spirit that would not be bound by the conventions of her time. A leader of the mystical, humanist Transcendentalist movement, she matched wits with the likes of Bronson Alcott, Henry David Thoreau and, especially, Ralph Waldo Emerson. She made frequent visits to the movement's experimental Brook Farm community in West Roxbury, Massachusetts; in Boston she conducted a renowned conversation series for women, in which she championed sexual equality. As a European correspondent for the *New York Tribune* (from 1846) she met many of the continent's leading literary and intellectual lights. Her letters to friends, including Emerson, reflect her unfettered attitudes and document her acquaintance with Edmund Spenser; Alfred, Lord Tennyson; Robert Browning and Elizabeth Barrett Browning; and other notables.

Margaret Fuller to Mrs. D. H. Barlow

Cambridge, November 19, 1830.

. . . Many things have happened since I echoed your farewell laugh. Elizabeth [Randall] and I have been fully occupied. She has cried a great deal, painted a good deal, and played the harp most of all. I have neither fertilized the earth with my tears, edified its inhabitants by my delicacy of constitution, nor wakened its echoes to my harmony; yet some things have I achieved in my own soft feminine style. I hate glare, thou knowest, and have hitherto successfully screened my virtues therefrom. I have made several garments fitted for the wear of American youth; I have written six letters, and received a correspondent number; I have read one book, — a piece of poetry entitled, 'Two Agonies,' by M. A. Browne, (pretty caption, is it not?) — and J. J. Knapp's trial; I have given advice twenty times, — I have taken it once; I have gained two friends and recovered two; I have felt admiration four times, honor once, and disgust twice. . . .

Margaret Fuller to an Unnamed Friend

July, 1841.

The more I think of it, the more deeply do I feel the imperfection of your view of friendship, which is the same Waldo E. takes in that letter on Charles's death. It is very noble, but not enough for our manifold nature. Our friends should be our incentives to Right, but not only our guiding, but our prophetic stars. To love by right is much, to love by faith is more; both are the entire love, without which heart, mind, and soul cannot be alike satisfied. We love and ought to love one another not merely for the absolute worth of each, but on account of a mutual fitness of temporary character. We are not merely one another's priests or gods, but ministering angels, exercising in the part the same function as the Great Soul in the whole, of seeing the perfect through the imperfect, nay, making it come there. Why am I to love any friend the less for any obstruction in his life? Is not the very time for me to love most tenderly when I must see his life in despite of seeming; when he *shows it me* I can only admire: I do not *give* myself. I am *taken captive.* How shall I express my meaning? Perhaps I can do so from the tales of chivalry, where I find what corresponds far more thoroughly with my nature than in these stoical statements. The friend of Amadis expects to hear prodigies of valor of the absent preux [chevalier]; but if he be mutilated in one of his first battles, shall he be mistrusted by the brother of his soul more than if he had been tested in a hundred? If Britomart finds Artegall bound in the enchanter's spell, can she doubt, therefore, him whom she has seen in the magic glass? A Britomart does battle in his cause, and frees him from the evil power; a dame of less nobleness sits and watches the enchanted sleep, weeping night and day, or spurs away on her white palfrey to find some one more helpful than herself. But they are always faithful through the dark hours to the bright. The Douglas motto, 'Tender and true,' seems to me the worthiest of the strongest breast. To borrow again from your Spenser, I am entirely suited with the fate of the three brothers, Diamond and the rest. I could not die while there was yet life in my brother's breast. I would return from the shades and nerve him with twofold life for the fight. I could do it, for our hearts beat with one blood. Do you not see the truth and happiness of this waiting tenderness?

Margaret Fuller to Ralph Waldo Emerson

November, 1843.

... I always thought the saddest position in the world must be that of some regal dame to whom husband, court, kingdom, world look in vain for an heir! She is only supposed to eat, breathe, move, think, nay! love, for this; the book of her life is only perused for the sake of its appendix. Meanwhile, she, perhaps, persists in living on, as if her life by itself were of any consequence, is the mother of no prince, or has even the impertinence to incumber the kingdom with a parcel of princesses, girls who must be 'weel-tochered' to make them of any value.

But what is this pathos compared to that perceptible in the situation of a Jove, under the masculine obligations of all-sufficingness, who rubs his forehead in vain to induce the Minerva-bearing headache! Alas! his brain remains tranquil, his fancy daughterless! Nature keeps on feeding him and putting him to sleep as if she thought the oak was of consequence, whether it bear the mistletoe or not!

Heaven help thee, my Druid! if this blessed, brooding, rainy day do not. It is a fine day for composition, were it not in Concord. But I trow the fates which gave this place Concord, took away the animating influences of Discord. Life here slumbers and steals on like the river. A very good place for a sage, but not for the lyrist or the orator.

Margaret Fuller to Mrs. Ripley

Sunday, February 21, 1841.

My dear friend, — I feel it more difficult to give on paper a complete outline of my plan for the proposed conversations than I expected. I find so much to say that I cannot make any statement satisfactory to myself, within such limits as would be convenient for your purpose. As no one will wish to take the trouble of reading a long manuscript, I shall rather suggest than tell what I propose to do, and defer a full explanation till the first meeting. The advantages of a weekly meeting for conversation might be great enough to repay attendance, if they consisted only in supplying a point of union to well-educated and thinking women, in a city which, with great pretensions to mental refinement, boasts at present nothing of the kind; and where I have heard many of mature age wish for some such place of stimulus and cheer; and those younger, for a place where they could state their doubts and difficulties, with a hope of gaining aid from the experience or aspirations of others. And if my office were only to suggest topics, which would lead to conversation of a better order than is usual at social meetings, and to turn back the current when digressing into personalities or commonplaces, so that what is most valuable in the experience of each might be brought to bear upon all, I should think the object not unworthy of the effort. But my ambition goes much farther. It is to pass in review the departments of thought and knowledge, and endeavor to place them in due relation to one another in our mind. To systematize thought and give a precision and clearness in which our sex are so deficient, chiefly, I think, because they have so few inducements to test and classify what they receive. To ascertain what pursuits are best suited to us, in our time and state of society, and how we may make the best use of our means for building up the life of thought upon the life of action. . . .

I believe I have written as much as any one will wish to read. I am ready to answer any questions which may be put, and will add nothing more here except,

Always yours truly,
S. M. Fuller

Charlotte Brontë

During the eighteenth and nineteenth centuries many European and American women formed romantic friendships that provided them with the kind of tenderness and intimacy they found lacking in their relationships with men. Among these friendships was that of Charlotte Brontë, author of *Jane Eyre*, and Ellen Nussey. In her letters to Nussey, Brontë confided her personal concerns about men, including Nussey's brother Henry and a certain flirtatious cad. She gave advice about marriage (for example, not to expect too much), gossiped about the family for whom she served as governess and described the circumstances surrounding her own engagement and marriage.

Charlotte Brontë to Ellen Nussey

Feb. 20, 1837.

I read your letter with dismay, Ellen — what shall I do without you? Why are we so to be denied each other's society? It is an inscrutable fatality. I long to be with you because it seems as if two or three days or weeks spent in your company would beyond measure strengthen me in the enjoyment of those feelings which I have so lately begun to cherish. You first pointed out to me that way in which I am so feebly endeavouring to travel, and now I cannot keep you by my side. I must proceed sorrowfully alone.

Why are we to be divided? Surely, Ellen, it must be because we are in danger of loving each other too well — of losing sight of the *Creator* in idolatry of the *creature*. At first I could not say, 'Thy will be done.' I felt rebellious; but I know it was wrong to feel so. Being left a moment alone this morning, I prayed fervently to be enabled to resign myself to *every* decree of God's will — though it should be dealt forth with a far severer hand than the present disappointment. Since then, I have felt calmer and humbler — and consequently happier. . . .

I have written this note at a venture. When it will reach you I know not, but I was determined not to let slip an opportunity for want of being prepared to embrace it. Farewell; may God bestow on you all His blessings. My darling — Farewell. Perhaps you may return before midsummer — do you think you possibly can? I wish your brother John knew how unhappy I am; he would almost pity me.

Charlotte Brontë to Ellen Nussey

12 March 1839

. . . You ask me, my dear Ellen, whether I have received a letter from Henry. I have, about a week since. The contents, I confess, did a little surprise me, but I kept them to myself, and unless you had questioned me on the subject, I would never have adverted to it. Henry says he is comfortably settled at Donnington, that his health is much improved, and that it is his intention to take pupils after Easter. . . . [Easter fell on March 31 that year.]

He then intimates that in due time he should want a wife to take care of his pupils, and frankly asks me to be that wife. Altogether the letter is written without cant or flattery, and in a common-sense style, which does credit to his judgement. . . .

Now, my dear Ellen, there were in this proposal some things which might have proved a strong temptation. I thought if I were to marry Henry Nussey, his sister could live with me, and how happy I should be. But again I asked myself two questions: Do I love him as much as a woman ought to love the man she marries? Am I the person best qualified to make him happy? Alas! Ellen, my conscience answered *no* to both these questions. I felt that though I esteemed, though I had a kindly leaning towards him, because he is an amiable and well-disposed man, yet I had not, and could not have, that intense attachment which would make me willing to die for him; and, if ever I marry, it must be in that light of adoration that I will regard my husband. . . .

. . . I was aware that Henry knew so little of me, he could hardly be conscious to whom he was writing. Why, it would startle him to see me in my natural home character; he would think I was a wild, romantic enthusiast indeed. I could not sit all day long making a grave face before my husband. I would laugh, and satirise, and say whatever came into my head first. And if he were a clever man, and loved me, the whole world weighed in the balance against his smallest wish should be light as air. Could I, knowing my mind to be such as that, conscientiously say that I would take a grave, quiet, young man like Henry? No, it would have been deceiving him, and deception of that sort is beneath me. So I wrote a long letter back, in which I expressed my refusal as gently as I could. . . .

Charlotte Brontë to Ellen Nussey

15th May 1840

I am fully convinced, Ellen, that he is a thorough maleflirt, his sighs are deeper than ever and his treading on toes more assiduous. — I find he has scattered his impressions far and wide — Keighley has yielded him a fruitful field of conquest, Sarah Sugden is quite smitten so is Caroline Dury — she however has left — and his Reverence has not yet ceased to idolise her memory — I find he is perfectly conscious of his irresistible-ness and is as vain as a peacock on the subject — I am not at all surprised at this — it is perfectly natural — a handsome — clean — prepossessing — good-humoured young man — will never want troops of victims amongst young ladies — So long as you are not among the number it is all right — He has not mentioned you to me, and I have not mentioned you to him — I believe we fully understand each other on the subject. I have seen little of him lately and talked precious little to him — now that he has got his spirits up and found plenty of acquaintances I don't care and he does not care either.

There is no doubt he will get nobly through his examination, he is a *clever* lad.

Charlotte Brontë to Ellen Nussey

November 20th, 1840.

My Dearest Nell, — That last letter of thine treated of matters so high and important I cannot delay answering it for a day. Now I am about to write thee a discourse, and a piece of advice which thou must take as if it came from thy grandmother. But in the first place, before I begin with thee, I have a word to whisper in the ear of Mr. Vincent, and I wish it could reach him. In the name of St. Chrysostom, St. Simon, and St. Jude, why does not that amiable young gentleman come forward like a man and say all that he has to say personally, instead of trifling with kinsmen and kinswomen. "Mr. Vincent," I say, "go personally, and say: 'Miss ——, I want to speak to you.' Miss —— will of course civilly answer: 'I am at your service, Mr. Vincent.' And then, when the room is cleared of all but yourself and herself, just take a chair nearer. Insist upon her laying down that silly . . . work, and listening to you. Then begin, in a clear, distinct, deferential, but determined voice: 'Miss ——, I have a question to put to you — a very important question: "Will you take me as your husband, for better, for worse. I am not a rich man, but I have sufficient to support us. I am not a great man, but I love you honestly and truly. Miss ——, if you knew the world better you would see that this is an offer not to be despised — a kind attached heart and a moderate competency." Do this, Mr. Vincent, and you may succeed. Go on writing sentimental and love-sick letters to ——, and I would not give sixpence for your suit." So much for Mr. Vincent. Now Miss——'s turn comes to swallow the black bolus, called a friend's advice. Say to her: "Is the man a fool? is he a knave? a humbug, a hypocrite, a ninny, a noodle? If he is any or all of these, of course there is no sense in trifling with him. Cut him short at once — blast his hopes with lightning rapidity and keenness. Is he something better than this? has he at least common sense, a good disposition, a manageable temper? Then consider the matter. Say further: "You feel a disgust towards him now — an utter repugnance. Very likely, but be so good as to remember you don't know him; you have only had three or four days' acquaintance with him. Longer and closer intimacy might reconcile you to a wonderful extent. And now I'll tell you a word of truth, at which you may be offended or not as you like." Say to her: "From what I know of your character, and I think I know it pretty well, I should say you will never love before marriage. After that ceremony is over, and after you have had some months to settle down, and to get accustomed to the creature you have taken for your worse half, you will probably make a most affectionate and happy wife; even if the individual should not prove all you could wish, you will be indulgent toward his little follies and foibles, and will not feel much annoyance at them. This will especially be the case if he should have sense sufficient to allow you to guide him in important matters." Say also: "I hope you will not have the romantic folly to wait for what the French call 'une grande passion.' My good girl, 'une grande passion' is 'une grande folie.' Mediocrity in all things is wisdom; mediocrity in the sensations is superlative wisdom." Say to her: "When you are as old as I am (I am sixty at least, being your grandmother), you will find that the majority of those worldly precepts, whose seeming coldness shocks and repels us in youth, are founded in wisdom."

No girl should fall in love till the offer is actually made. This maxim is just. I will even extend and confirm it: No young lady should fall in love till the offer has been made, accepted, the marriage ceremony performed, and the first half-year of wedded life has passed away. A woman may then begin to love, but with great precaution, very coolly, very moderately, very rationally. If she ever loves so much that a harsh word or a cold look cuts her to the heart she is a fool. If she ever loves so much that her husband's will is her law, and that she has got into a habit of watching his looks in order that she may anticipate his wishes, she will soon be a neglected fool.

Charlotte Brontë to Ellen Nussey

December 15th, 1852.

I inclose another note which, taken in conjunction with the incident immediately preceding it, and with a long series of indications whose meaning I scarce ventured hitherto to interpret to myself, much less hint to any other, has left on my mind a feeling of deep concern. This note you will see is from Mr. Nicholls.

I know not whether you have ever observed him specially when staying here. Your perception is generally quick enough — *too* quick, I have sometimes thought; yet as you never said anything, I restrained my own dim misgivings, which could not claim the sure guide of vision. What papa has seen or guessed I will not inquire, though I may conjecture. He has minutely noticed all Mr. Nicholls's low spirits, all his threats of expatriation, all his symptoms of impaired health — noticed them with little sympathy and much indirect sarcasm. On Monday evening Mr. Nicholls was here to tea. I vaguely felt without clearly seeing, as without seeing I have felt for some time, the meaning of his constant looks, and strange, feverish restraint. After tea I withdrew to the dining-room as usual. As usual, Mr. Nicholls sat with papa till between eight and nine o'clock. I then heard him open the parlour door as if going. I expected the clash of the front door. He stopped in the passage; he tapped; like lightning it flashed on me what was coming. He entered; he stood before me. What his words were you can guess; his manner you can hardly realise, nor can I forget it. Shaking from head to foot, looking deadly pale, speaking low, vehemently, yet with difficulty, he made me for the first time feel what it costs a man to declare affection where he doubts response. The spectacle of one ordinarily so statue-like thus trembling, stirred, and overcome, gave me a kind of strange shock. He spoke of sufferings he had borne for months, of sufferings he could endure no longer, and craved leave for some hope. I could only entreat him to leave me then and promise a reply on the morrow. I asked him if he had spoken to papa. He said he dared not. I think I half led, half put him out of the room. When he was gone I immediately went to papa, and told him what had taken place. Agitation and anger disproportionate to the occasion ensued; if I had *loved* Mr. Nicholls, and had heard such epithets applied to him as were used, it would have transported me past my patience; as it was, my blood boiled with a sense of injustice. But papa worked himself into a state not to be trifled with: the veins on his temples started up like whip-cord, and his eyes became suddenly bloodshot. I made haste to promise that Mr. Nicholls should on the morrow have a distinct refusal.

I wrote yesterday and got this note. There is no need to add to this statement any comment. Papa's vehement antipathy to the bare thought of any one thinking of me as a wife, and Mr. Nicholls's distress, both give me pain. Attachment to Mr Nicholls you are aware I never entertained, but the poignant pity inspired by his state on Monday evening, by the hurried revelation of his sufferings for many months, is something galling and irksome. That he cared something for me, and wanted me to care for him, I have long suspected, but I did not know the degree or strength of his feelings. Dear Nell, good-bye. — Yours faithfully,

C. Brontë.

Charlotte Brontë to Ellen Nussey

Haworth, April 11th, 1854.

Mr. Nicholls came on Monday, and was here all last week. Matters have progressed thus since July. He renewed his visit in September, but then matters so fell out that I saw little of him. He continued to write. The correspondence pressed on my mind. I grew very miserable in keeping it from papa. At last sheer pain made me gather courage to break it. I told all. It was very hard and rough work at the time, but the issue after a few days was that I obtained leave to continue the communication. Mr. Nicholls came in January; he was ten days in the neighbourhood. I saw much of him. I had stipulated with papa for opportunity to become better acquainted. I had it, and all I learnt inclined me to esteem and affection. Still papa was very, very hostile, bitterly unjust.

I told Mr. Nicholls the great obstacle that lay in his way. He has persevered. The result of this, his last visit, is, that papa's consent is gained, that his respect, I believe, is won, for Mr. Nicholls has in all things proved himself disinterested and forbearing. Certainly, I must respect him, nor can I withhold from him more than mere cool respect. In fact, dear Ellen, I am engaged.

Mr. Nicholls, in the course of a few months, will return to the curacy of Haworth. I stipulated that I would not leave papa; and to papa himself I proposed a plan of residence which should maintain his seclusion and convenience uninvaded, and in a pecuniary sense bring him gain instead of loss. What seemed at one time impossible is now arranged, and papa begins really to take a pleasure in the prospect.

For myself, dear Ellen, while thankful to One who seems to have guided me through much difficulty, much and deep distress and perplexity of mind, I am still very calm, very inexpectant. What I taste of happiness is of the soberest order. I trust to love my husband. I am grateful for his tender love to me. I believe him to be an affectionate, a conscientious, a high-principled man; and if, with all this, I should yield to regrets that fine talents, congenial tastes and thoughts are not added, it seems to me I should be most presumptuous and thankless.

Providence offers me this destiny. Doubtless, then, it is the best for me. Nor do I shrink from wishing those dear to me one not less happy.

It is possible that our marriage may take place in the course of the summer. Mr. Nicholls wishes it to be in July. He spoke of you with great kindness, and said he hoped you would be at our wedding. I said I thought of having no other bridesmaid. Did I say rightly? I mean the marriage to be literally as quiet as possible.

Do not mention these things just yet. I mean to write to Miss Wooler shortly. Good-bye. There is a strange half-sad feeling in making these announcements. The whole thing is something other than imagination paints it beforehand; cares, fears, come mixed inextricably with hopes. I trust yet to talk the matter over with you. Often last week I wished for your presence and said so to Mr. Nicholls — Arthur, as I now call him, but he said it was the only time and place when he could not have wished to see you. Good-bye. — Yours affectionately,

C. Brontë.

Charlotte Brontë to Ellen Nussey

August 9th, 1854.

Since I came home I have not had an unemployed moment. My life is changed indeed: to be wanted continually, to be constantly called for and occupied seems so strange; yet it is a marvellously good thing. As yet I don't quite understand how some wives grow so selfish. As far as my experience of matrimony goes, I think it tends to draw you out of, and away from yourself. . . .

Dear Nell, during the last six weeks, the colour of my thoughts is a good deal changed: I know more of the realities of life than I once did. I think many false ideas are propagated, perhaps unintentionally. I think those married women who indiscriminately urge their acquaintance to marry, much to blame. For my part, I can only say with deeper sincerity and fuller significance what I always said in theory, "Wait God's will." Indeed, indeed, Nell, it is a solemn and strange and perilous thing for a woman to become a wife. Man's lot is far, far different. Tell me when you think you can come. Papa is better, but not well. How is your mother? give my love to her. — Yours faithfully,

C. B. Nicholls.

Herman Melville

Herman Melville's letters to his mentor, Nathaniel Hawthorne, reflect a passion not only for the literary pursuits they shared but for the older novelist himself. The two were neighbors, Melville living in Pittsfield, Massachusetts, and Hawthorne a few miles away in Lenox. By the time Melville wrote the following letters, Hawthorne had achieved fame for his novels *The Scarlet Letter* and *The House of the Seven Gables*, and Melville was a popular novelist in his own right. As he completed *Moby-Dick* — which he called "my Whale," a book close to his heart but destined, he knew, to be misunderstood — Melville came to feel even more strongly about Hawthorne, who expressed an insightful admiration for the work. Although Hawthorne's replies have been lost, scholars know he felt ill at ease with Melville's intense affection, distancing himself from his protégé after 1851.

Herman Melville to Nathaniel Hawthorne

> *Pittsfield, Wednesday morning.*
> [March(?) 1851]

My dear Hawthorne, —

Concerning the young gentleman's shoes, I desire to say that a pair to fit him, of the desired pattern, cannot be had in all Pittsfield, — a fact which sadly impairs that metropolitan pride I formerly took in the capital of Berkshire. Henceforth Pittsfield must hide its head. However, if a pair of *bootees* will at all answer, Pittsfield will be very happy to provide them. Pray mention all this to Mrs. Hawthorne, and command me.

"The House of the Seven Gables: A Romance. By Nathaniel Hawthorne. One vol. 16 mo, pp. 344." The contents of this book do not belie its rich, clustering, romantic title. With great enjoyment we spent almost an hour in each separate gable. This book is like a fine old chamber, abundantly, but still judiciously, furnished with precisely that sort of furniture best fitted to furnish it. There are rich hangings, wherein are braided scenes from tragedies! There is old china with rare devices, set out on the carved buffet; there are long and indolent lounges to throw yourself upon; there is an admirable sideboard, plentifully stored with good viands; there is a smell as of old wine in the pantry; and finally, in one corner, there is a dark little black-letter volume in golden clasps, entitled "Hawthorne: A Problem." It has delighted us; it has piqued a reperusal; it has robbed us of a day, and made us a present of a whole year of thoughtfulness; it has bred great exhilaration and exultation with the remembrance that the architect of the Gables resides only six miles off, and not three thousand miles away, in England, say. We think the book, for pleasantness of running interest, surpasses the other works of the author. The curtains are more drawn; the sun comes in more; genialities peep out more. Were we to particularize what most struck us in the deeper passages, we would point out the scene where Clifford, for a moment, would fain throw himself forth from the window to join the procession; or the scene where the judge is left seated in his ancestral chair. Clifford is full of an awful truth throughout. He is conceived in the finest, truest spirit. He is no caricature. He is Clifford. And here we would say that, did circumstances permit, we should like nothing better than to devote an elaborate and careful paper to the full consideration and analysis of the purport and significance of what so strongly characterizes all of this author's writings. There is a certain tragic phase of humanity which, in our opinion, was never more powerfully embodied than by Hawthorne. We mean the tragedies of human thought in its own unbiassed, native, and profounder workings. We think that into no recorded mind has the intense feeling of the usable truth ever entered more deeply than into this man's. By usable truth, we mean the apprehension of the absolute condition of present things as they strike the eye of the man who fears them not, though they do their worst to him, — the man who, like Russia or the British Empire, declares himself a sovereign nature (in himself) amid the powers of heaven, hell, and earth. He may perish; but so long as he exists he insists upon treating with all Powers upon an equal basis. If any of those other Powers choose to withhold certain secrets, let them; that does not impair my sovereignty in myself; that does not make me tributary. And perhaps, after all, there is *no* secret. We incline to think that the Problem of the Universe is like the Freemason's mighty secret, so terrible to all children. It turns out, at last, to consist in a triangle, a mallet, and an apron, — nothing more! We incline to think that God cannot explain His own secrets, and that He would like a little information upon certain points Himself. We mortals astonish Him as much as He us. But it is this *Being* of the matter; there lies the knot with which we choke ourselves. As soon as you say *Me*, a *God*, a *Nature*, so soon you jump off from your stool and hang from the beam. Yes, that word is the hangman. Take God out of the dictionary, and you would have Him in the street.

There is the grand truth about Nathaniel Hawthorne. He says No! in thunder; but the Devil himself cannot make him say *yes*. For all men who say *yes*, lie; and all men who say *no*, — why, they are in the happy condition of judicious, unincumbered travellers in Europe; they cross the frontiers into Eternity with nothing but a carpet-bag, — that is to say, the Ego. Whereas those *yes*-gentry, they travel with heaps of baggage, and, damn them! they will never get through the Custom House. What's the reason, Mr. Hawthorne, that in the last stages of metaphysics a fellow always falls to *swearing* so? I could rip an hour. You see, I began with a little criticism extracted for your benefit from the "Pittsfield Secret Review," and here I have landed in Africa.

Walk down one of these mornings and see me. No nonsense; come. Remember me to Mrs. Hawthorne and the children.

H. Melville.

P.S. The marriage of Phoebe with the daguerreotypist is a fine stroke, because of his turning out to be a *Maule*. If you pass Hepzibah's cent-shop, buy me a Jim Crow (fresh) and send it to me by Ned Higgins.

Herman Melville to Nathaniel Hawthorne

[Pittsfield, June (?) 1851]

My dear Hawthorne, —

I should have been rumbling down to you in my pine-board chariot a long time ago, were it not that for some weeks past I have been more busy than you can well imagine, — out of doors, — building and patching and tinkering away in all directions. Besides, I had my crops to get in, — corn and potatoes (I hope to show you some famous ones by and by), — and many other things to attend to, all accumulating upon this one particular season. I work myself; and at night my bodily sensations are akin to those I have so often felt before, when a hired man, doing my day's work from sun to sun. But I mean to continue visiting you until you tell me that my visits are both supererogatory and superfluous. With no son of man do I stand upon any etiquette or ceremony, except the Christian ones of charity and honesty. I am told, my fellow-man, that there is an aristocracy of the brain. Some men have boldly advocated and asserted it. Schiller seems to have done so, though I don't know much about him. At any rate, it is true that there have been those who, while earnest in behalf of political equality, still accept the intellectual estates. And I can well perceive, I think, how a man of superior mind can, by its intense cultivation, bring himself, as it were, into a certain spontaneous aristocracy of feeling, — exceedingly nice and fastidious, — similar to that which, in an English Howard, conveys a torpedo-fish thrill at the slightest contact with a social plebian. So, when you see or hear of my ruthless democracy on all sides, you may possibly feel a touch of a shrink, or something of that sort. It is but nature to be shy of a mortal who boldly declares that a thief in jail is as honorable a personage as Gen. George Washington. This is ludicrous. But Truth is the silliest thing under the sun. Try to get a living by the Truth — and go to the Soup Societies. Heavens! Let any clergyman try to preach the Truth from its very stronghold, the pulpit, and they would ride him out of his church on his own pulpit bannister. It can hardly be doubted that all Reformers are bottomed upon the truth, more or less; and to the world at large are not reformers almost universally laughing-stocks? Why so? Truth is ridiculous to men. Thus easily in my room here do I, conceited and garrulous, revere the test of my Lord Shaftesbury.

It seems an inconsistency to assert unconditional democracy in all things, and yet confess a dislike to all mankind — in the mass. But not so. — But it's an endless sermon, — no more of it. I began by saying that the reason I have not been to Lenox is this, — in the evening I feel completely done up, as the phrase is, and incapable of the long jolting to get to your house and back. In a week or so, I go to New York, to bury myself in a third-story room, and work and slave on my "Whale" while it is driving through the press. *That* is the only way I can finish it now, — I am so pulled hither and thither by circumstances. The calm, the coolness, the silent grass-growing mood in which a man *ought* always to compose, — that, I fear, can seldom be mine. Dollars damn me; and the malicious Devil is forever grinning in upon me, holding the door ajar. My dear Sir, a presentiment is on me, — I shall at last be worn out and perish, like an old nutmeg-grater, grated to pieces by the constant attrition of the wood, that is, the nutmeg. What I feel most moved to write, that is banned, — it will not pay. Yet, altogther, write the *other* way I cannot. So the product is a final hash, and all my books are botches. I'm rather sore, perhaps, in this letter; but see my hand! — four blisters on this palm, made by hoes and hammers within the last few days. It is a rainy morning; so I am indoors, and all work suspended. I feel cheerfully disposed, and therefore I write a little bluely. Would the Gin were here! If ever, my dear Hawthorne, in the eternal times that are to come, you and I shall sit down in Paradise, in some little shady corner by ourselves; and if we shall by any means be able to smuggle a basket of champagne there (I won't believe in a Temperance Heaven), and if we shall then cross our celestial legs in the celestial grass that is forever tropical, and strike our glasses and our heads together, till both musically ring in concert,—then, O my dear fellow-mortal, how shall we pleasantly discourse of all the things manifold which now so distress us, —when all the earth shall be but a reminiscence, yea, its final dissolution an antiquity. Then shall songs be composed as when wars are over; humorous, comic songs, — "Oh, when I lived in that queer little hole called the world," or, "Oh, when I toiled and sweated below," or, "Oh, when I knocked and was knocked in the fight" —yes, let us look forward to such things. Let us swear that, though now we sweat, yet it is because of the dry heat which is indispensable to the nourishment of the vine which is to bear the grapes that are to give us the champagne hereafter.

But I was talking about the "Whale." As the fishermen say, "he's in his flurry" when I left him some three weeks ago. I'm going to take him by his jaw, however, before long, and finish him up in some fashion or other. What's the use of elaborating what, in its very essence, is so short-lived as a modern book? Though I wrote the Gospels in this century, I should die in the gutter. —I talk all about myself, and this is selfishness and egotism. Granted. But how help it? I am writing to you; I know little about you, but something about myself. So I write about myself, — at least, to you. Don't trouble yourself, though, about writing; and don't trouble yourself about visiting; and when you *do* visit, don't trouble yourself about talking. I will do all the writing and visiting and talking myself. — By the way, in the last "Dollar Magazine" I read "The Unpardonable Sin." He was a sad fellow, that Ethan Brand. I have no doubt you are by this time responsible for many a shake and tremor of the tribe of "general readers." It is a frightful poetical creed that the cultivation of the brain eats out the heart. But it's my *prose* opinion that in most cases, in those men who have fine brains and work them well, the heart extends down to hams. And though you smoke them with the fire of tribulation, yet, like veritable hams, the head only gives the richer and the better flavor. I stand for the heart. To the dogs with the head! I had rather be a fool with a heart, than Jupiter Olympus with his head. The reason the mass of men fear God, and *at bottom dislike* Him, is because they rather distrust His heart, and fancy Him all brain like a watch. (You perceive I employ a capital initial in the pronoun refering to the Deity; don't you think there is a slight dash of flunkeyism in that usage?) Another thing. I was in New York for four-and-twenty hours the other day, and saw a portrait of N. H. And I have seen and heard many flattering (in a publisher's point of view) allusions to the "Seven Gables." And I have seen "Tales," and "A New Volume" announced, by N.H. So upon the whole, I say to myself, this N.H. is in the ascendant. My dear Sir, they begin to patronize. All Fame is patronage. Let me be infamous: there is no patronage in *that*. What "reputation" H.M. has is horrible. Think of it! To go down to posterity is bad enough any way; but to go down as a "man who lived among the cannibals!" When I speak of posterity, in reference to myself, I only mean the babies who will probably be born in the moment immediately ensuing upon my giving up the ghost. I shall go down to some of them, in all likelihood. "Typee" will be given to them, perhaps, with their gingerbread. I have come to regard this matter of Fame as the most transparent of all vanities. I read Solomon more and more, and every time see deeper and deeper and unspeakable meanings in him. I did not think of Fame, a year ago, as I do now. My development has been all within a few years past. I am like one of those seeds taken out of the Egyptian Pyramids, which after being three thousand years a seed and nothing but a seed, being planted in English soil, it developed itself, grew to greenness, and then fell to mould. So I. Until I was twenty-five, I had no development at all. From my twenty-fifth year I date my life. Three weeks have scarcely passed, at any time between then and now, that I have not unfolded within myself. But I feel that I am now come to the inmost leaf of the bulb, and that shortly the flower must fall to the mould. It seems to be now that Solomon was the truest man who ever spoke, and yet that he a little *managed* the truth with a view to popular conservatism; or else there have been many corruptions and interpolations of the text. — In reading some of Goethe's sayings, so worshipped by his votaries, I came across this, *"Live in the all."* That is to say, your separate identity is but a wretched one, — good; but get out of yourself, spread and expand yourself, and bring to yourself the tinglings of life that are felt in the flowers and the woods, that are felt in the planets Saturn and Venus, and the Fixed Stars. What nonsense! Here is a fellow with a raging toothache. "My dear boy," Goethe says to him, "you are sorely afflicted with that tooth; but you must *live in the all,* and then you will be happy!" As with all great genius, there is an immense deal of flummery in Goethe, and in proportion to my own contact with him, a monstrous deal of it in me.

H. Melville.

P.S. "Amen!" saith Hawthorne.

N.B. This "all" feeling, though, there is some truth in. You must often have felt it, lying on the grass on a warm summer's day. Your legs seem to send out shoots into the earth. Your hair feels like leaves upon your head. This is the *all* feeling. But what plays the mischief with the truth is that men will insist upon the universal application of a temporary feeling or opinion.

P.S. You must not fail to admire my discretion in paying the postage on this letter.

Herman Melville to Nathaniel Hawthorne

November 17, 1851
Pittsfield, Monday afternoon.

My Dear Hawthorne,

People think that if a man has undergone any hardship, he should have a reward; but for my part, if I have done the hardest possible day's work, and then come to sit down in a corner and eat my supper comfortably — why, then I don't think I deserve any reward for my hard day's work — for am I not now at peace? Is not my supper good? My peace and my supper are my reward, my dear Hawthorne. So your joy-giving and exultation-breeding letter is not my reward for my ditcher's work with that book, but is the good goddess's bonus over and above what was stipulated for — for not one man in five cycles, who is wise, will expect appreciative recognition from his fellows, or any one of them. Appreciation! Recognition! Is love appreciated? Why, ever since Adam, who has got to the meaning of this great allegory — the world? Then we pygmies must be content to have our paper allegories but ill comprehended. I say your appreciation is my glorious gratuity. In my proud, humble way, — a shepherd-king, — I was lord of a little vale in the solitary Crimea; but you have now given me the crown of India. But on trying it on my head, I found it fell down on my ears, notwithstanding their asinine length — for it's only such ears that sustain such crowns.

Your letter was handed me last night on the road going to Mr. Morewood's, and I read it there. Had I been at home, I would have sat down at once and answered it. In me divine magnanimities are spontaneous and instantaneous — catch them while you can. The world goes round, and the other side comes up. So now I can't write what I felt. But I felt pantheistic then — your heart beat in my ribs and mine in yours, and both in God's. A sense of unspeakable security is in me this moment, on account of your having understood the book. I have written a wicked book, and feel spotless as the lamb. Ineffable socialities are in me. I would sit down and dine with you and all the gods in old Rome's Pantheon. It is a strange feeling — no hopefulness is in it, no despair. Content — that is it; and irresponsibility; but without licentious inclination. I speak now of my profoundest sense of being, not of an incidental feeling.

Whence come you, Hawthorne? By what right do you drink from my flagon of life? And when I put it to my lips — lo, they are yours and not mine. I feel that the Godhead is broken up like the bread at the

Supper, and that we are the pieces. Hence this infinite fraternity of feeling. Now, sympathizing with the paper, my angel turns over another page. You did not care a penny for the book. But, now and then as you read, you understood the pervading thought that impelled the book — and that you praised. Was it not so? You were archangel enough to despise the imperfect body, and embrace the soul. Once you hugged the ugly Socrates because you saw the flame in the mouth, and heard the rushing of the demon, — the familiar, — and recognized the sound; for you have heard it in your own solitudes.

My dear Hawthorne, the atmospheric skepticisms steal into me now, and make me doubtful of my sanity in writing you thus. But, believe me, I am not mad, most noble Festus! But truth is ever incoherent, and when the big hearts strike together, the concussion is a little stunning. Farewell. Don't write a word about the book. That would be robbing me of my miserly delight. I am heartily sorry I ever wrote anything about you — it was paltry. Lord, when shall we be done growing? As long as we have anything more to do, we have done nothing. So, now, let us add Moby Dick to our blessing, and step from that. Leviathan is not the biggest fish; — I have heard of Krakens.

This is a long letter, but you are not at all bound to answer it. Possibly, if you do answer it, and direct it to Herman Melville, you will missend it — for the very fingers that now guide this pen are not precisely the same that just took it up and put it on this paper. Lord, when shall we be done changing? Ah! it's a long stage, and no inn in sight, and night coming, and the body cold. But with you for a passenger, I am content and can be happy. I shall leave the world, I feel, with more satisfaction for having come to know you. Knowing you persuades me more than the Bible of our immortality.

What a pity, that, for your plain, bluff letter, you should get such gibberish! Mention me to Mrs. Hawthorne and to the children, and so, good-by to you, with my blessing.

Herman.

P.S. I can't stop yet. If the world was entirely made up of Magians, I'll tell you what I should do. I should have a papermill established at one end of the house, and so have an endless riband of foolscap rolling in upon my desk; and upon that endless riband I should write a thousand — a million — billion thoughts, all under the form of a letter to you. The divine magnet is on you, and my magnet responds. Which is the biggest? A foolish question — they are *One*.

P.P.S. Don't think that by writing me a letter, you shall always be bored with an immediate reply to it — and so keep both of us delving over a writing-desk eternally. No such thing! I sh'n't always answer your letters, and you may do just as you please.

Emily Dickinson

Always close to her sister, Lavinia (Vinnie), and her brother, Austin, Emily Dickinson formed an even more intimate bond with Austin's sweetheart, fiancée, and wife, Susan Gilbert. In her early twenties, around the time she started writing poetry, Emily Dickinson wrote a series of ardent letters to the woman whose affections she shared with her brother. The correspondence tapered off after Austin and Susan married, and as Emily donned her white dress and sequestered herself in her father's house, but the sisters-in-law continued to share a close, if more circumspect, attachment.

Emily Dickinson to Susan Gilbert Dickinson

[About February 6, 1852]

Will you let me come dear Susie — looking just as I do, my dress soiled and worn, my grand old apron, and my hair — Oh Susie, time would fail me to enumerate my appearance, yet I love you just as dearly as if I was e'er so fine, so you wont care, will you? I am so glad dear Susie — that our hearts are always clean, and always neat and lovely, so not to be ashamed. I have been hard at work this morning, and I ought to be working now — but I cannot deny myself the luxury of a minute or two with you.

The dishes may wait dear Susie — and the uncleared table stand, *them* I have always with me, but you, I have "not always" — *why* Susie, Christ hath saints *manie* — and I have *few*, but thee — the angels shant have Susie — no — no no!

Vinnie is sewing away like a *fictitious* seamstress, and I half expect some knight will arrive at the door, confess himself a *nothing* in presence of her loveliness, and present his heart and hand as the only vestige of him worthy to be refused.

Vinnie and I have been talking about growing old, today. Vinnie thinks *twenty* must be a fearful position for one to occupy — I tell her I dont care if I am young or not, had as lief be thirty, and you, as most anything else. Vinnie expresses her sympathy at my "sere and yellow leaf" and resumes her work, dear Susie, tell me how *you* feel — ar'nt these days in one's life when to be old dont seem a thing so sad —

I do feel gray and grim, this morning, and I feel it would be a comfort to have a piping voice, and broken back, and scare little children. Dont *you* run, Susie dear, for I wont do any harm, and I do love you dearly tho' I do feel so frightful.

Oh my darling one, how long you wander from me, how weary I grow of waiting and looking, and calling for you; sometimes I shut my eyes, and shut my heart towards you, and try hard to forget you because you grieve me so, but you'll never go away, Oh you never will — say, Susie, promise me again, and I will smile faintly — and take up my little cross again of sad — *sad* separation. How vain it seems to *write*, when one knows how to feel — how much more near and dear to sit beside you, talk with you, hear the tones of your voice; so hard to "deny thyself, and take up thy cross, and follow me" — give me strength, Susie, write me of hope and love, and of hearts that *endured*, and great was their reward of "Our Father who art in Heaven." I don't know how I shall bear it, when the gentle spring comes; if she should come and see me and talk to me of you, Oh it would surely kill me! While the frost clings to the windows, and the World is stern and drear; this absence is easier; the *Earth* mourns too, for all her little birds; but when they all come back again, and she sings and is so merry — pray, what will become of me? Susie, forgive me, forget all what I say, get some sweet little scholar to read a gentle hymn, about Bethleem and Mary, and you will sleep on sweetly and have as peaceful dreams, as if I had never written you all these ugly things. Never mind the letter Susie, I wont be angry with you if you dont give me any at all — for I know how busy you are, and how little of that dear strength remains when it is evening, with which to think and write. Only *want* to write me, only sometimes sigh that you are far from me, and that will do, Susie! Dont you think we are good and patient, to let you go so long; and dont we think you're a darling, a real beautiful hero, to toil for people, and teach them, and leave your own dear home? Because we pine and repine, dont think we forget the precious patriot at war in other lands! Never be mournful, Susie — be happy and have cheer, for how many of the long days have gone away since I wrote you — and it is almost noon, and soon the night will come, and then there is one less day of the long pilgrimage. Mattie is very smart, talks of you *much*, my darling; I must leave you now — "one little hour of Heaven," thank who did give it me, and will he also grant me one longer and *more* when it shall please his love — bring Susie home, ie! Love always, and ever, and true!

Emily —

Emily Dickinson to Susan Gilbert Dickinson

[April 5, 1852]

Will you be kind to me, Susie? I am naughty and cross, this morning, and nobody loves me here; nor would *you* love me, if you should see me frown, and hear how loud the door bangs whenever I go through; and yet it is'nt anger — I dont believe it is, for when nobody sees, I brush away big tears with the corner of my apron, and then go working on — bitter tears, Susie — so hot that they burn my cheeks, and almost scorch my eyeballs, but *you* have wept much, and you know they are less of anger than *sorrow*.

And I do love to run fast — and hide away from them all; here in dear Susie's bosom, I know is love and rest, and I never would go away, did not the big world call me, and beat me for not working.

Little Emerald Mack is washing. I can hear the warm suds, splash. I just gave her my pocket handkerchief — so I cannot cry anymore. And Vinnie sweeps — sweeps, upon the chamber stairs; and Mother is hurrying round with her hair in a silk pocket handkerchief, on account of dust. Oh Susie, it is dismal, sad and drear eno' — and the sun dont shine, and the clouds look cold and gray, and the wind dont blow, but it *pipes* the shrillest roundelay, and the birds dont sing, but twitter — and there's nobody to smile! Do I paint it *natural* — Susie, so you think how it looks? Yet dont you care — for it wont last so always, and we love you just as well — and think of you, as dearly, as if it were not so. Your precious letter, Susie, it sits here now, and smiles so kindly at me, and gives me such sweet thoughts of the dear writer. When you come home, darling, I shant have your letters, shall I, but I shall have *yourself*, which is more — Oh more, and better, than I can even think! I sit here with my little whip, cracking the time away, till not an hour is left of it — then you are here! And *Joy* is here — joy now and forevermore!

'Tis only a few days, Susie, it will soon go away, yet I say, go now, this very moment, for I need her — I must have her, Oh give her to me!

Mattie is dear and true, I love her very dearly — and Emily Fowler, too, is very dear to me — and Tempe — and Abby, and Eme', I am sure — I love them all — and I hope they love me, but, Susie, there's a great corner still; I fill it with that is gone, I hover round and round it, and call it darling names, and bid it speak to me, and ask it if it's Susie, and it answers, Nay, Ladie, Susie is stolen away!

Do I repine, is it all murmuring, or am I sad and lone, and cannot, cannot help it? Sometimes when I do feel so, I think it may be wrong, and that God will punish me by taking you away; for he is very kind to let me write to you, and to give me your sweet letters, but my heart wants *more.*

Have you ever thought of it Susie, and yet I know you have, how much these hearts claim; why I dont believe in the whole, wide world, are such hard little creditors — such real little *misers,* as you and I carry with us, in our bosoms every day. I cant help thinking sometimes, when I hear about the ungenerous, Heart, keep very still — or someone will find you out!

I am going out on the doorstep, to get you some new — green grass — I shall pick it down in the corner, where you and I used to sit, and have long fancies. And perhaps the dear little grasses were growing all the while — and perhaps they heard what we said, but they cant *tell!* I have come in now, dear Susie, and here is what I found — not quite so glad and green as when we used to sit there, but a sad and pensive grassie — mourning o'er hopes. No doubt some spruce, young *Plantain leaf* won its young heart away, and then proved false — and dont you wish *none* proved so, but little Plantains?

I do think it's wonderful, Susie, that our hearts dont break, *every day,* when I think of all the whiskers, and all the gallant men, but I guess I'm made with nothing but a hard heart of stone, for it dont break any, and dear Susie, if mine is stony, your's is stone, upon stone, for you never yield *any,* where I seem quite beflown. Are we going to *ossify* always, say, Susie — how will it be? When I see the Popes and the Polloks, and the John-Milton Browns, I think we are *liable,* but I dont know! I am glad there's a big *future* waiting for me and you. You would love to know what I read — I hardly know what to tell you, my catalogue is so small.

I have just read three little books, not great, not thrilling — but sweet and true. "The Light in the Valley," "Only," and A "House upon a Rock" — I know you would love them all — yet they don't *bewitch* me any. There are no walks in the wood — no low and earnest voices, no moonlight, nor stolen love, but pure little lives, loving God, and their parents, and obeying the laws of the land; yet read, if you meet them, Susie, for they will do one good.

I have the promise of "Alton Lock" — a certain book, called "Olive," and the "Head of a Family," which was what Mattie named to you. Vinnie and I had "Bleak House" sent to us the other day — it is like him who wrote it — that is all I can say. Dear Susie, you were so happy when you wrote to me last — I am so glad, and you will be happy *now,* for *all* my sadness, *wont* you? I cant forgive me ever, if I have made you sad, or dimmed your eye for me. I write from the Land of Violets, and from the

Land of Spring, and it would ill become me to carry you nought but sorrows. I remember you, Susie, *always* — I keep you ever here, and when *you* are gone, then I'm gone — and we're 'neath one willow tree. I can only thank "the Father" for giving me such as you, I can only pray unceasingly, that he will bless my Loved One, and bring her back to me, to "go no more out forever." "Herein is Love." But *that* was Heaven — *this* is but *Earth*, yet Earth so *like* to Heaven, that I would hesitate, should the true one call away.

> Dear Susie — adieu!
> *Emilie* —

Father's sister is dead, and Mother wears black on her bonnet, and has a collar of crape. A great deal of love from Vinnie, and she wants that *little note*. Austin comes home on Wednesday, but he'll only stay two days, so I fancy we shant go sugaring, as "we did last year." *Last year* is *gone*, Susie, did you ever think of *that?* Joseph [Lyman] is out south somewhere, a very great way off, yet we hear from him —

Emily Dickinson to Susan Gilbert Dickinson

[Early June 1852]

They are cleaning house today, Susie, and I've made a flying retreat to my own little chamber, where with affection, and you, I will spend this my precious hour, most precious of all the hours which dot my flying days, and the one so dear, that for it I barter everything, and as soon as it is gone, I am sighing for it again.

I cannot believe, dear Susie, that I have stayed without you almost a whole year long; sometimes the time seems short, and the thought of you as warm as if you had gone but yesterday, and again if years and years had trod their silent pathway, the time would seem less long. And now how soon I shall have you, shall hold you in my arms; you will forgive the tears, Susie, they are so glad to come that it is not in my heart to reprove them and send them home. I dont know why it is — but there's something in your name, now you are taken from me, which fills my heart so full, and my eye, too. It is not that the mention *grieves* me, no, Susie, but I think of each "sunnyside" where we have sat together, and lest there be no more, I guess is what makes the tears come. Mattie was here last evening, and we sat on the front door stone, and talked about life and love, and whispered our childish fancies about such blissful things — the evening was gone so soon, and I walked home with Mattie beneath the silent moon, and wished for you, and Heaven. You did not come, Darling, but a bit of Heaven did, or so it *seemed* to us, as we walked side by side and wondered if the great blessedness which may be our's sometime, is granted now, to some. Those unions, my dear Susie, by which two lives are one, this sweet and strange adoption wherein we can but look, and are not yet admitted, how it can fill the heart, and make it gang wildly beating, how it will take *us* one day, and make us all it's own, and we shall not run away from it, but lie still and be happy!

You and I have been strangely silent upon this subject, Susie, we have often touched upon it, and as quickly fled away, as children shut their eyes when the sun is too bright for them. I have always hoped to know if you had no dear fancy, illuminating all your life, no one of whom you murmured in the faithful ear of night — and at whose side in fancy, you walked the livelong day; and when you come home, Susie, we must speak of these things. How dull our lives must seem to the bride, and the plighted maiden, whose days are fed with gold, and who gathers pearls every evening; but to the *wife*, Susie, sometimes the *wife forgotten*, our lives perhaps seem dearer than all others in the world; you have seen flowers at morning, *satisfied* with the dew, and those same sweet flowers at noon with their heads bowed in anguish before the mighty sun; think you these thirst blossoms will *now* need naught but — *dew?* No, they will cry for sunlight, and pine for the burning noon, tho' it scorches them, scathes them; they have got through with peace — they know that the man of noon, is *mightier* than the morning and their life is henceforth to him. Oh, Susie, it is dangerous, and it is all too dear, these simple trusting spirits, and the spirits mightier, which we cannot resist! It does so rend me, Susie, the thought of it when it comes, that I tremble lest at sometime I, too, am yielded up. Susie, you will forgive me my amatory strain — it has been a very long one, and if this saucy page did not here bind and fetter me, I might have had no end.

I have got the letter, Susie, dear little bud, and all — and the tears came again, that alone in this big world, I am not *quite* alone. Such tears are showers — friend, thro' which when smiles appear, the angels call them rainbows, and mimic them in Heaven.

And now in four weeks more — you are mine, *all* mine, except I *lend* you a little occasionally to Hattie and Mattie, if they promise not to lose you, and to bring you back very soon. I shall not count the days. I shall not fill my cups with this expected happiness, for perhaps if I do, the angels, being thirsty, will drink them up — I shall only *hope*, my Susie, and *that* tremblingly, for hav'nt barques the fullest, stranded upon the shore?

God is good, Susie, I trust he will save you, I pray that in his good time we once more meet each other, but if this life holds not another meeting for us, remember also, Susie, that it had no *parting* more, wherever that hour finds us, for which we have hoped so long, we shall not be separated, neither death, nor the grave can part us, so that we only *love!*

Your *Emilie* —

Austin has come and gone; life is so still again; why must the storm have calms? I hav'nt seen Root this term, I guess Mattie and I, are not sufficient for him! When will you come again, in a week? Let it be a *swift* week!

Vinnie sends much love, and Mother; and might I be so bold as to enclose a *remembrance?*

Emily Dickinson to Susan Gilbert Dickinson

[June 11, 1852]

I have but one thought, Susie, this afternoon of June, and *that* of you, and I have one prayer, only; dear Susie, *that* is *for* you. That you and I in *hand* as we e'en *do* in heart, might ramble away as children, among the woods and fields, and forget these many years, and these sorrowing cares, and each become a child again — I would it were so, Susie, and when I look around me and find myself alone, I sigh for you again; little sigh, and vain sigh, which will not bring you home.

I need you more and more, and the great world grows wider, and dear ones fewer and fewer, every day that you stay away — I miss my biggest heart; my own goes wandering round, and calls for Susie — Friends are too dear to sunder, Oh they are far too few, and how soon they will go away where you and I cannot find them, *dont* let us forget these things, for their remembrance *now* will save us many an anguish when it is *too late* to love them! Susie, forgive me Darling, for every word I say — my heart is full of you, none other than you in my thoughts, yet when I seek to say to you something not for the world, words fail me. If you were here — and Oh that you were, my Susie, we need not talk at all, our eyes would whisper for us, and your hand fast in mine, we would not ask for language — I try to bring you nearer, I chase the weeks away till they are quite departed, and fancy you have come, and I am on my way through the green lane to meet you, and my heart goes scampering so, that I have much ado to bring it back again, and learn it to be patient, till that dear Susie comes. Three weeks — they cant last always, for surely they must go with their little brothers and sisters to their long home in the west!

I shall grow more and more impatient until that dear day comes, for till now, I have only *mourned* for you; now I begin to *hope* for you.

Dear Susie, I have tried hard to think what you would love, of something I might send you — I at last saw my little Violets, they begged me to let them go, so here they are — and with them as Instructor, a bit of knightly grass, who also begged the favor to accompany them — they are but small, Susie, and I fear not fragrant now, but they will speak to you of warm hearts at home, and of the something faithful which "never slumbers nor sleeps" — Keep them 'neath your pillow, Susie, they will make you dream of blue-skies, and home, and the "blessed countrie"! You and I will have an hour with "Edward" and "Ellen Middleton," sometime when you get home — we must find out if some things contained therein are true, and if they are, what you and me are coming to!

Now, farewell, Susie, and Vinnie sends her love, and mother her's, and I add a kiss, shyly, lest there is somebody there! Dont let them see, *will* you Susie?

Emilie —

Why cant I be a Delegate to the great Whig Convention? — dont I know all about Daniel Webster, and the Tariff, and the Law? Then, Susie I could see you, during a pause in the session — but I don't like this country at all, and I shant stay here any longer! "Delenda est" America, Massachusetts and all!

open me carefully

Emily Dickinson to Susan Gilbert Dickinson

27 June 1852

Susie, will you indeed come home next Saturday, and be my own again, and kiss me as you used to? Shall I indeed behold you, not "darkly, but face to face" or am I *fancying* so, and dreaming blessed dreams from which the day will wake me? I hope for you so much, and feel so eager for you, feel that I *cannot* wait, feel that *now* I must have you — that the expectation once more to see your face again, makes me feel hot and feverish, and my heart beats so fast — I go to sleep at night, and the first thing I know, I am sitting there wide awake, and clasping my hands tightly, and thinking of next Saturday, and "never a bit" of you.

. . . Be patient then, my Sister, for the hours will haste away, and Oh *so* soon! Susie, I write most hastily, and very carelessly too, for it is time for me to get the supper, and my mother is gone and besides, my darling, so near I seem to you, that I *disdain* this pen, and wait for a *warmer* language. . . .

Your *Emilie* —

Emily Dickinson to Susan Gilbert Dickinson

[About 1854]

Sue — you can go or stay — There is but one alternative — We differ often lately, and this must be the last.

You need not fear to leave me lest I should be alone, for I often part with things I fancy I have loved, — sometimes to the grave, and sometimes to an oblivion rather bitterer that death — thus my heart bleeds so frequently that I shant mind the hemorrhage, and I only add an agony to several previous ones, and at the end of day remark — a bubble burst!

Such incidents would grieve me when I was but a child, and perhaps I could have wept when little feet hard by mine, stood still in the coffin, but eyes grow dry sometimes, and hearts get crisp and cinder, and had as lief burn.

Sue — I have lived by this. It is the lingering emblem of the Heaven I once dreamed, and though if this is taken, I shall remain alone, and though in that last day, the Jesus Christ you love, remark he does not know me — there is a darker spirit will not disown it's child.

Few have been given me, and if I love them so, that for *idolatry*, they are removed from me — I simply murmur *gone*, and the billow dies away into the boundless blue, and no one knows but me, that one went down today. We have walked very pleasantly — Perhaps this is the point at which our paths diverge — then pass on singing Sue, and up the distant hill I journey on.

I have a Bird in spring
Which for myself doth sing —
The spring decoys.
And as the summer nears —
And as the Rose appears,
Robin is gone.

Yet do I not repine
Knowing that Bird of mine
Though flown —
Learneth beyond the sea
Melody new for me
And will return.

Fast in a safer hand
Held in a truer Land
Are mine —
And though they now depart,
Tell I my doubting heart
They're thine.

In a serener Bright,
In a more golden light
I see
Each little doubt and fear,
Each little discord here
Removed.

Then will I not repine,
Knowing that Bird of mine
Though flown
Shall in a distant tree
Bright melody for me
Return.

                              E —

Elizabeth Cady Stanton

Elizabeth Cady Stanton and Susan B. Anthony, leading feminists of the
nineteenth century alongside Lucy Stone, Antoinette Brown Blackwell and
others, formed one of the most productive political partnerships in American

history. Allied earlier with abolitionist William Lloyd Garrison, Stanton grew disillusioned with the antislavery movement because of its discrimination against women. Meeting in 1851, Stanton and Anthony labored on behalf of women's rights until Stanton's death in 1902, even though they sometimes disagreed about goals and methods. For the most part sequestered at home with her husband, Henry, and their children, Stanton wrote speeches that the unattached Anthony delivered; together they published *The Revolution,* a women's rights newspaper, and authored the massive *History of Women's Suffrage.* As they worked together, the two women developed a deep friendship that at times waxed romantic. The strength of their intellectual and emotional union is apparent in selected letters sent by Stanton to Anthony.

Elizabeth Cady Stanton to Susan B. Anthony

Seneca Falls, March 1, 1853.

Dear Friend, — I do not know whether the world is quite willing or ready to discuss the question of marriage. I feel in my innermost soul that the thoughts I sent the convention are true. It is in vain to look for the elevation of woman so long as she is degraded in marriage. I hold that it is a sin, an outrage on our holiest feelings, to pretend that anything but deep, fervent love and sympathy constitute marriage. The right idea of marriage is at the foundation of all reforms. How strange it is that man will apply all the improvements in the arts and sciences to everything about him, animate or inanimate, but himself. If we properly understood the science of life, it would be far easier to give to the world harmonious, beautiful, noble, virtuous children, than it is to bring grown-up discord into harmony with the great divine soul of all. I ask for no laws on marriage. I say with Father Chipman, remove law and a false public sentiment, and woman will no more live as wife with a cruel, bestial drunkard than a servant, in this free country, will stay with a pettish, unjust mistress. If lawmakers insist upon exercising their prerogative in some way on this question, let them forbid any woman to marry until she is twenty-one; let them fine a woman $50 for every child she conceives by a drunkard. Women have no right to saddle the state with idiots who must be supported by the public. You know that the statistics of our idiot asylums show that nearly all are the offspring of drunkards. Women must be made to feel that the transmitting of immortal life is a solemn, responsible act, and should never be allowed except when the parents are in the highest condition of mind and body. Man in his lust has regulated long enough this whole question of sexual intercourse. Now let the mother of mankind, whose prerogative it is to set bounds to his indulgence, rouse up and give this whole matter a thorough, fearless examination. I am glad that Catholic priest said of my letter what he did. It will call attention to the subject; and if by martyrdom I can advance my race one step, I am ready for it. I feel, as never before, that this whole question of woman's rights turns on the pivot of the marriage relation, and, mark my word, sooner or later it will be the topic of discussion. I would not hurry it on, nor would I avoid it. Good night.

Elizabeth Cady Stanton to Susan B. Anthony

Seneca Falls, July 20, 1857.

Dear Susan, — I was glad to hear of Lucy Stone. I think a vast deal of her and Antoinette Brown. I regret so much that you and Lucy should have had even the slightest interruption to your friendship. I was much interested in the extract from her letter; although I agree with her that man, too, suffers in a false marriage relation, yet what can his suffering be compared with what every woman experiences whether happy or unhappy? I do not know that the laws and religion of our country even now are behind the public sentiment which makes woman the mere tool of man. He has made the laws and proclaimed the religion; so we have his exact idea of the niche he thinks God intended woman to fill. A man in marrying gives up no right; but a woman, every right, even the most sacred of all — the right to her own person. There will be no response among women to our demands until we have first aroused in them a sense of personal dignity and independence; and so long as our present false marriage relation continues, which in most cases is nothing more nor less than legalized prostitution, woman can have no self-respect, and of course man will have none for her; for the world estimates us according to the value we put upon ourselves. Personal freedom is the first right to be proclaimed, and that does not and cannot now belong to the relation of wife, to the mistress of the isolated home, to the financial dependent.

Elizabeth Cady Stanton to
Susan B. Anthony

Seneca Falls, August 20, 1857.

Dear Susan, — I did indeed see by the papers that you had once more stirred that part of intellectual stagnation, the educational convention. The *Times* was really quite complimentary. Henry brought me every item he could see about you. "Well," he would say, "another notice about Susan. You stir up Susan, and she stirs the world." What a set of fools those schoolmarms must be! Well, if in order to please men they wish to live on air, let them. I was glad you went to torment them. I will do anything to help you on. If I do nothing else this fall I am bound to aid you to get up an antislavery address. You must come here for a week or two and we will accomplish wonders. You and I have a prospect of a good long life. We shall not be in our prime before fifty, and after that we shall be good for twenty years at least. If we do not make old Davies shake in his shoes we will make him turn in his grave.

Elizabeth Cady Stanton to
Susan B. Anthony

New York, September 10, 1865.

Dearly Beloved, — Of course your critics take no note of all you have been to me, though I have often told them what a stimulus and inspiration you were through years of domestic cares. But while I shall always be happy to write for you whatever document you desire, I am not willing to be bullied when I honestly differ from you in opinion, as I do in the matter you mention. Well, the human family is affording you abundant experience in the degradation of women; their littleness and meanness are the result of their abject dependence, their utter want of self-respect. But this must needs be so until they reach a higher development. Poor things! How can they be frank and magnanimous in view of their education? So let us expect nothing of the present generation of them, and then we shall not be disappointed. The past month's experience has taught me some deep spiritual lessons, and I rejoice more than ever that

I have been absorbed in some great question beyond wealth, position, and personal aggrandisement. You cannot imagine how much I miss you.

Elizabeth Cady Stanton to Susan B. Anthony

St. Louis, December 28, 1869.

My dear Susan, — As to changing the name of the *Revolution*, I should consider it a great mistake. If all these people who for twenty years have been afraid to call their souls their own begin to prune us and the *Revolution*, we shall become the same galvanized mummies they are. There could not be a better name than *Revolution*. The establishing of woman on her rightful throne is the greatest revolution the world has ever known or ever will know. To bring it about is no child's play. You and I have not forgotten the conflict of the last twenty years — the ridicule, persecution, denunciation, detraction, the unmixed bitterness of our cup for the past two years, when even friends crucified us. A journal called the *Rosebud* might answer for those who come with kid gloves and perfumes to lay immortal wreaths on the monuments which in sweat and tears others have hewn and built; but for us and for that great blacksmith of ours who forges such red-hot thunderbolts for Pharisees, hypocrites, and sinners, there is no name like the *Revolution*. It does not seem to me worth while for me to take that long trip to Washington when I have all I can do all winter out here in the West. This field is ripe for the harvest. I am doing more good in stirring up these Western women than in talking to those old Washington politicians. I do not want to manage other people, neither do I want other people to manage me. I stand ready to pay anybody you can get to go to Washington in my stead. But of course I stand by you to the end. I would not see you crushed by rivals even if to prevent it required my being cut into inch bits. If you will promise solemnly to let me free in May, I will wear the yoke a few months longer, bravely and patiently. But I do hate conventions, for I dislike to be in a position where any set of people have the right to say, "For the sake of the cause don't do this or that." In fact I had rather give you five hundred dollars than go to Washington. But if your life depends on me, I will be your stay and staff to the end. No power in heaven, hell or earth can separate us, for our hearts are eternally wedded together. Ever yours, and here I mean *ever.*

Elizabeth Cady Stanton to Susan B. Anthony

New York, June 27, 1870.

Dearest Susan, — Do not feel depressed, my dear friend. What is good in us is immortal, and if the sore trials we have endured for three years are sifting out pride and selfishness, we shall not have suffered in vain. How I long to see my blessed Susan! Not only have I finished my lecture on marriage and divorce, but I have delivered it. When I spoke in Brooklyn on this subject, I had a splendid audience, and since the Apollo Hall meeting I have received letters innumerable. Women respond to this divorce speech as they never did to suffrage. In a word, I have had grand meetings. Oh, how the women flock to me with their sorrows. Such experiences as I listen to, plantation never equaled. Speaking of divorce, the New York *Sun* has an article about you and me "having dissolved partnership." Have you been getting a divorce out in Chicago without notifying me? I should like to know my present status. I shall not allow any such proceedings. I consider that our relations are to last for life; so make the best of it. As to the newspapers — our critics have overdone their work in the *Tribune,* and the *Sun* has come out with a reply to one of the *Tribune's* attacks on me. With love and faith that all is for the best.

Elizabeth Cady Stanton to Susan B. Anthony

Tenafly, January 10, 1880.

Dear Susan, — You have not made me take your position. I repudiate it from the bottom of my soul. It is conservative, autocratic, to the last degree. I accept no authority of either bibles or constitutions which tolerate the slavery of women. My rights were born with me and are the same over the whole globe. I may be denied their exercise in the mines of Siberia, in the empire of China and in the State of New York, through force, fraud, and sophistry; but they remain the same everywhere. Does my watch cease to be mine because some thief has taken forcible possession thereof? Of the three branches of government, the legislative, representing the people, is the primal source of power. I perceive that one of the lawyers you have consulted admits one of my points — that the legislature is above the courts; and yet the courts can declare null and void the acts of the legislature. But if the legislature can be above the courts and yet at times be in conflict with them, why on the same principle can it not be above the Constitution and yet in conflict with it? How do you amend the Constitution? The legislature, directly representing the people, decides that the Constitution needs amending, frames the amendment and submits it to the people, the majority saying yea or nay. Now where is the primary source of power? In the majority of the people. All this seems so plain to me that I wonder you halt so long over it. Think of you accepting the man-made constitution, the man-interpretation thereof, the man-amendment submitted by a convention of aristocrats, and the old secession reverence for a constitution. Why Garrison, who kicked and cuffed the old document for forty years, would turn in his grave to see printed in our *History of Woman Suffrage* your present ideas as to the authority and majesty of any of those constitutions, state or national. Ah, beware, Susan, lest you become "respectable," you become conservative. One-half of the people have had no voice in the setting up of this constitution of New York, and I, for one, would not let a member of the legislature skulk behind the constitution so as to hold me at bay for years until that document were amended. On the contrary, I would say to him: "You represent me and it is your duty to see that justice is done. Set aside technicalities and accepted interpretations of special acts, and on broad principles recognize my citizenship." The legal rule of interpretation is in the spirit of the document. The legislature has the right to enfranchise the women of New York. Susan, you must rise to the dignity of Lord Mansfield who, when law, popular sentiment, religion, custom, everything and everybody, believed in slavery, declared that no slave could breathe on English soil. You may, if you choose, write ten thousand footnotes giving in your adhesion to these man-made constitutions and appending your own name thereto, but wherever in your last revision of the proofs you have made me responsible for such todyism, I shall always bow my head with shame and sorrow.

Walt Whitman

Walt Whitman met Peter Doyle one stormy 1866 night in Washington, D.C., when the forty-seven-year-old poet boarded an empty streetcar piloted by the twenty-year-old conductor. As Doyle later recalled, "We were familiar at once—I put my hand on his knee—we understood." Always fond of workingmen, Whitman had what Doyle described as "an irresistible attraction," and the two instantly became close companions. Whitman's classic *Leaves of Grass* had come out in 1855 and his Civil War collection *Drum Taps* in 1865, but American critics had greeted his work coolly. He continued to revise and expand the earlier volume (incorporating, among other things, the poems from *Drum Taps*) for the rest of his life, publishing numerous editions. Whitman's letters describe his life in New York and New Jersey and send love to Doyle, especially when the younger man becomes despondent as a result of a skin condition that mars his face.

Walt Whitman to Peter Doyle

New York, Oct. 9, 1868.

Dear Pete. It is splendid here this forenoon—bright and cool. I was out early taking a short walk by the river only two squares from where I live. I received your letter last Monday, also the *Star* same date, and glad enough to hear from you and the oftener the better, every word is good (I am grateful to these young men on the R. R. for their love and remembrance to me—Dave and Jim and Charley Sorrell, Tom Hassett, Harry on No. 11). I sent you a letter on the 6th which I suppose you received next day. Tell Henry Hurt I received his letter of Oct. 5th all right, and that it was welcome. Political meetings here every night. The coming Pennsylvania and Ohio elections cause much talk and excitement. The fall is upon us; overcoats are in demand. I already begin to think about my return to Washington. A month has nearly passed away. I have received an invitation from a gentleman and his wife, friends of mine, at Providence, R. I., and shall probably go down there and spend a few days latter part of October. Shall I tell you about it or part of it just to fill up? I generally spend the forenoon in my room writing, etc., then take a bath fix up and go out about 12 and loafe somewhere or call on someone down town or on business, or perhaps if it is very pleasant and I feel like it ride a trip with some driver friend on Broadway from 23rd Street to Bowling Green, three miles each way. (Every day I find I have plenty to do, every hour is occupied with something.) You know it is a never ending amusement and study and recreation for me to ride a couple of hours of a pleasant afternoon on a Broadway stage in this way. You see everything as you pass, a sort of living, endless panorama— shops and splendid buildings and great windows: and on the broad sidewalks crowds of women richly dressed continually passing altogether different, superior in style and looks from any to be seen anywhere else — in fact a perfect stream of people — men too dressed in high style, and plenty of foreigners — and then in the streets the thick crowd of carriages, stages, carts, hotel and private coaches, and in fact all sorts of vehicles and many first class teams, mile after mile, and the splendor of such a great street and so many tall, ornamental, noble buildings many of them of white marble, and the gayety and motion on every side: you will not wonder how much attraction all this is on a fine day, to a great loafer like me, who enjoys so much seeing the busy world move by him, and exhibiting itself for his amusement, while he takes it easy and just looks on and observes. Then about the Broadway drivers, nearly all of them are my personal friends. Some have been attached to me for years and I to them. But I believe I have already mentioned them in a former letter. Yesterday I rode the trip I describe, with a friend on a 5th Avenue stage — No. 26, a sort [of] namesake of yours, Pete Calhoun, I have known him 9 or 10 years. The day was fine and I enjoyed the trip muchly. So I try to put in something in my letters to give you an idea of how I pass part of my time and what I see here in New York. Of course I have quite a variety. Some four or five hours every day I most always spend in study, writing, etc. The other serves for a good change. I am writing two or three pieces. I am having finished about 225 copies of *Leaves of Grass* bound up, to supply orders. Those copies form all that is left of the old edition. Then there will be no more in the market till I have my new and improved edition set up and stereotyped, which it is my present plan to do the ensuing winter at my leisure in Washington. Mother is well, I take either dinner or supper with her every day. Remember me to David Stevens and John Towers. Tell Harry on No. 11 I will go to the hall again and see if I can find that man in the Sheriff's office. I send you my love and *so long* for the present. Yours for life, dear Pete (and death the same).

Walt Whitman to Peter Doyle

Brooklyn, N.Y., Saturday evening,
Aug. 21 [1869].

Dear Pete. I have been very sick the last three days — I don't know what to call it — it makes me prostrated and deadly weak, and little use of my limbs. I have thought of you, my darling boy, very much of the time. I have not been out of the house since the first day after my arrival. I had a pleasant journey through on the cars Wednesday afternoon and night — felt quite well then. My mother and folks are all well. We are in our new house — we occupy part and rent out part. I have a nice room, where I now sit writing this. It is the latter part of the afternoon. I feel better the last hour or so. It has been extremely hot here the last two days — I see it has been so in Washington too. I hope I shall get out soon — I hanker to get out doors, and down the bay. And now dear Pete for yourself. How is it with you, dearest boy — and is there anything different with the face? Dear Pete, you must forgive me for being so cold the last day and evening. I was unspeakably shocked and repelled from you by that talk and proposition of yours — you know what — there by the fountain. It seemed indeed to me, (for I will talk out plain to you, dearest comrade) that the one I loved, and who had always been so manly and sensible, was gone, and a fool and intentional suicide stood in his place. I spoke so sternly and cutting. (Though I see now that my words might have appeared to have a certain other meaning, which I didn't dream of — insulting to you, never for one moment in my thoughts.) But will say no more of this — for I know such thoughts must have come when you was not yourself but in a moment of derangement, — and have passed away like a bad dream. Dearest boy I have not a doubt but you will get well and entirely well — and we will one day look back on these drawbacks and sufferings as things long past. The extreme cases of that malady, (as I told you before) are persons that have very deeply diseased blood so they have no foundation to build on — you are of healthy stock, with a sound constitution and good blood — and I know it is impossible for it to continue long. My darling, if you are not well when I come back I will get a good room or two in some quiet place, and we will live together and devote ourselves altogether to the job of curing you, and making you stronger and healthier than ever. I have had this in my mind before but never broached it to you. I could go on with my work in the Attorney General's office just the same — and we would see that your mother should have a small sum every week to keep the pot a-boiling at home. Dear comrade, I think of you very often. My love for you is indestructible, and since that night and morning has returned more than before. Dear Pete, dear son, my darling boy, my young and loving brother, don't let the devil put such thoughts in your mind again — wickedness unspeakable — death and disgrace here, and hell's agonies hereafter — Then what would it be afterward to the mother? What to *me?* — Pete, I send you some money by Adams' Express — you use it, dearest son, and when it is gone you shall have some more, for I have plenty. I will write again before long — give my love to Johnny Lee, my dear darling boy. I love him truly — (let him read these three last lines) — Dear Pete, *remember* — WALT.

Walt Whitman to Peter Doyle

Brooklyn, Saturday afternoon,
July 30 [1870].

Dear Pete. Well here I am home again with my mother, writing to you from Brooklyn once more. We parted there, you know, at the corner of 7th St. Tuesday night. Pete there was something in that hour from 10 to 11 o'clock (parting though it was) that has left me pleasure and comfort for good — I never dreamed that you made so much of having me with you, nor that you could feel so downcast at losing me. I foolishly thought it was all on the other side. But all I will say further on the subject is, I now see clearly, that was all wrong. I started from the depot in the 7.25 train the next morning — it was pretty warm, yet I had a very pleasant journey, and we got in New York by 5 o'clock afternoon. About half an hour before we arrived, I noticed a very agreeable change in the weather — the heat had moderated — and in fact it has been pleasant enough every day since. I found mother and all as well as usual. It is now Saturday between 4 and 5 in the afternoon — I will write more on the other side — but Pete, I must now hang up for the present as there is a young lady down stairs whom I have to go with to the ferry and across to the cars.

Sunday, 6 p.m. Pete, dear boy, I will write you a line to-day before I go. I am going over to New York to visit the lady I went down to the ferry with — so you see I am quite a lady's man again in my old days — There is nothing special to write about — I am feeling in first-rate spirits and eat my rations every time. *Monday, Aug. 1.* The carrier brought quite a bunch this forenoon for the Whitman family, but no letter from you. I keep real busy with one thing and another, the whole day is occupied — I am feeling quite well all the time and go out a great deal, knocking around one place and another. The evenings here are delightful and I am always out in them, sometimes on the river sometimes in New York — There is a cool breeze and the moon shining. I think every time of you and wish if we could only be together these evenings at any rate. *Tuesday,*

Aug. 2. Well Pete, you will have quite a diary at this rate. Your letter came this morning — and I was glad enough to get word from you. I have been over to New York to-day on business — it is a pleasure even to cross the ferry — the river is splendid to-day — a stiff breeze blowing and the smell of the salt sea blowing up — (sweeter than any perfume to my nose) — It is now 2 o'clock, I have had my dinner and am sitting here alone writing this — Love to you, dear Pete — and I won't be so long again writing to my darling boy. WALT.

Walt Whitman to Peter Doyle

Brooklyn, Friday noon,
Feb. 23 [1872].

Dear Son. Your letter received this morning speaks of the mild weather there — but it has been and remains very cold here — so much so that I don't go around half as much as I would like. My cold hangs on, though not so bad as at first. The state of the weather, and my cold, etc., have rather blocked me from having my usual enjoyment here, so far — but I expect to make up for it by and by. Dear son, I see you are off — I take it by your letter that you are feeling well in health, and having as good a time as the law allows — I wish we could be together there, some of these moonlight nights — but here it is too cold for comfort — (the water pipes here froze again last night, causing trouble) — I go out a couple of hours middle of the day, but keep in nights — I have got the new edition of my book under way — and it will be satisfactory I think — It will be in one volume, and will make a better appearance than any of the former ones — Do you go up to the Debates in the Senate? — I see by the papers they are having high times — Senator Schurz appears to come out ahead of them all — he is a real good speaker — I enjoy the way he shakes them up, (very much like a first class terrier in a pit, with a lot of rats). Pete, I send you $10 enclosed, as you may need it — Should you want more, you write, as I have plenty — I am writing this up in my back room, home — have had a nice breakfast of hot potatoes and first-rate Oregon salmon, with the best coffee that's made — home-made bread and sweet butter — everything tip-top — get along well enough — you must try to do the same — so good-bye for this time, my own loving boy — WALT.

George Sand

The astonishingly prolific French novelist George Sand is as well known today for her habit of smoking cigars and wearing men's clothing as she is for her work. Born Amandine-Aurore-Lucile Dupin, she left her painfully dull husband soon after marrying, moved to Paris and adopted a masculine nom de plume. Her advocacy of feminism and free love and her numerous affairs shocked nineteenth-century France, but supporters agreed with Elizabeth Barrett Browning in her respect for "Thou large-brained woman and large-hearted man, self-called George Sand." Sand's letters to various correspondents, including the novelist Gustave Flaubert, evidence her considerable heart and mind in abundance.

George Sand to Madame d'Agoult

[La Châtre, July 10, 1836]

I started on foot at three in the morning, fully intending to be back by eight o'clock; but I lose myself in the lanes; I forget myself on the banks of the river; I run after butterflies; and I get home at midday in a state of torrefaction impossible to describe.

You have no idea of all the dreams I dream during my walks in the sun. I fancy myself in the golden days of Greece. In this happy country where I live you may often go for six miles without meeting a human creature. The flocks are left by themselves in pastures well enclosed by fine hedges; so the illusion can last for some time. One of my chief amusements when I have got out to some distance, where I don't know the paths, is to fancy I am wandering over some other country with which I discover some resemblance. I recollect having strolled in the Alps, and fancied myself for hours in America. Now I picture to myself an Arcadia in Berry. Not a meadow, not a cluster of trees which, under so fine a sun, does not appear to me quite Arcadian.

To throw yourself into the lap of mother nature: to take her really for mother and sister; stoically and religiously to cut off from your life what is mere gratified vanity; obstinately to resist the proud and the wicked; to make yourself humble with the unfortunate, to weep with the misery of the poor; nor desire another consolation than the putting down of the rich; to acknowledge no other God than Him who ordains justice and equality upon men; to venerate what is good, to judge severely what is only strong, to live on very little, to give away nearly all, in order to re-establish primitive equality and bring back to life again the Divine institution: that is the religion I shall proclaim in a little corner of my own, and that I aspire to preach to my twelve apostles under the lime-trees in my garden.

George Sand to a Young Poet

[Nohant, August 1842]

Never show my letters except to your mother, your wife, or your greatest friend. It is a shy habit, a mania I have to the last degree. The idea that I am not writing for those alone to whom I write, or for those who love them thoroughly, would freeze my heart and my hand directly. Everyone has a fault. Mine is a misanthropy in my outward habits — for all that I have no passion left in me but the love of my fellow-creatures; but with the small services that my heart and my faith can render in this world, my personality has nothing to do. Some people have grieved me very much, unconsciously, by talking and writing about me personally and my doings, even though favorably, and meaning well. Respect this malady of spirit.

George Sand to Gustave Flaubert

[Nohant, January 1869]

The individual called George Sand is quite well, enjoying the marvelous winter now reigning in Berry, gathering flowers, taking note of interesting botanic anomalies, stitching at dresses and mantles for her daughter-in-law, costumes for the marionettes, dressing dolls, reading music, but, above all, spending hours with little Aurore, who is a wonderful child. There is not a being on earth more tranquil and happier in his home than this old troubadour retired from business, now and then singing his little song to the moon, singing well or ill he does not particularly care, so long as he gives the *motif* that is running in his head . . . . . . He is happy, for he is at peace, and can find amusement in everything.

George Sand to M. Louis Ulbach

[Nohant, 1869]

For the last five-and-twenty years there is nothing more that is of interest. It is old age, very quiet and very happy, *en famille,* crossed by sorrows
entirely personal in their nature — deaths, defections, and then the general state of affairs in which we have suffered, you and I, from the same
causes. My time is spent in amusing the children, doing a little botany,
long walks in summer — I am still a first-rate pedestrian — and writing
novels, when I can secure two hours in the daytime and two in the
evening. I write easily and with pleasure. This is my recreation, for my
correspondence is numerous, and there lies work indeed! If one had
none but one's friends to write to! But how many requests, some touching, some impertinent! Whenever there is anything I can do, I reply.
Those for whom I can do nothing I do not answer. Some deserve that
one should try, even with small hope of succeeding. Then one must
answer that one will try. All this, with private affairs to which one must
really give attention now and then, makes some ten letters a day.

George Sand to Gustave Flaubert

Nohant, January 12, 1876

I have been meaning to write to you every day, but I have never had
time. Now at last I have a clear interval. We are simply buried in snow;
it is the weather I adore: this whiteness is like a general purification, and
indoor amusements are quieter and more intimate. Can one dislike the
country in winter? The snow is one of the most magnificent spectacles
of the year.

It seems that I do not make myself clear in my sermons; I have that
in common with the orthodox, but I am not of their persuasion, neither
have I any fixed ideas in the theories of equality or authority. You seem
to believe that I want to convert you to some doctrine. But no! I am not
thinking of such a thing. I respect everyone's right to a personal point of
view. I can give you the substance of mine in very few words: it is simply
not to stick myself behind a plate of opaque glass which gives no view
but a faint reflection of one's own nose. Then I try to see as far as

possible, to take in all good and evil, near and around, below and everywhere, to perceive the incessant gravitation of all tangible and intangible
things towards the necessity of goodness, truth, and beauty.

I do not say that humanity is on the path to the summits. I believe
it in spite of everything. But I will not argue the matter, for it is quite
useless, because everyone judges according to his own personal vision,
and the general aspect becomes momentarily poor and ugly. Besides I
have no need to be certain of the salvation of this planet and its inhabitants to believe in the necessity of the good and the beautiful. If the planet
broke away from that law it would perish: if its inhabitants refused to
obey the law, destruction would come upon them. Other stars and other
souls would crash across them. As for myself, I want to climb onwards,
until I draw my last breath, not exacting, not feeling certain of a good
place elsewhere, but because my only joy is to keep myself and my
children on the upward path.

In other words I flee from the sewers and I seek cleanliness, certain
that it is the law of my existence. After all, man is nothing very grand;
he is terribly close to the ape from which we are said to be descended.
So be it. All the more reason for doing our best to get away from him,
and to reach the very highest that our race is capable of, which is only a
very humble level to attain. Well, let us attain it, if possible and not allow
anything to debase us.

I think you and I agree there; but I practice my simple faith and
you do not, since you allow yourself to be cast down; your heart has not
been penetrated by it since you curse life and implore death like a
Catholic who hopes for compensation, be it only eternal rest. You are no
more secure than anyone else of that compensation. Eternal life may
mean eternal work. If it should be so, let us go bravely through this
stage. If it is otherwise and the personal spark perishes, let us at least
earn the credit of having got through our task — and that is, having done
our duty as we have no evident duties except those to ourselves and our
fellows. Anything we destroy in ourselves we destroy in others. Our falls
lower others and throw them down; we owe it to our fellows to keep
upright, in order that they too may keep their feet. To desire immediate
death is as much a weakness as to hope for a long life and I will not
allow you to go on thinking that you have the right to do it. I once
thought so too; yet I had the same beliefs that I hold today, but I lacked
force, and like you I said, "I can do nothing." But I was lying to myself.
One can do anything. One has strength that one never thought one had,
when one is dominated by the desire to rise, to mount one step of the
ladder every day. You ought to say: "Flaubert of tomorrow must be
better than Flaubert of yesterday, and the day after he must be better

and stronger still." Once your foot is on the ladder, you will mount rapidly. Little by little you will enter the most favorable stage of life: old age. It is then that art will reveal itself in gentle guise — when one is younger it brings much anguish into life. You prefer a polished phrase to the whole of metaphysics. I too appreciate a phrase which sums up the contents of several volumes, but one must have complete understanding of these volumes in order to be able to hit on the sublime formula which crystallizes their meaning, and becomes in consequence the highest expression of literary art; that is why we must never despise the smallest effort of the human brain to arrive at truth.

I say that because you have an excessive belief in words. You read and search and work much harder than I, or many others, do. You have acquired learning at which I shall never arrive. You are thus a hundred times richer than all of us, you are rich, and you whimper as if you were a beggar. Do be charitable to that beggar who has a mattress full of gold but wants to live on words and well-turned phrases. Foolish fellow! Stuff your hand into the mattress and use your gold. Nourish yourself on the feelings and ideas amassed in your head and your heart, then the words and phrases, the form that you make so much of, will come out without any trouble. You treat form as an end, it is only a means. Happy manifestations of *form* are only to be drawn from an emotion, and an emotion only comes from a conviction. One is not moved by anything that one does not believe in ardently.

I do not say that you have no belief; on the contrary, your whole life of affection, protection, and charming simple kindness proves that you are the most convinced individualist who ever existed. But no sooner do you touch literature than you become, I do not know why, a totally different man; a man who wants to hide himself, annihilate himself, have no existence. What an extraordinary mania! What a falsification of good taste! *Our work has always the same worth as ourselves.*

Who talks of your taking the stage and posing in publicity? That is nonsense if you like, unless it is done frankly as a performance. But what sick fancy is this attempt to withdraw your soul from what you are doing? To hide one's own opinion on the personages one creates and in consequence leave the reader doubtful as to what opinion he ought to have of them is to wish that one should not be understood, and henceforward the reader will desert you; for if he wants to listen to the story you are telling him, it is on condition that you will tell him plainly who is strong and who a weak character.

L'Education sentimental was a totally misunderstood book and I told you so with an insistence that you would not listen to. It either needed a short preface of some happily turned expression to show that you condemned evil, portrayed weakness, and acclaimed effort. All the characters of the book are feeble and miscarry, except those who have bad instincts and ruin noble efforts. When we are not understood it is always our own fault. The reader's first aim is to penetrate our thought and that is what you haughtily refuse him. He thinks that you despise him and are making fun of him. I understood you because I know you well. If your book had been brought to me without a signature I should have thought it fine, but strange, and I should have wondered whether you were an immoral being, a skeptic, an indifferent, or heart-broken. You say that it ought to be so and that M. Flaubert would be lacking in manners if he were to allow his thought and his literary aim to be evident. That is false, false as hell!

From the moment that M. Flaubert begins to write well and seriously one becomes attached to his personality and desires to be lost or saved with him. If he leaves one in doubt one can no longer take any interest in his work, one misunderstands and throws him aside.

I have already combated your favorite heresy, that of writing for a score of superior persons and snapping one's fingers at the rest. It is not a true one since the absence of all success irritates and afflicts. Besides, there were not twenty favorable critics to this remarkable and excellently written book. This means that one should no more write for twenty people than for three, or for a hundred thousand.

One ought to write for everyone who has any desire to read and can take advantage of good books. Thus you must make straight for morality, the highest that one can find within, and not make a mystery of the moral sense of one's volume which might profit something to someone.

Madame Bovary was considered immoral. But if one section of the public cried out as against a scandal, the saner and more widely spread party regarded it as a hard and striking lesson of a woman who had no conscience and no faith, a lesson to vanity and irrational ambition.

Art demanded that pity should be shown to her, but the lesson remained clear and it would have been clearer if you could have made it a lesson to *all*, if you had wished it by showing your own opinion of the wife, husband, and lovers, which would have indicated what opinion others were expected to have. This will to paint things as they are, the adventures of life as they present themselves to us, is not well reasoned in my opinion. To paint the inanimate as a realist or as a poet is all one to me, but when one comes to dealing with the human heart it is different. You cannot abstract yourself from this contemplation, for the author is yourself, and other men are readers. However hard you struggle, your story cannot be anything but a conversation between author and readers. If you coldly show him evil without ever showing him good, he will get angry. He will wonder who is evil, you or himself? You may try to move him and attach him to yourself, but you will never succeed unless you are moved yourself, nor will you succeed if you hide your emotion so well that he believes you indifferent. The reader is right. Supreme impartiality is an antihuman thing, and a novel should be human in the first place. If it is not, no one will want to give it credit for being well written, well composed, well observed in detail. The essential quality will be lacking. It will not be interesting. The reader also fails to attach himself to books in which all the characters are good without a shade of weakness; he can see perfectly well that it is not human either. I believe the special art of telling a story depends on this opposition of characters; but I want to see goodness triumph in the struggle; events may be allowed to crush the good man, but they must not soil him or belittle him, and if he must be sent to the slaughterhouse let him feel happier there than his butchers.

January 15, 1876

I have been writing this letter for three days and every day I have been on the point of throwing it into the fire. It is long and diffuse and probably useless. Natures which are opposed on certain points do not easily interpenetrate, and I am afraid you will not understand me any better today than you have done before. I am sending this scrawl all the same so that you may see that I am almost as much concerned for you as I am for myself. You need success after that bad luck which stirred you to the depths, and I will tell you how you can make success a certainty. Keep your excessive regard for form but do take more trouble about the foundations. Do not take real quality to be an inevitable accompaniment of impeccable form. Let it be represented in your work; dose the fools and idiots whom you love to deride with goodness and power. Show what is solid at the base of these intellectual experiments, and finally leave go of the conventions of realists and return to true reality, which is a mixture of the lovely and the hideous, of dullness and brilliancy, but in which the will to good inevitably finds its place and its use.

I send kisses from us all.

Nadezhda von Meck/Peter Tchaikovsky

The shy and foppish Peter Tchaikovsky had no doubts about his sexuality, but the Russian composer had the misfortune to attract female music fans' devotion. One such woman was Antonina Ivanovna Miliukova, whose fan letter he made the mistake of answering. Miliukova pursued Tchaikovsky relentlessly, even after he informed her he was gay. When she threatened suicide he relented, marrying her in 1877. Two miserable weeks later, the horrified artist tried to drown himself before fleeing his bride. His escape was made possible by funds advanced by Nadezhda Philaretovna von Meck, a patron who supported his career for the next thirteen years. But Tchaikovsky's trials were not yet over: von Meck also fell in love with him, and he faced the challenge of letting her down gently. Von Meck declared her love and Tchaikovsky tenderly rebuffed her via post.

Nadezhda von Meck to Peter Tchaikovsky

Brailov
Sept. 26, 1879
Friday at 8 A.M.

How sorry I am, my dearest, that you feel so badly in Petersburg, but — forgive me — I am glad you are homesick for Brailov. I doubt if you could ever understand how jealous I am of you, in spite of the absence of personal contact between us. Do you know that I am jealous in the most unpardonable way, as a woman is jealous of the man she loves? Do you know that when you married it was terribly hard for me, as though something had broken my heart? The thought that you were near that woman was bitter and unbearable.

And do you know what a wicked person I am? I rejoiced when you were unhappy with her! I reproached myself for that feeling. I don't think I betrayed myself in any way, and yet I could not destroy my feelings. They are something a person does not order.

I hated that woman because she did not make you happy, but I would have hated her a hundred times more if you had been happy with her. I thought she had robbed me of what should be mine only, what is my right, because I love you more than anyone and value you above everything in the world.

If this knowledge bothers you, forgive my involuntary confession. I have spoken out. The reason is, the symphony. But I believe it is better for you to know that I am not such an idealistic person as you think. And then, it cannot change anything in our relationship. I don't want any change. I should like to be sure that nothing will be changed as my life draws to its close, that nobody . . . But that I have no right to say. Forgive me and forget all I have said — my mind is upset.

Forgive me, please, and realize that I feel well and that I am in need of nothing. Good-by, dear friend; forget this letter, but do not forget your heartily loving,

N. von Meck

P.S. Would you mind, please, acknowledging the receipt of this letter?

Peter Tchaikovsky to Nadezhda von Meck

Grankino
Oct. 10, 1879

It is impossible to say how glad I was to see your handwriting and to know we were again in communication. Jurgenson forgot to tell me that the piano arrangement of our symphony had at last been published, so your letter was the first news I had of it. I am tremendously elated that you are satisfied with the arrangement, which in truth is well and skillfully done.

As for the music itself, I knew beforehand that you would like it; how could it have been otherwise? I wrote it with you constantly in mind. At that time, I was not nearly so intimate with you as now, but already I sensed vaguely that no one in the world could respond more keenly to the deepest and most secret gropings of my soul. No musical dedication has ever been more seriously meant. It was spoken not only on my part but on yours; the symphony was not, in truth, mine but ours. Forever it will remain my favorite work, as the monument of a time when upon a deep, insidiously growing mental disease, upon a whole series of unbearable sufferings, grief and despair, suddenly, hope dawned and the sun of happiness began to shine — and that sun was embodied in the person to whom the symphony was dedicated.

I tremble to think what might have happened if fate had not sent you to me. I owe you everything: Life, the chance to pursue freedom — that hitherto unattainable ambition, and such abundance of good fortune as had never occurred to me even in dreams.

I read your letter with gratitude and love too strong for expression in any medium but music. May I be able some time to express it thus!

Dear friend, may you keep well. I wish it for you more than for myself. Reading how our symphony caused you sleepless nights, I felt my heart constricted. I want my music henceforth to be a source of joy and consolation, and with all my strength I desire for you a spirit well and calm.

Yours,

P. Tchaikovsky

Algernon Swinburne

Algernon Swinburne, one of the leading English poets of the nineteenth century, enjoyed shocking Victorian readers with his subject matter. One of his volumes, *Poems and Ballads*, a celebration of the joys of sex, put him at the center of a literary scandal, particularly for its "Greek" overtones. Another, *Songs Before Sunrise*, espoused revolutionary democracy. In life as well as art Swinburne reveled in worldly pleasure, so compromising his health that he ultimately retired into the care of a friend, critic and poet Walter Theodore Watts-Dunton. He maintained a long relationship with poet and painter Dante Gabriel Rossetti, and counted novelist and poet George Meredith and poet Charles Baudelaire among his friends. Swinburne's letters to various friends reflect his wicked wit and his enthusiasm for life and literature. His 1864 letter to Richard Monckton Milnes, Lord Houghton, is charged with his devotion to the poet Walter Landor, who died that year, while other letters convey his admiration of Walt Whitman and Edgar Allen Poe.

Algernon Swinburne to Lord Houghton

[October 15, 1860]

. . . I have done some more work to *Chastelard*, and rubbed up one or two other things: my friend George Meredith has asked me to send some to "Once a Week," which valuable publication he props up occasionally with fragments of his own. Rossetti has just done a drawing of a female model and myself embracing — I need not say in the most fervent and abandoned style — meant for a frontispiece to his Italian translations. Everybody, who knows me already, salutes the likeness with a yell of recognition. When the book comes out, I shall have no refuge but the grave . . .

Algernon Swinburne to Lord Houghton

[March 4, 1864]

. . . If both or either should die tomorrow, at least today he has told me that my presence has made him happy: he said more than that — things for which of course I take no credit to myself but which are not the less pleasant to hear from such a man. There is no other man living from whom I should so much have prized any expression of acceptance or goodwill in return for my homage, for all other men as great are so much younger that in his case one sort of reverence serves as the lining for another. My grandfather was upon the whole *mieux conservé*, but he had written no "Hellenics." In answer to something that Mr. Landor said today of his own age, I reminded him of his equals and predecessors, Sophocles and Titian; he said he should not live up to the age of Sophocles, not see ninety. I don't see why he shouldn't, if he has people about him to care for him as he should be cared for. I should like to throw up all other things on earth and devote myself to playing valet to him for the rest of his days. I would black his boots if he were *chez moi*. He has given me the shock of adoration which one feels at thirteen towards great men . . .

Algernon Swinburne to Lord Houghton

Holmwood, Henley-on-Thames,
November 2nd [1866].

My dear Lord Houghton, — I am glad you like my *riposte*. I thought the sharper, and simpler in tone it was, the better. My motto is either to spare or strike hard. Mere titillation is lost on porcine hides.

The paper in *Fraser* I have not seen, but am expecting. I have had letters already from Ruskin and your friend Mr. Conway, who recalls our meeting under the auspices of the sea-beds (?), and intimates that having been fighting my battles in the *New York Tribune* he means to continue apropos of the *Notes*, of which I have sent him a copy. It is a very courteous and friendly letter.

If you have read the *Drum Taps* of his countryman, the great Walt (whose friends have published a pamphlet in *his* defense), I daresay you agree with me that his dirge or nocturne over your friend Lincoln is a superb piece of music and colour. It is infinitely impressive when read aloud. — Yours affectionately,

A. C. Swinburne.

Algernon Swinburne to Paul H. Hayne

Holmwood, Henley-on-Thames,
July 22nd, 1875

Dear Sir, — I received your letter with pleasure, and am sincerely obliged by your kind offer of Poe's autograph, which I should much value. Let me heartily congratulate you on the honour of having been the first to set on foot the project of a monument to that wonderful, exquisite poet. It was time that America should do something to show public reverence for the only one (as yet) among her men of genius who has won not merely English but European fame. As perhaps you know, Poe is even more popular, and in general more highly rated, in France than in England; thanks to the long, arduous, and faithful labour of his brother-poet and translator, my poor friend, Charles Baudelaire.

On your very flattering estimate of my own work I have, of course, no remark to offer; but you may be sure that the sympathy expressed in your letter was not lost upon me, and that the knowledge that I have made myself friends in the backwoods (as you say) of America, is much more to me than any average laudatory review.

Mr. Stedman's article, which you sent me some time since, is very far above such average; I read it with much genuine pleasure and admiration of his fine critical faculty and excellent style. One passage only renews a sense of disappointment, which I have felt before now, both in the writing and the conversation of American friends and authors; the lack of sympathy with us of the republican party in Europe, who are struggling to win what you have won. To use the old Catholic phrase, applied to the Church on earth and the Church in heaven: the Republic militant has surely some right to the good-will at least and fellow-feeling of the Republic triumphant. But of all your eminent men I know none but Whitman who has said a good word for us, sent us a message of sympathy nobly conceived and worthily expressed, paid in a memorial tribute to the countless heroes and martyrs of our cause. You see, therefore, that Mr. Stedman's comparative depreciation of my *Songs before*

Sunrise, at least his preference of my other books to this one, could not but somewhat disappoint me. For my other books are books; that one is myself.

You must excuse this opinion, as you have brought it upon yourself, and believe me, very sincerely yours,

A. C. Swinburne.

John Addington Symonds

Unusual for their frankness, the early letters of John Addington Symonds reveal the rapture and torment experienced by a young gay man in nineteenth-century England. Later in his life the historian, biographer and essayist would (with Havelock Ellis) pioneer the study of homosexuality and would advocate the liberalization of British sodomy laws, but in his youth he struggled to come to terms with his own sexuality. To curb his "pangs of passion" he married Catherine North in the fall of 1864, but husband and wife eventually agreed to a nonsexual union that left Symonds free to seek out male lovers. The selection of letters included here includes one to A. O. Rutson that describes April 7, 1858, the day Symonds first kissed a man — an experience he later recalled as the most ecstatic of his life — and retraces the course of that first love affair, with a choirboy named Willie Dyer. Laced with literary and historical references — many of them classical — the letters addressed to Henry Graham Dakyns narrate their author's alternating surges of joy and plunges into depression with extraordinary candor. He discusses his often homoerotic poems — notably "John Mordan" — and his admiration for contemporary poets Alfred, Lord Tennyson, and Walt Whitman.

John Addington Symonds to A. O. Rutson

[March 18, 1864]

There are a few things I sd like to say to you; because I, more than most people, can understand what you have written & are suffering, & can show you you must bear your unrest though I can not show you *how* to bear it.

i. I am not a woman. When you wonder whether, as you & I cannot be all in all to one another, you will ever find a wife to love you wholly, you quite mistake the sexes. You & she will love differently: and remember that you must not scorn human passion. It fuses two souls.

ii. If you yearn after the grace etc wh you seem to see in me, I admire the generosity, unselfishness, purity of imagination, & sympathy with good wh I know you to possess. Externally graceful, I am inwardly at war — the sport of a hundred wild desires wh you probably have never felt. This will explain why I love to have you near me. You do me good by giving me what I have not got. If I have at times felt your society irksome it is because my nature is at root male & passionate — I do not want to have strong affection given me wh I cannot return in kisses & all else that belongs to love — & great kindness suggests to the beast within me ineffable desires. Yet when this creature is at rest I turn to you with thanksgiving that I have a friend to guide me in the ways of Reason. Do not enquire into these words too deeply. You do not know the whole of me, as I do not know the whole of you. We are all everlastingly alone.

iii. You must learn to stand more alone. Since April 7 1858 — a day memorable in my life — I have never had a week without storms, struggles, infinite efforts to get near to some one. And this fails, & I am a wreck, a piece of useless seaweed, in consequence. Read Alastor. You are in his case, allowing for yr different cast of temper. Read Solomon, Faust, it is all the same.

iv. Be more confident: expect less: theorize less: be more content with a little. Though you *must* be alone, in Birth Life & Death, you can get great approach to perfect union, not by altering your nature, but by seeking to supplement it with another, & by remembering that the mysteries of marriage & of friendship are quite different.

v. Listen to the voice of my own struggles with Solitude: (2)

Ap: 5. 1858. "To have passed from *the mire of my own personality* into a hidden & uncommunicated Sympathy with another being is something." This was a brief delusion but the underlined words show that even at the age of 17 I yearned passionately, unrestingly, for what you now crave.

July 21, 1859. "His love for me is so vast, his purity so attractive, his strange influence so unimpaired, that I love him better than anyone else. The kind of love is strange. I w. rather he or I died." These I mention to show how early (in a disguised form) this Alastor feeling came upon me. The Diaries of 1860. 1861. 1862. are full of the same desire more passionate indefinite & disturbing. Continual reference is made to work impeded & annihilated, delirious nights, & long intense solitary walks filled with one thought. "I am weak & pale, & my spirit & memory are poor. Yet I must not complain. I can still battle on & strength has not yet failed me." Such an extract is common. Here are a few doggrels at the end of a poem on a man of my own age I never knew, but whom my father talked of after he had died.

> *We may not ask what secret end*
> > *In God's great World his dying wrought,*
> > *Nor tell what cycles of new thought*
> *His living promised to extend:*
> *It grieves me that I did not know*
> > *His Beauty, pure in life & limb;*
> > *My spirit yearns for such as him*
> *With uncommunicable woe.*
> *We sd have gauged each other's soul,*
> > *And learned the secrets of our blood;*
> > *He wd have taught me to be good,*
> *And I have loved his dear control.*
> *And living Learning's golden store,*
> > *From height to height we sd have clomb*
> > *Until we reached the arduous dome,*
> *Where Silence watches Wisdom's door:*
> *And throwing all her portals wide*
> > *With lavish hands we sd have stood*
> > *And showered on mortals all this good*
> *Till Truth & Peace were multiplied.*

As time went on the passion deepened. I called it "Seelensehnsucht" & treated it like a devil — as it was. "I have ceased to care about the Schools. My ship has sailed into a magic Sea with tempests of its own. On Entering it the outer storm lulled & now it raves on alien shores. But within is mourning & desolation & woe — self disdain & discontent, railing against heaven wild yearning after love." *Sept. 29. 1861.* All the records of this hunger of my Soul I cannot write. Here is a fragment. *Sept. 15. 1862.* "I have said that my life is nought & my spirit within me corruption. Misery, misery! To be selfbound worse than a drunkard! My imagination turns all thoughts to gall & sucks up the vigour of youth into one fiery phantom of impossible delight. Per noctis vigilos clamavi, et lacrymis terram irrigavi. Mane lucem spectare odi et sub vespere tenebras perhorreo. Quod non est desidero, quod est fastidior praeterita respicio nec tamen laetus sum. Praesentia cruciant. Futura timeo. Amare nequeo quos amare debeo. Amore inamabili eorum quos amare nunquam possim ardeo. Lux me taedet, nox me terret, libri fatigant, homines contemnunt. Nihil est quod vulnus medeat, nihil est quod scire foream, nihil est quod osculer, nihil est quod quaeram. Cur terram onero?"[1]

Sept. 16. 1862. This I cannot write out. It is too beautiful even in the Past. These things are far from having ceased. If you cd have seen my Soul all through last night — from 10 p.m. to 8 a.m. you wd have pitied me. The end is not yet. We have both much to bear you & I, differently in form, the same in essence. Return this paper. I do not wish you to keep, & I will have it back again.

(1) If what you saw recorded in my diary has the Truth, spoken to myself, what I have here written down of you was the Truth, spoken in the same breath to others — as I cd prove, if need were, from my letters written from Rome to Clifton.

(2) Out of these Diaries & out of my memory of a continual battle, in wh the one thought ever present was "Oh that cd get Love, that I cd cease to be alone, or die!"; in wh sleep & Art, two forms of the same power, showed One Beauty, & reason told of one hopelessness, & Duty spoke of one plain method of avoidance; in wh the outer world at last came rudely like a great blast of wind to make my strife more arduous & painful, opening my secret parts to daylight & imposing on me scornfully the burden under wh already secretly & by myself I was staggering [out of this History I have often thought that, if I lived to do nothing else, I should write confessions wh w. be better for the world to read than Rousseau's & not less interesting. I sometimes think that I am being trained for this.

(3) At this very moment, as I write, I sit like Hercules between the two Powers. Ere I see you again one more victory may have been gained, or as often before an amnesty on equal terms concluded.

---

[1] "I complained aloud through the night watches, and I watered the earth with my tears. In the morning I hate to see the light and at evening I dread the shadows. I desire what is not, I look back on the past with revulsion and yet I am not happy. The present torments me. I fear the future. I am not able to love whom I ought to love. I burn with a disgusting desire for those I could never love. Light offends me, night terrifies me, books weary me, men despise me. There is nothing to heal my wound, nothing which I would say to know, nothing which I value, nothing which I would seek. Why do I burden the earth?"

John Addington Symonds to
Henry Graham Dakyns

[Clifton]
Tuesday March 29. 1864

My dear Dakyns

I too felt as if it wd be better not to say again Goodbye to you, for such last moments are never what they mean to be.

I cannot now tell you exactly as I wish how deeply I feel the more than kindness of your words, & yet how much I fear them. I know I am not worthy of them. I dread lest they should make me selfish, & lest a time should come when I might have to cry in vain for them & be alone. — Still they are gifts wh I take as I sh take any great gift of God wh came to me & made me live. I will not talk much of your letter. You know now that to be loved is what I desire more than anything on earth. But I rarely can hope to find one so unselfish, so true, & so pure as you, to love me. By saying this I meant to tell you how much I value what your words express.

I am your affectionate

J. A. Symonds

Write to me as often as you can, & be long suffering if you are able, for I am not reckoned a good correspondent.

John Addington Symonds to
Henry Graham Dakyns

London
Sunday April 3. 1864.

My dear Dakyns

Today has been wet, & I have had some opportunity of seeing how dreary it is possible for London to look, without sun, without shops, without movement. Within & without have been equally dismal. I begin to think I must be like the liver wh Plato describes in the Timaeus — a greedy & restless animal wh is kept polished & bright to receive all images that may be reflected on its surface. I vary so painfully with the circumstances in wh I am placed. Nor do I ever seem to live in time. Each moment is an eternity to me, whether of pain or of pleasure. I do not see beyond it: it absorbs me, makes me what I for the minute am, to the exclusion of past & future or of any alleviating considerations. This comes, I suppose, of having no faith, no firm recess of Soul whether in stress of affliction or in gust of enjoyment to retire. It makes me of one man a thousand; so that I am not I, but a thousand bubbles, reflecting various colours in their perfect spheres, & then becoming nought as briefly as they sprang into existence. I dare not divide the nightmare of life by suicide. It would be most wicked to those whose love has given me such exquisite delight. And for myself it w. be infinitely sad forever to forego the dear remembrance of a happy Past. "Forever to forego" — how impossible it is to break the spell of Self. B.[ishop] Butler said that Personal Identity depended solely on the Memory. But here I by hypothesis annhilate the Memory, & yet I still suppose a blank & vacant Self. Without the power of recollection, without sense or thought, in the dull cold voiceless unresounding grave, we yet are forced to conceive some empty shadow type & symbol of ourselves — some husk different from all other husks, some void incubus among a troop of helpless & insensible idola, wh can perish never. This is the hideous nightmare of immortality. This we clothe with heaven & hell & fiend & angel, translating all our pains & fears & hopes & joys in large dim charactery to that unsubstantial realm. Then we gloat over the idea, & cling to it, so passionately do we relish life, & even from that horrible phantasmal dream we draw a wormy satisfaction. Death & peace in truth are hidden from us. That trance, wh I spoke of to you, was no annihilation of the World or Self — that cd not be, for both are deathless despots — but it was a question asked of How, Why, Whence & Whither; the answer to wh being lost & indiscoverable, self & the world became mere senseless phantoms, the mind lost its hold on things & on its relation to men & on its own identity, became a stray waif in the whirl of chance, an atom that had wandered from the path & found it had no longer any place, amid the tempest driven snowflakes blown through Space. "Blown" — who blows them? "Space" — where is it? "Tempest" — is there any motion, or is all the world & I myself a dream from whence I may awaken on Adonis beds of amaracus & find that all is calm? The whirligig of this trance I can follow no further. I never cd put it into words. But a point in it always is reached by me when I have to start & leap & run or pinch my hands & tie myself once more to the Ixion wheel of life.

Then a beautiful shape stands before me, full of love & light, & beckons, & I cry out —

> *I will arise & come to thee! the juice*
> > *Of gravest herbs, poppy & pale henbane,*
> > *Shall bead my forehead & confuse my brain*
> *With fierce intoxication, life's long truce.*
> *Too true there is no road to peace but Death*
> > *And that perhaps to Nothing; yet blank nought*
> > *Were better than the anguish of such thought*
> *As we draw daily with our deepest breath.*
> *I know what compels me; but thy form*
> > *Still beckons, & I hear a voice that says*
> > *"Pass forth: forever flow the lengthening days,*
> *Forever swells the elemental storm,*
> > *And thou art Nothing; lay thee on the knees*
> > *Of Doom, & take thine everlasting ease."*

The idea of self, well reflected on, pushed to its utmost limits, conceived in all its gloomy despotism & oppressive omnipresence, is one wh goes nigh to drive one mad. Men have made religions to escape from it; to contemplate Self, not in Itself, not cheek by jowl, within the limits of their own circumference, but outside itself, far off in dim reflections & impersonalities, binding up the eternity omnipresence & infinity wh the idea implies within these shadowy & unsolved possibilities whereof this life is called upon to give no explanation & wh we term God & Immortality. — Oh God! To Thee I turn. Show me thyself or I must perish. Shine forth, irradiate me, breathe upon me with the breath of life, or I die suffocated in darkness. Cry aloud & call me, break the portals of my ears, & flood me with the music that forever sounds outside & wh I cannot hear. Help me ere I be turned to stone. I have sought thee under a thousand phantom shapes. I have served for thee more years than Jacob served for Rachel. But I still clasp clouds, & the happiness I clutch at is cold consolation. — But the storm of chance still drives the snowflakes of creation over the Chaotic Sea: my helm is broken, my sails torn; & like the wretch in that chorus of the Eumenides καλω π ρὸς ἀκούοντας ονδέν.[1] Let this suffice for my Sunday sermon.

I am yr aff
J. A. Symonds

[1] I call to him who hears nothing.

John Addington Symonds to
Henry Graham Dakyns

Freshwater [Isle of Wight]
Nov: 23. 1864.

My dear Dakyns

I have been today to Farringford. I only saw the setting. Tennyson was in London. But as the Play of Hamlet even if given without Hamlet's part, leaves Ophelia Polonius & Laertes, the terrace at Elsinore & the ghost, — so of Farringford. Mrs Tennyson & the boys I saw, & the rooms full of works of Art intense. She is a strange woman: I love her from the little I have seen, almost monastic in her shy retirement, plain drapery, & worn heavenly face. But those boys: when I saw them, & thought (with Mephistophiles) of each:

> *Staub nuss er essen ünd mit Lüst*
> *Wie meine Mühme, die berühmte Schlange.*[1]

My heart bled & my soul yearned to them. They filled me with a love sadly deep even at first sight. It seems folly to say so. Yet I am not in a vein of sentimentality. I felt as if I knew them. And I knw that if I saw them daily they would find in me strong sympathy. I touched their hands & I looked at them & I spoke three or four words. That was all. But there was something in the light that ran over Hallam's face, in Lionel's grace, & in the delicate fibre of both felt through their fingertips, wh revealed them to me. You say they have "la maladie du Siècle" already. But good God! do you know what form this will take with one or both of them? I see it. In this I am not apt to be mistaken. But the bitterest cup may be kept from them. Would I could die for you, my brothers. Or has it not sufficed the Everpardoning that one should suffer for a hundred? There is such waste of sorrow in the world. A worm like me lives through one misery: and after he is safe he sees angels beginning the same life & cannot save them. Why could not his little body, wrung through all its length, & suffering anguish no less fiery than the pangs of cherubim — since pain is one to all — have sufficed? There is no type of sin & shame & torment. Each soul renews them, & a man going forth for specimens need not break up rocks or dig deep: he finds them broadcast,

[1] He must eat dust, and with delight,
  As does my old aunt, the famous snake.

the earth not being weary of repeating them & making her best forms their matrix.

I am purposely obscure. For I would say things I am not sure of, & prophesy. Wh is folly.

Tell me about these boys. I will never forget them.

I am yr ever aff
J. A. Symonds

Nov: 24.
This letter is rather wild, written in style to be avoided. But I felt it last night & you do not misunderstand. I hope to be in Clifton next Wednesday.

John Addington Symonds to Henry Graham Dakyns

London
Jan 29 1865

My dear Graham

I fear my long silence after yr last letter may have pained you. But we know each other too well for me really to think that you will have fancied me oblivious or offended or uninterested. I thank you very much for what you said. Such expressions of affection I value very highly. They are a blessing to me for wh I am thankful not without humility.

When I said you were fratzenhaft I meant to indicate a certain restless inability to be as others are wh sometimes forces itself in you on my attention. But do not weigh the word.

I should have written before but for two reasons wh are really one. I wrote very hard as Hastings in the midst of dissipations on "the Greek Life" & then an article on "Landscape painting in England" for the Cornhill. The latter I wrote having relinquished the former in order to get a too exciting subject out of mind. But it remained & has produced a kind of nervous crisis wh I can only compare to what I had heard of delirium tremens — exremely painful, exhausting, & involving much despair.

I am getting better but I am very weak.

Ever yr aff
J. A. Symonds

48 Oxford Terrace Hyde Park is our address.

John Addington Symonds to
Henry Graham Dakyns

[Clifton] *Jan. 18. 1866.*
[Thursday] *Night*

Sat: Please meet me at 2:30
on the Observatory if it is
fine. If not. I come to you.

My dear Graham

I cannot go to bed without writing to you — after reading your letter of last night & Arthur's [Sidgwick].

I think *I* know now a little what you mean when you say you cannot write. My poor facility, framed for poor thoughts & shallow feelings, will not bear me up.

I want to tell you that I love you & love him, & that I have a reverence for you that is something sacred & for him also — I mean dear Arthur of Rugby — after reading his letter greater than I ever had before.

My dear friend, I have very much indeed to learn & you must teach me. I seem only just embarking on that great wide sea of Love wh has tossed you for years, wh Arthur clearly, simply, more emphatically than I could, has called Genius.

I have in me a tincture of Philistinism awfully strong. I know it & have some times hugged it to my bosom. I fail also in Love.

But I cannot tell you all I mean. Let me write my Amen at the foot of what Arthur has said of you.

2 I scarcely think Percival is quite the fool you take him for. He does not understand, but then you require from him sensibilities too finely set. They are uncommon. Ecce Homo is his Gospel — & a good one, believe me.

3 If you care for John Mordan, please keep the verses. Make me a poet. I would give many things to write one good thing in prose or verse before I die.

4 You are never burdensome to me. Rather let me say that I find great sweetness in you, a perfection of love which makes my selfishness blush.

5 And now of what is next your heart. What shall I say? You only know your own bitterness, & any hand I can lay on it is harsh. The letter of this evening I understand. It is very sad: but I do not sorrow for you as one who has no hope. I cannot help looking at your relation to him

from an outside point of view. I cannot help fearing that you expect too much here also — I do not mean, idealize him — but that you are not enough content with the inevitable limitations & deficiencies of boyhood. Still I know that you are master: I do not believe the formula "As yet" = "now & for ever." You must still be unwearied & you shall conquer. I saw him & her: but things were unsatisfactory today — I, they, the late return last night, & Lyria. —

O my dear Graham I do understand yr letter of tonight. I cannot preach a Philistine's comfort. But that of *you* the Lord is mindful I cannot doubt; & in that faith I am calm. It is so easy to be calm about another: & you, poor friend, even now are with your "despair to brood over the livelong night" — more tempestuous than that scornful sunset, or the red glare on the clouds from a burning city.

Yet again the Καιρος [time] shall come. Why did you not go together to the Madrigals tonight? If you had told me yesterday I could have got him a ticket. Believe me things were wrong today in Sutherland House — not you: it was the nature of things that deserved damning.

As if I did not know the bitterness of two little words — "as yet" or "ah me"! There is no bitterness in a folio equal to it.

Goodnight, yr most affectionate friend

J.A.S.

John Addington Symonds to
Henry Graham Dakyns

[Clifton]
Jan 20 1866

Dear Graham

I add one line to my father's. It is, that if Lionel [Tennyson] comes to stay in this house I shall be very happy to hear him his lessons, *provided always I am still here.* I cannot offer to look after him altogether; but he cd sit in my study & at least be kept out of mischief.

Arthur's [Carré's] Idyll is good — chiefly in that is is simple & expresses a strong truth. I do not intend to discuss his conduct much more. I shall long to hear of him, every new thing; & I believe in his goodness. But that he is in a dangerous position cannot be denied; when I think of him I range the matter somehow in questions & answers like the following —

Is this ερως [love] Greek? No.

If it were Greek, is it what Plato would allow? No.

Is it established in modern Society? No.

Is it what the world at large would call romantic, sentimental, effeminate, on the verge of vice? Yes.

Supposing the world wrong in a special instance, may not its general verdict be right? I think so.

What is the source of Arthur's love? Is it intellectual sympathy? No. Is it moral good? No. Is it consentaneity of tastes? No. Is it chiefly aesthetical enjoyment & the pleasure of highly refined sensuousness? Yes. Are these likely to produce moral & intellectual strength? No. Are they capable of producing moral or intellectual debility? Yes, *capable.* What has yr experience been of this ερως? That if uncontrolled it is evil. In all cases of possible harm, what does Duty say? Avoid all appearance of evil. Is this Duty increased or diminished by Arthur's position? Increased. In case moral injury were to accrue, where wd the evil fall most heavily? On the boy, & if on him then through him on his fellow boys.

Does Arthur expose himself to external danger? Yes, to a very gt extent.

These questions by no means settle or exhaust the matter. It is a case of absolutely new casuistry. There is no rule by wh to measure it as yet.

I shall come to see you today at 2, if you are unengaged. But send to say so if you are engaged.

Yr aff
J.A.S.

John Addington Symonds to
Henry Graham Dakyns

[Clifton]
Monday Jan. 22. 1866.

My dear Graham

Your prophecy realized itself in part at least. The thorn of my flesh sprang up & wreathed itself into a crown about my forehead. I maddened myself with the sweetness of strange thought. And I have been ill since I saw you. One fruit of this illness is a second part of John Mordan, wherein I poured out some fire hitherto unexpressed of past passion. The Ms is locked up beyond my reach now & Catherine holds the key. Yet even so I have in some sense triumphed though "my thoughts like hounds pursue their father & their prey." If only I might be a poet! Then I would not mind having to pour forth my heartsblood & brainsmarrow. But to do this, & to fail of being a poet, that is sorrow.

Send your Hours: also send me your Idylls.

I am yr aff
J.A.S.

John Addington Symonds to Henry Graham Dakyns

Union Club. [London]
S.W.
Oct 22. 1866.

Yes, my best beloved, thou shalt have Arthur's poem back — that sweet wild swallow of another land from wh I have already plucked one feather. Lo in my breast I bear it!

But for poems from me; the fount of them is very dry & they do not gush forth in this dark country. A few, such as are left from brighter days, I will send.

Thy letter was itself a Poem & gladdened my heart like the song of birds in May. For when thou singest I sing, & when thy heart is glad I too am light of heart — even though the days are dark, the eyes weary, & the brain oppressed. Let us thank God for the good that hath fallen to thee, the good for wh thou wast made, the good of others & thy own. Yea & thou shalt have greater good than this. Even for thyself shall it be poured forth more abundantly. "For in the wilderness shall waters gush forth & streams in the Desert." These are to me not words but Music.

Write me more about the deep things of thy soul. Cry unto me as one deep crieth to another deep, when the rains of the Lord are above them & the noises of many waters go abroad. I have less to say except thanks & sympathy wh cannot be dried up.

Day by day I sit & commune with the might dead — to me most mighty, though the world discerns them not. I fit my optic glasses & make dim my eyes with poring on that Constellation whose spherical music enchants my soul. I count its stars & call them by their names & cannot weigh them in my balance for they are too great. But when I write on paper their times & seasons, their risings & settings, & say "this was called Ben Jonson, & that fiery planet had the name of Marlowe," then the spirit fails within me, & I falter, wondering whether it was not the tears of my eyes or the imperfections of my glasses wh surrounded them with a fictitious irridescence. Then comes the doubt of self, & I behold those mighty masters as my rainbow. So it must be: for the course of my work goes by fits & starts of burning impulse & weary flagging, of unselfish genuflections, & conceited self reflections, of swift flights & dull day labour.

On Thursday night at 8 they will perform at Covent Garden the Sinfonia Eroica of Beethoven & more of that soul stirrer. Wilt thou come?

John Addington Symonds to
Henry Graham Dakyns

Union Club. [London]
S.W.
Nov 2 1866

My dear Graham

I feel inclined to write you a biographical letter. I have just returned from a visit to Rugby & to Oxford. Of such days I feel that if I should ever be alone & without friends they would to me be "dear as remembered kisses after death." Environed as I now am by friends they are to me as sweet as love.

Arthur [Sidgwick] was very well; & each of the three nights I spent with him found us at two oclock still talking. There was a disagreement between him & Robertson wh caused him some pain. But before I left the current of their friendship was again flowing smoothly, if not so strongly & swiftly as before. Some indignation had gathered in Robertson's mind περι τών έρωτίκων,[1] and for a time he seemd to look on Arthur as the destroyer of his peace. He is a man of fewer thoughts & interests than Arthur, & the soul of his love is not so scientific. But Arthur treated him with wisdom, & the sore heart & proud spirit have returned to the companionship of him whom we call third.

I saw A. J. Lushington at breakfast. He struck me as being manifestly elect for the fall & rising of many in Israel. ἐνέβλεθέ τέ μοι τοῖς ὀφθαλμοῖς. ἁμήχαιδν τι οἶον.[2]

Arthur took me into his School moreover, where I sat in the seat of the teacher while Arthur made his boys construe Caesar. You shall do this for me one day at Clifton. The ὄψις ἀστράπτοσδα[3] was beside me, a face & form of unimaginable beauty, haunted by thoughts & passions wh as yet are undeveloped. Fancy a form of loveliness over wh its own predestinated soul of power & passion hovers; not as poets have dreamed, the dead clay haunted by its ancient spirit, but the just dawning lif environed by cloud shadows of the youth & strength to be. Such is A.J.L. Yet I see that my words cannot express the incubation of a future soul wh struck me in the boy.

Many & various were our discourses; & often did we talk of you. For this is our symbol, & I care not where you put the names.

It grieves me greatly that intercourse is so inadequate. Each of us is like a spider giving from its entrails here a thread & there a thread. You take one thread from me & make a cobweb, Arthur another. But no man can seize the whole threads of another & hold by them all. To my friends I should like to give my whole soul & that not of cobweb stuff but adamant.

When I left Rugby I immersed myself in the other atmosphere of Oxford. Jowett & [T.H.] Green were the two notes wh I principally struck. But I need not tell you much of this part. It was very good. I got new ideas for my own work & heard much of theirs. A few really solemn minutes I passed by myself in my old Balliol rooms. They have now their third occupant since me: but the chairs & tables are substantially the same, & I remembered "that my youth was half divine." Of Caecilius [Cecil Boyle] I would hear somewhat. Much music is soon coming. You shall be told. I am anxious for you about him. Write.
Catherine's love: & mine: Yr ever aff.

J. A. Symonds.

---

[1] About love matters.
[2] I have seen with my own eyes something irresistible.
[3] The lightning-like apparitions.

John Addington Symonds to
Henry Graham Dakyns

London
Nov. 20. 1866.

My dear Graham

Please do not disobey me but destroy J.[ohn] M.[ordan] *The Cretan Idyll & what remains of the other 3*. Destroy them with fire. I repent in dust & ashes of their unholiness, and until I hear from your lips that they are burned I rest not crying Miserere. Do not disobey me. They remain engraved on my mind & in Paradise we will repeat them when Sin is no more that hath set so sad a separation between the parts of our Souls. Do not disobey me, but write at once that it is done. A letter from Arthur [Sidgwick] has stung me to this recoil upon myself. It is all really well with him, but wild fire is abroad in the world & who am I that I should offend against God's elect?

ever yours
J.A.S.

John Addington Symonds to
Henry Graham Dakyns

47 N. Sq. [London]
April 15. 1867

My dear Graham

A line to ask you where you are, when you will come to London.

I am not in one of my depression fits exactly. But I cannot recover tone or strength. The old irritation is again established in my lung, & the great chest doctor whom I have been consulting this morning repeats the old story of absolute repose, pure air, & the necessity of straining no nerve & taking no cold. It is hard — a plain tough fact that I am tethered.

J'ai perdu ma force et ma vie.

I went to see M D Conway on Saturday. We soon became friends.

He presented me with a volume containing all that W. W. has written —
much new matter besides Drum Taps, & the old poems rearranged. You
will like to see the book. I am proud of having it: for it has been sent to
Conway by W. W. himself to be given to some worthy proselyte. Conway
is singularly like Tennyson, on a smaller scale, but laid out in the same
fashion. He talked much about W. W. & discussed him as a man & as a
poet. I cd not get him to say anything explicit about Calamus. This, I
think, means that Calamus is really very important & that Conway refuses to talk it over with a stranger. He cannot be oblivious of its plainer
meanings. I shall, if I see him again, consult him about a few passages
in the book including the enigmatical warning in the 2d (?) part of
Calamus.

Arthur [Sidgwick] has written a very jolly letter in reply to my
tirade.

Whether I shall be able to go with you is still doubtful. I am so
weak & dull; & if the pain in my side does not abate, I had better wait
here & see what comes.

Yr ever aff *J.A.S.*

John Addington Symonds to Henry Graham Dakyns

47 N. Sq. [London]
May 19 1867

My dear Graham

Io son si stanco sotti il fascio antico delle mie colpa e dell' usanza via[1]
that I have been unable to write to you, & I am now reminded most
strongly of old times in wh I was more pure & loving & able to say things
of better meaning & nobler purpose. If my last letter to you was foolish,
as it really was, please forgive it: written 3 weeks since. I have never had
a day's health since then. I have been lying mere inutilis alga[2] & rotting
all the time. Mrs [Josephine] Butler writes that I do not know how my
coldness & indifference repell & grieve those who cross my path. But if
I am cold it is the frost of bitter disappointment about me; & if I seem
indifferent it is merely the self repression of despair. If I were to open
my lips I should only cry "Imus Imus praecipites"[3] or "Death under the

breast bones. Hell under the skull bones"; and people by this time are too well accustomed to my "depression fits." Therefore I keep silence & am called cold. They do not know how I love them & how I loathe myself. At a great London dinner party last night I was among Marshalls Monteagles Myerses & Spring Rices, & they all talked & seemed to think that I had something to say too. It was all I cd do to withold myself from falling flat upon the floor & crying out to them: Behold I am a scarecrow a thread paper a hypocrite, I am not what I look tear off the clothes & flesh & find the death & hell inside; if anyone of you have got a God let him first search me, let him scatter me to the winds & discover my emptiness.

It is no good to heap on sackcloth & wear ashes. It is no good to go wailing every day & to cry Lord Lord. Temo di mancar tra via.[4]

I am not now in a depression fit or any fit. It is more than that. If only I cd see my way out & find an end of all this Schooling! Will the bird of dawning never sing? I have heard nothing of you. I fear that even over you perhaps the uggia of my mean nature & selfishness has fallen. If so, take some whip & scourge me: say some hard words to me: I need a spur.

I long to hear of you & yours, of your father, of your mother, of your Cecil [Boyle]. I deserve to hear nothing for I wrote last to you mere insolence moonshine — the priggishness of a pedantic pedagogue. Not a single line has been written by me, not a song sung, not a sight seen except one almost unparalleled for sublimity. The only book I have read is Petrarch.

If you write write about yourself & on thin paper. I am going to Poitiers [France] perhaps on Tuesday. It is still uncertain. But I die so daily that it is thought necessary to move me elsewhere.

I hear nothing from Arthur [Sidgwick].

I am yr ever loving
J.A.S.

> *Quanti miseri in ultima vecchiezza!*
> *Quanti felici songià morti in fascia*
> *Alcun dice: beato è chi non nasce.*[5]

---

[1] I am so fatigued under the old bundle of my guilt and the customary road. . . .
[2] Useless seaweed.
[3] "We are, we are falling."
[4] "I am afraid to fail in life."
[5] How much happiness would ring dead in swaddling bonds
    How much wretchedness in the final oldness!
    Someone says: blessed is he who is not born.

John Addington Symonds to Henry Graham Dakyns

Cannes —
Jan. 4. 1868.

My dear Graham

ἀασάμην — I have sinned, done foolishly, & spoken folly, to you, my dearest friend.

I am very miserable — self convicted, self humiliated. The fear of hell & horror of damnation is a consciousness that dreads its own continuity as the worst torment.

Please do not write. I do not want to hear from you. For I see things clearly. And I have perfect faith in you & perfect patience — a momentary surcease from selfishness.

God bless you. I am your ever most affectionate for your love is exceedingly precious to me.

J. A. Symonds —

Gerard Manley Hopkins/ Richard Watson Dixon

In 1878, thirty-three-year-old poet and Jesuit priest Gerard Manley Hopkins wrote a fan letter to Richard Watson Dixon, a fellow poet and Church of England parish priest. Dixon, who had once been a master at Hopkins's school, was associated with the pre-Raphaelite painters Edward Burne-Jones, William Morris, and Dante Gabriel Rossetti, and his work was admired also by Algernon Swinburne. Although little read in his own time and subsequently, Dixon elicited breathless admiration from Hopkins — a more talented poet, who remained unpublished in his own lifetime. The two men launched a warm relationship by post that lasted until Hopkins's death in 1889, probably meeting only once in adulthood. Their letters center around discussions of poetry and theology, into which Hopkins sublimated his repressed homosexual feelings. Indeed, sometimes Hopkins's work failed to veil his feelings; it variously extols the glories of "the breathing bloom of a chastity in mansexfine," "limber liquid youth" and naked boys at play in a swimming hole.

Gerard Manley Hopkins to
Richard Watson Dixon

Stonyhurst College, Blackburn. June 4, 1878.

Very Rev. Sir; — I take a liberty as a stranger in addressing you, nevertheless I did once have some slight acquaintance with you. You will not
remember me but you will remember taking a mastership for some
months at Highgate School, the Cholmondeley School, where I then
was. When you went away you gave, as I recollect, a copy of your book
Christ's Company to one of the masters, a Mr. Law if I am not mistaken.
By this means coming to know its name I was curious to read it, which
when I went to Oxford I did. At first I was surprised at it, then pleased,
at last I became so fond of it that I made it, so far as that could be, a part
of my own mind. I got your other volume and your little Prize Essay too.
I introduced your poems to my friends and, if they did not share my own
enthusiasm, made them at all events admire. And to shew you how
greatly I prized them, when I entered my present state of life, in which I
knew I could have no books of my own and was unlikely to meet with
your works in the libraries I should have access to, I copied out *St. Paul,
St. John, Love's Consolation,* and others from both volumes and keep them
by me.

What I am saying now I might, it is true, have written any time
these many years back, but partly I hesitated, partly I was not sure you
were yet living; lately however I saw in the *Athenaeum* a review of your
historical work newly published and since have made up my mind to
write to you — which, to be sure, is an impertinence if you like to think
it so, but I seemed to owe you something or a great deal, and then I
knew what I should feel myself in your position — if I had written and
published works the extreme beauty of which the author himself the
most keenly feels and they had fallen out of sight at once and been (you
will not mind my saying it, as it is, I suppose, plainly true) almost wholly
unknown; then, I say, I should feel a certain comfort to be told they had
been deeply appreciated by some one person, a stranger, at all events
and had not been published quite in vain. Many beautiful works have
been almost unknown and then have gained fame at last, as Mr. Wells'
poem of *Joseph,* which is said to be very fine, and his friend Keats' own,
but many more must have been lost sight of altogether. I do not know of
course whether your books are going to have a revival, it seems not
likely, but not for want of deserving. It is not that I think a man is really
the less happy because he has missed the renown which was his due, but

still when this happens it is an evil in itself and a thing which ought not to be and that I deplore, for the good work's sake rather than the author's.

Your poems had a medieval colouring like Wm. Morris's and the Rossetti's and others but none seemed to me to have it so unaffectedly. I thought the tenderness of *Love's Consolation* no one living could surpass nor the richness of colouring in the 'wolfsbane' and other passages (it is a mistake, I think, and you meant henbane) in that and *Mark and Rosalys* nor the brightness of the appleorchard landscape in *Mother and Daughter.* And the Tale of Dauphiny and 'It is the time to tell of fatal love' (I forget the title) in the other book are purer in style, as it seems to me, and quite as fine in colouring and drawing as Morris' stories in the *Paradise,* so far as I have read them, fine as those are. And if I were making up a book of English poetry I should put your ode to Summer next to Keats' on Autumn and the Nightingale and Grecian Urn. I do not think anywhere two stanzas so crowded with the pathos of nature and landscape could be found (except perhaps there are some in Wordsworth) as the little song of the Feathers of the Willow: a tune to it came to me quite naturally. The extreme delight I felt when I read the line 'Her eyes like lilies shaken by the bees' was more than any single line in poetry ever gave me and now that I am older I could not be so strongly moved by it if I were to read it for the first time. I have said all this, and could if there were any use say more, as a sort of duty of charity to make up, so far as one voice can do, for the disappointment you must, at least at times, I think, have felt over your rich and exquisite work almost thrown away. You will therefore feel no offence though you may surprise at my writing.

I am, Very Rev. Sir, your obedient servant

Gerard M. Hopkins S.J.

(I am, you see, in 'Christ's Company').

Richard Watson Dixon to Gerard Manley Hopkins

Hayton Vicarage, Carlisle. 8 June 1878.

Reverend and most Dear Sir, — I received your Letter two days ago, but have been unable to answer it before, chiefly through the many and various emotions which it has awakened within me. It is probable that I shall not be able to finish this letter of answer tonight, & that you will receive it at a later date than might be expected from the date which you read at the top. You cannot but know that I must be deeply moved, nay shaken to the very centre, by such a letter as that which you have sent me: for which I thank you from my inmost heart. I place and value it among my best possessions. I can in truth hardly realise that what I have written, which has been generally, almost universally, neglected, should have been so much valued and treasured. This is more than fame: and I may truly say that when I read your Letter, and whenever I take it out of my pocket and look at it, I feel that I prefer to have been so known & prized by one, than to have had the ordinary appreciation of many. I was talking to my friend Burne Jones the painter a while ago, about three weeks: who said among other things, 'One only works in reality for the one man who may rise to understand one, it may be ages hence'. I am happy in being understood in my life-time. To think that you have re-volved my words, so as to make them part of yourself, and have actually copied out some of them, being denied books, is to me indescribably affecting.

I think that I remember you in the Highgate School. At least I remem-ber a pale young boy, very light and active, with a very meditative & intellectual face, whose name, if I am not vastly mistaken, was yours. If I am not deceived by memory, that boy got a prize for English poetry. I may be deceived in this identification: but, if you have time to write again, I should like to know. I little thought that my gift to Mr. Lobb, which I had quite forgotten, would bear such fruit.

With what you say about mifsing fame, I cordially agree. It is often a disadvantage to rise into fame, at least immediate fame; it leads a man to try to excell himself, or strike out something new incefsantly, or at least not to work so naturally and easily as he would if he did not know that the world was watching to see what he will do next.

I may just add that I received a letter of warm & high approbation & criticism from Rossetti (whom you mention in your letter) about three years ago, when he read my poems, which he had not seen before. Beside that letter I place yours.

But I am ashamed of writing so much of myself: none is so conscious of my defects as I am. Let me rather regard with admiration the arduous and self-denying career which is modestly indicated in your Letter & signature: and which places you so much higher in 'Christ's Company' than I am.

Believe me yours, with every sentiment of gratitude and esteem.

R. W. Dixon.

Gerard Manley Hopkins to Richard Watson Dixon

> The Catholic Church, St. Giles's, Oxford.
> March 29 1879

Very Reverend and Dear Sir; — I now send my pieces: please return them when done with, as I have no other copies. It is best to read the *Eurydice* first, which is in plain sprung rhythm and will possess you with the run of it. The *Deutschland,* earlier written, has more variety but less mastery of the rhythm and some of the sonnets are much bolder and more licentious. The two pieces written here at Oxford have not their last finish.

I hope you will like them.

Believe me your sincere friend

> *Gerard M. Hopkins S.J.*

Richard Watson Dixon to Gerard Manley Hopkins

> Hayton Vicarage, Carlisle. 5 April 1879.

Reverend and Most Dear Sir — I have your Poems and have read them I cannot say with what delight, astonishment, & admiration. They are among the most extraordinary I ever read & amazingly original. I write to say this, not in answer to your letter, to which I will reply when I can: and say more of the Poems.

It seems to me that they ought to be published. Can I do anything? I have said something of the institution of your Society in my next volume of Church History, which is not yet published. I could very well give an abrupt footnote about your poems, if you thought good. You need not answer about this before you hear from me again, as I shall not be ready for the Prefs for a year. You may think it odd for me to propose to introduce you in the year 1540, but I know how to do it. My object would be to awaken public interest & expectation in your as yet unpublished poems: or your recently published, if you think of publishing before that time.

By the way, I should have told you before that I have no title to be called *Very* Reverend. I have somehow always neglected or forgotten this at the time of writing.

Believe me with the sincerest admiration

Your friend

R. W. Dixon

I have delayed posting this by accident.

Gerard Manley Hopkins to Richard Watson Dixon

St. Wilfrid's, Preston. Palm Sunday [April 2,] *1882*

My Dear Friend, — I am still lingering at Preston, expecting to go south tomorrow or next day. I was detained here and closely employed, or I shd. have dropped you a line before to thank you, which I never did, for your kind entertainment at Carlisle.

I wish our meeting cd. have been longer for several reasons, but to name one, I fancied you were shy and that time would have been needed for this to wear off. I think that for myself I have very little shyness left in me, but I cannot communicate my own feeling to another.

I have nothing more to say now, but when I see anything settled you shall hear. In the meantime as long as I am at Roehampton, at least in the character of a novice, I do not ask to see *Mano* or anything important of yours — which nevertheless, in MS or print, I do of course earnestly hope to see.

Believe me your affectionate friend

Gerard M. Hopkins S.J.

To Gerard Manley Hopkins

Hayton, Carlisle. 13 Ap. 1882

My dear Friend, — I ought to have written before: but things have been in the way: to say how very glad I am to have seen you & to have a full knowledge of what you are like. So far as I can remember, you are very like the boy of Highgate. I dare say I seemed 'shy': I have an unfortunate manner: & am constantly told that I am too quiet: I have often tried to overcome it: but the effort is always apparent to those with whom I am, & never succeeds. You must therefore forgive it: it is not from want of feeling or affection.

I feel the death of Rofsetti most acutely. I have known him for twenty years: he was one of my dearest friends, though I only saw much of him at one period, & that not a long one. It leaves an awful blank.

I am now called out, so good bye: wishing you every pofsible happinefs, & among others that you may soon be at liberty to write, & may write poems.

I am My dear Friend Ever your affec.^te

R. W. Dixon

Robert Louis Stevenson

The author of *Treasure Island, Dr. Jekyll and Mr. Hyde, Kidnapped* and other adventure stories wrote letters of corresponding vigor and imagination. Born to the Scottish upper class, Stevenson preferred canoe trips through France and trips to California and the South Pacific to the lawyer's life he was expected to lead. In his travels he met many of the leading literary figures of his day, including the English writers Edward Gosse, Allan Monkhouse and J. M. Barrie, and the American writer Henry James. Stevenson's letters reflect his unconventional approach to letter writing and his spirited view of life in general.

Robert Louis Stevenson to Edmund Gosse

The Cottage (late the late Miss M'Gregor's),
Castleton of Braemar, August 10, 1881.

My dear Gosse, — Come on the 24th, there is a dear fellow. Everybody else wants to come later, and it will be a godsend for, sir — Yours sincerely.

You can stay as long as you behave decently, and are not sick of, sir — Your obedient, humble servant.

We have family worship in the home of, sir — Yours respectfully.

Braemar is a fine country, but nothing to (what you will also see) the maps of, sir — Yours in the Lord.

A carriage and two spanking hacks draw up daily at the hour of two before the house of, sir — Yours truly.

The rain rains and the winds do beat upon the cottage of the late Miss Macgregor and of, sir — Yours affectionately.

It is to be trusted that the weather may improve ere you know the halls of, sir — Yours emphatically.

All will be glad to welcome you, not excepting, sir — Yours ever.

You will now have gathered the lamentable intellectual collapse of, sir — Yours indeed.

And nothing remains for me but to sign myself, sir — Yours,

Robert Louis Stevenson

N.B. — Each of these clauses has to be read with extreme glibness, coming down whack upon the "Sir." This is very important. The fine stylistic inspiration will else be lost.

Robert Louis Stevenson to Edmund Gosse

The Cottage, Castleton of Braemar,
August 19, 1881.

If you had an uncle who was a sea captain and went to the North Pole, you had better bring his outfit. *Verbum sapientibus.* I look towards you.

R. L. Stevenson.

Robert Louis Stevenson to Edmund Gosse

[Braemar], *August 19, 1881.*

My dear Weg, — I have by an extraordinary drollery of Fortune sent off to you by this day's post a P. C. inviting you to appear in sealskin. But this had reference to the weather, and not at all, as you may have been led to fancy, to our rustic raiment of an evening.

As to that question, I would deal, in so far as in me lies, fairly with all men. We are not dressy people by nature; but it sometimes occurs to us to entertain angels. In the country, I believe, even angels may be decently welcomed in tweed; I have faced many great personages, for my own part, in a tasteful suit of sea-cloth with an end of carpet pending from my gullet. Still, we do maybe twice a summer burst out in the direction of blacks . . . and yet we do it seldom. . . . In short, let your own heart decide, and the capacity of your portmanteau. If you came in camel's hair, you would still, although conspicuous, be welcome.

The sooner the better after Tuesday. — Yours ever,

Robert Louis Stevenson.

Robert Louis Stevenson to Cosmo Monkhouse

La Solitude, Hyères-les-Palmiers, Var,
March 16, 1884.

My dear Monkhouse, — You see with what promptitude I plunge into correspondence; but the truth is, I am condemned to a complete inaction, stagnate dismally, and love a letter. Yours, which would have been welcome at any time, was thus doubly precious.

Dover sounds somewhat shiveringly in my ears. You should see the weather *I* have — cloudless, clear as crystal, with just a punkah-draft of the most aromatic air, all pine and gum tree. You would be ashamed of Dover; you would scruple to refer, sir, to a spot so paltry. To be idle at Dover is a strange pretension; pray, how do you warm yourself? If I were there I should grind knives or write blank verse, or — But at least you do not bathe? It is idle to deny it: I have — I may say I nourish — a growing jealousy of the robust, large-legged, healthy Britain-dwellers, patient of grog, scorners of the timid umbrella, innocuously breathing fog: all which I once was, and I am ashamed to say liked it. How ignorant is youth! grossly rolling among unselected pleasures; and how nobler, purer, sweeter, and lighter, to sip the choice tonic, to recline in the luxurious invalid chair, and to tread, well-shawled the little round of the constitutional. Seriously, do you like to repose? Ye gods. I hate it. I never rest with any acceptation; I do not know what people mean who say they like sleep and that damned bedtime which, since long ere I was breeched, has rung a knell to all my day's doings and beings. And when a man, seemingly sane, tells me he has "fallen in love with stagnation." I can only say to him, "You will never be a Pirate!" This may not cause any regret to Mrs. Monkhouse; but in your own soul it will clang hollow — think of it! Never! After all boyhood's aspirations and youth's immoral day-dreams, you are condemned to sit down, grossly draw in your chair to the fat board, and be a beastly Burgess till you die. Can it be? Is there not some escape, some furlough from the Moral Law, some holiday jaunt contrivable into a Better Land? Shall we never shed blood? This prospect is too grey:

> *"Here lies a man who never did*
> *Anything but what he was bid;*
> *Who lived his life in paltry ease,*
> *And died of commonplace disease."*

To confess plainly, I had intended to spend my life (or any leisure I might have from Piracy upon the high seas) as the leader of a great horde of irregular cavalry devastating whole valleys. I can still, looking back, see myself in many favourite attitudes; signalling for a boat from my pirate ship with a pocket-handkerchief, I at the jetty end, and one or two of my bold blades keeping the crowd at bay: or else turning in the saddle to look back at my whole command (some five thousand strong) following me at the hand-gallop up the road out of the burning valley: this last by moonlight.

Robert Louis Stevenson to Henry James

Skerryvore, Bourneymouth,
October 28, 1885.

My dear Henry James: —

At last, my wife being at a concert, and a story being done, I am at some liberty to write and give you of my views. . . .

And now to the main point: why do we not see you? Do not fail us. Make an alarming sacrifice and let us see "Henry James's Chair" properly occupied. I never sit in it myself (though it was my grandfather's); it has been consecrated to guests by your approval, and now stands at my elbow gaping. We have a new room, too, to introduce to you — our last baby, the drawing-room; it never cries and has cut its teeth. Likewise, there is a cat now. It promises to be a monster of laziness and self-sufficiency. . . . Now, my dear James, come — come — come. The spirit (that is me) says, come; and the bride (and that is my wife) says, come; and the best thing you can do for us and yourself and your work is to get up and do so right away.

Yours affectionately,
Robert Louis Stevenson.

Robert Louis Stevenson to Edmund Gosse

Skerryvore, Bournemouth, Jan. 2nd, 1886.

That is the hard part of literature. You aim high, and you take longer over your work, and it will not be so successful as if you had aimed low and rushed it. What the public likes is work (of any kind) a little loosely executed; so long as it is a little wordy, a little slack, a little dim and knotless, the dear public likes it: it should (if possible) be a little dull into the bargain. I know that good work sometimes hits; but, with my hand on my heart, I think it is by an accident. And I know also that good work must succeed at last; but that is not the doing of the public; they are only shamed into silence or affectation. I do not write for the public: I do write for money, a nobler deity; and most of all for myself, not perhaps any more noble, but both more intelligent and nearer home.

Let us tell each other sad stories of the bestiality of the beasts whom we feed. What he likes is the newspaper; and to me the press is the mouth of a sewery where lying is professed as from an university chair, and everything prurient, and ignoble, and essentially dull, finds its abode and pulpit. I do not like mankind; but men, and not all of these — and fewer women. As for respecting the race, and, above all, that fatuous rabble of burgesses called "the public," God save me from such irreligion! — that way lies disgrace and dishonour. There must be something wrong in me, or I would not be popular.

This is perhaps a trifle stronger than my sedate and permanent opinion. Not much, I think. As for the art that we practise, I have never been able to see why its professors should be respected. They chose the primrose path; when they found it was not all primroses, but some of it brambly, and much of it uphill, they began to think and to speak of themselves as holy martyrs. But a man is never martyred in any honest sense in the pursuit of his pleasure; and *delirium tremens* has more of the honour of the cross. We were full of the pride of life, and chose, like prostitutes, to live by a pleasure. We should be paid if we give the pleasure we pretend to give; but why should we be honoured?

I hope some day you and Mrs. Gosse will come for a Sunday; but we must wait till I am able to see people. I am very full of Jenkin's life; it is painful, yet very pleasant, to dig into the past of a dead friend, and find him, at every spadeful, shine brighter. I own, as I read, I wonder more and more why he should have taken me to be a friend. He had many and obvious faults upon the face of him; the heart was pure gold. I feel it little pain to have lost him, for it is a loss in which I cannot believe; I take it, against reason, for an absence; if not to-day, then to-morrow, I still fancy I shall see him in the door; and then, now when I know him better, how glad a meeting! Yes, if I could believe in the immortality business, the world would indeed be too good to be true; but we were put here to do what service we can, for honour and not for hire; the sods cover us, and the worm that never dies, the conscience, sleeps well at last; these are the wages, besides what we receive so lavishly day by day; and they are enough for a man who knows his own fraility and sees all things in the proportion of reality. The soul of piety was killed long ago by the idea of reward. Nor is happiness, whether eternal or temporal, the reward that mankind seeks. Happinesses are but his way-side campings; his soul is in the journey; he was born for the struggle, and only tastes his life in effort and on the condition that he is opposed. How, then, is such a creature, so fiery, so pugnacious, so made up of discontent and aspiration, and such noble and uneasy passions — how can he be rewarded but by rest? I would not say it aloud; for man's cherished belief is that he loves that happiness which he continually spurns and passes by; and this belief in some ulterior happiness exactly fits him. He does not require to stop and taste it; he can be about the rugged and bitter business where his heart lies; and yet he can tell himself this fairy tale of an eternal tea-party, and enjoy the notion that he is both himself and something else; and that his friends well yet meet him, all ironed out and emasculate, and still be lovable, — as if love did not live in the faults of the beloved only, and draw its breath in an unbroken round of forgiveness! But the truth is, we must fight until we die; and when we die there can be no quiet for mankind but complete resumption into what? God, let us say — when all these desperate tricks will lie spell-bound at last.

Here came my dinner and cut this sermon short — *excusez.*

R.L.S.

Robert Louis Stevenson to J. M. Barrie

Vailima, July 13, 1894.

My dear Barrie, — This is the last effort of an ulcerated conscience. I have been so long owing you a letter, I have heard so much of you, fresh from the press, from my mother and Graham Balfour, that I have to write a letter no later than to-day, or perish in my share. But the deuce of it is, my dear fellow, that you write such a very good letter that I am ashamed to exhibit myself before my junior (which you are, after all) in the light of the dreary idiot I feel. Understand that there will be nothing funny in the following pages. If I can manage to be rationally coherent. I shall be more than satisfied.

In the first place, I have had the extreme satisfaction to be shown that photograph of your mother. It bears evident traces of the hand of an amateur. How is it that amateurs invariably take better photographs than professionals? I must qualify invariably. My own negatives have always represented a province of chaos and old night in which you might dimly perceive fleecy spots of twilight, representing nothing; so that, if I am right in supposing the portrait of your mother to be yours, I must salute you as my superior. Is that your mother's breakfast? Or is it only afternoon tea? If the first, do let me recommend to Mrs. Barrie to add an egg to her ordinary. Which, if you please, I will ask her to eat to the honour of her son, and I am sure she will live much longer for it, to enjoy his fresh successes. I never in my life saw anything more deliciously characteristic. I declare I can hear her speak. I wonder my mother could resist the temptation of your proposed visit to Kirriemuir, which it was like your kindness to propose. By the way, I was twice in Kirriemuir, I believe in the year '71, when I was going on a visit to Glenogil. It was Kirriemuir, was it not? I have a distinct recollection of an inn at the end — I think the upper end — of an irregular open place or square, in which I always see your characters evolve. But indeed, I did not pay much attention; being all bent upon my visit to a shooting-box, where I should fish a real trout-stream, and I believe preserved. I did, too, and it was a charming stream, clear as crystal, without a trace of peat — a strange thing in Scotland — and alive with trout; the name of it I cannot remember, it was something like the Queen's River, and in some hazy way connected with memories of Mary Queen of Scots. It formed an epoch in my life, being the end of my trout-fishing. I had always been accustomed to pause and very laboriously to kill every fish as I took it. But in the Queen's River I took so good a basket that I forgot these niceties;

and when I sat down, in a hard rain shower, under a bank, to take my sandwiches and sherry, lo! and behold, there was the basketful of trouts still kicking in their agony. I had a very unpleasant conversation with my conscience. All that afternoon I persevered in fishing, brought home my basket in triumph, and sometime that night, "in the wee sma' hours ayont the twal," I finally forswore the gentle craft of fishing. I dare say your local knowledge may identify this historic river; I wish it could go farther and identify also that particular Free kirk in which I sat and groaned on Sunday. While my hand is in I must tell you a story. At that antique epoch you must not fall into the vulgar error that I was myself ancient. I was, on the contrary, very young, very green, and (what you will appreciate, Mr. Barrie) very shy. There came one day to lunch at the house two very formidable old ladies — or one very formidable, and the other what you please — answering to the honoured and historic name of the Miss C—— A——'s of Bulnamoon. At table I was exceedingly funny, and entertained the company with tales of geese and bubblyjocks. I was great in the expression of my terror for these bipeds, and suddenly this horrid, severe, and eminently matronry old lady put up a pair of gold eye-glasses, looked at me awhile in silence, and pronounced in a clangorous voice her verdict. "You give me very much the effect of a coward, Mr. Stevenson!" I had very nearly left two vices behind me at Glenogil — fishing and jesting at table. And of one thing you may be very sure my lips were no more opened at that meal.

July 29th.

No, Barrie, 'tis in vain they try to alarm me with their bulletins. No doubt, you're ill, and unco ill, I believe; but I have been so often in the same case that I know pleurisy and pneumonia are in vain against Scotsmen who can write. (I once could.) You cannot imagine probably how near me this common calamity brings you. *Ce que j'ai toussé dans ma vie!* How often and how long have I been on the rack at night and learned to appreciate that noble passage in the Psalms when somebody or other is said to be more set on something than they "who dig for hid treasures — yea, than those who long for the morning" — for all the world, as you have been racked and you have longed. Keep your heart up, and you'll do. Tell that to your mother, if you are still in any danger or suffering. And by the way, if you are at all like me — and I tell myself you are very like me — be sure there is only one thing good for you, and that is the sea in hot climates. Mount, sir, into "a little frigot" of 5,000 tons or so, and steer peremptorily for the tropics; and what if the ancient mariner, who guides your frigot should startle the silence of the ocean with the cry of land ho! — say, when the day is dawning — and you should see the turquoise mountain-tops of Upolu coming hand over fist above the horizon? Mr. Barrie, sir, 'tis then there would be larks! And though I cannot be certain that our climate would suit you (for it does not suit some), I am sure as death the voyage would do you good — would do you *Best* — and if Samoa didn't do, you needn't stay beyond the month, and I should have had another pleasure in my life, which is a serious consideration for me. I take this as the hand of the Lord preparing your way to Vailima — in the desert, certainly — in the desert of Cough and by the ghoul-haunted woodland of Fever — but whither that way points there can be no question — and there will be a meeting of the twa Hoasting Scots Makers in spite of fate, fortune, and the Devil. *Absit omen.*

My dear Barrie, I am a little in the dark about this new work of yours: what is to become of me afterwards? You say carefully — methought anxiously — that I was no longer me when I grew up? I cannot bear this suspense: what is it? It's no forgery? And AM I HANGIT? These are the elements of a very pretty lawsuit which you had better come to Samoa to compromise. I am enjoying a great pleasure that I had long looked forward to, reading Orne's "History of Indostan"; I had been looking out for it everywhere; but at last, in four volumes, large quarto, beautiful type and page, and with a delectable set of maps and plans, and all the names of the places wrongly spelled — it came to Samoa, little Barrie. I tell you frankly, you had better come soon. I am sair failed a'ready; and what I may be if you continue to dally, I dread to conceive. I may be speechless; already, or at least for a month or so, I'm little better than a teetoller — I beg pardon, a teetotaller. It is not exactly physical, for I am in good health, working four or five hours a day in my plantation, and intending to ride a paper chase next Sunday — ay, man, that's a fact, and I havena had the hert to breathe it to my mother yet — the obligation's poleetical, for I am trying every means to live well with my German neighbours — and, O Barrie, but it's no easy! To be sure, there are many exceptions. And the whole of the above must be regarded as private — strictly private. Breathe it not in Kirriemuir: tell it not to the daughters of Dundee! What a nice extract this would make for the daily papers! and how it would facilitate my position here! . . .

August 5th.

This is Sunday, the Lord's Day. "The hour of attack approaches." And it is a singular consideration what I risk; I may yet be the subject of a tract, and a good tract too—such as one which I remember reading with recreant awe and rising hair in my youth, of a boy who was a very good boy, and went to Sunday Schule, and one day kipped from it, and went and actually bathed, and was dashed over a waterfall, and he was the only son of his mother, and she was a widow. A dangerous trade, that, and one that I have to practise. I'll put in a word when I get home again, to tell you whether I'm killed or not. "Accident in the (Paper) Hunting Field: death of a notorious author. We deeply regret to announce the death of the most unpopular man in Samoa, who broke his neck at the descent of Magagi, from the misconduct of his little raving lunatic of an old beast of a pony. It is proposed to commemorate the incident by the erection of a suitable pile. The design (by our local architect, Mr. Walker) is highly artificial, with a rich and voluminous Crockett at each corner, a small but impervious Barrièer at the entrance, an arch at the top, an Archer of a pleasing but solid character at the bottom: the colour will be genuine William-Black; and Lang, lang may the ladies sit wi' their fans in their hands." Well, well, they may sit as they sat for me, and little they'll reck, the ungrateful jauds! Muckle they cared about Tusitala when they had him! But now ye can see the difference; now, leddies, ye can repent, when ower late, o' your former cauldness and what ye'll perhaps allow me to ca' your *tepeedity!* He was beautiful as the day, but his day is done! And perhaps, as he was maybe gettin' a wee thing fly-blawn, it's nane too shüne.

Monday, August 6th.

Well, sir, I have escaped the dangerous conjunction of the widow's only son and the Sabbath Day. We had a most enjoyable time, and Lloyd and I were 3 and 4 to arrive; I will not tell here what interval had elapsed between our arrival and the arrival of 1 and 2; the question, sir, is otiose and malign; it deserves, it shall have no answer. And now without further delay to the main purpose of this hasty note. We received and we have already in fact distributed the gorgeous fahbrics of Kirriemuir. Whether from the splendour of the robes themselves, or from the direct nature of the compliments with which you had directed us to accompany the presentations, one young lady blushed as she received the proofs of your munificence. . . . Bad ink, and the dregs of it at that, but the heart in the right place. Still very cordially interested in my Barrie and wishing him well through his sickness, which is of the body, and long defended from mine, which is of the head, and by the impolite might be described as idiocy. The whole head is useless, and the whole sitting part painful: reason, the recent Paper Chase.

> *"There was racing and chasing in Vailile plantation,*
> *   And vastly we enjoyed it,*
> *But, alas! for the state of my foundation,*
> *   For it wholly has destroyed it."*

Come, my mind is looking up. The above is wholly impromptu. —
On oath.

Tusitala.

August 12, 1894.

And here, Mr. Barrie, is news with a vengeance. Mother Hubbard's dog
is well again — what did I tell you? Pleurisy, pneumonia, and all that
kind of truck is quite unavailing against a Scotchman who can write —
and not only that, but it appears the perfidious dog is married. This
incident, so far as I remember, is omitted from the original epic —

> *"She went to the graveyard*
> *To see him get buried,*
> *And when she came back*
> *The Deil had got married."*

It now remains to inform you that I have taken what we call here
"German offence" at not receiving cards, and that the only reparation I
will accept is that Mrs. Barrie shall incontinently upon the receipt of this
Take and Bring you to Vailima in order to apologize and be pardoned
for this offence. The commentary of Tamaitai upon the event was brief
but pregnant: "Well, it's a comfort our guest-room is furnished for two."
This letter, about nothing, has already endured too long. I shall just
present the family to Mrs. Barrie — Tamaitai, Tamaitai Matua, Teuila,
Palema, Loia, and with an extra low bow,

Yours,
Tusitala.

Oscar Wilde

A towering figure in gay history, Irish writer Oscar Fingal O'Flahertie Wills
Wilde poured as much of his unique wit into creating himself as into creating

his prose, his poetry and plays such as *Salomé* and *Lady Windermere's Fan*. He numbered among the most visible celebrities of the late nineteenth century, but with fame came the notoriety that ultimately ruined him. Brief and sparkling, Wilde's letters to various friends in the arts and literary communities trace his rise and fall in his trademark style. His animated spirit buckled during his imprisonment on sodomy charges, which he described in *Ballad of Reading Gaol* and *De Profundis*. Traveling under the pseudonym Sebastian Melmoth after his release, Wilde finally succumbed to grim poverty and social ostracism. Included here are notes to his friend and biographer, Robert H. Sherard, to the artist Will Rothenstein and to Lord Alfred (Bosie) Douglas, his lover.

Oscar Wilde to Robert H. Sherard

[1891(?)]

Dear Robert, — Your letters are charming, they are iridescent, and everything you see or hear seems to become touched with colour and tinged with joy. I think of you often wandering in violet valleys with your honey-coloured hair, and meditating on the influence of paradoxes on the pastoral mind; but you should be here. One can only write in cities, the country hanging on one's walls in the grey mists of Corot, or the opal mornings that Daubigny has given us: not that I have written here — the splendid whirl and swirl of life in London sweeps me from my Sphynx. I am hard at work being idle; late midnights and famishing morrows follow one another. I wish I was back in Paris, where I did such good work. However, society must be amazed, and my Neronian coiffure has amazed it. Nobody recognises me, and everybody tells me I look young: that is delightful, of course.

My book you will have next week — it is a great pleasure to give it to anyone so sympathetic as you — poet to poet. I give you my work because your joy in it makes it more dear to me.

Who is your young man who likes what I said of the primrose?

My pen is horrid, my ink bad, my temper worse. — Write soon, and come soon to London.

Oscar.

Oscar Wilde to Will Rothenstein

> 51 Friedrich's Promenade
> Bad-Homburg
> [1892]

My dear Will,

The *Gaulois*, the *Echo de Paris*, and the *Pall Mall* have all had interviews.
I hardly know what new thing there is to say. The Licenser of Plays is
nominally the Lord Chamberlain, but really a commonplace official — in
the present case a Mr. Pigott — who panders to the vulgarity and hypocrisy of the English people, by licensing every low farce and vulgar melo-
drama — he even allows the stage to be used for the purpose of the
caricaturing of the personalities of artists, and at the same moment when
he prohibited *Salome*, he licensed a burlesque of *Lady Windermere's Fan* in
which an actor dressed up like me and imitated my voice and manner!!!
The curious thing is this: all the arts are free in England, except the
actor's art; it is held by the Censor that the stage degrades and that the
actors desecrate fine subjects — so the Censor prohibits not the publication of *Salome* but its production: yet, not one single actor has protested
against this insult to the stage — not even Irving, who is always prating
about the art of the actor — this shows how few actors are artists. All the
dramatic critics except Archer of *The World* agree with the Censor that
there should be a censorship over actors and acting! This shows how
bad our stage must be, and also shows how Philistine the English jour-
nalists are.
I am very ill, dear Will, and can't write any more.

> Ever yours,
> *Oscar Wilde.*

Oscar Wilde to Lord Alfred Douglas

> January 1893[?]
> Babbacombe Cliff

My Own Boy,

Your sonnet is quite lovely, and it is a marvel that those red rose-leaf lips
of yours should have been made no less for music of song than for

madness of kisses. Your slim gilt soul walks between passion and poetry. I know Hyacinthus, whom Apollo loved so madly, was you in Greek days.

Why are you alone in London, and when do you go to Salisbury? Do go there to cool your hands in the grey twilight of Gothic things, and come here whenever you like. It is a lovely place — it only lacks you; but go to Salisbury first.

Always, with undying love, yours

Oscar

Oscar Wilde to Robert H. Sherard

L.P.
C.4

From Wilde,
H. M. Prison,
Holloway,
16-4-1895.

B.2-4
3.56

My Dear Robert, — You good, daring reckless friend! I was delighted to get your letter, with all its wonderful news. For myself, I am ill — apathetic. Slowly life creeps out of me. Nothing but Alfred Douglas' daily visits quicken me into life, and even him I only see under humiliating and tragic conditions.

Don't fight more than 6 duels a week! I suppose Sarah is hopeless; but your chivalrous friendship — your fine, chivalrous friendship — is worth more than all the money in the world. — Yours,

Oscar.

Oscar Wilde to Lord Alfred Douglas

Hôtel de la Plage, Berneval-sur-Mer
Friday, 4 June 1897 2:30

My dear Boy,

I have just got your letter, but Ernest Dowson, Dal Young, and Conder are here, so I cannot read it, except the last three lines. I love the last words of anything: the end in art is the beginning. Don't think I don't love you. Of course I love you more than anyone else. But our lives are irreparably severed, as far as meeting goes. What is left to us is the knowledge that we love each other, and every day I think of you, and I know you are a poet, and that makes you doubly dear and wonderful. My friends here have been most sweet to me, and I like them all very much. Young is the best of fellows, and Ernest has a most interesting nature. He is to send me some of his work.

We all stayed up till three o'clock; very bad for me, but it was a delightful experience. Today is a day of sea-fog, and rain — my first. Tomorrow I go with fishers to fish, but I will write to you tonight.

Ever, dear boy, with fondest love

Oscar

Oscar Wilde to Will Rothenstein

From M. Sebastian Melmoth
Hôtel de la Plage
Berneval-sur-Mer
Dieppe

Wednesday [June 9, 1897]

My dear good Friend,

I cannot tell you how pleased I was to get your kind and affectionate letter yesterday, and I look forward with real delight to the prospect of seeing you, though it be only for a day. I am going into Dieppe to breakfast with the Stannards, who have been most kind to me, and I will send you a telegram from there. I so hope you can come tomorrow by the daily boat, so that you and your friend can dine and sleep here. There is no one in this little inn but myself, but it is most comfortable, and the chef, there is a real chef — is an artist of great distinction; he walks in the evening by the sea to get ideas for the next day. Is it not sweet of him? I have taken a chalet for the whole season for £32, so I shall be able I hope to work again, and write plays or something. I know, dear Will, you will be pleased to know that I have not come out of prison an embittered or disappointed man. On the contrary. In many ways I have gained much. I am not really ashamed of having been in prison: I often was in more shameful places: but I *am* really ashamed of having led a life unworthy of an artist. I don't say that Messalina is a better companion than Sporus, or that the one is all right and the other all wrong: I know simply that a life of definite and studied materialism, and philosophy of appetite and cynicism, and a cult of sensual and senseless ease, are bad things for an artist: they narrow the imagination, and dull the more delicate sensibilities. I was all wrong, my dear boy, in my life. I was not getting the best out of me. *Now,* I think that with good health, and the friendship of a few good, simple nice fellows like yourself, and a quiet mode of living, with isolation for thought, and freedom from the endless hunger for pleasures that wreck the body and imprison the soul, — well, I think I may do things yet, that you all may like. Of course I have lost much, but still, my dear Will, when I reckon up all that is *left* to me, the sun and the sea of this beautiful world; its dawns dim with gold and its nights hung with silver; many books, and all flowers, and a few good friends; and a brain and body to which health and power are not denied — really I am *rich* when I count up what I still have: and as for money, my money did me horrible harm. It wrecked me. I hope just to have enough to enable me to live simply and write well.

So remember that you will find me in many respects very happy — and of course by your sweetness in coming to see me, you will bring me happiness along with you.

As for the silent songs on stone, I am charmed at the prospect of having society of yours. It is awfully good of you to think of it. I have had many sweet presents, but none I shall value more than yours.

You ask me if you can bring me anything from London. Well, the salt soft air kills my cigarettes, and I have no box in which to keep them. If you are in a millionaire condition and could bring me a box for keeping cigarettes in, it would be a great boon. In Dieppe there is nothing between a trunk and a *bonbonnière.* I do hope to see you tomorrow (Thursday) for dinner and sleep. If not, well Friday morning. I am up now at 8 oc. regularly!

I hope you never forget that *but for me* you would not be *Will*

Rothenstein: *Artist.* You would simply be *William* Rothenstein, *R.A.* It is one of the most important facts in the history of art.

I look forward greatly to seeing Strangman. His translating *Lady Winder-mere* is delightful.

> Your sincere and grateful friend,
> *Oscar Wilde*

Will Rothenstein, Esquire, Artist,
53 Glebe Place, Chelsea, S.W.,
Londres, Angleterre.

Oscar Wilde to Will Rothenstein

> *Berneval-sur-Mer*
> *August 24th, 97*

My dear Will,

Of course I only did it to oblige you. My name was not to be appended, nor was there to be any honorarium of any kind. It was to oblige you I did it — but with me, as with you, as with all artists, one's work *est à prendre ou à laisser.* I couldn't go into the details of coarse and notorious facts. I know Henley edited the *National Observer,* and was a very bitter and in some respects a cowardly journalist in his conduct: I get the historical Review regularly, and its silliness and stupidity are beyond words. I am only concerned with the essence of the man, not with his accidents — miry or other.

When I said of W.E.H. that his prose was the prose of a poet, I paid him an undeserved compliment. His prose is jerky, spasmodic, and he is incapable of the beautiful architecture of a long sentence, which is the fine flower of prose-writing, but I praised him for the sake of an antithe-sis — 'his poetry is the beautiful poetry of a prose-writer' — that refers to Henley's finest work: the Hospital Poems — which are in *vers libres* — and *vers libres* are prose. The author by dividing the lines shows you the rhythm he wishes you to follow. But all that one is concerned with is *literature:* poetry is not finer than prose, nor prose finer than poetry — when one uses the words poetry and prose, one is merely referring to certain technical modes of word-music, the melody and harmony one might say — though they are not exclusive terms — and though I praised Henley too much, too extravagantly, when I said his prose was the beautiful prose of a poet, the latter part of the sentence is a subtle aesthetic appreciation of his *vers libres* which W.E.H., if he has any critical faculty left, would be the first to appreciate. You seem to me to have misunderstood the sentence — Mallarmé would understand it. But the matter is of no importance. Everybody is greedy of common panegyrics — and W.E.H. would much sooner have a long list of his literary failures chronicled with dates.

I am still here though the wind blows terribly — your lovely lithographs are on my walls, and you will be pleased to hear that I do not propose to ask you to alter them, though I am *not* the Editor of a 'paying Publication'.

I am delighted to hear the Monticelli is sold, though Obach does not say for how much. Dal Young is coming out here tomorrow and I will tell him. He seems to be under the impression that he bought it. Of course I know nothing about the facts of the case.

Robbie Ross had to go back to England on Thursday last, and I fear will not be able to come again this year.

I don't know where I shall go myself. I am not in the mood to do the work I want — and I fear I shall never be. The intense energy of creation has been kicked out of me. I don't care now to struggle to get back what, when I had it, gave me little pleasure.

Ever yours,
Oscar.

Oscar Wilde to Will Rothenstein

Hôtel de Nice
Rue des Beaux-Arts
Paris
[1898]

My dear Will,

I cannot tell you how touched I am by your letter, and by all you say of my poem. Why on earth don't you write literary criticisms for papers? I wish the Ballad had fallen into your hands. No one has said things so *sympathiques,* so full of delicate insight, so large, from the point of view of art, as you. Your letter has given me more pleasure, more pride, than anything has done since the poem appeared.

Yes: it is something to have made a 'sonnet out of skilly' — (Cunninghame Graham will explain to you what skilly is. You must never know my personal experience). And I *do* think the whole affair 'realised' — and that is triumph.

I hope you will be in Paris some time this spring, and come and see me. I see by the papers that you are still making mortals immortal — and I wish you were working for a Paris newspaper, and that I could see your work making kiosques lovely.

Ever yours,
Oscar.

Oscar Wilde to Robert H. Sherard

[Paris, 1898]

I am sending you a copy of my Ballad — first edition — which I hope you will accept in memory of our long friendship. I had hoped to give it to you personally, but I know you are very busy, tho' I am sorry you are too busy to come and see me, or to let me know where you are to be seen.

Aubrey Beardsley

Enormously popular at the end of the nineteenth century, English artist Aubrey Beardsley traveled in social circles that included Oscar Wilde and Max Beerbohm. Critics denounced his work for the erotic androgyny of his male and female figures, which seemed to them obscene, but their views held no sway with an adoring public. Beardsley's illustrations for Wilde's *Salomé* particularly irked the pillars of the artistic community, perhaps as much for their connection to Wilde as for their aesthetic qualities. This selection of Beardsley's letters opens with two — one to his mother and the other to his sister, Mabel — written at the age of seven, and then skips ahead to one written to Robert Ross, a lover of Wilde's, in 1893. The letters spanning the years 1895 to 1898 (when Beardsley died, at the age of twenty-six), are addressed to close friend and patron André Raffalovich, a wealthy Russian who wrote *L'Uranisme: Inversion Sexuelle Congénitale*, an essay on homosexuality. Beardsley often addressed Raffalovich as Mentor and signed himself Télémaque, a reference to Homer's *Odyssey*, in which Odysseus's friend Mentor gives advice to Telemachus.

Aubrey Beardsley to Ellen Beardsley

1 October [1879]
Hamilton Lodge, Hurstpierpoint

My dear Mother,

I hope you are quite well. I am getting on quite well. The boys do not tease me. I like Hurst very much. I met Mrs C. Cook one day. I do not do very many lessons. I go lots of times in to the playground. I hope Mabel is quite well. How do you like Margate? My knee is better. I am quite well. I received your letter this morning; thank you for it. I am very happy. I hope Mabel is quite well. I think the old man who had two umbrellas must have taken Mrs Cook's. Good-bye.

Your loving Aubrey

Aubrey Beardsley to Mabel Beardsley

15 October [1879]
Hamilton Lodge

My dear Mabel,

Thank you for your letter. We have pudding every day. The drilling master [comes] every Thursday. I like the lessons very much. We drill on a lawn. We have a dog named Fido, he comes out with us every day. I like the walks very much. I am quite well. Give my love to Mother and to Father. I will write to Mother next week. I hope you feel better for your trip to Margate. I like some of the boys very much.

Miss Wise reads out of a book about French and English ships.

Good-bye.
Your loving brother Aubrey

Aubrey Beardsley to Robert Ross

[Late] *November* [1893]
114 Cambridge Street

Dear Bobbie,

Many thanks for your letter. I haven't found a moment to answer it sooner. How beastly dull you must be on the top of Mont Blanc or wherever you are. I do wish I could have managed to get over to see you.

I suppose you've heard all about the *Salomé* row. I can tell you I had a warm time of it between Lane and Oscar and Co. For one week the numbers of telegraph and messenger boys who came to the door was simply scandalous. I really don't quite know how matters really stand now. Anyhow Bozie's name is not to turn up on the Title. The book will be out soon after Christmas. I have withdrawn three of the illustrations and supplied their places with three new ones (simply beautiful and quite irrelevant). *Masques* is going to be A 1.

I have just turned out a very amusing frontispiece to *Vergilius the Sorcerer* (Nutt), also a really wonderful picture for *Scaramouch in Naxos*.

This morning Pennel has been giving me lessons in etching. Verlaine is over here, I met him at the Harlands'. He is a dear old thing. Moore's article about him was a downright libel.

My *Girl and a Book Shop* at the N.E.A.C. has received very amusing notices; *Public Opinion* sets me down as belonging to the Libidinous and Asexual School.

Whibley is meditating a violent attack on the Birmingham School. I do hope it will come off, idiots are beginning to say nice things about Gaskin, Batten and all those hopeless people. Wratislaw has just published rather a clever volume of verse. I think he's really not a bad sort.

By the way Bozie is going to Egypt, in what capacity I don't quite gather; something diplomatic I fancy. Have you heard from either him or Oscar? Both of them are really very dreadful people.

I long for your return.

In January I shall be over in Paris for a short time. There is a very jolly exhibition of French work at the Grafton now. Affiches, lithographs, and all that sort of thing. Let me have a line and tell me something about your vegetable life. I suppose you see papers, can I send you any books?

Ever yours Aubrey Beardsley

Kindest remembrances from my mother and sister.

Aubrey Beardsley to André Raffalovich

[Circa May 16, 1895]
114 Cambridge Street

My dear Mentor,

First for your sonnet a thousand thanks. You shall have one in return when my thoughts can find 'a shape in which to wander forth', meantime your verses lie amongst my treasures. How charming of you to send me these letters of Meredith, they are full of his splendid manner. Of course I shall value them enormously — but I feel I am robbing you.

I am delighted with the idea of making your portrait; it must be in pastel on brown paper — full length. I shan't plague you with long sittings as I draw very quickly.

Monday evening I am free and will be very pleased to spend it with you.

Yours till Saturday morning Télémaque

I am beginning the frontispiece — a literal rendering of the first line — .

Aubrey Beardsley to André Raffalovich

[May 28, 1895]
114 Cambridge Street

My dear Mentor,

Thank you for your letter and the photograph which interests me very much.

The frontispiece is quite finished and looks pretty.

Sarah's first night was a huge success. I have never seen such a reception as she got. She played superbly. What a pity though she did not start with *Fedora*. It would have been such a splendid reply to Mrs Patrick Campbell who really turns out to be the most incompetent creature. How I should love to come to Berlin, but I'm afraid it will be impossible with all the work I have to get through. By the way, some lovely flowers came to me yesterday from Goodyear's — thanks so much. I saw the prospectus for *Pan* when I was in Paris, of course it interested me enormously; it would be quite delightful to do anything for it.

Your advice as to work, food and sleep is not wasted on me. I have plenty of each. I suppose the result of the Oscar trial is in the German papers — two years' hard. I imagine it will kill him.

On Friday I am going to hear *Tannhäuser.* I look forward to it with mixed pleasure for it puts me most terribly out of conceit with my own little variations on the same theme.

Best remembrances to John Gray.

Yours Télémaque

Please give my kindest regards to Miss Gribbell.

Aubrey Beardsley to André Raffalovich

[November 1896]
Pier View, Boscombe.

My Dear***

This morning's post brought me Stendhal's fragments on Napoleon, & two magistral volumes, edited by Masson & Biagi, of Napoleon's student writings, & notes upon his early life. I need not tell you how grateful I am for them, & how delighted with the prospect of reading.

I was tremendously interested to hear about your correspondence with the beautiful Rachilde, & will look forward to her new novel, documented from your book.

No, you never told me anything about a blind man with a romantic history; still I am sorry he has taken to drink.

Sudermann's play must be charming in Cosmopolis.

It is most kind of Father — to write to the Fathers down here about me. A Father called, & was most charming & sympathetic.

I am indeed interested to hear all news of your controversy on nonconformity. I hope you will resume all that is being said for & against in some future edition of your book.

I have just been lent a study of mœurs antique entitled Aphrodite. It is by Pierre Louÿs. You have I expect read it.

Yours very affecly
Aubrey Beardsley

Aubrey Beardsley to André Raffalovich

(December, 1896)
Pier Veiw, Boscombe

My Dear***

I have not had many returns of blood since the first & rather violent outbreak. You are quite right in your expectation that the attacks would now be thrown off more easily. My breathing was only affected on the first day, & has since become (what I have grown to look upon) as normal. Still it makes me nervous about getting out. The weather too is against me. I have been whiling away my semi-convalescent moments with Zola's Rome, in its thoroughly bad English dress. I always melt over descriptions of the South & sunshine. You have of course read the book, & will recollect the very ludicrous passages about Botticelli.

I have been suffering dreadfully from depression, a condition which seems to me next door to the criminal.

I am yours always affectionately
Aubrey Beardsley.

Aubrey Beardsley to André Raffalovich

Sunday [? 7 February 1897]
Muriel, Bournemouth

My dear André,

I was so delighted to receive a letter of yours again. Many congratulations on the hand's recovery. Arsenic is to my mind an atrocious drug. My doctor has insinuated it into several of my medicines, with signal failure. I have at last rebelled formally against its presence in any prescription. I hope the effects of the overdose have by this time quite passed away.

I was greatly interested in the portrait you sketched me of your little friend, designated for the priesthood. I sympathize with him utterly in all his school troubles, for I know how much more bitter are these troubles to bear than any others that come in later life. I rejoice with him in his escape from so much anguish. There will be no more tears, I am sure, at St Mary's College.

I am beginning to think cheerfully of the coming spring, to hope that I may be well enough to enjoy the sight of new leaves. Last year I was robbed shamefully of my April and May; I believe that accounts entirely for my persistent wretchedness ever since.

Is it true that Ed. Toulouse, who wrote the book you sent me on Zola, has been able to find no one else to submit to his questionings, and that Sarah Bernhardt turned him indignantly out of her house? I have been reading a very charming little volume of Crébillon's *La nuit et le moment*, a perfectly delightful piece of work. My chances of recovery improve every day. Tomorrow I am to go out in a chair, if the weather is kind and gentle.

I am yours very affectionately Aubrey Beardsley

I have just received your letter of Sunday. Many thanks. We are so pleased that the proposed visit to Bournemouth is to be paid so soon.

Aubrey Beardsley to André Raffalovich

Wednesday [February 24, 1897]
Muriel, Bournemouth

My dear André,

So many thanks for your kind letter. Father Bearne came to see me yesterday, but unfortunately I had not the opportunity of talking to him as much as I should have wished. He was most charming and promised to come to see me often. I felt much drawn towards him and I believe he will be a good friend of mine. He has lent me a long life of Saint Ignatius Loyola, and I am reading for the first time a history of the growth and foundation of the Company. Master Oswald's letter is admirable. I can appreciate all his wants, except the one for a watch. To live in South Audley Street and to serve as an acolyte at Farm Street, is certainly an ingenious programme. I am touched to think of his childish prayers for me. I hope some day I shall have the pleasure of meeting my little beadsman. I wonder whether it would amuse him to receive some little present and a letter from a stranger? You could tell me if there was any story or picture book, or something of that sort that might please him. Do let me know. I hope he will not have too severe tumbles in the skating gallery of Mount St. Mary's.

It is so good of you, my dear André, to inquire about rooms for me.

This letter will I suppose cross one of yours with some news of Manchester Street. The weather has been a littler colder here, so I have not ventured out today. I shall miss a very kind friend at my side next time I am charioted up to the east cliff. I was so interested in what you tell me of Reichmann's book, and the remarks of Havelock Ellis in English.

Thank you very much for the *Journal*. It is really so kind of you to send it me. It interests me hugely every morning. I look forward to the book about George Sand, I am all gratitude. I did not know that Huysmans had announced a new work. How thoughtful you are, dear André. I can never thank you enough for your care for my well being and progress. I *do* hope I am the most grateful of creatures.

I am yours always affectionately Aubrey Beardsley

Aubrey Beardsley to André Raffalovich

Thursday [February 25, 1897]
Muriel, Bournemouth

My dear André,

Mariéton's very interesting volume arrived this morning. Thank you so much for it. What a nice ample creature George Sand is. Like a wonderful old cow with all her calves. I recollect, long ago, in my first boyhood, beginning a novel, the heroine of which became sadly spoiled by reading *Lélia*. She also refused to eat at meals, but carried bonbons and sweet biscuits about with her in her pocket. I have quite forgotten her name. I am reminded of her by the first pages of the *Histoire d'Amour*, and by the pangs of hunger I am suffering just at this moment. Dinner not to appear for another hour, and no confiserie at hand.

Spring cleaning is going forward at Muriel today, which has made me nervous and cross, it is so trying to hop about from one room to another.

I had a letter from Mabel this morning. She seems in better spirits, but I am aghast at the amount of travelling she has to get through before the tour comes to an end. I do hope she won't "knock up" while she is over there. Of course I don't like to advise her to come back. Still I believe it would be best for her to do so. What a pity the other tour did not end normally.

I am receiving long lectures here, from pillars of the Anglican faith, à propos of my communications with the kind Fathers of the Sacred Heart.

Please give my kindest remembrances to Miss Gribbell and to John Gray.

I am always yours very affectionately Aubrey Beardsley

Aubrey Beardsley to André Raffalovich

Saturday [April 10, 1897]
Hôtel Voltaire, Paris

My dearest Brother,

Our travelling went off so capitally, thanks to the kind care of Dr Phillips. I don't know what we should have done without him.

I felt a little unwell in the train on the way to Dover but nothing happened.

The sea was beautifully calm and unruffled. From Calais to Paris my spirits and appearance improved every half hour. This hotel has *no* lift but they seem very willing to carry me up and down stairs, and they carry me, by the way, quite nicely. Our proper rooms have not been allotted to us yet. I will give you full particulars about them when we are installed.

I think Dr Phillips was surprised at the way in which I got through the move. I don't feel in the least tired.

My little stay in London was such a bright and happy one, now I [am] again looking forward to seeing you. Paris you will find looking perfectly sweet. Such delicious tender green upon the trees. From my window I have a view which pleases me more than I can say. I think of you, dear André, at every turn with affection and with gratitude. Love from us to all. With much love,

Very affectionately Aubrey Beardsley

Aubrey Beardsley to André Raffalovich

[1897] *Hôtel Cosmopolitain,
Menton, Decr. 30th*

My Dearest Brother

. . . Among many things your goodness has taught me is a greater care &
wisdom in the spending of money. How hot my face gets when I think
how wildly & uselessly one scattered one's money once. I am glad to say
life is comparatively cheap here, much cheaper for instance than at such
a place as Dieppe.

I am delighted at your success with the works of [J.A.] Symonds.
There is much to be said for a writer who may be sold profitably at
second hand.

Yes there is a library here but not a very good one. However I
belong to it as I found a dozen books or so on the catalogue that I was
anxious to read, & were worth the expenditure of six francs.

Oh how good of you to think of sending me some scraps from
Archbishop Ullathornes life, but have you really the time to copy them
out! For the last twenty four hours we have had a pitiless drench of
rain, & the Mentonese are rejoicing for the sake of their oranges &
lemons. But I am grumbling dreadfully at being kept indoors.

With the greatest affection, & gratitude for your brotherly care &
love.

Aubrey Beardsley.

Aubrey Beardsley to André Raffalovich

[1898]
*Hôtel Cosmopolitain,
Menton, Jan. 11th.*

My Dearest Brother

Thank you so much for your kind letter. Yes I am in a land of sunshine
again, & the spell of wet weather does not seem to have done me the
least hurt. Menton is a truly sociable little place, & the strong English
contingent here furnishes me with quite a number of people to talk to.

There is a famous egyptologist here who looks like a corpse, has looked like one for fourteen years, who is much worse than I am, & yet lives on & does things. My spirits have gone up immensely since I have known him.

Both the Priests who visit me here have been invalids like myself & are so kind & sympathetic. Neither of them are French. The Abbé Luzzani is German & Italian, & Father Orchmans is Belge. The curé of Menton is an old dear but I see very little of him.

Your year's waiting will surely be attended with the greatest graces, as are even the least acts of obedience.

With our best love to all

Yours always most affectionately
Aubrey Beardsley.

Max Beerbohm/Will Rothenstein

A keen observer of the English literary and social scene during the first third of the twentieth century, Max Beerbohm was a leading drama critic, satirist and caricaturist. His letters to friends such as gadabout and conversationalist Reggie Turner and the portraitist Will Rothenstein combine the tongue-in-cheek camp and astute discernment that distinguished his published writing. Like so many other gays of the time, Beerbohm struggled with the issue of marriage and experienced a string of broken engagements. Surrounded by the celebrities of his day — such as Oscar Wilde, Aubrey Beardsley, Lord Alfred (Bosie) Douglas and the "Bloomsbury donkeys," as he called Virginia Woolf's crowd — Beerbohm provides an eye-opening peek into the English gay and lesbian scene. The letters reveal his familiarity with Wilde's companion Robert Ross, with Alfred Taylor (whose home was a popular meeting place for gay men), and with male prostitutes, known as "renters." Wilde's arrest, at which Turner was present, his trials at the Old Bailey, his famous "love that dare not speak its name" speech and his eventual death are narrated in heartbreaking and humorous detail.

Max Beerbohm to Will Rothenstein

The Bodley Head, Vigo Street, London
August 24, 1893

My dear Will

Whilst I write I am coming of age: I was born twenty one years ago today and am ever so sorry that I cannot possibly come & live with you in Scarborough as you so charmingly ask me. I have to go into the country tomorrow for a week to stay with relations & cannot possibly put them off. Why do I write on this odd paper? Because it was wrapped up with two very lovely drawings by Aubrey Beardsley which J. Lane has just given me. They lie before me as I write: I am enamoured of them. So is John Lane: he said "How lucky I am to have got hold of this young Beardsley: look at the technique of his drawings! What workmanship! *He never goes over the edges!*" He never said anything of the kind but the criticism is suggestive for you, dear Will? And characteristic of Art's middleman, the Publisher — for of such is the Chamber of Horrors. How brilliant I am! I forget whether you like Salomé or not — Salomé is the play of which the drawings are illustrative? I have just been reading it again — and like it immensely — there is much, I think, in it that is beautiful, much lovely writing — I almost wonder Oscar doesn't dramatise it.

But brilliancy to the winds! I am in love — in love with Cissie Loftus and, oh my dear Will, though it may not seem paradoxical to say so, it is very very charming to be in love: you may not believe me — I could not have foretold it two weeks ago but now my whole being is changed: I have become good and am really happy at last.

My moral sense has awakened. The other night I 'interviewed' her for an imaginary newspaper: she is not fifteen yet and wears a pink ribbon in her hair. I am utterly changed. Do write and be sympathetic with me. She let me hold her hands, telling them by palmistry, for a long time and the whole thing was quite a little idyll in its way.

I must see you to rave about her; you would hardly know me. But you must not see her: a caricature might dissillusionise me. Oh my dear Will I am so happy and good. Yours Max.

She has a small oval face and long eyes and full lips: her hair is quite straight as it falls over her shoulders and she has been in a convent for four years. As yet, in spite of her great success in art, she is utterly unspoiled. My love for her is utterly reverent: you, I know, regard woman simply as the accusative after the second auxiliary verb: or do I wrong you? I could not ever wrong *her;* but I should love to marry her. I am so good and changed. Yours again Max.

All love to you in Scarborough: how I wish I could have come.

Max Beerbohm to Reggie Turner

The Chicago Club, Chicago
[Postmark March 3, 1895]

My dear Reg,

Poor, poor Oscar! How very sad it is. I cannot bear to think of all that must have happened — the whisperings and the hastenings hither and thither — before he could have been seduced into Marlborough Street. I suppose he was exasperated too much not to take action. I am sorry he has not got George Lewis, wonder if Bosie has returned, what evidence will be brought in for the defence — and so forth. It is awful not to be upon the spot. Do let me hear *real long* details — *full accounts.* Do please not mind writing many pages — I am parched for news — the head-lines are so short here and so relentless: "Gives Oscar what's-for," "The Pretty Poet and the Mocking Marquis," "Mrs Wilde sticks to him," etc. etc. — quite dreadful. Do not, I beg you, get mixed up in the scandal. I was *so* deeply interested in your account of the first night, but do not curtail anything about this matter.

Dear Chicago! I quite like it and am being rather lionised. I am (not a word to dear Mrs Leverson) in love with a certain Miss Conover in my brother's company — a dark Irish girl of twenty, very blunt and rude, who hates affectation and rather likes me. We only knew each other during this tour and have seen a good deal of each other. On the car from N. York to Chicago we sat together all the time. I made her cry on the first afternoon by telling her circumstantially that she was known at the Garrick as "Kill-Scene-Conover" — and immediately fell in love with her. There were two sleeping cars, one entirely for the actors and the other for the actors and actresses, who slept in berths partitioned off by ineffectual curtains that were perpetually withdrawn to let people pass. Miss Conover looked extremely pretty in her night-gown and gave me an apple from her hamper. Miss Cockerell, who slept by her in the same berth, looked very pretty too, I am bound to confess. Miss Cockerell threw me a banana. It was like being in a girls' school. Do you remember the big girls' school on the road to Rouen and our speculations about it? Here in Chicago I see Miss Conover perpetually and have asked her to be my wife, but as we have always been upon terms of chaff, she is only just beginning to realise that I am in earnest — which perhaps I am not — who knows? I took her to a theatre here last night and in the cab home we held each other's hands all the way. I have her photograph in my little green case now. I really am very much in love with her and she will be very much in love with me, I think, soon. Do be sympathetic.

The climate, you will be sorry to hear, does not agree with Charles Allan. He cannot get bread-and-milk well made here and has to substitute negus at night. (He says that negus comes extremely expensive.) I heard him use the expression *"Fiddle-de-dee"* to a black waiter the other day.

Last night Herbert gave a large supper to the critics: afterwards Herbert and I and Brough were taken to see a town-ball — a scene of vast and hideous debauchery. Also we visited certain houses where black-women danced naked to the sound of the piano — and one where French women gambolled with one another in a room cushioned with blue silk, just as the bells began ringing for early mass. I did not get to bed til six just as the sun began his daily task of rising & setting.

This is Sunday evening at six and I feel rather feverish as I used to feel on the Sunday after a wine. I wish that this huge club in which I am writing were the little room at Adamson's and that the younger X would soon come in stamping in his great-coat and Y with the debauch of last night in his small blue eyes and Z looking forward to his champagne, and you smiling at me. Dear Oxford! Dear Chicago! My great love to you.

Ever your
Max

Max Beerbohm to Reggie Turner

19 Hyde Park Place
[Postmark May 3, 1895]

My dearest Reg,

I am very sorry I have not written before. Ever since I arrived I have been all day at the Old Bailey and dining out in the evening — and coming home very tired. Please forgive me. Oscar has been quite superb. His speech about the Love that dares not tell his name was simply wonderful, and carried the whole court right away, quite a tremendous burst of applause. Here was this man, who had been for a month in prison and loaded with insults and crushed and buffeted, perfectly self-possessed, dominating the Old Bailey with his fine presence and musical voice. He has never had so great a triumph, I am sure, as when the gallery burst into applause — I am sure it affected the gallery. Public opinion too has undergone a very great revulsion, so everyone seems to think — nine out of the twelve jurors were for him. Today they renew application for bail, but I don't think they can get it. Somebody has written to Ned Clarke offering Oscar the sole use of his house and grounds at Camberwell or somewhere. Ned Clarke has done splendidly and is very much implected with Hoscar — and talks of shaving his whiskers. Hoscar stood very upright when he was brought up to hear the verdict and looked most leonine and sphinx-like. I pitied poor little Alfred Taylor — nobody remembered his existence, and Grain made a very poor speech and he himself a poor witness. Hoscar is thinner and consequently finer to look at. Willie has been extracting fivers from Humphreys. It was horrible leaving the court day after day and having to pass through a knot of renters (the younger Parker wearing Her Majesty's uniform — another form of female attire) who were allowed to hang around after giving their evidence and to wink at likely persons: Trelawny is raising money for the conduct of the case. Leverson has done a great deal. Clarke and Humphreys are going to take no fees. The Leversons have got the full-length portrait of Hoscar and Rothenstein's pastel of Bosie and also of him and a larger nude picture by Ricketts. Rothenstein is most sympathetic and goes about the minor clubs insulting everyone who does not happen to be clamouring for Hoscar's instant release.

I saw Bosie the night before his departure. He seemed to have lost his nerve. The scene that evening at the Leversons' was quite absurd. An awful New Woman in a divided skirt (introduced by Bosie) writing a pamphlet at Mrs Leverson's writing-table with the aid of several whiskey-and-sodas: her brother, a gaunt man with prominent cheek-bones from Toynbee Hall who kept reiterating that "these things must be approached through first principles and through first principles alone:" two other New Women who subsequently explained to Mr Leverson that they were there to keep a strict watch upon New Woman number one, who is not responsible for her actions: Mrs Leverson making flippant remarks about messenger-boys in a faint undertone to Bosie, who was ashen-pale and thought the pamphlet (which was the most awful drivel) admirable: and Mr Leverson explaining to me that he allowed his house to be used for these purposes not because he approved of "anything unnatural" but by reason of his admiration for Oscar's plays and personality. I myself exquisitely dressed and sympathising with no one.

Dear Miss Conover! I see a great deal of her and love her very much. I think you would like her. *Do,* for God's sake, come back again. I long to have a cosy day or two at *l'Auberge Clement.* Also I am sure it would be much better for you, as I suppose you must have been more or less talked about as you were in the garden of Gethsemane at the supreme moment. Why not shew yourself on English territory. I must say I think it is rather bad luck that you — a comparatively new friend of Oscar — should have been with him at that unpleasant crisis. Do come back. How is Charley Hickey? Do come back.

> Your loving
> *Max*

Max Beerbohm to Reggie Turner

> *Saturday* [Postmark December 1, 1900]
> *48 Upper Berkeley Street*

My dear Reg,

I got your letter this morning, and read it before I read my newspaper — before I knew that poor Oscar really was dead. I am, as you may imagine, very sorry indeed; and am thinking very much about Oscar, who was such an influence and an interest in my life. Will you please lay out a little money for me in flowers for his grave? I will repay you, having (for me) quite a large sum of money in the bank. I hope to be able to write something nice about Oscar in my next article for the *Saturday.* Of course I shall have to ask Hodge, first, whether he has any objection. I think he is the kind of man who will not place any obstacles. In this morning's *Chronicle* there is a rather nice obituary and editorial note.

I suppose really it was better that Oscar should die. If he had lived to be an old man he would have become unhappy. Those whom the gods, etc. And the gods *did* love Oscar, with all his faults.

Please give my sympathy to Bobbie, and tell him how much less happily Oscar might have died.

> In great haste
> Yours affectionately
> *Max*

Will has just come in and sends his love to you both.

Max Beerbohm to Reggie Turner

Wednesday [Postmark December 30, 1903]
48 Upper Berkeley Street

My dearest Reg,

By the way: please don't breathe to Bobbie or anyone about my engagement to Constance. I want it to be a *dead secret.* The position of fiancée to
Max Beerbohm is rather a ridiculous position, after poor Miss Conover's
experience, and I don't want Constance to be placed in it publicly. So
we mean to be married quite suddenly (so far as the public is concerned).
If anyone asks about Miss Conover and me, then you can say that we
have agreed to dissolve our engagement, and if anyone asks whether
Miss Collier has anything to do with it, of course say "no." But don't
volunteer the information.

I am just home from the Court Theatre, frozen through.

Your affectionate
Max

Max Beerbohm to Reggie Turner

48 Upper Berkeley Street
15 April 1910

My dearest Reg,

This time I have not merely the excuse of being a bad correspondent — a
person who *wants* to write and puts off the writing because he feels his
letter will be dull. I have the good excuse that I did not wish to write
without giving you a piece of news about myself which you of all people
ought to hear — a piece of news which, from day to day, I thought I
might be in a position to divulge, but which till now I have had to keep
secret.

And this news (as perhaps you are already guessing) is that I am
going to be married! Whether in a church or in a registry-office, is not
settled. Nor is it settled on *which* day of next week the ceremony will be.
Probably Wednesday. I am very happy in the prospect of it. Florence is
the one woman with whom I could be always and wholly happy, and the

one woman apart from whom I could not be happy. I count myself extraordinarily fortunate in having, after my various driftings and pleasantries and narrow escapes, had Florence vouchsafed to me. To me she represents the achievement of happiness, happiness for good and all. We shall be rather poor, financially, but able to live without discomfort or anxiety: neither of us has "expensive tastes." Very likely we shall live in Italy. In tomorrow's *Saturday* appears my valedictory article. I have some money "in hand"—some of it from (this is a dead secret. Don't breathe it to Carfax or to anyone) "Leicester Brown" on the strength of a retrospective exhibition of my caricatures, to be held next year. And other money is in prospect (Kegan Paul, per Frederick Whyte, wants the right of pre-emption of "Meanwhile"—which will amount to a tidy sum). Florence and I will be all right, in point of bread and butter. I think I shall be able to do a good deal of work, now that I am quit of dramatic criticism. I shall first devote myself to the Alexander play. My mother and Con and Aggie are all very much delighted, though I suppose they will miss me. Dearest Reg, dearest of all my friends, I am sure you will be glad at my happiness.

Your affectionate
Max

All this is to you alone. Except you and my family, no one is to know till after the event.

Max Beerbohm to Reggie Turner

Savile Club
Monday [Postmark April 18, 1910]

My dearest Reg,

What can I say to thank you? You will have had my wire: "overwhelmed." I very truly am. It is *much* too good of you. I don't feel I ought to take it; and at the same time I am afraid to send it back. Nobody but you would have thought of giving me a present like that, and not even from you should I ever have expected a present like that. I have not seen Florence yet today: she will be as staggered as I am (and as my people are!). I wired "date Monday." And on Monday the marriage will be. I do hope you will be there: I did not like to *ask* you to come, because I thought you might not want to be hauled out of your beloved Paris. But

without your presence the marriage would seem hardly valid. Meanwhile, don't breathe it to a soul: I am telling *no one* outside the family. I
shall just have an announcement in *The Times* or somewhere, a day or
two after. Florence and I equally hate anything in the nature of a to-do.
Also, don't mention that we *may* live in Italy. One thing is certain: we
shan't live in *London*, but somewhere that is uncomplicated and pleasant
and easy and un-fussy and lets one be oneself. And wherever it is, there
must be a great deal of my dearest Reg. Just what you say of Florence,
she has often said of you — almost in the same words. Of all my charming
and un-charming acquaintances I want to get rid: they are a charming
or un-charming nuisance, taking up one's time — clogs and drags. Henceforth I am going to be as exclusive as the Duchess of Buccleuch. . . .

Will Rothenstein to Max Beerbohm

Iles Farm, Far Oakridge, nr. Chalford Gloucestershire
May 4, 1913

My very dear Max — it is awful to think of the stream of letters that
flows from a man's pen during a lifetime, & of how few he writes of those
he wishes to write de coeur, from feelings of admiration & affection.
Here have I been meaning to write ever since the day I stepped into the
Leicester Galleries, walking in through mud & rain & out upon air, a
new joy running through my veins & a grateful acknowledgement to
the Divine Power upon my lips for giving the poor human heart such
easement & relief. How often have I told you over the space of years
how richly gifted you are; but how much more delightfully than most
men you return your gifts to the Gods, through us mortals happily, in
kind. Without hurting anyone you seem to observe everything, where
the rest of us would be assailed as spies & hirelings, for you possess the
divine art of understanding. Tout comprendre c'est tout pardonner; you
are a living witness to the truth of that epigram & we murmur it as we
rub the Elliman [liniment] upon our rainbow bruises.

  You have never done such delightful drawings or seen more profoundly. I keep on marvelling at the amazing subtlety of the Fry drawing
— the mouth & eye curling together, and the Bennett formula is quite
perfect. My acquisitive passion is not perhaps quite so unreasonable as
it was, but I did long to carry off the whole collection bodily, to be
enjoyed at my ease, with no one just looking at the drawing I want to

see & read from — let no one say, after a visit to your show, that this is an age of rush & hurry. I feel humbled when I realise how quite definite & irresistible is the appeal of really finished art. The days when one considered oneself an artist by the grace of God & the public a fool by the same grace are long gone by. Some faith I still have in my own work not because I am gifted but because I care so much for what I am doing that I believe that this caring will in one way or another show itself to some few here & there, but I do exult in the richer gifts of others always & always feel under a definite personal debt to people like yourself, dear Max. Do you realise it is just 20 years since we first met? You were already so much wiser & more finished a person than myself, but I was even then alive to the existence of all the qualities you have developed so triumphantly since. It is pleasant to think that after 20 years' intimate friendship I can look upon you with an even richer & riper affection & admiration. I was glad to see red marks (Lord, have mercy upon us!) on Albert's frame & mine. I suppose the doors are now closed & the Academy's opened. My love & homage to your dear wife. Ever your affectionate friend Will.

George Bernard Shaw/Lord Alfred Douglas

Thirty tears after the death of Oscar Wilde, the Irish playwright George Bernard Shaw and Lord Alfred (Bosie) Douglas, Wilde's famous lover, looked back on the tragedy in an animated correspondence. Frank Harris's publication of a Wilde biography, which included Shaw's recollections and took a critical view of Douglas's role in Wilde's downfall, prompted Douglas to argue his case with Shaw. At the same time, Douglas was planning the release of his autobiography, in which he intended to give his side of the story. When the book came out it largely convinced Shaw of Douglas's innocence, but a new edition of Harris's book kept their letters spicy. In the course of their literary and biographical debate, the correspondents shed a great deal of light on the story of Oscar Wilde.

George Bernard Shaw to Lord Alfred Douglas

[April 1931]
[The Grand Hotel, Venice]

Dear Lord Alfred Douglas,

It is a pity that Wilde still tempts men to write lives of him. If ever there was a writer whose prayer to posterity might well have been 'Read my works; and let my life alone' it was Oscar.

It is inevitable that you should appear in these biographies as a sort of *âme damnée* beside him, not in the least because you were a beautiful youth who seduced him into homosexuality (how enormously better it would have been for him if you had: you might have saved him from his wretched debaucheries with guttersnipes!) but because you were a lord and he was a snob. Judging from the suppressed part of *De Profundis* (Carlos Blacker lent me his copy) I should say that you did one another far more harm socially than you could possibly have wrought by any extremity of sensual affection. You had much better have been at the street-corner with me, preaching Socialism.

However, you need not worry. Your *Autobiography* and your book anticipating the publication of *De Profundis* in full (I have read both of them attentively) have made your position quite clear; and you need not fear that any biographer will be powerful enough to write you down.

Harris threatens *me* with a biography. I have deleted the allusion to you in the letter which he used as an appendix to his book on Wilde (in case he should republish it). They were not unjust as statements of what we felt at the time. Your hatred of your father may have been very natural, and richly deserved; but you were very young then; and if you had been older and unblinded by that passion, you would have made Oscar ignore the card left at the club as the act of a notorious lunatic lord, and clear out before the police could be moved to proceed. Consequently we were all rather down on you at the time. Harris's advice was sound. And I still think his memoir of Wilde, and incidentally his revelation of himself (which should have appealed to your sense of humour), much the best intimate portrait that is likely to be drawn. It may be unjust to you; but you have had a very full hearing in defence; and anyhow why should you, who have been so unjust to many good men, expect justice for yourself? Are you not wise enough yet to pray God to defend you from it? Does your conscience never reproach you for the reckless way in which you exploited Crosland's phobia for calumny in the *Academy?*

I have been forced to leave many hundreds of letters unanswered by the limits of time and working power; but I have no recollection of your being among the sufferers. They all have to forgive me; and so must you.

Your picture has not been sent on to me: I shall find it in London on my return presently. I wonder, is there any man alive except yourself who would take such a step as a defence against a diagnosis of narcisism! That flowerlike sort of beauty must have been a horrible handicap to you: it was probably Nature's reaction against the ultra-hickory type of your father.

Ross did not get his testimonial for nothing. Only a great deal of good nature on his part could have won over that distinguished and very normal list of names to give public support to a man who began with so very obvious a mark of the beast on him. A passage in one of my prefaces on the influence of artistically cultivated men on youths who have been starved in that respect, and their liability to be imposed on by mere style, was founded on a conversation I had with Ross one afternoon at Chartres in which he described the effect produced on him by Wilde, who, in the matter of style, always sailed with all his canvas stretched. Let Ross alone: the world has had enough of that squabble.

Roman Catholicism was not what you needed: you should have turned Quaker. I still hold that Creative Evolution is the only religion in all the associations and implications whereof a fully cultivated modern man can really persuade himself to believe. Unless, indeed, he can content himself with Marxism.

This time you cannot reproach me for leaving you unanswered. Faithfully

G. Bernard Shaw

Lord Alfred Douglas to George Bernard Shaw

35 Fourth Avenue, Hove
27 May 1931

Dear Mr Bernard Shaw,

I told my publisher, Martin Secker, that I had asked you to write a preface for the new edition of my *Autobiography*. [He thinks] if you will write a preface my book will get the circulation in America which so far has been denied it. As it is precisely in America that Harris's malignant lies about me and my 'ill treatment' of Oscar have been most widely circulated (largely owing to your collaboration with Harris) I appeal to your sense of justice to do this for me. The injury to me in America is *incalculable,* and unless I can get Americans to read my book while I am still alive (I have no fear that it will not be read all over the world after my death) I shall go down to my grave under a burden of false witness and calumny. I don't ask you to 'boost' my book. If you would say substantially what you said in your letter, or give me permission to quote the letter it would be a good action on your part. Yours most sincerely

Alfred Douglas

George Bernard Shaw to Lord Alfred Douglas

4 Whitehall Court, London
4 July 1931

Dear Lord Alfred Douglas,

Why has Heaven afflicted me with this infantile complex of yours which keeps you making 'a low-spirited noise', like Mrs MacStinger's baby, down the ages because somebody has been unkind to you — this eternal 'moreover the plaintiff here, the offender, did call me ass', and now this intolerable 'Oo dave Frank a bit of cake and oo won't dive me my piece'. You are worse than the tailor who got into London society on the strength of having once been kicked by Count D'Orsay, because he, poor chap, had nothing else to say for himself, whereas you started with all the advantages, social and personal. You are the literary Man from Shropshire, who died, a universally execrated nuisance, of his grievance. I tell you, you must never have a grievance. Never excuse yourself, never deny, never explain, never moan; and seize every opportunity to apologize (the most effective and popular of public attitudes) and to embrace every accusation and expose yourself to every reproach until your enemies are tempted to shift all the sympathy to your side by slapping your always-turned-other-cheek as hard as they can while you are good-humouredly knocking them out with the disengaged side.

I have revised your two galley slips; and on your life, do not restore a word I have struck out or alter a word I have put in. If you cannot produce an impression that I am on your side, don't advertise me as being against you.

As to that notice of *Getting Married*, I honestly believed that you had not written it; and when, to my genuine surprise, you said you had, I said:

> *If boozy be bosie, as some folks miscall it*
> *Then Bosie is boozy, whatever befall it.*

You must have been as drunk as a boiled owl on that occasion; and if you were to tell the whole story, couplet and all, exactly as it occurred it would amuse your readers much more than your allusion to it as it stands. But I shall never make a good controversialist of you. You will always raise that wail———!

By the way, that retraction [the *New Preface*] that you induced Harris to perpetrate was judged from its style as being the work of Alfred Douglas, the signature alone being Frank's. And if you want to convince your readers that Frank is unscrupulous, you could do it much more effectively by owning up to the dictation than by implying that the retraction has the smallest value to you. In great haste — don't be so ungrateful as to reply and argue.

G. Bernard Shaw

Lord Alfred Douglas to George Bernard Shaw

35 Fourth Avenue, Hove
6 July 1931

Dear Mr Bernard Shaw,

Thanks for the proof, which I will leave exactly as you have corrected it. No, I was not 'drunk' when I wrote the notice of *Getting Married* in the *Academy.* (By the way, you don't specify whether you assume that I was 'drunk' when I wrote the notice or when I saw the play or both.) Why should you suggest that I was drunk then or at any other time? I will not say that I have never been drunk in my life (donkeys' years ago) but I have certainly never been drunk when I was sitting in the stalls of a theatre, nor when I was writing an article in my editorial office. I hated your play. It bored and exasperated me, and I expressed exactly what I thought about it at the time. In the notice you will perhaps remember it is explained that I only lasted through two acts. Talk about narcissism! You are such a mental Narcissus that you cannot believe that anyone who is not drunk can possibly fail to fall down and worship you. You have the advantage of me in this sort of 'back-answering' because I am politer and more tender-hearted than you and cannot bring myself to be rude or to say wounding things except when I am really angry (which never happens nowadays).

I never know whether what you say is meant to be taken seriously (you probably don't know yourself), but in case you really mean what you say about Harris and the preface, I will give you my word of honour that I did not write or dictate a solitary word of it (leaving out my letter to Harris of course).

I am sure you are right about my infantile complex which makes 'a low-spirited noise'. You will find the same phenomenon in most of the great poets, not excluding Shakespeare (in the sonnets). All real poets have an infantile complex. Also, there is the best authority for believing that the possession of an infantile complex is the only way to get into the Kingdom of Heaven. Yours very sincerely

Alfred Douglas

George Bernard Shaw to Lord Alfred Douglas

Ayot St Lawrence
19 July 1938

Dearest Childe,

You will drive me crazy.

Don't blather like all the rest of them about Harris's malicious lies. They are imaginary. Put your finger on one of them; and I shall know what grievance you have left.

I have all your notes made when you went through the text. They were very useful. I did all you required and more. I must now have something definite to bully you about.

I never read Harris's preface. I have read the sulky and hostile letter with which he introduced the two AWFUL letters from you which appear in the Covici edition.

Do you want that to hold the field?

Why did you not agree to an English edition when you and he apparently had it out at Nice?

I am completely done up — too much work this morning — and can no more.

G. B. S.

Lord Alfred Douglas to George Bernard Shaw

1 St Ann's Court, Hove
27 July 1939

My dear St Christopher,

I saw in the papers that yesterday was your birthday, so many happy returns, and a candle to St Anthony will be lit today for you. I saw a picture of you looking extraordinarily well and vigorous. I hope you really are well.

I have been going through perfect hell, because I have been writing this book for Duckworth about Wilde. . . . I very nearly wrote to Duckworth returning his advance and saying I couldn't possibly do it. However now I have written twenty-two thousand words (all written in a week). The book is only to be thirty thousand and I am going tomorrow to stay with A. J. A. Symons at Brick House, Finchingfield, Essex, till Monday. He can help me with dates and facts and I hope to finish the book there. I came to the conclusion that in order to do the book in an original way (and to prevent it from being just a 'guidebook') I *must* deal with the whole question of homosexuality. So I start off with the first three chapters all on the subject. I would awfully like you to read what I have written, and very nearly posted off the carbon typescript copy of what I have written (eight chapters) to you last night. But then it occurred to me that you would curse me and think me an awful bore if I did! I know what it is to have unsolicited manuscripts fired at me. So I refrained. I saw Symons in London yesterday (you know he is doing a full-length biography of Wilde) and he read what I had written. He told me he thought it quite excellent and that it "filled him with jealousy". This was an enormous relief (if he really meant it and was not just trying to 'buck me up'), as I really hadn't an idea whether what I had written was any good at all. I still feel nervous about it. For one thing I don't know whether Duckworth and the public will stand for my chapters about homosexuality. Of course I do not defend it, but my argument is that it is a moral offence (a sin) and not a crime and that therefore the law ought not to take any cognizance of it (as is the case with the Code Napoléon in France). I have quoted what you say in your Harris preface about Wilde's attitude to it which is admirable and completely true. Also said some nice things about you. . . . Your ever devoted

Childe Alfred

P.S. I spent the week-end before last at a place called Wadhurst Park (a place that used to belong to the Murrietas) with Grant Maclean and his wife (very rich). They had a Hollywood film magnate to meet me (he controls Paramount) and he wants me to do a film scenario about Wilde. I don't know whether anything will come of it, but he seems very keen and has written to me twice since I met him. If it came off I would make a lot of money.

George Bernard Shaw to
Lord Alfred Douglas

4 Whitehall Court, London
16 August 1939

Dear Childe,

To come down to tin tacks.

You must rearrange that idiotic book as follows. You must begin with Wilde's birth and follow his history to his grave as matter-of-factly as the *Dictionary of National Biography*. Then, when the reader is in full possession of all that Wilde was and exactly what happened to him, you can moralize about him to your heart's content; for not until then will your alarums and excursions be intelligible.

You must explain why the new biography is needed in spite of the admirable work by Harris, revised by yourself and, considering its date, a model of what a biography should be (just as your manuscript is a model of what it shouldn't be).

You must explain that Harris and Sherard were hampered by the fact that in their time it was generally believed that homosexuality involved the most horrible depravity of character, and was unnatural and unmentionable. Since then the work done in England by Havelock Ellis and Edward Carpenter and abroad by Freud and the psychoanalysts has completely changed all that. Not only have sexual subjects become mentionable and discussable (compare Thackeray's novels with D. H. Lawrence's) but it is now known that a reversal of the sex instinct occurs naturally, and that the victim of it is greatly to be pitied and may be a person of the noblest character. Wilde's life must therefore be taken out of the old atmosphere in which Harris and Sherard wrote, and retold with a healthy objectivity which was impossible before the war.

In doing this you must clear your mind of Sodom and Gomorrah and the Catholic categories of sin-as-distinguished-from-crime and all the rest of it. You will have to explain that Wilde was prosecuted not for sodomy but for offences under the Criminal Law Amendment Act for the protection of boys, as to which he was guilty. It is not necessary to pester the reader with assurances that you are bound as a Catholic to proclaim Pickwickian opinions and values that are now obsolete, irrelevant and ridiculous.

You must cut out the sentimental rubbish about Mrs Wilde, which is just like Sherard. She was not a pretty woman, and never can have been; but she was not ugly: her appearance simply calls for no comment. As for its being her duty to stick to Wilde, did your mother think it *your* duty to stick to Wilde? You forget that Constance had two sons to bring up, much younger than the one son your mother felt responsible for. To combine your pious condemnation of Mrs Wilde with your disclosure of Holland's parentage is unspeakable.

You are bound not only to narrate the trial with documentary calm, but to tell the important and indispensable truth that Wilde, like Edmund Kean, [Thomas] Robson and Dickens, died of an attempt to live on alcohol for the sake of the extraordinary power it gave to him as an actor.

You must make up your mind as to whether *De Profundis* is a forgery or not. If it is, you have no grounds for complaining that Wilde attacked you; and all that stuff must come out. If you accept it as genuine, which it obviously is, you have no ground for describing it as a fake. As nobody now remembers anything about Ross, your weakness for vulgar abuse really does him a resurrectional service.

Your spluttering letter needs no reply. My sketch of what any intelligent and not unfriendly publisher's reader would report was meant to open your eyes to the effect your book must make. Years have passed and oblivion has thickened since your autobiography was published. Symons was right in concluding that what you wanted was not criticism but adulation; and he laid it on accordingly. He ought to be ashamed of himself. Now go and rearrange your book exactly as I tell you, and be damned to you. I do not enjoy having my time wasted.

G. B. S.

P.S. As you have rashly sent the book to Duckworth without waiting for my instructions you had better send him my 'reader's report' also and ask him whether he agrees. You will thus get an independent opinion. Of course he will agree with every syllable of it.

You are an exceedingly troublesome Childe.

Lord Alfred Douglas to
George Bernard Shaw

1 St Ann's Court, Hove
18 August 1939

My dear St Christopher,

Why don't you write a life of Wilde yourself in thirty thousand words and see how you make out on it? Whatever you made of it, it could not be a greater failure or have a more devastating 'press' than your edition of Harris's imbecile work (redeemed of course by your brilliant preface) which you (absolutely alone as *Bernardus contra mundum*) persist in considering the best life of Wilde. Seriously why do you want to turn me into a sort of little Bernard Shaw? Nothing could be more absurd and more fatal than for me to write a life of Wilde on your lines, and from your point of view which is almost the exact opposite of mine. I write as a devout Catholic (although I have the advantage of having known all about the homosexual question long before your Havelock Ellises and Freuds turned their attention to it) and, as regards my friendship with Oscar, a sentimentalist. I am not going to change my views just to please you. It would take a twenty-page letter to answer all the absurdities of your 'reader's report' (which has gone into the waste-paper basket) or your letter received this morning. You are utterly unscrupulous in argument. You just say anything that comes into your head. In your utter inability to appreciate any point of view but your own you remind me forcibly of my father! e.g., on a quite minor point, you say that Mrs Wilde was not pretty. Well, which of the two, you or I, is more likely to be a judge of that point? I who spent weeks at a time in her house, played tennis with her, danced with her and saw her continually on and off for more than four years, or you who hardly knew her and cannot have seen her more than a few times, generally in the distance? However, I utterly decline to be lured into a slinging match with you. I don't suppose I should have a chance, because I hate hurting anyone's feelings and you thoroughly enjoy it. I remain quite devoted to you, and if you like me at all you must make up your mind, like a schoolboy, to 'know all about me and still go on liking me'. You can't have me on any other terms.

I sent in my book to Duckworth's three days ago and so far have only a formal acknowledgment. I don't intend to alter it at all except on minor points (e.g., I will, if you like, mention that you deny disliking

Wilde and that Lady Wilde, from the Irish point of view, was a *grande
dame*) and if Duckworth's don't like it, *tant pis*. I know that Secker would
be delighted to publish it if they don't want it. Your devoted

Childe

P.S. It is characteristically unfair of you to say that you 'don't like having
your time wasted'. I asked you if you would like to see my book and you
replied by return of post saying you would. I then, at your request, sent
it to you. So why am I *wasting your time?* What about *my* time, to say
nothing about my nerves, and my self-esteem, which (although I have
some of the virtue of humility, to which you are a complete stranger) is
hurt by your vicious kicks?

George Bernard Shaw to Lord Alfred Douglas

4 Whitehall Court, London
15 February 1940

Dear Childe,

There may be a job for you in this. Why not persuade your publisher, or
some publisher, to bring out a volume entitled *The Famous Comedies of
Oscar Wilde*, edited by you, with a long preface by you. I believe it would
sell; and anyhow the publisher would not lose by it and would gain
prestige.

It is so long since I have seen or read a play of Wilde's that I shall
not commit myself until I have refreshed my memory. Only the other
day a manager who was looking out for revivals (tempted by the success
of *The Importance*) told me that he had looked up *A Woman of No Importance* and found it utterly impossible and obsolete. My own recollection of
them from their first production is that they were of a godlike brilliancy
compared to the fashionable pieces of that day: they were not only witty
but literature with a large 'L'. If Wilde had not been up against Ibsen,
who reduced even Shakespeare to flapdoodle, they would have been
epoch making. I must read them again: Oscar sent me copies; and I must
have them somewhere.

Oscar's superiority to Sheridan and Congreve lies in the fact that
he was an original moralist, whereas, though Sheridan could create char-

acters like Sir Peter Teazle, Joseph Surface, Bob Acres, Sir Anthony Absolute, Mrs Candour, Mrs Malaprop, etc., etc., Oscar couldn't or at any rate didn't, Sheridan's morality being of the most barren conventionality, with the result that his virtuous heroine, Lady Teazle, is now a dirty little cad, and his hero, Charles Surface, a vaurien feebly redeemed by the touch of feeling that made him refuse to sell his uncle's portrait. Sheridan, it is true, named him Surface, but that was meant not for him but for Joseph.

As to Congreve, he had literary and dramatic talent; but how are you to class a playwright whose notion of humour was to ridicule cuckolds and lecherous old women, and to make a laughing matter of syphilis? Wilde was heavens high above that. There is plenty of writing-up for you to do here.

Goldsmith, who in *The Deserted Village* and *The Vicar of Wakefield* anticipated Karl Marx, was by far the biggest of the Irish bunch, the only one who cuts a noble figure. In *The Goodnatured Man,* the failure of which crushed him as a playwright, he made the first move in the direction of Ibsen and Wilde by challenging the moral valuations of the bourgeoisie, but unfortunately accepted the convention that a play must have a plot, and killed his play with it.

When next you explode on the subject of the Irish plantations, remember that *all* the Irish are planted. The extreme type, which used to be caricatured in the English papers with long upper lip, is as obviously a Spanish muleteer as the Duke of Wellington was a gentleman of the garrison. Both are planted on Irish soil; and the climate makes both of them as completely Irish as I am, though I have lived for sixty-three years in England and only twenty in Ireland. The odd thing is that two years spent in Ireland will change an Englishman into a different person; but a century will not rub the Irish mark off an Irishman. Therefore be careful not to be led away into Hitleresque nonsense about race.

However, that is not to the present point, which is to emulate Heming and Condell by producing a first folio Wilde. I presume you have all the quartos.

G. Bernard Shaw

Henry James

The boundless devotion of American novelist Henry James to his friends shines through in his letters, which are filled with an at times lighthearted and at times intense affection. Among his many correspondents were the English poet Arthur C. Benson, a Norwegian-American sculptor named Hendrik Andersen and the English novelist Hugh Walpole. James's letters encouraged these men in their work, amused them with quick wit and lavished upon them a tenderness moving in its candor and simplicity.

Henry James to A. C. Benson

34 De Vere Gardens, W.
June 10th, [1895]

My Dear Arthur B.,

I like your letters much, but I like your dinner almost as much. You give, in such a case, with your so liberal welcome, in your so romantic home, much more than you can receive. What is the use moreover of "being friends" except in the belief that giving and taking are all one, that exact accounts are a loathsome pedantry and that indistinguishable obligations are the law of the affair? My too abbreviated dash at you was pure satisfaction and excellent poetry. I was all the better the next morning — you wholly routed the gout-fiend. I'm glad I've *seen* you — what I call seeing: I hadn't done so till then. Well, it's very fine — but I *should*, I repeat, have liked to show you. Don't be afraid — I *will! Then* you'll not write in a day or two in a spirit of sublimity; but perhaps in "natural irritation". *Basta.* Your rhetorical question opens up deeps. *Cette jeunesse!* — over what gulfs it swallow-plunges. Just for to-day let me say that I think I find myself at a point where the difference between sadness and cheer, interest and detachment, lies behind in the road like a shuffled coil. It's all one, it's all life, it's all fate, it's all — everything! And yet after all there is perhaps something more grossly primitive, and less "painfully acquired" in the sentiment with which I ask you to consider your hand as grasped by

Yours evermore,
Henry James

Henry James to A. C. Benson

Osborne Hotel,
Torquay, August 5th, 1895

Dear Arthur Benson,

I have read them bang off and you must put up with a little politeness. All your verses touch me no less than their predecessors. They seem to me to have truth and charm and distinction and a particular something which I can perhaps best call loveability. I am hideously, corrosively critical and am always wanting things to be what they are not — i.e., (or e.g.,) when they have the lyric egotism and confidentiality I want them to be hard and detached and impersonal — stony-hearted triumphs of objective form. When they are real masterpieces of *that* (which so often happens!) I want them to be quivering and throbbing and human, lyrical cries and emotional realities. So I have no business to speak of anything. None the less there are things I *would* speak of if you were here — so much more easily would it be to talk them, in many tones, than it is to write them in none. Why aren't you here to take a good Devonshire walk with me? I hang over a green garden and a blue sea from a big balcony where I smoke solitary cigarettes. There would be room on the balcony even for your inches or cigarettes, even for Apollo's lips. I fled down hither immediately after that almost violently supererogatory social occasion at H. Sturgis's — where it was a wonder that anything so simple could be so almost painfully complicated. I have had a much-needed bath of silence and solitude — of bland air and unmassacred work. Unfortunately I have, from the 15th, to spend ten days in town. *Is* there a chance of seeing you there for an hour? No — you are starting for the Jungfrau or some other pure eminence. I envy you the scented pines of Switzerland. I shall probably return *here* for September, etc. To-morrow I shall read the Professor again. He's a little too ghostly a professor — but he's massive compared with *her.* She is of a pearly paleness. But together they make a very interesting eloquent A. C. B. Hang it who *should* turn on his bed of pain if not the restless poet? Rise, however, *surge tandem*, from that couch of green curtains and snowy sheets. I wish the Jungfrau were in S. Devon. Yes, indeed, what a block burden of a postman's pack you must carry! Let me not add to it by the weight of a single stamp — and only accommodate your shoulders in silence to the friendliest pressure of the very illegible hand of

Yours always,
Henry James

Henry James to A. C. Benson

Osborne Hotel,
Torquay, September 24th, 1895

My Dear Arthur,

The other day — 5 or 6 ago — Edmund Gosse, in town, where I had occasion to spend a few hours, told me what it was that had happened to you on the glacier. Ever since then I have wanted just to tell you that now at last I *know* it; but the desire to spare you a letter has continually carried the day. Now it is — that desire — only superficially vanquished: the letter that I still spare you is the smallest rejoinder to this. I *particularly* request of you to make none: *entendez-vous bien?* All the more that absolutely the only thing I want to remark to you is that I *do*, and with a still more relentless grip, hold you faster than ever. Gosse's story didn't do for me at all: I pay the penalty of my magnificent imagination. Will it in future, or ever, be anything of a motive to you to happen to think of that? But you will answer this question only *viva voce*. And you will utterly forget, please, in the meanwhile, yours constantly but contingently,

Henry James

Henry James to A. C. Benson

34 De Vere Gardens, W.
Thursday [January 16, 1896]

My dear Arthur,

I am divided between 2 sensations — panting for to-morrow p.m. and blushing for all the hours of all the past days. I ought to have acknowledged your beautiful letter (after your last being here,) about — about everything. But I have been so taken up with living in the future and in the idea of answering you with impassioned lips. This however is (besides saying, so feebly, *that*, to be able to face you at all) to say, more forcibly, that you are not to worry in the faintest degree about the question of my conveyance to-morrow, meeting me, causing me to be met, or getting me over at all. I can with utter ease procure myself to be transported. I shall *come* — "that is all you know — and all you need to know." *Voilà.* I shall in the meantime weave spells over your house and its inmates.

Yours almost uncontrollably,
Henry James

Henry James to A. C. Benson

34 De Vere Gardens, W.
1st October, 1897

My dear Arthur,

I return you with this — or rather separately — the charming Diary; which you will think perhaps I have kept too many days. But I have only been waiting, amid much occupation, for the right hour to give it the right sentiment. That is what — this last — I *have* finally given it. It has been, for me, a very friendly, happy, delightful contact; almost a tangible substitute for never, never seeing you. Give me more in time; give me a great deal more, give me as much as you can. I like it enough for that. With my voracity for personal introspections, I find in your existence a great deal to feed upon. The fault of the record is of course that it's not really private enough; but that is the fault of all confidences. At any rate, I welcome it as a document, a series of data, on the life of a young Englishman of great endowments, character and position at the end of the 19th century. There is nothing I like better than that others should live *for* me, as it were, — in case, of course, I can catch them *at* it. Therefore, in short, continue to live, and *do* continue to let me catch you. I will do anything — everything — munificently — to keep you going to this end. Bear that in mind, and put in all you can. I have read, of course, every word — and I think have had real inspirations in the way of making you out. There is absolutely not a word I have lost. Your episode at Hawarden is a prodigy of *reportage:* how grand of you to be able to feel you have such a loaf upon the shelf in case the mothers, and even the sons, ever become too many for you! I would read the newspapers then.

I am much touched by your delightful friendliness about my little old house. Your taste in these things would not, I think, be afflicted by my little undertaking. I don't think it could be so exactly the right thing for me if it were not rather decent. But I won't willingly pander in this manner to any such sympathy (as you may benignantly drop upon me) as will help you in the least not to come down and see it for yourself the very first, or at most the very second or very third, time I try to make you. The merit of it is that it's such a place as I may, when pressed by the pinch of need, retire to with a certain shrunken decency and wither away in — in a fairly cleanly and pleasantly melancholy manner — toward the tomb. It is really good enough to be a kind of little becoming, high-door'd, brass-knockered *façade* to one's life. This gives me an advantage, for I feel — after the Journal — as if I had got a little behind *your* knocker. Why is the great interest of Mr Gladstone somehow so awfully uninteresting? *Vale.*

Yours always,
Henry James

Henry James to Hendrik C. Andersen

105 Pall Mall S.W.
February 9th 1902

My dear, dear dearest Hendrik.

Your news [of your brother's death] fills me with horror and pity, and how can I express the tenderness with which it makes me think of you and the aching wish to be near you and put my arms around you? My heart fairly bleeds and breaks at the vision of you *alone*, in your wicked and indifferent old far-off Rome, with the haunting, blighting, unbearable sorrow.

The sense that I can't *help* you, see you, talk to you, touch you, hold you close and long, or do anything to make you rest on me, and feel my participation — this torments me, dearest boy, makes me ache for you, and for myself; makes me gnash my teeth and groan at the bitterness of things. I can only take refuge in hoping you are *not* utterly alone, that some human tenderness of *some* sort, some kindly voice and hand *are* near you that may make a little the difference.

What a dismal winter you must have had, with this staggering blow at the climax! I don't of course know *what* fragment of friendship there may be to draw near to you, and in my uncertainty my image of you is of the darkest, and my pity, as I say, feels so helpless. I wish I could go to Rome and put my hands on you (oh, how lovingly I should lay them!)

but that, alas, is odiously impossible. (Not, moreover, that apart from *you*, I should so much as like to be there now.)

I find myself thrown back on anxiously and doubtless vainly, wondering if there may not, after a while, [be] some possibility of your coming to England, of the current of your trouble inevitably carrying you here — so that I might take consoling, soothing, infinitely close and tender and affectionately-healing *possession* of you. This is the one thought that relieves me about you a little — and I wish you might fix your eyes on it for the idea, just of the possibility.

I am in town for a few weeks but I return to Rye April 1st, and sooner or later to *have* you there and do for you, to put my arm round you and *make* you lean on me as on a brother and a lover, and keep you on and on, slowly comforted or at least relieved of the first bitterness of pain — this I try to imagine as thinkable, attainable, not wholly out of the question. There I am, at any rate, and there is my house and my garden and my table and my studio — such as it is! — and your room, and your welcome, and your place everywhere — and I press them upon you, oh so earnestly, dearest boy, if isolation and grief and the worries you are overdone with become intolerable to you. There they are, I say — to fall upon, to rest upon, to find whatever possible shade of oblivion in.

I will *nurse* you through your dark passage. I wish I could do something *more* — something straighter and nearer and more immediate but such as it is please let it sink into you. Let all my tenderness, dearest boy, do *that*. This is all now. I wired you three words an hour ago. I can't *think* of your sister-in-law — I brush her vision away and your history with your father, as I've feared it, has haunted me all winter. I embrace you with almost a passion of pity.

Henry James

Henry James to Hugh Walpole

[April 15, 1911]

I congratulate you ever so gladly on Mr. Perrin — I think the book represents a very marked advance on its predecessors. I am an atrocious reader, as you know — with a mania for appreciation, or in other words for criticism, since the latter is the one sole gate to the former. To appreciate is to appropriate, and it is only by criticism that I can make a thing in which I find myself interested at all *my own*. But nobody that I have encountered for a long time seems to have any use for any such process — or, much rather, does almost every one (and exactly the more they "read") resent the application of it. All of which is more or less irrelevant, however, for my telling you that I really and very charmedly made your book very *much* my own. It has life and beauty and reality, and is more closely *done* than the others, with its immense advantage, clearly, of resting on the known and felt thing: in other words on depths, as it were, of experience. If I weren't afraid of seeming to you to avail myself foully of your supine state to batter and bruise you at my ease (as that appears to have been for you, alas, the main result of my previous perusal of your works) I should venture, just on tiptoe — holding my breath, to say that — well, I should *like* to make, seated by your pallet and with your wrist in my good grasp and my faithful fingers — or thumb — on your young pulse, one or two affectionately discriminative little remarks. One of these is to the effect that, still, I don't quite recognise here the *centre of your subject,* that absolutely and indispensably fixed and constituted point from which one's ground must be surveyed and one's material wrought. If you say it's (that centre) in Mr. P's exasperated consciousness I can only reply that if it *might* be it yet isn't treated as such. And, further, that I don't quite understand why, positing the situation as also a part of the experience of Mr. Traill, you yet take such pains to demonstrate that Mr. Traill was, as a vessel of experience, absolutely *nil* — recognizing, feeling, knowing, understanding, appreciating, that is, absolutely nothing that happened to him. Experience — reported — is interesting, is *recorded* to us, according to some vessel (the capacity and quality of such,) that contains it, and I don't make out Mr. Traill's capacity at all. And I note this — *shall* you feel, hideously? — because the subject, your subject, *with* an operative, a felt centre, would have still more harmoniously and effectively expressed itself. Admirable, clearly, the subject that you had before you; and which, when all is said, dearest, dearest Hugh, has moved you to write a book that will give a great push to your situation.

Henry James to Hugh Walpole

[October 1913]

Beautiful must be your Cornish land and your Cornish sea, idyllic your Cornish setting, this flattering, this wonderful summer . . .

It will be the lowest kind of "jinks" — so halting is my pace; yet we shall somehow make it serve. Don't say to me, by the way, apropos of jinks — the "high" kind that you speak of having so wallowed in previous to leaving town — that I ever challenge you as to *why* you wallow, or splash or plunge, or dizzily and sublimely soar (into the jinks element,) or whatever you may call it: as if I ever remarked on anything but the absolute inevitability of it for you at your age and with your natural curiosities, as it were, and passions. It's good healthy exercise, when it comes but in bouts and brief convulsions, and it's always a kind of thing that it's good, and considerably final, to *have* done. We must know, as much as possible, in our beautiful art, yours and mine, what we are talking about — and the only way to know is to have lived and loved and cursed and floundered and enjoyed and suffered. — I think I don't regret a single "excess" of my responsive youth — I only regret, in my chilled age, certain occasions and possibilities I *didn't* embrace. Bad doctrine to impart to a young idiot or a duffer; but in place for a young friend (pressed to my heart,) with a fund of nobler passion, the preserving, the defying, the dedicating, of which always has the last word: the young friend who can dip and shake off and go his straight way again when it's time. But we'll talk of all this — it's abominably late. Who is D. H. Lawrence, who, you think, would interest me? Send him and his book along — by which I simply mean Inoculate me, at your convenience (don't address me the volume:) so far as I can *be* inoculated. I always *try* to let anything of the kind "take."

Henry James to Hugh Walpole

[September 11, 1914]

Dearest, dearest Hugh,

I am deeply moved by your news, and only a bit heartbroken at the thought you will have left London, I gather, by the time this gets there — though I write it but an hour after receipt of your note; so that the best I can do is to send it to the Garrick to be "forwarded." You will probably be so much forwarder than my poor pursuing missive always, that I feel the dark void shuttng me out from you for a long time to come — save as I shall see your far-off light play so bravely over the public page. Your adventure is of the last magnificence of pluck, the finest strain of resolution, and I bless and cheer and honour it for all I am worth. It will be of the intensest interest and of every sort of profit and glory to you — which doesn't prevent however my as intensely yearning over you, my thinking of you with all the ache of privation. But of such yearnings and such aches, such privations and such prides, is all our present consciousness made up; and I wait for you again with a confidence and courage which I try to make not too basely unworthy of your own. Feel yourself at any rate, dearest boy, wrapped round in all the affection and imagination of your devotedest old

Henry James.

George Moore

A relatively minor philosopher, George Moore nonetheless occupied a prominent position in the intellectual and literary circles of his day. He came from an elite English family and attended Cambridge University, where as a member of the secret society known as the Apostles he mixed with leading men of letters. Among its various interests and activities, the society nurtured a fascination with homosexuality, and many of its members were overtly gay or at least enjoyed "posing as sodomites." Among these were Roger Fry, Lowes Dickinson and Bertrand Russell; later members would include E. M. Forster, Lytton Strachey, John Maynard Keynes, Ludwig Wittgenstein and Rupert Brooke. Moore also had a startling near encounter with Algernon Swinburne, which he described in a letter to Edmund Gosse, who wrote a biography of the poet. Moore started the letter by recounting an incident involving the French poet Stéphane Mallarmé.

George Moore to Edmund Gosse

121 Ebury Street, S. W.
2nd December, 1912.

My Dear Gosse — You say you have been waiting a whole week for the Mallarmé-Swinburne note, and that you want it instantly. Well, my dear friend, you can have it instantly, but I am afraid you will be disappointed. Anecdotes of the kind are well enough in conversation, but when we take up the pen to transcribe them, they seem slightly too slight for transcription. But since you must have it, here goes!

One night at Mallarmé's — he received on Tuesday night, but in the 'seventies he was not a celebrity and very few came to his receptions; I think we generally spent Tuesday night together, *tête-à-tête*. One night the conversation turned on Swinburne, and he showed me a long correspondence, written on sheets of blue foolscap paper, in a shaky handwriting, about the poem which Swinburne was asked to contribute, and which he did contribute to *La Republique des Lettres*, "Une Nocturne," a sestina written in French. Swinburne had asked Mallarmé to alter anything that seemed to him to need alteration, and Mallarmé consequently altered the second line of the poem, and the alteration drew from Swinburne at least three voluminous epistles. Other alterations were made by Swinburne at Mallarmé's suggestion; these I do not remember, but Mallarmé's I remember quite well. Swinburne wrote:

> *La nuit écoute et se penche sur l'onde*
> *Pour recueillir rien qu'un souffle d'amour.*

"Pour recueillir rien" did not sound agreeable to Mallarmé's French ear, and his alteration of the line shows exquisite taste. He altered the line to *"pour y cueillir rien,"* etc. Swinburne discussed the alteration with Mallarmé, maintaining that his reason for using *recueillir* was that it seemed to him that *cueillir* would be more properly applied to apples and pears than to a breath of love. Whether the verse appeared in *La Republique des Lettres* as corrected by Mallarmé or in its original form I do not know, but in the volume you will find Mallarmé's correction.

There was another line later on, in the last stanza but one I think, of which we could make nothing. The first word seemed to us like *l'orme*, and Mallarmé asked me if there was any word in English like *l'orme*. He could think of nothing in French except the elm, and the elm of course did not come into the sentence. In a subsequent letter Swinburne sent half a dozen versions for Mallarmé to select from. I think the line now reads:

> *"Le sang du beau pied blessé de l'amour."*

One phrase in the letters I remember. He had heard that some French writer had said, speaking of his (Swinburne's) French verses, that they were *les efforts géants d'un barbare*. This phrase inspired many grand rolling sentences. He was unwilling as unable to accept the praise implied by the word *géant*, for his verses in French were those of a barbarian, etc. Though he knew of course that the word was used in the Greek sense, still it was not a foreigner's verses that he wished to send, etc. I wish I could remember the torrent of words that he poured forth on this subject. You must get the letters. Of course *ses vers sont des vers d'un barbare.* What else could they be? And if I may be allowed to carry the Frenchman's criticism a little further I will say that they seem to me to be French verses written by a man who could not speak French. I cannot help thinking that his French verses wear the same sort of deadly pallor that the Latin of a mediaeval poet would wear if a great poet had written in the Middle Ages.

I never saw Swinburne but once, and I cannot remember whether it was before or after the publication of the sestina. We were all carried away on the hurricane winds of Swinburne's verses in the 'seventies, and I think it was the ambition of everybody who wrote verses to see the poet. Rossetti, William Michael it must have been, told me that all I had to do was to go and present myself and that I should find Swinburne very agreeable and pleased to see me. It was William Michael who gave me the address. As well as I can recollect he said Bedford Row. You tell me that he lived in Great James Street, which is near Bedford Row; that may be so, no doubt is so. I remember that one entered the house by an open doorway, as in the Temple, and that I went upstairs, and on the first floor began to wonder on which Swinburne lived; thinking to see a clerk engaged in copying entries into a ledger I opened a door and found myself in a large room in which there was no furniture except a truckle bed. Outside the sheets lay a naked man, a strange, impish little body it was, and about the head, too large for the body, was a great growth of red hair. The fright that this naked man caused me is as vivid in me to-day as if it had only occurred yesterday, possibly more vivid. I had gone to see Swinburne, expecting to find a man seated in an arm-chair reading a book, one who would probably ask me if I smoked cigarettes or cigars, and who would talk to me about Shelley. I had no idea what Swinburne's appearance was like, but there was no doubt in my mind that the naked man was Swinburne. How I knew it to be Swinburne I cannot tell. I felt that there could be nobody but Swinburne who would look like that, and he looked to me like a dreadful caricature of myself. The likeness was remarkable, at first sight; if you looked twice I am sure it disappeared. We were both very thin, our hair was the same colour, flaming red; Swinburne had a very high forehead and I had a very high forehead, and we both had long noses, and though I have a little more chin than Swinburne, mine is not a prominent chin. It seemed to me that at the end of a ball, coming downstairs at four o'clock in the morning, I had often looked like the man on the bed, and the idea of sitting next to that naked man, so very like myself, and explaining to him that I had come from William Michael Rossetti frightened me nearly out of my wits. I just managed to babble out, "Does Mr. Jones live here?" The red head shook on a long thin neck like a tulip, and I heard, "Will you ask downstairs?" I fled and jumped into a hansom, and never heard of Swinburne again until he wrote to Philip Bourke Marston a letter about *A Mummer's Wife* which Philip Bourke Marston had sent him. Of that letter I remember a phrase: "It was not with a chamber pot for buckler and a spit for a spear that I charged the Philistines." He afterwards wrote to me explaining away this letter which did not annoy me in the least. The absurd epithets that he piled up in his prose could not annoy anybody; they merely amused me. He wrote the worst prose ever written by a great poet.

Now, my dear Gosse, I have sent you the note which you asked for. It seems to me to be without any interest, but that is not my affair, it is yours. It may, however, induce you to go to Paris and try to persuade Mallarmé's daughter to give you copies of Swinburne's letters to her father; or if you like I will go there as a missionary on your behalf. — Very sincerely yours,

George Moore.

Edmund Gosse/André Gide

During a friendship that spanned twenty-four years, starting in 1904 and ending at Gosse's death in 1928, the writers Edmund Gosse and André Gide wrote approximately one hundred letters. Like so many relationships between writers, theirs was founded on mutual admiration of each other's work. It survived the First World War, when the dangers of travel between France and England limited contact between the two friends and made even a postal relationship difficult. After the war, Gide published his most challenging works — *Corydon* (written before the war), *Si le grain ne meurt* and *Journal des Faux-Monnayeurs* — autobiographical meditations on morality that addressed homosexuality in general and Gide's own in particular. These books deeply troubled Gosse, who worried that perhaps Gide should have kept certain opinions and experiences to himself. Indeed, Gide at first showed *Corydon* to no one and *Si le grain ne meurt* only to his most trusted friends. Nevertheless, Gosse supported Gide's work, concluding that hypocrisy and concealment are more corrupt than any "instinctive abnormality." But until the publication of *Si le grain ne meurt* in 1926, the two friends never broached the topic of homosexuality, allowing it to remain a silent third party to their correspondence.

Edmund Gosse to André Gide

[March 7, 1910, from London]

My Dear Monsieur Gide, Two little books of yours, "Le Retour de l'Enfant Prodigue" and "Oscar Wilde" have reached me through your kindness, and have given me immense pleasure. They have — different as they are — the same kind of beauty, the beauty of pure thought, strong and clear expression, and that moral elevation which is so characteristic of your genius. There is no one now writing in France whose works give me more pleasure than yours, — perhaps no one at this moment who gives me so much.

Of course, I had already read most of the "Oscar Wilde" in your admirable "Pretextes."

There has been a great deal of folly written about Wilde. I like the complete sanity of your picture. Of course he was not "a great writer." A languid romancier, a bad poet, a good (but not superlatively good) dramatist, — his works, taken without his life, present, to a sane criticism, a mediocre figure. But the man was consistent, extraordinary, vital even to excess, and his strange tragedy will always attract the consideration of the wise.

Some time ago I sent you my book "Father and Son." I never heard that you read it. I should be disappointed to think that you could never find time to do so, for I put the whole passion of my mind into it, and I should like to think that you, for whom I have so great a sympathy, had some sympathy for me.

Believe me always, with the greatest esteem,

Yours sincerely,
Edmund Gosse

André Gide to Edmund Gosse

[December 31, 1911, from Paris(?)]

Bien Cher ami

Here it is the last day of the year. Before I let it slip away I dwell once more on the memories it has left me.

"While joy recaptures many a province fair, flowing, and luminous, and debonair . . ."

And among the best things the year has brought me I find the blessing of your friendship.

Since my last letter I have received your volume of poems; almost every evening I have read one or two of them, recovering in your lines the sound of your voice, with its depth and gentle warmth of inflection.

But since I have read them mostly in their printed order, could you believe that not until the day before yesterday did I discover the poem at the head of which you have put my name! It was late at night; everything about me was still; I could not keep back my tears. I do thank you with all my heart, my dear friend.

Much better than the photograph of the Sargent portrait of you I like the fine photograph in front of the *Father and Son* that you gave me, the likeness is still so marvelously close.

I managed to see Davray a few days ago; the translation of *Père et Fils* was on his table, nearly ready for book publication.

But — I think it is a pity that such a work could not come out in the *Revue des Deux Mondes* formerly, and I cannot understand how Davray doesn't get it, for you as important as you are. I am very ashamed on my national pride and pray you for excusing it.

How are you, dear friend, and Madame Gosse? Please kindly give her my regards and best wishes. — I take the permission to write in my native language this last sentence, because I noticed the compliments seem always awkward when translated. I dont hope to say in English all that I feel for you in my heart. — How much I wish to see you again! But when? and where?

Votre dévoué *André Gide*

Edmund Gosse to André Gide

[January 2, 1914, from London]

My dear Gide, Conceive the impatience with which, yesterday morning, I tore open the Nouvelle Revue Française and read the opening chapters of "Les Caves du Vatican."

I have awaited this book with unspeakable impatience, with hope and fear mingled. Now all is hope, and joy! Your novel opens with a magnificent originality. I believe this is perhaps *by far* — the greatest thing you have written. All is your own; no other writer could have written one of these pages; your sign-manual is on them all.

The conversion of Anthime is superb. Nothing could be led up to better, nothing could be more surprising, more brilliant, vivid with a more sparkling irony. The characters of the women — so finely contrasted, — the soft, passive Veronique, the more acid, active and absurd Marguerite. The child Julie promises an admirable character; I see in her a continuation of the force of her grandfather Juste-Agénor. Lafcadio is at present a box of puzzles, anything may come out of him.

There is a singular air of mystery and mystification about these early chapters. I hold my breath in expectation of what that is paradoxical, that is saugrenu, will come out of it all, and I can hardly endure the strain of waiting till February for a continuation.

Bravo! and bravo! This, I am sure, my dear friend, is a book which will be enormously attacked, widely *discussed, finally immortal.*

Have you forgotten me entirely? Months have passed and you have not given me a sign of your existence. I thought you would have written to me in November, but not a word. You do not realise how much your friendship is to me. I am miserable if I think that you have ceased to think of me with indulgence.

We are well, at last. Both my wife and I had long illnesses since the summer. We were in Paris in August, and then in Wiesbaden for four weeks, ill and unhappy. Since then I have been extremely busy, and much has happened to me. I had the great surprise of a most unexpected and brilliant recognition from the French Government. You did not write. Perhaps you disapproved?

My wife begs to be remembered to Madame Gide and to you. How is everybody? Has the new theater been a success? I hear nothing from any of my French friends — a conspiracy of silence! I wish you would come to London.

Ever sincerely yours,
Edmund Gosse

André Gide to Edmund Gosse

[January 8, 1914, from Paris(?)]

My dear friend, your letter fills me with both embarrassment and delight: embarrassment in quantity, delight in greater quantity for what a friend you are being! Bless you for not being cross with me for my disappearance.

My hope of getting to London for the Christmas holidays, as I did last year — and, thanks to you, what lovely memories I have of that trip! — has considerably lengthened my silence.

I should have taken such pleasure in wishing you and Mrs. Gosse a Merry Christmas and giving Mrs. Gosse by word of mouth* my best wishes for the New Year. A persistent cold has kept me in Auteuil; but for days and days it was a toss-up: do I go, or do I not go? — with me daring neither to tell you that I would be there nor to make up my mind to forgo the pleasure.

I meant to take with me the whole text of my *Caves*, which I am on tenterhooks to have you know complete — especially now that I know the beginning of it did not disappoint you. How often I thought of you while writing it! wishing, hoping, *willing* that you might be able to find pleasure in it. Your praise [not only] somewhat puffs up my pride, but truly strengthens me, for now I *know* that my book is not a failure.

Wanting in this letter to purge myself of my misdoings, I will tell you that my not having before now congratulated you on your decoration was a consequence of my hearing about it very belatedly. Once I had missed being among the first to applaud, I chose, out of damaged self-esteem, not to applaud at all. And, anyway, it was not so much you that I felt like congratulating as my dear fine France for managing to show recognition of the wise and beautiful friendship you have unceasingly and faithfully shown her. I was happy, too, because it seemed to me that by this gesture France was drawing you a little closer, as one holds a friend back by the coat sleeve, and that you yourself were going to feel, after that, even a little more French. How strange that we are not of the same country! If we lived in the same city, no doubt I should feel a little less shy. I lead a more and more solitary life. Still, thanks to my friends of the theater and of the magazine, I do not feel lonely. The Théâtre du Vieux-Colombier and the *Nouvelle Revue Française* continue to be the focal points of so many friendships and loyalties and enthusiasms! Yes, the theater is doing well, indeed much better than we had ventured to hope; our only worry is seeing Copeau so dreadfully overworked; he cannot allow himself a single day off, and the shortage of actors in the little company compels him to act himself almost every night.

There is nothing to tell you about last summer. The Balkan troubles kept me from getting to Constantinople and Brusa as I had intended; I just tamely fell back on Italy and then came back to Normandy, where my wife had stayed peacefully with her brothers and sisters, waiting for me. If only I had known *where* in England and could have thought I might join you somewhere without instrusion, I do believe I should have crossed the Channel. Yes, I really did think about it seriously, and I came near writing you at that point. Your letter gives me the consolation of finding that you were in Wiesbaden.

* and in English!

No, my dear friend, don't imagine that I am forgetting you or that my fondness for you lessens. When you see me again you will perceive at once that I remain and shall remain unchanged, despite these lapses into silence in which I lose all awareness of time. Au revoir. I am going to say, whether or no, *à bientôt*. My wife wants to be remembered to Mrs. Gosse. Please give her my regards.

André Gide

Edmund Gosse to André Gide

[May 30, 1915, from London]

My dear Gide, Miss Stephens has sent me your graceful and touching article, "Les Réfugiés," which I have enjoyed putting into my best colloquial English and sending back to her. How delightful it is, dear and noble friend, for me to be allowed to collaborate with you in your admirable piety! My thoughts go out to you often and often. When shall we meet again? Surely this horror will some day, or some year, be overpast?

Every English heart goes out in warmest union of heart with you in France. But how terrible it is! We have lost, and are daily losing, our most gallant and splendid young men, the very brain and nerve of England, dying on the fields of Flanders.

God bless you and keep you. Mrs. Gosse sends her warmest regards to you and to Madame Gide.

Yours very affectionately, *Edmund Gosse*

Do you know that the Marcellus of our age, the most promising of all the young English poets, has fallen in the Dardanelles? This was Rupert Brooke, who lies buried in Tenedos.

André Gide to Edmund Gosse

[July 7, 1915, from the Foyer Franco-Belge, Paris]

Bien cher ami

These last sonnets of Brooke's are very fine. I should be glad to translate them, and undoubtedly a selection of his poems along with them; these, with a biographical sketch of Rupert B. and translations of a few more articles or letters of his, would quickly eke out a volume that the Nouvelle Revue Française would publish. Out of considerations as much sentimental as literary, we should want to take very special pains with this publication. Are you by any chance in a position to ask either the family or the publisher for the translation rights in my behalf, so that I could begin work right away? I should be most grateful to you.

My wife is with me for four days. (The Foyer will keep me in Paris all summer, while other duties are keeping my wife in Cuverville.) She joins me in sending you and Mrs. Gosse our best regards.

André Gide

André Gide to Edmund Gosse

[September 20, 1916, from Paris]

Bien cher ami,

I come posthaste from Cuverville, where I got your letter day before yesterday. I can't endure the thought of your coming to France without my seeing you.

However official your trip may be, you will nevertheless manage, I am sure, to find a moment to give to friendship. I should already be waiting for you on the arrival of your train this evening if I did not think someone will be there to welcome you.

In any event I shall come here tomorrow morning around eleven to inquire for you; and if that is not convenient, maybe you could leave a note naming some other time? I am in Paris for no reason but to see you again.

Even if it were for but a moment. How good of you to have come! What a grand friend you are — I mean, friend of France; and how happy I am to be a Frenchman!

Votre *André Gide*

Edmund Gosse to André Gide

[August 15, 1920, from London]

My dear Gide, Thank you for the gift of your "Symphonie Pastorale." I have read it with the deepest emotion and admiration! I am about to review it, and therefore will say no more today.

How long, -- how long, it is since I saw you or heard from you! I hunger for the pressure of your hand, my dear, exquisite friend! I wish you would write to me. We are passing through dreadful days, in which the pillars of the world seem to be shaken and all in front of us seems to be darkness and hopelessness. It is much harder to bear than the War was, because there is no longer the unity which sustained us nor the nobility which inspired hope and determination. What is to come of the angry, distracted world? I feel very old and very helpless.

Do write me a good, long letter. I think of you constantly.

Your affectionate friend, *Edmund Gosse*

Edmund Gosse to André Gide

[August 25, 1924, from London]

My dear Gide, For a long time past I have been intending to thank you for the gift of your "Incidences," but I have been prevented by the mass of work which I have had in hand, and by a certain indolence which creeps over my old age. I will delay no longer.

In reading "Incidences" I have once more found myself listening to the voice which (almost more than any other) fascinates and allures me. Many of the little essays I have read before in the N.R.F. but they gain a new accent, a fresh significance in re-reading. Your mind is excessively limpid. I see strange and beautiful things moving in its depths, as in the hyaline of a pacific sea.

I will not specify more particularly what pleases me than to say that no one has written so well (*nearly* so well) on Proust as you have. "Si désintéressée, si gratuite," nothing could be more excellent. Your article on Gautier interests me very much, because, when I was quite young, about 1873, his prose and verse exercised a violent influence over me, which a little later, the preface to "Les Fleurs du Mal" accentuated. Now

I cannot read Gautier any more; Theodore de Banville has faded for me also but not nearly so much as Gautier. It is like the pleasure one takes in Fragonard's pictures: the thing may not be very well worth doing, but no one does it better than Banville. But all through "Incidences" I enjoy your line of thought: it goes *leaping* along, with great *jumps*, and I joyously jump with it.

You did not send me "Corydon," so I had to buy it. Perhaps you thought I should be "shocked." But that is not my way. There is nothing in the whole diversity of life which serious men can not seriously discuss. I think you show great courage in writing this book, although I do not quite know *why* you wrote it. But that is your business, and I read with sympathy and respect everything you choose to write. No doubt, in fifty years, this particular subject will cease to surprise any one, and how many people in the past might wish to have lived in 1974.

You will have seen that we have lost Conrad, a beautiful figure. But he had said all he had to say, and went on writing in order to make money. He will live in half a dozen of his early books. Here in England, literature is in a deplorable state, dying of collectivism and emptiness. Well, well! I wish you would write to me, but at least I am glad that you have not forgotten me. I am always

Sincerely yours, *Edmund Gosse*

André Gide to Edmund Gosse

[September 12, 1924, from Cuverville]

Mon cher Edmund Gosse,

I am greatly warmed by your fine letter and no end gratified that you should write to me in such terms. My long silences, it seems, have not lessened your sympathetic awareness, which I value above all things. What you tell me about my *Incidences* enchants me.

Your not receiving *Corydon* means I did not send it to anyone. But if I had done so, I really must confess to you that you are one of my friends to whom I should not have dared give it. That is why I am especially moved by your few lines about this little book. Various deplorable misconceptions and calamitous misunderstandings that have cost a good deal of pain were what drove me to write it; also other considerations that you will understand, or so I hope, when you read the completion of *Si le Grain ne meurt* (next spring, probably). This is another book that I mean to send to *no one* — only I shall give you a copy of it as witness to my gratitude and my deferential and steadfast friendship.

André Gide

P.S. Dent had asked me for an introduction to the new edition of *Tom Jones;* I admire Fielding so much that I had assented with enthusiasm. Alas, the proposed translation was discovered to be so wretched that this splendid undertaking had to be given up. Every time I am captivated by an English author it turns out that he is the subject of an essay, introduction or analysis of yours. What a genial arrangement, this coming upon you again in every corner of my library!

Edmund Gosse to André Gide

[August 22, 1926, from London]

My dear Gide, It gave me great pleasure to receive your letter from Cuverville. I did get your earlier letter from central Africa, but did not know how to respond to it, as you seemed moving across incalculable deserts over pathless sands! But I welcome you back in France, and I hope you will give us impressions of your strange adventures such as you, alone, are capable of doing.

You must write them soon, if you please, for if you delay too long, I shall not be here to welcome them. In a few days I shall complete my 77 years, and although I am not conscious as yet of any mental infirmity, my body gets more and more "crawxy" (as we say). I shall certainly never come to France again, but I hope to see you in London.

I read everything you publish, and always with admiration of your sincerity and your courage. I do not always agree with you, but that is another thing. I admire extremely your rectitude, and it is all the more marked because most of contemporary literature seems to me to be cowardly and conventional. It all tends to be standardised and the only salvation for us is to specialise, — to say clearly and boldly what we, individually, believe and feel. I should like you to know that I sympathize deeply with your determination to see things as they are to you.

May I venture to wish, however, that you would try to release yourself from your bondage to the Russians, and particularly to Dostoevski? We have all in time been subjected to the magic of this epileptic monster. But his genius has only led us astray, as I should say to any

young writer of merit who appealed to me. Read what you like, only
don't waste your time reading D. He is the cocaine and morphine of
modern literature.

Do not be long before writing to me again. Tell me what works you
are projecting and what use you are going to make of your African
travels. Will you not come over to London; say towards the end of
October? I should like to organise a public dejeuner in your honour.
Will not that tempt you?

Your affectionate Friend, *Edmund Gosse*

Edmund Gosse to André Gide

[December 19, 1926, from London]

My dear Gide, I am very angry with you! You have published a book ("Le
Grain ne meurt") which all the world is talking about. You have not sent
it to me, —your earliest and most loyal admirer. Pfui! I know all about it
and I must read it. Send it to me *at once:* if you do not, I shall know that
you have no confidence in my discretion or my indulgence.

Ever sincerely yours, *Edmund Gosse*

André Gide to Edmund Gosse

[December 22, 1926]

Mon cher Edmund Gosse,
No, don't be disconcerted at not having received *Si le Graine ne meurt.* I
did not send it to *anyone,* and I have not let the N.R.F. distribute any
review copies.

But you ask me for the book in so warmhearted and irresistible a
way that I am going to make an exception in your favor as soon as an
attack of grippe will let me get out to pick up a copy at the N.R.F.

I sent you just lately a superfine copy of the *Journal des Faux-
Monnayeurs.* and I hope it hasn't gone astray, for the book has now come
to be very rare and hard to find. — My most intimate friends protested
emphatically against publishing *Si le Grain ne meurt;* that is what led me

not to send it to them and, at the same time, to withhold it from all and sundry. Just the same, I can't manage to persuade myself that I was wrong to have it come out — and some of the most opposed have already begun to change their original opinion.

All best wishes for the New Year to you and yours.

André Gide

Edmund Gosse to André Gide

[December 26, 1926, from London]

My dear Gide, It was very neglectful of me not to thank you at once for "Le Journal des Faux-Monnayeurs," which I read with great interest, and prize. You will perhaps be intrigued to hear that we have at this moment a case of a closely parallel kind. A Club of school-boys has been discovered by the fact that they forced one of their number to commit suicide. The circumstances were very much like what you describe in your novel. They called themselves the Red Avengers! The ringleaders (boys of 14 to 16) are now to be tried for murder.

I look forward with keen anticipation to your gift of "Si le Grain ne meurt." I regard you as the most important artist now writing in France and I cannot afford to miss any movement of your mind.

I hope la grippe is better. My Wife joins me in warmest greetings.

Yours always *Edmund Gosse*

André Gide to Edmund Gosse

[December 30, 1926, from Cuverville]

Cher grand ami

Do you know, I came near to being put "out of sorts" by your letter.

So you ask me if I know *Father and Son!!!* — a book that I read and reread and made others read, I don't know how many times; a book that I have lived with and felt was written *for me,* one with the power to stir up the most intrusive echoes. In my time I must have discussed it with you at length and tried to take in some sort of your father's side against you. But that was a long time ago — before the war.

You will find if you keep on reading *Si le Grain ne meurt* — and oh, I almost wish you would stop it short — one feature in common with your book, one more important than the kaleidoscope; and that is the wonderment in the presence of the marine fauna and flora that, I remember, you describe superbly in *Father and Son*. My own book evokes both enthusiasm and resentment. I believe it deserves both; but I tell you now that if, after you had finished reading it, you were to revoke your respect and your friendship, it would be one of the great regrets of my life.

André Gide

My wife asks you please to give Mrs. Gosse her regards and best wishes. To them I add mine, most cordially.

Edmund Gosse to André Gide

[January 7, 1927, from London]

My dear Gide, I have now read "Si le grain ne meurt" very carefully to the end. I have already read much of it twice. Up to page 44 of Tome III I have nothing but admiration of your art, your originality, your exquisite manner of writing. There are passages here which will bear comparison with the best modern literature.

But when I read the "Deuxième Partie" I am confronted by an immense difficulty. What can I say? Yet I must not leave what I feel unsaid. I pray you to bear with me.

The *facts* here related offer me no surprise, since I divined the truth when I read "L'Immoraliste" more than twenty years ago, while later publications have confirmed my knowledge. This has not affected my feeling, personal or literary, since I have never allowed the idiosyncrasies of my friends to blind me to their qualities. I am not a critic of temperaments, nor so ignorant as to believe myself fitted to be a judge.

But now you have gone much further, and I cannot help asking myself, in the face of this narrative. — Was it wise? Was it necessary? Is it useful? I am incapable of answering these questions, which leaves me in a very painful perplexity.

Heaven forbid that I should be such a prig as to put my instinct in the matter before yours. You have acted not without reflection, certainly not without a marvellous courage. You possess so unusual a genius that perhaps it may claim to be a law to itself. But *why* have you done it, and what advantages to any one can accrue from it?

If you think that my old (and undiminished) affection gives me a right to ask you this question, I beg you to send me a full and clear reply. I do not ask it from curiosity, or in a priggish or dictatorial spirit; I ask it in deep sympathy and in an earnest wish to comprehend your position.

I am, my dear Gide, now as ever,

Your attached friend, *Edmund Gosse*

André Gide to Edmund Gosse

[January 16, 1927, from Roquebrune — Cap Martin]

Mon cher Edmund Gosse

What a fine letter I have from you, and how deeply I am moved by it!

Why did I write this book? Because I thought I *had* to write it.

What advantages do I expect from it? I expect nothing but consequence painful to me (and not only to me, alas). And of course the moral obligation had to be more than a little imperious to make me persist; but in truth it would have seemed to me cowardly to let myself be stopped by contemplation of the distress, or of the risk. I had the feeling that I could not have died in peace if I had kept all this locked up in me.

My dear friend, I abominate falsehood. I can't endure having a share in the customary camouflage that deliberately belies the writing of X, Y, and many another. I wrote this book to "create a precedent," to set an example of candor; to enlighten some persons, hearten others, and compel public opinion to reckon with something of which it is oblivious or pretends to be, to the immense impairment of psychology, morality, art — and society.

I wrote this book because I had rather be hated than be beloved for what I am not. "I would willingly come from the other world, to give him the lie, that should frame me other than I had beene: were it he meant to honour mee," Montaigne said.

I will add that I printed but one quickly exhausted edition of the book and that I am not minded to have it reprinted — at least, for a long time to come — except with the elimination of everything censurable. But I did not want to die without knowing that it is *there.*

I am talking to you without strain and without fear, and I am actually happy to be talking to you. Please do see in all I am telling you a testimony to my deep respect and steadfast friendship.

André Gide

Liane de Pougy/Natalie Barney/ Renée Vivien/Dolly Wilde

Among the ranks of the world's greatest and most notorious lovers, Natalie Barney occupies a prominent place. Although she wrote poetry, the France-based American expatriot gained fame in her lifetime largely for her long string of lesbian conquests, which included almost everyone who was anyone in the first half of the twentieth century. The first great love of her life was Liane de Pougy, a courtesan who served the richest and most powerful men in Europe, and who commemorated their affair in a poem called "Sapphic Idyll." The troubled and jealous poet Renée Vivien (Pauline Tarn) claimed Barney's heart for a time before fleeing into the arms of "La Brioche," a grotesque but enormously wealthy countess so nicknamed for her obesity. Along the way Barney had love affairs with the novelist Colette, the spy and exotic dancer Mata Hari, the painter Romaine Brooks and Dolly Wilde, the niece of Oscar Wilde. She also sustained acquaintances and friendships with Virginia Woolf—who is described at length in a letter from Dolly—with Gertrude Stein and with Alice B. Toklas. The letter fragments included here reveal the phenomenal ardor Barney inspired in her lovers as well as the profound heartache caused by her ever-wandering eye.

Liane de Pougy to Natalie Barney

[1899]

The carriage wheels barely go round twice, grinding in the sand, and my Nattie is gone, carried off; my pretty blonde vision finished . . . I go back inside, where I'm handed your flowers, red and white roses, pansies, especially cornflowers, daffodils, forget-me-nots.

You are my very own lover, and you are sad, but you'll come tomorrow and together we'll go for a walk, veiled, in a corner of Paris.

I feel far from everything, from everyone. Natty, do you love me? Fridays are always sad, and when it rains. Little Natty, what's the use of doing what I do? Give me courage, caress my aching soul, put me to sleep, Natty, for a long, long time, and wake me in May, in the warm sun. Good-bye. And then . . . not to take too seriously the word good-bye, to say it, repeat it, always fearing it, to hope for it, to desire it, deny it, use it according to my whim.

Natty, my flower-sister.

Until tomorrow morning.

Liane de Pougy to Natalie Barney

[1899]

What a life! What a world. . . . Even the water here, the waves, the beaches, the sun, everything seems artificial, suspect and crippled.

. . . God! And I'm so resentful toward the people who have dragged me here. I am paralyzed, chilled, my eyes take in horrible things, my soul is locked in distrust, my thoughts probe painfully, and I feel in the situation of that poor little princess, pale and white, led to the witches' Sabbath! My heart leaps at the harshness of the hatreds and jealousies. This blue, this gold, these merry women and crazy men begin to appear like monsters armed with thorns and poisoned arrows, while the flowers, even the fragile flowers, seem like traps to me . . . And I want to turn away, hide, flee! Yet I stay, pinned down, dead, praying for night, obscurity, ignorance, repose, peace, and finding myself surrounded by a cruel brightness which allows me to notice and fear everything. I ask myself: why am I here? Why am I me? Ah! That half-light of Paris in cold February, sad, gray, dull and morose. The stagnant water of the Seine, trapped between its banks, the acrid smoke of the big city, the shouts of hurried pedestrians, all that is less false, less evil and sometimes one may even happen on a smile that brings an unexpected calm, the gentleness of a sincere look. Come, Moonbeam, come take me and carry me off. I no longer am made for these things since I learned to believe, since I doubted, and wondered even if I believed. Come fetch me, Moonbeam, for a month you will take me far away from everything that exists . . . You will lead me where you please. Come take me. I am just right for you now, as you want me, the way you dream of me.

Please come, I am weeping, come, I am dying, come, they are killing me, come, they are murdering me, come help me to revive, my little one.

We will go back together to Paris toward our dreams. Come, you will buy two dresses less, me too, and we'll earn a little happiness for ourselves, a bit of freedom for our dreams. Come quickly to awaken the flower of my soul. Your voice will lull me, singing of sweet things that never happen but for which one hopes and always waits; I will desire and I will wait. You see then, I'm forgetting my work, my new duties and they break my heart. Here, I am the mistress of a clubman who smokes fat cigars and spends his days and nights gambling . . . I wait for him in my bed, unable to sleep, feverish, unable to dream, saddened . . . in a painful materiality. However, the courtesan in me ought to be content for he has just given me a necklace of the white pearls I love, worth one hundred thousand francs. Well, my little one, I suffer on all sides with all of my being. I suffer by wanting to die.

Why this dividing of myself?

Why am I not whole like these men, like the women?

Where does my sadness come from, my revolt, my pain? I am suffering. Come take me, save me. I will go off with you, far from them all, the men, the women. I am not where I belong, and "the man bewitched by a passing shadow always carries with him the punishment of having wanted to change places." There! My place is in you, Moonbeam, spiritually in you, in the softness of your golden fleece, of your tender rays.

Come take me. And after having revived in the sun, we will go and see the first little leaves sprout in Paris, in the woods, on the lake; you will carry me off on a little skiff, frail and light, and we will drift afar, to other places, by coming closer to ourselves.

Ah! The prison of ourselves! Who could have said that? Only in myself do I find space, infinity. *Prison is the others*, the world, society, life. Roses of Jericho. Ashes that scatter at the slightest breath. Come Natty, come, Moonbeam.

You see, I received pearls and I am weeping.

Natalie Barney to Liane de Pougy

[1899]

Will was saying that you were so well known, so famous, that in my madness, I was going to compromise myself and then he couldn't marry me anymore. I began to think about that and I succeeded in converting him to the sweet pleasures of our love, making him appreciate its beauty

and especially those two divine functions so well described by Pierre
Louÿs: the Caress and the Kiss. He officially promised never to take me,
to expect from me only chaste and intellectual enjoyment. Sometimes I
tested him to the point of martyrdom, he kept his word, afterward soothing himself with beautiful slaves.

Liane de Pougy to Natalie Barney

[1899]

You will give up your little petticoat ribbons for me, my Natty, and other
things . . . It's nice, so nice of you, and if I had the swift wings of the
faithful swallow, I would quickly return to your warm blond nest, which
I will do at the end of the month, you may be sure.

My darling, think about it if you like and ready the blessed little
nook where we will love each other; words, caresses, light touching, all
that is us.

Natalie Barney to Liane de Pougy

[1899]

My Liane,

Since you are spiritually happy and physically chaste, I must be that way
too . . . To tire myself out (I know more agreeable, but less innocent,
ways), I take long rides. Yesterday I went twenty-eight kilometers looking for some beauty on which to feast my eyes, tired of the monotony of
my surroundings. I saw pipes, piles of stones, old women and cows. I
also saw some sheep: one of them refused to walk like or with the others
. . . and they were beating him. A moral lesson which I certainly don't
appreciate. Was I like that sheep? The voice of my reason sharply answers yes. Then there were villages where I felt I had to dismount to
taste their cider and the patois of the region. Two years ago I would have
found these inns picturesque, but now they simply seem dirty. A sure
sign of age, when uncleanliness no longer has any artistic appeal. Must I
confess that I have never known the youthful madness of he who sang:

"In a loft, how happy one is at twenty." I'm still only twenty-three, but I already think that one is better off "elsewhere." In your bed, for example.

In coming here, I was hoping that the Bretons would look something like you. Still another disillusionment.... But I do see you, my beloved, in the flowers of your country. These things that I respect are independent of time and are all over. They grow as easily in the immense garden of the Infinite as in the secret of your soul. While I kiss, nibble and inhale the ones around me, do you know what I'm thinking about?

It's time for me to take another ride on my horse. Good-bye. Your . . . and for always.

Natty

Natalie Barney to Liane de Pougy

[1899]

Ah! always to be able to freely love the one whom one loves! To spend my life at your feet like our last days together. To protect you against imaginary satyrs so that I can be the only one to throw you on this bed of moss. We'll go back other times . . . and often, what about it? We'll find each other again in Lesbos, and when dusk falls, we'll go deep in the woods to lose the paths leading to this century. I want to imagine us in this enchanted island of immortals. I picture it as being so beautiful. Come, I'll describe for you those delicate female couples, and far from the cities and the din, we'll forget everything but the Ethics of Beauty.

Liane de Pougy to Natalie Barney

[1899]

Everyone tells me to let you go. *Everyone* is wise and resigned when it comes to the suffering of others.

So my revolt against society and its principles and laws and falsehoods and pettiness is not in essence so ugly.

The *means* alone are disgusting. Laugh at everyone . . . and you won't cry anymore.

I don't know what to tell you.

At every moment, I send you thoughts that you must feel deeply and understand.

I dreamed about you last night. When I woke up, I was happy to be alone and to be able to write to you. And why all that?

Only the beast ought to exist in me.

Good-bye, Natty, I love you.

Liane de Pougy to Natalie Barney

[1900]

I am learning so much about you. Ugh. You present yourself as Flossie. You don't even have the courage to use your name and to show yourself without a mask. If you are ashamed of what you are doing, why do you do it?

And I who thought you so beautiful and who believed in you. And you are thinking about coming to me.

I am worth more than you, Flossie-Natty. I'm prettier, you are ugly with your yellow skin and reddish eyes. Your head of hair, yes, it's ashamed of the rest of you. Your heart . . . doesn't exist. You're stuffed with phrases, and you're believed, and paid attention to.

I don't want to think about you anymore for a very long time. Your reputation is sullied everywhere and from all sides. There is nothing real in you. What I used to love doesn't exist and I'm mad at you for having made me discover it . . .

Take care that I never run into you, for I would take off your mask in front of everybody.

Good-bye.

I no longer believe.

I no longer hope.

I no longer love.

And this evening, I'm going to sell myself to a very rich and very ugly Jew.

Liane de Pougy to Natalie Barney

[1901]

The Idyll has seen the light and the public is scrambling, that's the word, for these scraps of us and our former desires. Everyone is writing to me; men and women, anyone with a soul has been moved by our charm. The most cherished and exquisite memory that has been given to me like a caress, is that evening when I wrote the word "end." ("The end of everything is good," wrote Zarathustra.) And our ending, Natty, purifies all that was too human in *Us.*

We were on the beach at Saint . . . but I don't want to spoil by naming it, that landscape which was like a dream, where we ran, close, very close to each other . . . You told me this would happen, that, and I still wanted to work, forever, this, that too.

The sea became silent, the night muffled all the sounds around us as if out of respect for the ardor of our illusions, the sky clouded over. Your hair, oh, your lovely hair, Natty, its softness brushed against me, an enigma of parallel lines united by disorder . . . I drank in your words, heady with your ideas. The brightness of your hair, the smell of the sea breeze, I see all of it this evening. I love to remember . . . You must see other things. Me, I stopped there. Ah! how soft the sand was . . . How we would have loved to suddenly bury ourselves in it and disappear down to the core of us.

I am getting married, I'm delaying as long as I can, but *I'm going to do it.* Write me your address legibly. When I'm married, I will let you know.

Natty, I would still like to work. Help me, with a little spiritual light that can transcend space and forgetting. Tell me what to read, write me every week, help me to move on.

My little beloved. My fair-haired sweetness, I have your portrait in front of me. You have already made me take a big step in my life. But we are so small beneath the stars.

I go horseback riding two hours a day, if you return it will be a new sensation for our "togetherness." It's to accompany my fiancé and especially my son whom I've taught. Natty, what are you doing? When will you return? Good-bye my Natty, my blond sweetness, my little flaxen flower, Moonbeam. Charm the clouds, enlighten me a little: from afar, it will be lovely, and nearer, still lovelier, wouldn't it be? my sister. Your shadow will cross mine so gently . . . Write to me at the Hotel Cecil in London, my fiancé has given me back your letter. He's good and desires nothing else but to walk with me side by side all my life.

Renée Vivien to Natalie Barney

[1902]

I had the touching joy to receive your nice telegram and your delicious letter, my Little One. I could never tell you what balm it was for my feverish anguish, how refreshing and hopeful . . . I almost seemed to find some tenderness, real tenderness in your heart in what you were so prettily saying and I was happy in the midst of my sorrow. You are such a dear little being, I think with such tenderness of all the beautiful things in you, in your mysterious soul, my pretty Little One, and now I'm afraid, knowing that you are there alone. It seems to me that you must need my useless love. In that case, you will telegraph me immediately, won't you, my dearest soul? Don't feel alone, I love you, I love you deeply, I'll come quickly, quickly. I love you too much to ever abandon you. I will always return.

I feel almost for the first time how much my life is tied to yours. I miss you horribly at every moment. I realize how mad it was for us to separate . . . and yet not, since I finally know you are indispensably dear to me. I can't live without you, my blond Sweetness.

What's happening over there? What are you doing? I so much need to have news of you. Is Eva as passionately beautiful as ever? I'm afraid that you are sad. If this isn't one of the nightmares of an exiled lover, let me know quickly. I only let you leave because I thought you happy without me, no longer forced to have me constantly around you. But I'll come at your first call, don't forget.

What are you doing, Pretty Blond Vision? I am anxious about the distance between us.

The days are slow and long and heavy. It seems to me that it's already been several years since you left.

What a sweet little thing you were that last morning. I keep your beauty in my dazzled eyes, your memory tightly held to my heart. Wherever you go, whatever you do, my arms will be around you, always, and my kisses will remain in your hair. I think about the marvelous mystery that you are. Why haven't I been able to understand you since I have loved you so passionately?

My soul is in your hands, keep it, have pity on it.

I love you, my love, unchangingly.

I would like to tell you infinite things and I'm already at a loss for words. It seems to me that my love ought to be able to express itself eternally and there it is, already breathless.

Little thing, so sorrowfully dear, I adore you.

Renée Vivien to Natalie Barney

[1902]

My Little-One, I was very surprised to learn that you had sent me a telegram telling me to come . . . I never received it. You must have written the wrong address; in that case, it will be returned to you. It could be perhaps that it arrived when I was in Paris, and that my family opened and kept it from me during my absence . . . but I don't want to accuse them before I have proof. Ask the post office what became of it and try to find out whether or not it arrived at Hyde Park Street.

If I had received it, not knowing what it was all about, I would have rushed to you right away, my dear child. But your letter cleared things up for me, and in reading it, I see that it's only a caprice of yours — alas!

I'm sad that you haven't kept the promise that you made before leaving. You had promised not to call me just so that I could amuse you for a boring hour, only to call if you needed me to comfort you, to help you in a bad time. Now there is no reason for my coming. Nothing serious has come up in your life, you don't need support or comfort, you call me for the simple pleasure of still testing your power over me, or for still having a suffering type around you, an easy dupe whom you will continue to use for your amorous and fantastic enterprises.

I am saddened to the depths of my soul to have to tell you this, to you whom I still love in spite of everything. But you forget just how much you made me a martyr, the anguish, the humiliations, the wounds that you inflicted; you forget that I am still bleeding and bruised by all that you made me suffer and that I don't have the strength to immediately bear fresh woes that you might like to have me undergo, unconsciously perhaps, but inevitably. Far away from you, I don't suffer with the same intensity of pain, of jealousy, of the anxiety that I endure when I see you handing out smiles and provocative looks to every woman, and man, as if you were dealing in kisses. There is such bitterness in my soul, you see, that it is overflowing, even in this letter which I would like to be very gentle and tender, almost a letter from a loving friend.

No, my Darling and my Adored, I won't come yet because the moment isn't right. Later, yes, when you call me with all your soul. Not now, for a whim, simply because you are at loose ends.

Here are all the reasons, one after another, that prevent me from coming . . . .

Then the lesser ones: I decided to devote this month to my family. God knows that I've never been so bored in my life, that the days are interminably gloomy, that I hate my country and that I'm waiting for the moment to leave it like my deliverance. But after all I promised, and I'm determined to make this sacrifice for them, which I'm doing with all the patience possible.

Then, forgive me for mentioning these details, but there is, my beloved child, the vulgar question of money. I'm not rich, alas! as you know and everything is so expensive in your country of millionaires that if I undertake an expensive voyage, I won't have almost anything left to spend for my apartment! and you know how I've dreamed of having my little place, a flimsy shelter, a place of refuge and calm, someplace on earth that belongs to me and that is personal, where I will be the mistress and the ruler, where I will be entirely free. In addition, I have taken this apartment; I'll have to furnish it some time or another, and now would be preferable. But all that wouldn't be anything if, in a moment of sadness or grief, you had said to me: "Come, my best friend, cheer me up and comfort me, for I need your tenderness." You didn't say this word because the time hasn't come when it will spring from your heart.

The word you haven't been able to read is "unchangingly," which doesn't mean the same thing as "unfailingly" in the language of love. Yes, my Sweetness, I love you with a love that doesn't change, which persists despite sorrow and disappointment and disillusionment; I will always love you, but not anymore with that blind love of our beginnings. I love you now with a more bitter, darker, more skeptical love (to say right off that ugly word); I no longer have an unreasoning faith; I doubt and I try to know what truth there is at the bottom of lies — what is false at the heart of truth — for you are such a complex being that you are never entirely true or false. But it's love, always, and it will be 'til the day of my death.

Don't be mad at me for seriously refusing you something for the first time, for telling you: "later," when you call me right away. But I beg you, leave me a little peace, let me bathe in solitude and silence and regain some strength. Don't call me this way out of the caprice of a spoiled child who only wants something because he doesn't have it, and disdains it as soon as he has it in his hand. Be very gentle, let me wait for you, don't force me to endure new sorrows.

Don't you understand, then, won't you ever understand what pain it is to love without being loved? and that friendship is a pitiful exchange for love? Write me: "My friend, I'm not mad at you, I understand that this separation is necessary for the future of our love and even in its interest; give your soul some peace, forget with time the sufferings that I inflicted on you without wanting to perhaps, and come back to me calmer, more confident, composed, better."

Do you understand that, my Little One?

To come back to you for a time, just to leave again, what madness! I couldn't do it, I wouldn't have the courage to be separated a second time. There are sacrifices one cannot do over. I had the courage — I must have the will to benefit from it — it has to serve some purpose. To leave again, sadder than ever, more cruelly painful than to never see you, don't you feel that it's impossible? I am tormented beyond what I can say. Nevertheless, this letter doesn't betray any of my deepest anxieties. If you could see me suffering from writing you: that's impossible, you would tell yourself that you should take pity and let me live after having tortured me for so long. I am a cowardly being, weak, contemptible; but that isn't a reason for doing away with myself — and the weak ought to have the right to exist like the strong.

I'm suffering, Little One, that is why I'm mean, but believe me when I tell you again that I love you "unchangingly" and that if I don't come, it's through reason, through duty, and not because of a lack of tenderness and passion. *I* love you, I love you the way I always will.

Liane de Pougy to Natalie Barney

[1902]

The other evening at the Moulin-Rouge an ugly little blond, who looked like a startled rabbit, wished me a good day on your behalf. I said it wasn't true because it annoyed me to see that horror between us. I have such a lovely memory of you and your hair.

My new friend is nice. Life is good with her near me. She's as dark as you were blond; she never leaves me, I'm her sole love and her only reason for being. She grows on one for she is *deep and reliable* . . . which doesn't prevent me from often thinking of you, Natty, my dear little friend, so light and supple, suave and tempting. You were a lovely spring-time morning, it couldn't last long, those fleeting returns.

It would be a joy to see you again. If I've changed, it's to become better. Life is purifying. Come back sometime, as for me, I never feel very far from you.

Your Liane.

P.S. Renée is with la Brioche (you know, *née*...). La Brioche has just published a book of poetry, *Effeuillements* (When the Leaves Fall). No comment.

Natalie Barney to Liane de Pougy

[1902]

You were right to tell the "ugly little blond" who stupidly wished you good day on my behalf that it wasn't true. First of all, I don't know any ugly little blonds, and then, it would take very pretty lips and mind for me to entrust them with a message for you.

You're also right to stand by your memory of me. The past is such a subtle thing. In the end, nothing else exists. Everything is made of the past, even the future, and if I'm still living and am happy or unhappy, it's from having been that way.

I'm glad that you have a friend of depth and reliability. Be good to her, Liane, love is an awesome gift. If it's true that you are her whole horizon, be limitless and always beautiful.

Strange that you should mention Pauline and la Brioche. Oh! Lianou, I'm sad. And one has to forget so many things in order to be able to remember a little.

You my tender friend, my distant beloved, "it couldn't last," and nevertheless, and always, your

Natalie.

Renée Vivien to Natalie Barney

[1904]

I feel a bit of shame and much sadness in writing you this letter, my blond siren. But it's necessary. And I am obeying.

First of all, there's one thing you must know: *She* alone is master of my fate. She is my strength and my will. I depend on her, I live through her, I breathe through her. I can't live without her. Thus whatever happens, I remain her thing. She has taken hold of me as much as a human being can . . . . If you want to see me again (although that seems impossible to me after these too truthful confessions that I have just made), I will see you every two weeks with my friend's permission . . . . Leave me to my uneasy future, knowing that a single being possesses my heart and my body. She alone.

I write badly, stupidly, brutally, because I'm telling the truth which is never good to say.

And then ... one regret ... that of perhaps having caused you a little pain.

Dolly Wilde to Natalie Barney

[1931]

Cambridge on a frosty night. The Dean's room in King's College, firelight, books, sober colours, elegance and a group of charming people holding conversation. We are waiting for dinner when someone says "Leonard and Virginia are very late." The smooth waters of my mind are ruffled by fear by this unexpected remark, and my heart beats percepti bly quicker. The chief Lama of Thibet will be here any moment — easy manners must give place to decorum, familiar friendship be brought stiffly to attention. Then the door opens and a tall gaunt figure, grey-haired, floats into the room. Her age struck me first, and then her prettiness — shock and delight hand in hand. How explain? There is something of the witch in her — as in Edith Sitwell — with the rather curved back and sharp features. She is dressed in black, old fashioned elderly clothes that make me feel second-rate in my smart clothes — her feet are very long and thin encased in black broché shoes with straps of the Edwardian period. All is faded and grey about her, like her iron grey hair parted in the middle and dragged into a 'bun' at the back. And yet immediately one sees her *prettiness* and a lovely washed away ethereal look making all of us look so gross and sensual. The eyes are deep-sunk and small the nose fine and pointed, a little *too* pointed by curiosity, but the feature that most strikes one is the mouth — a full round mouth, a pretty girl's mouth in that spinster face. It is so young, young like her skin that is smooth and soft. She greets Honey and me without looking at us and at dinner never once makes us the target of her eyes — there is embarrassment around the table and she only talks to her intimates. She is witty and kindly malicious. Then suddenly I say something that makes her laugh and the curtain of her eyelids are raised and we talk together, flippantly delightfully. I had once been told one must never mention her books and as we threaded byeways of humour I thought of your letters about her so much. I saw her, too, all the time as such a pretty little girl in a big hat, and Kew Gardens with the governess planting a kiss on the back of her neck — do you remember? — which was the parent of all the kisses in her life. . . .

She has nothing to do with maternal life — is supposed to be a virgin, to have experienced no physical contact even with Orlando. She says she has no need of experience — knows everything without it: and this impression she gives as one meets her. I felt cruelty in her, born of humour — tiredness, great tiredness and her eyes *veiled* with visions rather than brightened by them.

Natalie Barney to Gertrude Stein and Alice B. Toklas

74, Rue Raynouard, Paris — 16,
End of May, 1946

Dear Gertrude and Alice dear,

Here I am at last, but with my sister in the 16th, instead of 20 rue Jacob in the 6th with my souvenirs — and near you! But I am near you all the same as I've "Wars I have seen.". . . . My half faithful servant Berthe (her other half is occupied by dress-making) greeted me at the station (Gare de Lyon: Florence-Paris direct) with "il pleut sur le lit de Mademoiselle" — so as I'd been most comfortable in my wagon-lit I decided not to rough it until my old pavilion is put in comparative order and repaired. I long to be your 'voisine' again and resume our night-walks — and be greeted by Alice, and revisit your lovely home rue Christine in the meantime; — when shall that be? The newly arrived have very little to do, except moon about, and like the newly married reacquaint themselves with things strangely familiar, realized as in a dream. I have dreamed of getting back to our old quarter so long, that, like a somnambulist, I shall find my way to your door, and see the doves of your bedroom flutter, and the easy chairs contain us as before, and your portrait seating you above us looks down: uniting past & present to whatever future we have yet to live through — may it be in Paris — although my visa is only *via* France! . . .

"Au revoir" is a nice word, and let it be soon. Just tell Berthe or telephone or send me a note to say when I can find you in. And ever most attentively and appreciatively your friend

Natalie

Radclyffe Hall

Radclyffe Hall, author of the lesbian classic *The Well of Loneliness*, spent twenty-eight years with sculptor Una Troubridge, but at the tender age of twenty-one (eight years before she met Troubridge) she carried a torch for Violet Hunt. The socialite daughter of a noted pre-Raphaelite painter, Hunt was eighteen years older than Hall and the erstwhile object of a young Oscar Wilde's affections. Hall fell hard for Hunt and sent her this note, knowing her beloved did not share her amorous feelings.

Radclyffe Hall to Violet Hunt

[1907]

I do not know just how much you are likely to be bored by my affection which you never after all sought, for perhaps even now you are thinking me impertinent, as you read this letter. I can't help it Violet I must risk that, if I can't always say the things I am feeling when we are together it is because you have built a brick wall around yourself and I must not venture to get inside it. No doubt you have many good reasons for wishing it to be there. I have never met any one who could so repulse affection as you can in your quiet sweet way. If you are angry with me, what can I say except that I am so fond of you? I will never bother you to read this sort of thing again. Forgive it this once. Don't bother to answer. I will call for you Thursday unless you stop me.

Leonard Woolf/Lytton Strachey/Virginia Stephen Woolf

Among the many tangled relationships within the Bloomsbury literary circle, the triangular friendship of the biographer Lytton Strachey and the novelist-publishers Leonard and Virginia Woolf is typical. The two men shared an essentially platonic friendship in which their mutual homosexuality was a point of commonality; one focus of their correspondence was the debate over which of them should marry Virginia Stephen, the only woman with "enough brains." Likewise, the early correspondence of Leonard and Virginia directly addresses the advantages and pitfalls of potential marriage, even as a deep affection and respect emerges. Included here as well are Virginia's despondent last letters, sent to Leonard shortly before her suicide.

Leonard Woolf to Lytton Strachey

Palatupana
Ceylon
[Postmarked February 1, 1909]

I have just received your last letter in a hut in the middle of the jungle. I am on my way to the Game Sanctuary a vast area of forest which the government in its forethought for the villager & as much for the sportsman has reserved: no one may shoot in it or live in it & so the buffalo lies down with the elephant & the elephant with the leopard & the leopard with the deer. I trail along with my caravan of carts & mudaliyars [district chiefs] & tents; there are no villages & no people & if I don't go out & shoot something my dinner is sardines & eternal chicken.

You have the atmosphere into which you launch your thunderbolts. It is a fairly simple frame of mind to walk 10 miles with a rifle in your hand & the only thought in your head to shoot a deer. And then you suddenly come with all the violence & the intricacies of feelings which after all perhaps after 4 years I understand. But I don't agree with you. The most wonderful of all would have been to marry Virginia. She is I imagine supreme & then the final solution would have been there, not a rise perhaps above all horrors but certainly not a fall, not a shirking of facts. Of course I suppose it is really impossible for the reason (if for no other) that I cannot place you in it — & that for me makes it impossible or shows only perhaps that everything has gone beyond me — but it certainly would be the only thing. It is undoubtedly the only way to happiness, to anything settled, to anything not these appalling alternations from violent pleasures to the depths of depression. I am sure of it for myself &, as I perpetually now live on the principle that nothing matters, I don't know why the devil I don't. But something or other always saves me just at the last moment from these degradations — their lasciviousness or their ugliness probably — though I believe if I did I should probably be happy. Do you think Virginia would have me? Wire to me if she accepts. I'll take the next boat home; & then when I arrived I should probably come straight to talk with you. You don't know what it is not to have talked to anyone for four years. By the bye one of the saddest things in Moore's letter I thought was this. He said that Ainsworth seemed so happy at being engaged. 'I wished I could be engaged too'. God! I wish I could write like that!

A curious little thing with regard to your previous letter may amuse you. There was one thing in it about D[uncan Grant] which on reading it first actually struck me with a horror. And then I suddenly remembered that a woman had once done it to me & it hadn't struck me as a horror at all. Two things are quite clear from this & one is that what I always say is true, reality is nothing, it is only in writing & imagination that things are wonderful or horrible or supreme, in reality they are sometimes just beautiful, nearly always ugly & always vague & dire.

I wonder if after all Virginia marries Turner.

Your

L.

I never thanked you for the books. I do read on these circuits in the middle of the day & they are a godsend especially as I have just got to the end practically of the last batch I ordered out. I suddenly thought I must now read Maupassant again & when I reread the tale about the child who is pinched on the buttocks by the adulterating captain I thought I was right. I also read [the Earl of Cromer's] *Modern Egypt* & you can deduce my state of mind by the fact that I think it is the greatest book written in the last 25 years. I wish you wouldn't write introductions but when you do you must send them to me. What do you think of this

> *When I am dead & you forget*
> *My kisses in the stirring air*
> *Will you not shudder when my touch,*
> *Grown nothing now, just stirs your hair?*
> *Will you not shudder when you feel*
> *My arms about you in the mist;*
> *You will not know the dead man's lips*
> *You will not know that you have kissed*
> *A dead man. Only there may come*
> *A memory of a foreign land*
> *Of wind & sun & how you lay*
> *By the salt marshes in the sand*
> *With someone. Some forgotten name*
> *May murmur in the wind: but I*
> *Amid the havoc of all things*
> *Know that our bodies never die.*

Lytton Strachey to Leonard Woolf

Feb 19th 1909

Your letter has this minute come — with your proposal to Virginia, and I must write a word or two of answer, though the post is all wrong. You are perfectly wonderful, and I want to throw my arms around your neck. Everything you say is so tremendously to the point! Isn't it odd that I've never really been in love with you? And I suppose never shall. You make me smile and shudder — oh! and long for you to be here. It's curious — are you after all happier than I am? In spite of the silence of four years? This is all rubbish, but I'm rather ill and rather excited — by your letter.

The day before yesterday I proposed to Virginia. As I did it, I saw that it would be death if she accepted me, and I managed, of course, to get out of it before the end of the conversation. . . . I think there's no doubt whatever that you ought to marry her. You *would* be great enough and you'll have the immense advantage of physical desire. . . . If you came and proposed she'ld accept. She really would.

Your poem disproves your theory. Imaginations are nothing; facts are all. A penis *actually* erected — on becoming erect — is cataclysmal. In imagination it's a mere shade. That, in my view, is the point of art, which converts imaginations into actualities. But I'm sleepy and ill, and I've got to write on Swift, Stella, & Vanessa for the *Spectator.*

Your
Lytton

Lytton Strachey to Leonard Woolf

21 August 1909

. . . Your destiny is clearly marked out for you, but will you allow it to work? You must marry Virginia. She's sitting waiting for you, is there any objection? She's the only woman in the world with sufficient brains: it's a miracle that she should exist: but if you're not careful you'll lose the opportunity. At any moment she might go off with heaven knows who — Duncan? Quite possible. She's young, wild, inquisitive, discontented, and longing to be in love. If I were you I should telegraph. But at any rate come and see her before the end of 1910. . . .

Aug. 24th . . . Write to me again for the Lord's sake, and quickly. I want to talk to you far more than to anyone else. If it weren't for the hideous expense I'd start tomorrow for Hambantota. . . .

Your loving
Lytton

Leonard Woolf to Virginia Stephen

[Frome]
Jan 12 [1912]

I find the post doesn't go out until evening, so I can try & write about what, with you sitting there, it was so difficult to discuss calmly & dispassionately. I dont think I'm selfish enough not to be able to see it from your side as well. From mine, I'm sure now that apart from being in love, I should be right to say — & I would — that if I were in love, it would be worth the risk of everything to marry you. That of course — from your side — was the question you were continually putting yesterday & which probably you ought to. Being outside the ring of fire, you should be able to decide it far better than I inside it. God, I see the risk in marrying anyone & certainly me. I am selfish, jealous, cruel, lustful, a liar & probably worse still. I had said over & over again to myself that I would never marry anyone because of this, mostly because, I think, I felt I could never control these things with a woman who was inferior & would gradually enfuriate me by her inferiority & submission. (I have had to be motored to Bath & back & it is now evening again.) It is because you aren't that that the risk is so infinitely less. You may be vain, an egoist, untruthful as you say, but they are nothing compared to your other qualities: magnificence, intelligence, wit, beauty, directness. After all too we like one another, we like the same kinds of things & people, we are both intelligent & above all it is realities which we understand & which are important for us. You wanted me to give you reasons for my state of mind: here they are & damnably truthful at any rate. I feel like knocking nails — with Walter & Sydney — into my coffin. I would even go so far — in the cause of truth — as to admit the possibility of my desire for you blinding me to the knowledge that no woman ought to marry me — but I don't believe it in your case — if you ever did love me.

As you dont, you ought to be able to know now exactly what the risk would be if you were & married me.

The people have come for the post so I must stop.

Yr
L.

Leonard Woolf to Virginia Stephen

[38 Brunswick Square]
29 April 1912

Dearest Virginia, I cant sleep not from desire but from thinking about you. I've been to the opera but for all that I heard of it I might have been sitting in this room. I've read two of your MSS from one of which at any rate one can see that you might write something astonishingly good. I want to see you to talk with you & now, though I suppose I shouldn't, I'm going to write utterly miserable what I should want to say to you & probably couldnt.

Since yesterday something seemed to rise up in you against me. It may be imagination on my part; if it is, you must forgive me: I dont think even you realize what it would mean to me. God, the happiness I've had by being with you & talking with you as I've sometimes felt it mind to mind together & soul to soul. I know clearly enough what I feel for you. It is not only physical love though it is that of course & I count it the least part of it, it isn't only that I'm only happy with you, that I want to live with you; it's that I want your love too. It's true that I'm cold & reserved to other people; I don't feel affection ever easily: but apart from love I'm fond of you as I've never been of anyone or thing in the world. We often laugh about your lovableness but you don't know how lovable you are. It's what really keeps me awake far more than any desire. It's what worries me now, tears me two ways sometimes — for I wouldn't have you marry me, much as I love you, if I thought that it would bring you any unhappiness. Really this is true though it hurt me more than the worst physical pain your mere words that you told Vanessa that probably you would never marry anyone.

There is nothing that you've done which hasn't seemed to me absolutely right which hasn't made me love you more. I've never for a single moment thought you were treating me badly & I never shall, whether you marry me or not. I love you more for not deciding — I know the reasons. You are far finer, nobler, better than I am. It isn't difficult to be in love with you & when one is in love with anyone like you one has to make no allowances, no reservations. But I've many beastly qualities — though I've shown them to you deliberately often because I'm too fond of you not to want you to know that they do exist. For me to know that they do exist & to be in love with someone like you, that's where the pain comes in.

I don't want you to decide until you've finished your novel [*The Voyage Out*], I think you're right not to. I can go on as we've been doing for six months even, if you want it, or if you ever for a moment feel it would be easier, I will go away for a week or a month or longer — though not seeing you for a day makes me miserable now. But I believe I know how you feel now & one should speak out what one thinks. I should like to say it to you, only when I'm with you all sorts of feelings make it so difficult to say exactly what I mean — so that it's a good thing perhaps that I am writing to you. I believe you might very easily be in love now & almost equally easily never be — with me at any rate. I dont think much of the physical part of it though it must come in — but it's so elusive. If one happens to be born as I am, it is almost certain to be very strong, but even then it becomes so merged with one's other feelings. It was the least strong of my feelings for you when I feel in love & when I first told you. It has grown far more violent as my other feelings have grown stronger.

I think we're reaching a point at which everything will tremble in the balance. Sometimes I suppose you don't know exactly what you feel & really unimportant things become magnified. I have faults, vices, beastlinesses but even with them I do believe you ought to marry me & be in love — & it isn't only because so often I feel that if you never are, the best thing in life will have gone. I shall never be like you, never anything like it, but you seem to purge my faults from me. And I have the fire in me at any rate & the knowledge. I want to live & get the best things in life & so do you. You are the best thing in life & to live it with you would make it ten thousand times more worth living. I shall never be content now with the second best. And you, I'm sure, you see that if it could be lived like that by two people who know how to live — God, the chance of it is worth any risk almost.

Virginia, I don't know where I've got to. I'm just writing as I think. It's nearly 3 in the morning. I shall go for a walk & post this & then go to bed again. I only hope there's nothing in it to worry you. At any rate you must know that I love you as much as it is possible for one human being to love another. I would rather do anything than harm you in the slightest possible way. You mustn't worry or hurry — there's no need for it. You must finish your novel first & while you are doing it you must not try to decide. If you dont try to decide & we go on as we have been, I shall get plenty of happiness in the next two months. After all I've had more happiness in the last two months than in all the rest of my life put together.

And writing like this to you is like talking to you, it makes all depression go. I shall go to bed happy & sleep peacefully. I hope you are.

L.

Virginia Stephen to Leonard Woolf

Asheham, [Rodmell, Sussex]
May 1st [1912]

Dearest Leonard,

To deal with the facts first (my fingers are so cold I can hardly write) I shall be back about 7 tomorrow, so there will be time to discuss — but what does it mean? You can't take the leave, I suppose if you are going to resign certainly at the end of it. Anyhow, it shows what a career you're ruining!

Well then, as to all the rest. It seems to me that I am giving you a great deal of pain — some in the most casual way — and therefore I ought to be as plain with you as I can, because half the time I suspect, you're in a fog which I don't see at all. Of course I can't explain what I feel — these are some of the things that strike me. The obvious advantages of marriage stand in my way. I say to myself. Anyhow, you'll be quite happy with him; and he will give you companionship, children, and a busy life — then I say By God, I will not look upon marriage as a profession. The only people who know of it, all think it suitable; and that makes me scrutinise my own motives all the more. Then, of course, I feel angry sometimes at the strength of your desire. Possibly, your being a Jew comes in also at this point. You seem so foreign. And then I am fearfully unstable. I pass from hot to cold in an instant, without any reason; except that I believe sheer physical effort and exhaustion influence me. All I can say is that in spite of these feelings which go chasing each other all day long when I am with you, there is some feeling which is permanent, and growing. You want to know of course whether it will ever make me marry you. How can I say? I think it will, because there seems no reason why it shouldn't — But I don't know what the future will bring. I'm half afraid of myself. I sometimes feel that no one ever has or ever can share something — Its the thing that makes you call me like a hill, or a rock. Again, I want everything — love, children, adventure, intimacy, work. (Can you make any sense out of this ramble? I am putting down one thing after another). So I go from being half in love with you, and wanting you to be with me always, and know everything about me, to the extreme of wildness and aloofness. I sometimes think that if I married you, I could have everything — and then — is it the sexual side of it that comes between us? As I told you brutally the other day, I feel no physical attraction in you. There are moments — when you kissed me the other day was one — when I feel no more than a rock. And yet your caring for me as you do almost overwhelms me. It is so real, and so strange. Why should you? What am I really except a pleasant attractive creature? But its just because you care so much that I feel I've got to care before I marry you. I feel I must give you everything; and that if I can't, well, marriage would only be second-best for you as well as for me. If you can still go on, as before, letting me find my own way, as that is what would please me best; and then we must both take the risks. But you have made me very happy too. We both of us want a marriage that is a tremendous living thing, always alive, always hot, not dead and easy in parts as most marriages are. We ask a great deal of life, don't we? Perhaps we shall get it; then, how splendid!

One doesn't get much said in a letter does one? I haven't touched upon the enormous variety of things that have been happening here — but they can wait.

D'you like this photograph? — rather too noble, I think. Here's another.

Yrs.
VS

Leonard Woolf to Virginia Woolf

The Lacket
Lockeridge
13 March 1914

Sweetest Mandy, Do you know that I almost cried when I got your letter just now? Merely from longing for you. Is that foolish, dearest? I've been depressed & wanting you so much today.

It's a wretched day & my head has been worrying me again, not very bad, but it's disappointing that it does not go. However I suppose one must expect ups & downs.

I think I shall go to Bella. I dont think it does to stay too long here. Lytton is very nice but he's exacting. I very nearly enraged him this morning because I said I saw no reason to believe that the Greeks didn't love women! Also this isn't really a very comfortable house: there's only one comfortable chair & no sofa, so that it's rather miserable if one is not feeling well.

There is no doubt of one thing, beloved, & that is that we do suit each other in some amazing way. I've never been alone with anyone else for a few days without irritating & being irritated. And yet you can day after day & all day give me perfect happiness.

Lytton read me last night what he had written about Manning. It's very good & amusing. We argue & talk about books & Vanessa & Clive & Roger & Adrian. He thinks Nessa by nature a virgin & Adrian a cretin. He has a tremendous opinion of Mistress Mandril. He said this morning that your handwriting was the most "eminent" he had ever seen. I think sometimes he is rather jealous of your old Mongoose.

Don't think, dear one, that I'm ill. I'm not. Really I'm even today much better than I was when I came here. But I'm lonely without you. You cant realize how utterly you would end my life for me if you had taken that sleeping mixture successfully or if you ever dismissed me.

Some of the country round here is very good. Very open & rolling downs, & then there are very mystic mounds & tombs of prehistoric kings. But it doesn't 'dispose itself' in that amazing way of Sussex. It hasn't the character or the atmosphere.

I think you might like to read Purcell's life of Manning & W. Ward's life of Newman & another amusing book I looked at here is Hurrell Froude's *Remains*. I have read partly Newman's *Apologia;* he seems to me a self-sentimentalist. But Haultain's Goldwin Smith is the gem.

I feel the usual post-Stracheyan conviction of dust in my mouth & that it is useless for me ever to try to write again.

It is worth going away from you I always say in order to come back, but it's hard being away from you.

Your M.

Love to Ka. Will you thank her for her letter? Has Cascara acted?

Virginia Woolf to Leonard Woolf

[Monk's House, Rodmell, Sussex]
Tuesday [March 18(?) 1941]

Dearest,

I feel certain that I am going mad again: I feel we cant go through another of those terrible times. And I shant recover this time. I begin to hear voices, and cant concentrate. So I am doing what seems the best thing to do. You have given me the greatest possible happiness. You have been in every way all that anyone could be. I dont think two people could have been happier till this terrible disease came. I cant fight it any longer, I know that I am spoiling your life, that without me you could work. And you will I know. You see I cant even write this properly. I cant read. What I want to say is that I owe all the happiness of my life to you. You have been entirely patient with me and incredibly good. I want to say that — everybody knows it. If anybody could have saved me it would have been you. Everything has gone from me but the certainty of your goodness. I cant go on spoiling your life any longer.

I dont think two people could have been happier than we have been.

V.

Virginia Woolf to Leonard Woolf

[Monk's House, Rodmell, Sussex]
[March 18(?) 1941]

Dearest,

I want to tell you that you have given me complete happiness. No one could have done more than you have done. Please believe that.

But I know that I shall never get over this: and I am wasting your life. It is this madness. Nothing anyone says can persuade me. You can work, and you will be much better without me. You see I cant write this even, which shows I am right. All I want to say is that until this disease came on we were perfectly happy. It was all due to you. No one could have been so good as you have been, from the very first day till now. Everyone knows that.

V.

You will find Roger's letters to the Maurons in the writing table drawer in the Lodge. Will you destroy all my papers.

Rupert Brooke

Bursting onto the English literary scene in 1911, the young poet Rupert Brooke enjoyed dazzling success for three short years. In 1914, at the age of twenty-eight, he died on a World War I hospital ship, a loss that shocked those who recognized his phenomenal talent. His death was made all the more poignant by the publication of his war poems, including "The Soldier," that depicted the lonely lives of fighting men. Brooke became an emblem of the obscene sacrifice of young talent during the First World War. He wrote the following letter at the pinnacle of his short life, during an extended trip to the islands of the Pacific.

Rupert Brooke to Edward Marsh

Somewhere near Fiji
November 15 (?), 1913

Dear Eddie, I'm conscious I haven't written to you for a long time: — though, indeed, my last letter was *posted* only a short time ago. When it, or when this, will get to you, God knows. About Christmas, I suppose, though it seems incredible. My *reason* tells me that you'll be slurring through London mud in a taxi, with a heavy drizzle falling, and a chilly dampness in the air, and the theatres glaring in the Strand, and crowds of white faces. But I can't help *thinking* of you trotting through crisp snow to a country church, holly-decorated, with little robins picking crumbs all around, and the church-bells playing our brother Tennyson's *In Memoriam* brightly through the clear air. It may not be: it never has been: — that picture-postcard Christmas. But I shall think of you so.

You think of me, in a loin-cloth, brown and wild in the fair chocolate arms of a Tahitian beauty, reclining beneath a bread-fruit tree, on white sand, with the breakers roaring against the reefs a mile out, and strange brilliant fish darting through the pellucid hyaline of the sun-saturated sea.

Oh, Eddie, it's all true about the South Seas! I get a little tired of it at moments, because I am just too old for Romance. But there it is: there it wonderfully is: heaven on earth, the ideal life, little work, dancing and singing and eating, naked people of incredible loveliness, perfect manners, and immense kindliness, a divine tropic climate, and intoxicating beauty of scenery.

I came aboard and left Samoa two days ago. Before that I had been wandering with an "interpreter" — entirely genial and quite incapable of English — through Samoan villages. The last few days I stopped in one, where a big marriage-feast was going on. I lived in a Samoan house (the coolest in the world) with a man and his wife, nine children, ranging from a proud beauty of 18 to a round object of 1 year, a dog, a cat, a proud hysterical hen, and a gaudy scarlet and green parrot, who roved the roof and beams with a wicked eye; choosing a place whence to —, twice a day, with humorous precision, on my hat and clothes.

The Samoan girls have extraordinarily beautiful bodies, and walk like goddesses. They're a lovely brown colour, without any black Melanesian admixture; their necks and shoulders would be the wild envy of any European beauty; and in carriage and face they remind me continually and vividly of my incomparable heartless and ever-loved X. Fancy moving among a tribe of X's! Can't you imagine how shattered and fragmentary a heart I'm bearing away to Fiji and Tahiti? And, oh dear! I'm afraid they'll be just as bad.

And Eddie, it's all True about, for instance, Cocoanuts. You tramp through a strange vast dripping tropical forest for hours, listening to weird liquid hootings from birds and demons in the branches above. Then you feel thirsty, so you send your boy up a great perpendicular palm. He runs up with utter ease and grace, cuts off a couple of vast nuts and comes down and makes holes in them. And they are chock-full of the best drink in the world.

Romance! Romance! I walked 15 miles through mud and up and down mountains, and swam three rivers, to get this boat. But if ever you miss me, suddenly, one day, from lecture-room B. in King's, or from the Moulin d'Or at lunch, you'll know that I've got sick for the full moon on these little thatched roofs, and the palms against the morning, and the Samoan boys and girls diving thirty feet into a green sea or a deep mountain pool under a waterfall — and that I've gone back.

Romance? That's half my time. The rest is Life — Life, Eddie, is what you get in the bars of the hotels in 'Frisco, or Honolulu, or Suva, or Apia, and in the smoking-rooms in these steamers. It is incredibly like a Kipling story, and all the people are very self-consciously Kiplingesque. Yesterday, for instance, I sat in the Chief Engineer's cabin, with the first officer and a successful beach-comber lawyer from the white-man's town in Samoa, drinking Australian champagne from breakfast to lunch. "To-day I am not well." The beach-comber matriculated at Wadham, and was sent down. Also, he rode with the Pytchley, quotes you Virgil, and discusses the ins and outs of the Peninsular campaign. And his repertoire of smut is enormous. Mere Kipling, you see, but one gets some good stories. Verses, of a school-boy kind, too . . . *Sehr primitiv.* The whole thing makes a funny world.

I may pick up some mail, and hear from you, when I get to New Zealand. I'm afraid your post as my honorary literary agent, or grass-executor, is something of a sinecure. I can't write on the trail.

There's one thing I wanted to consult you about, and I can't remember if I mentioned it. I want some club to take an occasional stranger into, for a drink, and to read the papers in, and, sometimes, to have a quiet meal in. Where do you think I should go? . . . I want somewhere I needn't always be spick and span in, and somewhere I don't have to pay a vast sum.

There's nothing else in the way of my European existence, I think. That part of it which is left, out here, reads Ben Jonson. Kindly turn up his "New Inn" (which is sheer Meredith) and read Lovel's Song in Act IV. The second verse will dispel the impression of the first, that it is by Robert Browning. The whole thing is pure beauty.

No more. My love to everyone, from Jackson down to ——if you've made her acquaintance yet — Helena Darwin Cornford. And to such as Wilfred (Gibson) and Denis (Browne) and yourself and a few more poor, pale-skinned stay-at-homes, a double measure. I have a growing vision of next summer term spent between King's and Raymond Buildings: a lovely vision. May it be.

Manina! Tofa!
Thy
Rupert

Katherine Mansfield/Virginia Woolf

Born in New Zealand, short story writer Katherine Mansfield sent the lesbian vignette "Leves Amores" to her friend Vere Bartrick-Baker at the

age of twenty. After moving to England she became popular with the Bloomsbury crowd. There, in the last twelve years of her short life, she published
several story collections while battling the tuberculosis that eventually killed
her. Mansfield became close friends with Virginia Woolf as well as with
Dorothy Brett, Lady Ottoline Morrell and Anne Estelle Rice, and married
John Middleton Murry in 1918. Sometimes wryly and sometimes lyrically,
her letters reflect her great affection for her women friends as well as the
inescapable reality of her illness.

Katherine Mansfield to Vere Bartrick-Baker

"Leves Amores"
[1908]

I can never forget the Thistle Hotel. I can never forget that strange
winter night.

I had asked her to dine with me, and then go to the Opera. My
room was opposite hers. She said she would come but — could I lace up
her evening bodice, it was hooks at the back. Very well.

It was still daylight when I knocked at the door and entered. In her
petticoat bodice and a full silk petticoat she was washing, sponging her
face and neck. She said she was finished, and I might sit on the bed and
wait for her. So I looked round at the dreary room. The one filthy
window faced the street. She could see the choked, dust-grimed window
of a wash-house opposite. For furniture, the room contained a low bed,
draped with revolting, yellow, vine-patterned curtains, a chair, a ward-
robe with a piece of cracked mirror attached, a washstand. But the
wallpaper hurt me physically. It hung in tattered strips from the wall. In
its less discoloured and faded patches I could trace the pattern of roses
— buds and flowers — and the frieze was a conventional design of birds,
of what genus the good God alone knows.

And this was where she lived. I watched her curiously. She was
pulling on long, thin stockings, and saying 'damn' when she could not
find her suspenders. And I felt within me a certainty that nothing beautiful could ever happen in that room, and for her I felt contempt, a little
tolerance, a very little pity.

A dull, grey light hovered over everything; it seemed to accentuate
the thin tawdriness of her clothes, the squalor of her life, she, too, looked
dull and grey and tired. And I sat on the bed, and thought: 'Come, this
Old Age. I have forgotten passion, I have been left behind in the beauti-

ful golden procession of Youth. Now I am seeing life in the dressing-room of the theatre.'

So we dined somewhere and went to the Opera. It was late, when we came out into the crowded night street, late and cold. She gathered up her long skirts. Silently we walked back to the Thistle Hotel, down the white pathway fringed with beautiful golden lilies, up the amethyst shadowed staircase.

Was Youth dead? . . . *Was* Youth dead?

She told me as we walked along the corridor to her room that she was glad the night had come. I did not ask why. I was glad, too. It seemed a secret between us. So I went with her into her room to undo those troublesome hooks. She lit a little candle on an enamel bracket. The light filled the room with darkness. Like a sleepy child she slipped out of her frock and then, suddenly, turned to me and flung her arms round my neck. Every bird upon the bulging frieze broke into song. Every rose upon the tattered paper budded and formed into blossom. Yes, even the green vine upon the bed curtains wreathed itself into strange chaplets and garlands, twined round us in a leafy embrace, held us with a thousand clinging tendrils.

And Youth was not dead.

K. Mansfield.

Katherine Mansfield to Dorothy Brett

Wednesday
141a Church St., Chelsea
August 1, 1917

. . . If this weather goes on, my girl, I'm afraid you'll have to make a canvas boat of your picture and I will have to turn my writing table upside down and float out of the window. But perhaps God in His goodness will allow us to bob near each other for a moment. I have been informed by my great-aunt Charlotte (of Bangalore, Worple Avenue) that all those who are saved have expected a recurrence of the flood ever since the Kaiser was recognized to be Anti-Christ. And are Fully Prepared for it. Can't you see them "done up in impervious cases, like preserved meats" — like the Micawber family starting off for Australia? . . .

I spent a mournful half morning yesterday being thumped and

banged and held up by the heels by my doctor, who gave me no comfort at all, but half hinted, in fact, that given another hearty English winter or two the chances were that I'd bend and bow under my rheumatism until I become a sort of permanent croquet hoop. . . .

So, if in a year or two (I don't think the rain will stop before then) you *should* come through my gate and find me in the garden as a sort of decorative arch with a scarlet runner growing over me you will know then that the *worst* has happened.

Good-bye for now, mia bella. Salute my friends, frown on my enemies.

Katherine Mansfield to Virginia Woolf

August 1917

I had a last glimpse of you just before it all disappeared and I waved; I hope you saw.

Thank you for letting me see Asheham. It *is* very wonderful and I feel that it will flash upon one corner of my inward eye for ever.

It was good to have time to talk to you; we have got the same job, Virginia, and it is really very curious and thrilling that we should both, quite apart from each other, be after so very nearly the same thing. We are, you know; there's no denying it.

Don't let THEM ever persuade you that I spend any of my precious time swopping hats or committing adultery. I'm far too arrogant and proud. However, let them think what they like. . . . There's a most wonderful greengage light on the tree outside and little white clouds bobbing over the sky like rabbits. And I wish you could see some superb gladioli standing up in my studio very proud and defiant like Indian braves.

Yes, your Flower Bed is *very* good. There's a still, quivering, changing light over it all and a sense of those couples dissolving in the bright air which fascinates me —

Old Mother Gooseberry, my char from Ludgate Hill, has hung up her beetle bonnet: "Please m'm, if you would let me have the place to myself." So I am chased off, to sit among those marble pillars of brawn at the Library and read, *not* Henry James.

Katherine Mansfield to Dorothy Brett

[May 2, 1918]

It will be Great Fun, Larks and Jollifications. I am wearing, of course, a Simple Robe of White Crêpe de Chine and Pearl Butterfly presented by *our dear Queen*. Murry, naturally, top hat and carnation buttonhole.

Blessings on thee — I hope thou wilt be Godmother to my First Half Dozen —

Katherine.

P.S. We have decided (owing to the great war) to have a string band without brasses.

Katherine Mansfield to Lady Ottoline Morrell

Tuesday
47 Redcliffe Road
June 1918

It is simply dreadful that you should suffer so much and that doctors should be such useless fools. . . . What can one say? I know so devilishly well the agony of feeling perpetually ill and the longing — the immense longing just to have what everybody else takes so easily as their portion — health — a body that isn't an enemy — a body that isn't fiendishly engaged in the old, old "necessary" torture of — breaking one's spirit —

"Why won't you consent to having your spirit broken?" it wonderingly asks. "Everybody else yields without a murmur. And if you'd only realise the comfortable, boundless numbness that you would enjoy for ever after —" I wonder sometimes how it will end. One will never give in and so — All the same it would be more tolerable if only people understood — ever so little — but *subtly* — not with a sort of bread jelly sympathy — but with exquisite, rare friendship. (Oh, dear, I *still* believe in such a thing and *still* long for it.)

You see, I cannot help it. My secret belief — the innermost "credo" by which I live is — that *although* Life is loathsomely ugly and people are terribly often vile and cruel and base, nevertheless there is something at the back of it all—which if only I were great enough to understand would make *everything*, everything, indescribably beautiful. One just has glimpses, divine warnings—signs—Do you remember the day we cut the lavender? And do you remember when the Russian music sounded in that half-empty hall? Oh, those memories compensate for more than I can say—

Katherine Mansfield to Anne Estelle Rice

Monday
January 13, 1919

My darling Anne
After my Plan
For New Year's Day fell through,
I gave up hope
Of catching a rope
Which would land me down near you.
Since then I've been
(Pulse one sixteen
Temperature one o three)
Lying in bed
With a wandering head
And a weak, weak cup of tea.
Injections, chère
In my derrière
Driven into a muscular wad
With a needle thick
As a walking stick —
How can one believe in God!
Plus — pleurisy
And je vous dis
A head that went off on its own
Rode a circular race
That embraced every place
I ever shall know or have known.
I landed in Spain
Went to China by train

And rounded Cape Horn in a gale
Ate an ice in New York
Caught the boat for Majourke
And went up the Nile for a sail. . . .

Light refreshments, bouillon, raw eggs and orange juice were served on the journey. M. came in, fell over the screen, went out again, came back, dropped a candle, groaned, and went again, and the Faithful One changed the hot-water bottles so marvellously often that you never had a hot-water bottle at all. It was always being taken or brought back.

All this, Anne darling, is a new treatment that my new doctor has started — a treatment by injections. He is a wonderful man. In April he says I ought to go to a place like Corsica. Switzerland is impossible, tank de Lord. So I think I shall. . . . Well, Anne dearest, I'll keep on thinking and thinking about you, and wishing you all the luck there is. I shall be no good after to-day till the end of this week for I have another consignment shipped into me to-morrow. But I'll write again then. Quelle vie!

Katherine Mansfield to Virginia Woolf

April 1919

I have burned to write to you ever since you were here last. The East Wind made my journey in the train an impossibility; it set up ponds and pools in my left lung wherein the Germs and the Toxins — two families I detest — bathed and refreshed themselves and flourished and multiplied. But since then so many miracles have happened that I don't see how one will be able to bear real, full Spring. One is almost tired already — one wants to swoon, like Charles Lamb, before the curtain rises — Oh God! to look up again and see the sun like a great silver spangle, big bright buds on the trees, and the little bushes caught in a net of green. But what I chiefly love, Virginia, is to watch the people. Will you laugh at me? — it wrings my heart to see the people coming into the open again, timid, airing themselves; they idle, their voices change and their gesture. A most unexpected old man passes with a paper of flowers (for whom?), a soldier lies on the grass hiding his face, a young girl *flies* down a side street on the — positive — *wing* of a boy —

On April 5th our one daffodil came into flower and our cat, Charlie Chaplin, had 2 kittens.

Charles Chaplin

Athenæum   April

Athenæum is like a prehistoric lizard, in very little. He emerged very strangely — as though hurtling through space — flung by the indignant Lord. I attended the birth. Charles implored me. He behaved so strangely: he became a beautiful, tragic figure with blue-green eyes, terrified and wild. He would only lie still when I stroked his belly and said, "It's all right, old chap. It's bound to happen to a man sooner or later." And, in the middle of his pangs, his betrayer, a wretch of a cat with a face like a penny bun and the cat-equivalent of a brown bowler hat, rather rakish over one ear, began to *howl* from outside. "Fool that I have been!" said Charles, grinding his claws against my sleeve. The second kitten, April, was born during the night, a snug, compact little girl. When she sucks she looks like a small infant saying its prayers and *knowing* that Jesus loves her. They are both loves; their paws inside are very soft, very pink, just like unripe raspberries. . . .

Virginia, I have read your article on Modern Novels. You write so *damned* well, so *devilish* well.

But I positively must see you soon. I want to talk over so much — Your room with the too deep windows — I should love to be there now. Last time the rambler roses were nearly over and there was a sound of someone sawing wood.

Katherine Mansfield to Anne Estelle Rice

December 26, 1920

The parcel arrived on Xmas morning but it was a separate fête by itself, just your letter and the two enchanting sketches. I love them, Anne. They remind me of our spring together and the laburnum seems hung with little laughs. If you knew how often I think of that time at Looe, our picnic, the white-eyed kaffir, the midget infant hurling large pieces of Cornwall into the sea on the beach that afternoon! It's all as clear as to-day.

But you know, don't you? that all the times we have ever spent together are clear like that. And here — I am always sending you greetings, always sharing things with you. I salute you in tangerines and the curved petals of *roses-thé* and the crocus colour of the sea and in the moonlight on the *poire sauvage*. Many, many other things. It will *always* be so with me, however seldom I see you. I shall just go on rejoicing in the fact of you. And loving you and feeling in that family where Monsieur Le Beau Soleil est notre père nous sommes des soeurs.

I am still hard at the story-writing and still feeling that only now do I begin to see what I want to do. I am sending you my book. It is not a good one. I promise the next will be better but I just wanted you to have a copy. Living solitary these last months with a servant who is a born artist and says, "Un ou deux bananes font plus *intrigant* le compotier," and who returns from market with a basket, which just to see on the kitchen table is *food* for the day, makes work a great deal easier to get at. The *strain* is removed. At last one doesn't worry any more. And fancy one's domestique having an idea of what work is! She won't even let a person talk at the front door if I am working. She whispers to them to go to la porte de la cuisine . . . "parceque c'est très énervant pour Madame d'entendre causer quelqu'un pendant qu'elle travaille!" It's like being in heaven with an ange gardienne.

Katherine Mansfield to Anne Estelle Rice

Christmas Eve, 1921

Suddenly this afternoon as I was thinking of you there flashed across my inward eye a beautiful poppy that we stood looking at in the garden of the Hotel at Looe. Do you remember that marvelous black sheen at the base of the petal and the big purplish centre? Then that took me back to our improvised café — just the same table with a bottle on it, and ourselves, out of space and time . . . for the moment! And from that I began to think of your très blue eyes that I love so and your neck, and the comb you wore in your hair the last time you dined with us and a pink pinny you had on the first time I saw you in the studio in Paris. These things are not the whole of my Anne, but they are signs and tokens of her and for the want of a thousand others what wouldn't I give at this moment to put my arms round her and give her a small squeeze.

I shall be in Paris, I hope, from May on this year. Will you by any chance be there? I am going on a preliminary visit almost at once to see a specialist there — a *Russian* — and to have some teeth pulled out and pulled in again. Then I come back here to save pennies for my flight in

May. I believe this Russian cures people with my complaint. He sounds wonderful.

It's so long since I have heard of any of the *old set.* Where are they? New friends are not — never can be — the same, and all mine seem to be people I know as a writer, not as a common garden human being. Whether they care personally for the smell of tangerines or not I haven't the least idea. I can't really care for people who are cut off at the head. I like them to exist as far as their hearts *au moins.* Don't ever come to Switzerland, Anne. It's all *scenery.* One gets the same on a Mountain Railway at 6d. a go and get off after the last bumping. But the Swiss!! They are always cutting down trees and as the tree falls the hausfrau rushes out of the kitchen to see, waving a pig-knife and shouting a joyful *voilà!* I believe they are full of virtue but virtue is a bad boisson to be *full* of.

Hugh Walpole/Rebecca West/Joseph Conrad/ Katherine Mansfield/Virginia Woolf

The English novelist Hugh Walpole began his career in 1909 at the age of twenty-five, with the publication of *Wooden Horses.* The event swept him into the vibrant literary community of London, where he met H. G. Wells, Max Beerbohm, Harold Nicholson, Katherine Mansfield, Vita Sackville-West and Violet Hunt, among many others. An aging Henry James became one of Walpole's mentors and Robert Ross — an intimate of the late Oscar Wilde — one of his closest friends. A string of successes followed, including *Mr. Perrin and Mr. Traill* in 1911, *Fortitude* in 1913 and *The Dark Forest* in 1916. Popular with readers as well as with most critics, Walpole wrote more than a dozen additional books in his lifetime, adapting some as plays. His correspondence encompassed almost all the English literary lights of his time, including Joseph Conrad and (of course) Virginia Woolf.

Hugh Walpole to His Mother

[September 1909]

Dearest Mother,

A very little line so that you shouldn't think that I'd disappeared altogether into some mysterious limbo, never to emerge. H. J. wants me to
stay here more or less indefinitely—but I shall have to come back to
town tomorrow and perhaps will return here later.

We have had some extraordinary talks. You can imagine what it
must be to hear all about Thackeray, Stevenson, Dickens, Carlyle and
the rest intimately from first hand. And then all his talk about the Novel
and his own things is quite amazing. It is a wonderful thing for me and
will of course alter my whole life. He is, I think, a really great man. The
honour is all the greater as Mrs Prothero, wife of the editor of the
Quarterly, told me yesterday that I am now supposed to have more influence over him than anyone, and say things to him that no one else can—
and so I get given messages to give *him* and act the diplomatist. He wants
to come to tea at Lambeth and see all of you. I'm sure you would love him.

You'll all be interested to know that *Maradick* was finished on Monday. I feel curiously lost without it.

I'll see you soon I hope.

Love to all,
Yr. loving
Hugh.

Joseph Conrad to Hugh Walpole

[Fall 1920]

My dear Hugh,

I left the "civilities" to Jessie who has no doubt written to you already.
This is only to tell you that I have read the book—which is a book—a
creation—no small potatoes indeed—très chic; and if the truth must be
told très fort even—considerable in purpose, successful in execution and
deep in feeling—a genuine Walpole, this, with an unexpected note of
maturity in design and composition; and holding the interest from page
to page, which in itself is not a common quality. O! dear, no!

Katherine Mansfield to Hugh Walpole

[Fall 1920]

Dear Hugh Walpole,

Please do not praise me. But—let me say how I look forward to that talk, one of these days. The fact that you care about writing as you do, that "you are working," is such happiness that all my good wishes and my sympathy cannot repay you for letting me know.

Your from-this-time-forth *"constant reader,"*

Katherine Mansfield.

Violet Keppel Trefusis

From November 1918 to March 1919 English society was rocked by the culmination of a passionate love affair in its midst. Wildly infatuated, Violet Keppel (rumored to be the illegitimate daughter of King George V) and writer Vita Sackville-West eloped to France. The affair continued after Violet's 1919 marriage to Denys Trefusis, who finally forced his wife to give up her lover. The affair and its aftermath forever branded Sackville-West, in particular, a "Sapphist," a label she does not seem to have rejected. In 1923, in fact, she published the novel *Challenge*, a thinly veiled account of her affair with Violet. She and Violet exchanged numerous ardent love letters, but only those received and preserved by Vita survive. Furious over the episode, Denys Trefusis burned almost all those from Vita to Violet.

Violet Trefusis to Vita Sackville-West

[1918]

My beautiful,

Because there's no getting away from the fact that you are beautiful. I become inarticulate when I look at you—at the splendid ivory column of your neck, of your eyes like smouldering jewels, at your mouth with its voluptuously chiselled lips, palely red, like some fading wine stain.

I may be writing rubbish, but then I am drunk. Drunk with the beauty of my Mitya! All today I was incoherent. I tell you, there is a barbaric splendour about you that conquered not only me, but everyone who saw you. You are made to *conquer*, Mitya, not to be conquered. You were *superb*. You could have the world at your feet. Even my mother, who is not easily impressed, shared my opinion. *You have also changed*, it appears? They said, this evening after you had gone, that you were like a dazzling Gypsy. My sister's words, not mine. A Gypsy potentate, a sovereign — what you will, but still a Gypsy.

They also said they noticed a new exuberance in you, something akin to sheer animal spirits — that never was there before. You may love me, Mitya, but anyone would be *proud* to be loved by you, even if they were to be thrown aside and forgotten — for somebody new.

Everyone is vulgar, petty, "mesquin," beyond all words, in comparison with you. It would be an unpardonable *impudence* to limit you to one life, one love, one interest. Yours are *all* lives, *all* loves, *all* interests! Beloved, my beautiful, I have shown myself naked to you, mentally, physically and morally.

Good God alive! No one in this earth has as much claim to you as I have. *No one in this world*.

Yours, *Lushka*

Violet Trefusis to Vita Sackville-West

[1919]

Men tiliche,

I have been talking all the evening about Paris — Paris when we first arrived there — Knoblock's flat — O Mitya! It makes me drunk to remember it, and the hoard of days, weeks and months we had ahead of us.

I shall never forget the mad exhilaration of the nights I spent wandering about with Julian as long as I live! Even Monte Carlo was not better. As good, but not better. It makes my brain reel to remember! The night we went to the Palais Royal and the night we went to *"La Femme et le Pantin"* were the happiest in my life. I was simply drunk with happiness. We were just bohemians, Julian and I, with barely enough to pay for our dinner, free, without a care or a relation in the world. O god! I was happy! I thought it would never come to an end. I was madly, insatiably in love with you.

Julian was a poet *sans sou ni maille:* I was Julian's mistress. One day Julian would write great poetry and make money — but, *en attendant,* we just had enough to live on. I worshipped Julian. The Paris of François Villon, *Louise, La Bohème,* Alfred de Musset, all jumbled up, lay at our feet: we were part of it, essentially.

As much part of it as the hairy concierge and the *camelots* who wear canvas shoes and race down the boulevards nasally screaming, "La Petue! La Presse!" and "La Femme et le Pantin." I lay back in an abandonment of happiness and gave myself up to your scandalously indiscreet caresses, in full view of the whole theater!

Not ladylike perhaps! But then I had never known what it was like to be a lady!

Then we drove back in the dark taxi, and the chauffeur smiled knowingly and sympathetically at you. I'm sure he thought: *"C'est pas souvent qu'ils doivent se payer ça, pauvres petits . . ."* Then the flat, the deserted, unutterably romantic Palais Royal, Julian's impatience, Julian's roughness, Julian's clumsy, fumbling hands . . . My God! I can't bear to think of it!

Mitya . . . Mitya . . . How I adored you! Our life, our blessed bohemian life! It *can't* be at an end! It can't. It *can't.* I love you as feverishly, as passionately as I did then. I love you with a passion that only increases, never diminishes.

As Professor Ross said to me tonight, you are made for passion, your perfectly proportioned body, your heavy-lidded brooding eyes, your frankly sensual mouth and chin. You are made for it and so am I.

I said to Professor Ross that I thought you were one of the most moral people I knew. He spat with derision: "Pah! With that mouth, with that chin. With those antecedents! Tell me another!" (Professor Ross cheered me up considerably while he was here.)

My beautiful, my lovely, I want you so. . . .

Violet Trefusis to Vita Sackville-West

Golf Hotel, St Jean de Luz
July 1919

At last I got a letter from you this morning. I hadn't heard since Friday, I quite agree with all you say about us, darling, but I cannot feel your serenity. How can there be serenity without contentment? How can I be contented? I see nothing but strife ahead of us. But, O! I *do* feel all you say to be true of us. You say you were at Hendaye. When were you at Hendaye and with whom?

Mitya, you don't know to what a pitch I have brought my truthfulness with L. This is the sort of conversation that takes place constantly:

L: What are you thinking about?
Me: V
L: Do you wish V. were here?
Me: Yes
L: (All this actually happened.) You don't care much about being with men, do you?
Me: No, I infinitely prefer women.
L: You are strange, aren't you?
Me: Stranger than you have any idea of.

The above conversation took place word for word last night and it is a typical one. I will *not* lie to L., save in an absolute extremity. I know the truth hurts him frightfully, but I should feel absolutely beneath contempt if I lied to him. I almost think that if he asked me point blank to tell him the whole truth from beginning to end, without omitting a single detail, I should do so. It would kill him, you know what I mean, but he is essentially a person one cannot lie to.

I have never felt the smallest scruple about lying to anyone else. Almost everything I say makes him wince, poor thing, but it is better than the other alternative. I know it is. Darling, you hold different views, don't you? And I know if you could overhear some of our conversations, you would be desperately sorry for Loge.

I will never deceive you, but *you* must never deceive me. *Tu me dois cela.* Don't think it amuses me to see L. writhe in agony sometimes. It does *not* — nothing has ever amused me less, but I know the answer to things he asks me, if it is the truthful one, will hurt terribly, and I know I would be disloyal to *mea*——to withhold it or to modify it in any way, so I never hesitate.

Everything is infinitely painful,
et plus ça va, plus je t'aime.

O Mitya, you must be straight with H. about me! *You must.* It is *so* despicable to tell lies to someone who cares for one. All the time I have been here I have neither done nor said anything you could possibly have taken exception to. Are you as straight with H?

O darling, I fear not . . . *Accorde moi cela, et je me montrerai si infiniment reconnaissante . . .*

I can't tell you how marvellous the sea is. It is blazing hot and there is a thunderstorm coming from the Spanish coast ... I can hear the thunder rumbling through the mountain passes.

Violet Trefusis to Vita Sackville-West

February 14, 1920
Hotel Ritz, Paris

My darling beloved,

I am simply dazed and sodden with pain; it seems incredible that I should go on living — how *can* I bear it, how can I bear it?

My God, my God, and happiness was so near. *Nous l'avons assurs* — Mitya, I shall go mad. I know I shall, and we'd gone, we'd gone, we had *got away* — and my darling, my darling, my heart is simply breaking. I can scarcely hold the pen. It's too dreadful, it's too dreadful. If I had thought I was never going to see you again, I would have drowned myself tonight. If you don't write to me I shall still. What is so perfectly *awful* to me is the feeling that our separation is partially due to a misunderstanding. There has NEVER never never in my life been any attempt at what you thought from that person. *Never* —

He said his pride wouldn't allow him to say more, and he particularly doesn't want anyone to know that there has never been anything of that nature and scarcely anything of the other. I loathe having to write this, but what I told you this evening is exactly true down to the minutest detail. O God — if only I — or he — could have explained. I told him I hated him and that I would rather go to St. Moritz than stay alone with him if neither Pat nor Bagnold can come. At the present moment he is sobbing next door.

I told him I was going to write to you all the time, and you to me. I *will* force him to answer your letter. I feel absolutely merciless towards him. He has completely and irrevocably done for himself and he knows it. I told H. to tell you that it was against my will, but now you know more about it than he does, thank God. O Mitya Mitya, Why didn't you give me time to explain? It was even less than you imagine now. You must know, you must know. It kills me to write it, but you *must* know all this.

I am going to try to speak to you on the telephone tomorrow morning. That man has ordered a motor at 11 to go to Toulon — it will take days — but I don't care what I do or where I go. It's Toulon, because I've asked Pat to meet me there. Mitya, Mitya, and you are so near and so supremely unavailable you might be on another continent. Mitya, it is breaking me. I feel I must die.

I don't know where you're going or anything. Try to go somewhere by yourself. I don't know where to write to. You must let me know. O my beloved, my beloved, I feel there has never been sorrow or pain or suffering for me till now.

Violet Trefusis to Vita Sackville-West

[October 1920]
Clingendaal, Holland

Mitya, I wish you weren't so beautiful! Supposing I had ceased to care for you and had dismissed you, trait by trait — finally there would come the insurmountable stumbling block of your beauty, and I should be as hopelessly inveigled as ever I was!

I dread it, because it is without flaw. Of its "school" quite perfect. You are just as undeniably beautiful as the cathedral in Seville or the "view from the Acropolis." There can be no two opinions about that. You are indomitably, incorrigibly beautiful and I wish to Heaven you weren't because it is the only thing I can't resist.

Violet Trefusis to Vita Sackville-West

October 14, 1920
Clingendaal, Holland

I love nothing in the world but you. Test after test is applied to my love, and test after test is vanquished triumphantly. For you I would commit any crime; for you I would sacrifice any other love. My love for you terrifies and overpowers me.

I am writing this for myself, not for you. I am so hypersensitive where you're concerned that not the slightest inflection of your voice, not the subtlest nuance of your letters, escapes me. I got one yesterday that was cold, almost impersonal. I worried myself almost sick over it.

My love for you is all-engrossing. There is no other love in my life — no other occupation. Everything else is of such mediocre importance compared to you that it is hardly worth mentioning.

You might so easily kill me.

My life is in your hands. If you deceived me in any vital issue, you could kill me.

You must not deceive me. I don't deserve that you should. My whole life is *yours*. I never do anything which does not indirectly concern you. You are never out of my thoughts. You must be ill for it is a crime to deceive the person one loves.

E. M. Forster/Virginia Woolf

A complicated and principled man, E. M. Forster wrote subtle novels that probed the nature of personal relationships and raised questions about English society. Gracefully and fearlessly, he told the truth as he knew it in works such as *A Passage to India* and *Maurice*. *A Passage to India* manifests Forster's fascination with India, originally sparked by his Indian friend Syed Ross Masood, while the posthumously published *Maurice* sheds light on his gay identity. Forster expressed concerns about *Maurice* in a January 23, 1915, letter to Forrest Reid. He wrote also to his lover, a handsome, athletic policeman named Robert (Bob) Buckingham. Two essential aspects of his character, his homosexuality and his belief in the importance of personal and civic integrity, impelled him to campaign against censorship on behalf of other writers' works, notably James Hanley's *Boy* and D. H. Lawrence's *The Rainbow*. An extensive correspondence delineates Forster's contact with the Bloomsbury crowd — including Lytton Strachey, Lady Ottoline Morrell and Vanessa Bell — as well as his acquaintance with Christopher Isherwood and Tennessee Williams. He also maintained a tangled literary camaraderie with Virginia Woolf that yielded a short, simple, yet deeply affecting note of condolence to Leonard Woolf after her 1941 suicide.

E. M. Forster to Syed Ross Masood

Harnham, Monument Green, Weybridge
5 December 1914

Dearest SRM

Are you going to give me a Xmas present? I meant to give you nothing, but have lately thought of 'Georgian Verse' which has made some stir over here, so shall send it to you, packed up with mother's book. It will keep you in touch with latest developments, though you will scarcely care for them.

Dodo Morison is at present the sole authority for your latest — the rest of us marvel and are silent. O many sided youth! I am very fit and well — occasionally have wretched fits of longing to see you, followed by days when I don't think about you at all. I expect that's much what you feel about me. In the bottom of my heart I long to see you always.

Masood, a young lady has fallen in love with me — at least so I judge from her letters. Awkward is it not — awkward and surprising. You would be flattered and twirl your moustache, but I am merely uncomfortable. I wish she would stop, as she is very nice, and I enjoyed being friends. What an ill constructed world this is! Love is always being given where it is not required.

I have just been to Oxford for a week end, but saw little; an Indian to tea — Hindu, I forget his name. The Universities grow more & more concerned about your compatriots; it is indeed a problem. We have lost the art of digesting you that we had in your father's time. I can hardly hear of any cases in which an Englishman & Indian have become real friends.

ever thine
Morgan

E. M. Forster to Forrest Reid

23 January 1915

Oh my dear Reid, I have been in the most awful gloom lately, and who do you think finally raised me from it? You will be so contemptuous of me. D. H. Lawrence. Not the novels, but their author, a sandy haired passionate Nibelung, whom I met last Thursday at a dinner party. He is really extraordinarily nice.

I'm not going to write about him though, but about a pretty serious matter which I have not had the spirit to tackle until now. I would rather have talked about it to you than written, but my chances of Ireland recede. I have written a novel which cannot be published, and if you were willing to read it I could send it you. You would, in some way, sympathise with it, but I know that in other ways it might put a severe strain on our friendship, which terrifies me. My attitude — I realise more fully than you can — is not yours. I have heard you feel things I cannot,

and draw distinctions that mean nothing to me. I should be very miserable indeed if your feelings towards me altered as the result of reading
this book, even though I should think (as I do think) that they ought not
to alter, for I have not written one word of which I am ashamed. I am
taking quite a grave risk for two reasons — first one's ordinary desire to
be read and secondly my knowledge that you will be glad to know I have
written *something,* and am not as sterile as I am obliged to pretend to the
world.

Whatever your decision, you will not mention the book's existence
to anyone, I know.

Yours ever
E.M.F.

E. M. Forster to Sir Henry Newbolt

Harnham, Monument Green, Weybridge
7 November 1915

Dear Newbolt

D. H. Lawrence, whom I regard as a man of genius and a serious writer,
tells me that his novel *The Rainbow* (Methuen) has been confiscated by
the authorities. I haven't read the book nor shall I have time to do so
before leaving England; but I don't think that either that or the fact that
certain passages in it would probably offend me, makes any difference
to my indignation. I write in great haste — which please excuse — and I
am not sure what your attitude over the matter will be. But I venture at
all events to bring it to your notice, remembering all your frankness and
sympathy while we walked on the downs. Some people would say "Oh
but *this* isn't the time to make a fuss"; I feel myself that the right to
literary expression is as great in war as it was ever in peace, and in far
greater danger, and I write on the chance of your being willing and able
to protect it.

I am off to Egypt on Red Cross work. If all goes well I shall come
and see you next spring. With best wishes and remembrances:

Yours very sincerely
E. M. Forster

You'll probably dislike *The Rainbow* — I make no appeal on that
ground. But it represents over a year's hard and sincere work, I know.

E. M. Forster to Virginia Woolf

24 October 1922

Dear Virginia,

I like *Jacob's Room* and am sure it is good. You have clean cut away the difficulties that so bother me and that I feared in *Night & Day* were gaining on you — all those Blue Books of the interior and exterior life of the various characters — their spiritual development, income, social positions, etc. etc. The danger is that when cut away these detach with them something that ought to remain — at least according to my notion of a novel, namely the reader's interest in at least one of the characters as a character — if that goes we merely swing about among blobs of amusement or pathos. You keep this interest in Jacob. This I find a tremendous achievement — the greatest in the book and the making of the book. I don't yet understand how, with your method, you have managed it, but of course am reading the book again. Have only just finished it; and am confused by wondering what developments, both of style and form, might come out of it, which is of course outside the present point. The book was quite long enough — ! this means not what it looks, but that some of your odd new instruments gave hints of scratches and grinds towards the end. e.g. the Proper Nomenclature. Having once taken such an instrument up you couldn't possibly lay it down, its occasional application to the surface was imperative. This is a minor point though, for the damage done by the scratches is too little to count. They disappear in the general liberation. — One very important thing is that most of the book is seen through happiness; you have got quite clear from the sensitive sorrower whom novelists cadge up to as the easiest medium for observations.

I will now say no more except that my favourite pages are 63–4.

I will return Percy Lubbock next week.

A muddle of plans seems ahead. I think I won't come to your old ladies this early November. But I should like to, later. You may wear my pyjamas until I arrive.

I much enjoyed my visit.

Thank you very much for giving me the book. I do think it an amazing success, and it's full of beauty, indeed is beautiful.

Morgan

E. M. Forster to Syed Ross Masood

[May 23, 1923]

Dearest SRM,

I seem to need you more than usual today. It is a year since Mohammad died, and I have just had another blow though slight in comparison as Vicary, of whom I am fond is going to Canada on Saturday. I am left with plenty of trusty acquaintances and relatives, but life is alarmingly empty in other respects, and no doubt will continue to empty itself as I grow older. All that remains positive, is the expression of oneself through art, and this at present I cannot attain to. Art seems the only true vent for our sorrows and for the dissatisfactions that are somehow more painful, even than our sorrows. It alone redresses the bias against romance that runs through the material of the world. Personal relations succeed in this way less and less. It is my faith — not other people's. I bring less and less to them. You are the only person to whom I can open my heart and feel occasionally that I am understood.

Twelve chapters of my novel are in typescript and have been shown to the Publisher who has offered £500 in advance of royalties — good terms. When eighteen are in typescript I shall send them to you. They will give you a good deal of work, especially the police part of which I am innocent, despite Mr. Goad. I wonder whether anything should be added to the dedication ('To Syed Ross Masood'). I don't want to *exhibit* our intimacy, yet it might be important to indicate its length and solidity. Otherwise the reader may think it's some temporary intimacy; 'in Memory and in Expectation' occurred to me. Or 'in Remembrance of the past sixteen years and in Certainty of the years to come'. I can't quite get what I want. I shall in any case be guided by your wishes in the matter.

Thanks for your letter. I am glad your prospects are no worse. I am well, 'successful', and cheerful outwardly, but my heart aches.

Thine dear boy,
Morgan

E. M. Forster to Virginia Woolf

The Union Society, Cambridge
5 June 1927

Dear Virginia,

I don't arrange my thoughts about your book easily and am not sure that it invites arrangement. I should like to come and see you and talk some time if I may. It is awfully sad, very beautiful both in (non-radiant) colour and shape, it stirs me much more to questions of whether and why than anything else you have written. The uneasiness of life seems to well up between all the words, the excitement of life on the other hand to be observed, stated. This I believe to be right: excitement would dry up those little winds. I must now read it again — am inclined to think it your best work (my mother by the way is sure it is — she took to it immensely). Thank you again for giving it me.

I am up here taking my part in the Life of the College, and, after so many years peaceful cadging, not enjoying it very much. Such a dirty place, always washing one's hands, and bad complicated food.

Morgan

E. M. Forster to W. J. H. Sprott

West Hackhurst, Abinger Hammer, Dorking
16 July 1931

Dearest Sebastian.

As for the flat, do come for the 22nd as well as the 23rd. If I want to sleep there myself on the 23rd, will be there be room [sic], or does Les come? I have got muddled. (Don't on any account put him off.) And if the flat should be wanted at 12.0. midday on the 24th (not by me!) is it possible to you to leave it empty by that time? I am coming up on the 23rd to lunch with Dobrée, and if flat's full shall either proceed to Cambridge or sleep at Joe's — no difficulty in either.

What think you of Maisie her letter as apart from her handwriting? Like you, I am not much worried over the thing except by it's being there, which one resents, and it is annoying to think that I have enhanced him in her eyes. Such a thing to get to know a writer! On the other hand this sort of thing is inevitable for him, and I got to know him just when, and only because, he had broken off an engagement. So the class of events one calls Fate have worked more for me than against. I'm quite sure that his feeling for me is something he has never had before. It's a spiritual feeling which has extended to my physique — pardon, cher maitre, such nomenclature; I desire to convey that it's something he calls MORGAN he's got hold of, so that my lack of youth and presence, which in other relationships might hinder or depress me, are here no disadvantage, in fact the reverse. He must be made to see that there can't be a menage à trois, which I think is his dream, and, for the moment, possibly hers too; but he should easily see this when told.

Yes, the flat in the rain must have been dreary, but what price Gwen Lally at Tewkesbury? Here I lay happily in bed, or read, or finished Voltaire, or talked pleasantly with my mother. I enclose the £20; judging by the paper this morning you and I can be the only people left who have any money. If there is not the general crash, I shall send you some more at Christmas. If there is, I suppose we may all be much where we are.

Oh the Bells, the Woolves — or rather Virginia, for I do like Leonard! Oh how I do agree, and if to become anti-Bloomsbury were not to become Bloomsbury, how I would become it! But to turn one's backside to them is the only course — they will never have the grace to penetrate it, their inquisitiveness never had any spunk, that is why one loathes it so. Turned well away from them, let one read their books, which are *very* good, and look at their mural designs, which may be good too, and that is the end. I am sorry at what you say about Lytton, and surprised — I thought his curiosity was of the pardonable type, and that he was getting both solid and charming. What was it you mean? Ottoline I like better, now that you do, and I look forward to seeing her, which I certainly usen't to, but I 'don't altogether trust her' — helpful phrase. It's excellent news that the Bells &ct are ravaged by fear; now that's the sort of thing I should never have thought of!

Had a lot more to say, but can't remember, so had better stop. I believe, since I began to write, that Les does come on the 23rd, so I definitely won't come for the night, though I may see you during the day.

Much pleased with my own Voltaire article.

Love to your mother. Love to Velda.

Love to you
M.

E. M. Forster to W. J. H. Sprott

West Hackhurst, Abinger Hammer, Dorking
4 December 1931

Dearest Sebastian,

You are warmly invited to lunch here on the 14th, but now do you want to come? For I don't think I want to come up to town that night, since I must be up for the night of the 15th. What *I want* then is for you to lunch here on the 14th (or tea, if it suited your routes better), and to lunch with me in town on the 15th.

Will you do what I want?

Nay, I have been greatly tossed by the Waives, and you will be delighted to hear that I was *repelled* by the emotion emanating from Percival, told Leonard so, and he told Virginia. But moderate your content. With this repulsion mingles the conviction that the book will be a classic, and while you will pertly pipe up 'Well why not?' the gap isn't, for a *person of culture*, so easy to skip. For there is emotion, and I was interested to learn that Vanessa too was overcome by it, though in a favourable sense. The position is that I have got to being bored by Virginia's superciliousness and maliciousness, which she has often wounded me with in the past, and with this boredom comes a more detached view of her work. A new book of hers is affects me like a newly discovered manuscript. One unrolls the papyrus — yes! this time a masterpiece. This too I have told her. I don't know what she makes of the gap.

Your remark about her hatred interests and cheers me, and perhaps it is true.

Love from *meorgan*.

I put in cheque for £10, which I mentioned for December, and I will write again on the subject of money in the New Year, when I shall know better how I stand. Mother sold her furniture well — £115 when they expected £80 — and is selling the house for £1750 — probably worth £2000, but what a blessing to have found a purchaser.

E. M. Forster to Robert J. Buckingham

W[est] H[ackhurst].   *29 May 1940*

Dear Bob, what a lovely day we spent together. I don't think I have ever been happier with you, the weather, the rowing, the flowers, all made it into a sort of poetry. Siegfried's poem 'Everyone suddenly burst out singing' came into my mind at Kew, and I felt the trees &^{ct} were all taking flight into a better place and taking us with them. I don't often feel like that at my age, but you probably understand since you appreciated the curiousness and the timelessness of time in Priestley's play. I haven't lived as much as I might have in that country, indeed it isn't easy to get there except in the company of someone whom one loves. It is so easy to go on inside a little case of wisecracks and sneers and being slightly tough lest one gets hurt. What a thing to have someone whom you're fond of and can trust! Even that sad and lovely film we saw in the evening seemed to belong — compassion and enjoyment are joined up together somehow, though one doesn't feel them both at the same time. It must be grand to have the eye that *sees* things, like yourself: i.e. colours, shapes of clouds, &^{ct}. As soon as I look I start to think — though I am better at that since knowing you, it is one of the things you've shown me.

Mrs Mawe is stopping on indefinitely, which means that Wolfgang's visit is off unless he cares to go to that flat and be partly alone, which I don't suppose he will. I have written him.

Florence seemed in trouble over the phone, over some Dutch relative who had been interned. I could not make out. I hope you'll ring her some time.

I am to do the pamphlet, as now the B.B.C. (i.e. Malcolm) want me to broadcast regularly to India. I may also be doing Local Defence! funny if I was in the field before you. I don't expect it will have to come to anything, as I cannot fire a gun. Bone and the rabbit-cartridges are to go out tonight.

Stephen Spender did not bore me at lunch, for the reason that he was in Devonshire — 'Horizon' is to be shifted.

If I can get up next week, can you see me any morning, or are some dates impossible. Let me know soon, and also (which goes without saying) let me know whenever it is possible for you to stay.

Forrest Reid's new vol. of biography, 'Private Road' is one of the best things he's ever done. I'm just enchanted by it, also it's very witty and well written. It really ought to have got into the first paragraph of this letter, for it's a sort of poetry too.

Love
Morgan

E. M. Forster to Leonard Woolf

Fletton Tower, Peterborough
3 April 1941

Dear Leonard,

I have just seen the Times feel a bit trembly and unable to think of anyone but myself, I will write again to you. As I daresay you know she had invited me to come and I had suggested doing so ~~Later~~ later in this month. I am just going to Cambridge, dear Leonard, it will seem empty and strange, I can't write any more now, only send my deepest love and sadness. Leslie Humphry came over that very day, and we talked a great deal about Virginia, he will be desolated like so many of all generations.

Morgan

E. M. Forster to Christopher Isherwood

25 June 1948

Dearest Christopher

Tennessee Williams got up too late to reach Cambridge. Vidal arrived and I wish hadn't, as I disliked him a lot. I hope anyhow he returned you Gerald's *Street Car.* I am looking forward to seeing it on the stage, where its colour, violence, and seedfulness should be effective. I did not find the characters alive (my old whimper), but that is where actors and actresses are so useful. Alive themselves, often through no wish of their own, they are compelled to vivify the dramatist's ideas. I shouldn't have thought it was a good play — with the chief character an invalid who ought to have been looked after earlier. Still the stage is always surprising me into a good deal of pleasure. The poker scene might look lovely.

What I am really writing about though is *Maurice*. I should very much like a talk alone with you during the next week or so. I am ashamed at shirking publication but the objections are formidable. I am coming up on Tuesday for a night or probably two. Wednesday should be all right. If you wish to drop me a line here, do so. Otherwise I will ring you in London.

Lovely letter from Ben. Herring &c comes to Cambridge at the end of the month.

Love
Morgan

Harold Nicholson/Vita Sackville-West

Like Leonard and Virginia Woolf, Vita Sackville-West and Harold Nicholson entered marriage with their eyes wide open and on remarkably equal terms. Deeply fond of each other, they understood their shared need for gay connections and gave each other the freedom to pursue outside interests. Harold had his affairs and, indeed, contracted a nasty venereal disease in the process, but it was Vita's amours that received the lion's share of attention in their correspondence. These letters between Harold and Vita show their agreement at work during Vita's affairs with Violet Trefusis and Virginia Woolf.

Harold to Vita

Foreign Office
2 September 1918

Hadji has got a brilliant idea which she mustn't laugh at. It is this. Mar is to get a little cottage in Cornwall or elsewhere — and it is to be a Padlock cottage: and the Padlock is to be that Hadji never goes there, or sees it. It will just have two or three rooms, and will be hers absolutely, and she can go there when she likes and be quite alone and have whom she wants. Then the Padlock is that Hadji never goes there and can't (by the rules of the Padlock) even be asked — or even know when she is there or who she has got with her. It will make it a real escape from the

YOKE [of marriage]. And when I am rich, I shall have one too, just the same and on the same condition.

Darling, take the idea seriously and think over it.

Vita Sackville-West to Harold Nicholson

Bordighera, Italy
5 December 1919

I feel it's such a mockery my writing you superficial letters, and I dread writing you *real* ones; that's really why I have written so little. I hate unreality and convention, especially between you and me. It's an insult to us both. So I'm going to write you a real letter now, a long one, and, please, you must realise that I'm writing quite sanely, and not think that anything I say is hysteria or theatrical, or anything but the sober fact and truth.

You see, I don't think you realise except in a very tiny degree what's going on or what's been going on. I don't think you have taken the thing seriously. (Of course, I know you have hated my being away and all that, but I think you have looked on it all as more or less transitory and "wild oats" — your own expression.) But surely, darling, you don't think I would have gone away from you and risked all that I *have* risked — your love, B.M.'s love, Dada's love, and my own reputation — for a whim? (I don't really care a damn about the reputation, but I do care about the rest.) Don't you realise that only a very great force could have brought me to risk these things? Many little things have shown me that you don't realise it. For instance: you talked of "wild oats." You talked of my being away as a holiday. You write of V. as Mrs Denys Trefusis — don't you realise that that name is a stab to me every time I hear it? every time I see it on an envelope? Yet you write of her as that as a joke.

There is another thing you don't realise. When I come back this time, V. and I [will] give each other up for ever. It is the only thing we can do, but it is going to break me for the time being. I'm not grumbling about it, or suggesting any other course; only, simply, there it is . . . Please, darling, don't write to me and say why is this necessary? *please* don't do that, or refer to it; I know you are such an angel that you wouldn't ever want me to do anything so drastic, but you must let me decide this for myself, and I *have* decided.

This brings me to the question of my coming to Paris. It is quite true that I shan't be well, and I really won't travel sitting up all night under those conditions. Denys is coming to Cannes on the 15th. I will come back then. [She didn't.] I don't want to write any more about this. I am infinitely sorry to know B.M. will be in Paris. I should have liked to be alone with you, or failing that, by myself.

Then, oh Hadji, my darling darling Hadji (you *are* my darling Hadji, because if it wasn't for you I would go off with V.), there's another thing. You say you only want to *tromper* me with myself. But that's *impossible,* darling; there can't be anything of *that* now — just now, I mean. Oh Hadji, can't you realise a little? I *can't* put it into words. It isn't that I don't love you; I do. I do! How much you will never know.

The whole thing is the most awful tragedy, and I see only too clearly that I was never fit to marry somebody so sane, so good, so sweet, so limpid, as yourself; it wasn't fair on you. If you had asked me to live with you, I would have done so. It is all I am fit for. But at least I love you with a love so profound that it can't be uprooted by another love, more tempestuous and altogether on a different plane.

Hadji, I don't want to hurt you, I can't *really* hurt you, can I, when I tell you I love you so infinitely much?

Oh dear, all the fount of anguish with which I started this letter seems to have exhausted itself and I must stop. Don't think it a 'rattled' letter, it's so much graver than that, if you only knew. And don't be afraid I shall do anything awful.

Mar

Vita Sackville-West to Harold Nicholson

Dover
[February 9, 1920]

Hadji, since I wrote to you this afternoon things have happened. I went out to send some telegrams and to post my letter, and then I was standing looking at the sea when I saw Denys [Trefusis] coming towards me. He asked me where Violet was. I said I had promised not to tell him. He said he would find out, or stay with me till I left Dover and come wherever I went because he knew I would join her sooner or later. So I told him, as it seemed useless to conceal it. So he and I are going there [Amiens] tomorrow, and he is going to ask her whether she will go back to him. I shall try my utmost to make her, O God, O God, how miserable and frightened I am — and if she refuses, he says he will never have anything to do with her again. I do not for a moment think she will consent, as I urged her *so* much this morning and she refused so positively; she said she would never live with him even if I did not exist. I will try to make her, I will, I will, I will; I will only see her in front of Denys, and he shall see that I will try.

If she consents, and goes with him, I shall come to you. I am trying to be good, Hadji. I want so dreadfully to be with her, and I cannot *bear* to think of her being with him, but I shall try to make her. We are going to France. I nearly had a fit when I saw him. I can't help seeing the ludicrous side of this journey with him — will we go in the same railway-carriage or what? The whole thing is so unreal; everything is unreal except the pain of it. He has spent all the afternoon and most of the evening walking up and down my room in this filthy little hotel. I do not believe she will go back to him, and he says he will have nothing more to do with her if she won't. Hadji, it is the most extraordinary situation I have ever been in; I think you would think so too if you were me.

But the point is that if, after all his arguments and all my persuasion, she still refuses, he will go away leaving her for good. And she *will* refuse, I am almost sure she will refuse.

Hadji, I will try, I swear I will try, both for your sake and a little bit for his as I think he is too fine a person to be broken, but of course it is for you really. I *will* try, I feel strong, I did this morning and I can keep it up.

Poor Denys, he is really a very splendid person, though I know you think he is mad.

O darling, there's such an awful wind and the sea is so dreadfully rough.

How terrified she will be when she sees me arrive with him.

How worried you will be by all this. I am thankful you are not in the middle of it, as things always seem a little less vivid when one isn't there.

O darling, it's awfully lonely here.

I must write to B.M. now and Dada.

Your *Mar*

Vita Sackville-West to Harold Nicholson

Long Barn
9 November 1926

Oh dear, Virginia . . . You see, Hadji, she is very very fond of me, and
she says she was so unhappy when I went to Persia that it startled and
terrified her. I don't think she is accustomed to emotional storms, she
lives too much in the intellect and imagination. Most human beings take
emotional storms as a matter of course. Fortunately she is the sensible
sort of person who pulls themselves together and says, "This is absurd."
So I don't really worry. (Rather proud, really, of having caught such a
big silver fish.) I look on my friendship with her as a treasure and a
privilege. I shan't ever fall in love with her, *padlock*, but I am absolutely
devoted to her and if she died I should mind quite, quite dreadfully. Or
went mad again.

Vita Sackville-West to Harold Nicholson

Long Barn
30 November 1926

I'm alone. It is very cold and wet. I have got Virginia coming for the
weekend. Darling, I know Virginia will die, and it will be too awful. (I
don't mean *here*, over the weekend; but just die young.) I went to Tavistock Sq. yesterday, and she sat in the dusk in the light of the fire, and I
sat on the floor as I always do, and she rumpled my hair as she always
does, and she talked about literature and Mrs Dalloway and Sir Henry
Taylor, and said you would resent her next summer. But I said no, you
wouldn't. Oh Hadji, she *is* such an angel; I really adore her. Not 'in love'
but just love — devotion. I don't know whether it annoys you that I
should write so often about her? One has to be so careful at this distance;
but really Hadji shouldn't be annoyed, because her friendship does en-
rich me so, and she is so completely un-silly. I absolutely long for you to
know her better. I don't think I have ever loved anybody so much, in the
way of friendship; in fact, of course I haven't. She knows the mars adore
each other; I've told her so, and so has Tray. Oh my sweet, they do, don't
they? God, how I want to *talk* to you; just talk and talk and talk. Yes,

'the time' is a real personal thing — like a snowman that dwindles very, very slowly. But still dwindles.

Harold Nicholson to Vita Sackville-West

Teheran
3 December 1926

You *do* promise to tell me if there is a muddle with Virginia! I am so worried about that. It is *such* a powder magazine. I am far more worried for Virginia and Leonard's sake than for ours. I *know* that for each of us the magnetic north is the other — and that though the needle may flicker and even get stuck at other points — it will come back to the pole sooner or later. But what dangers for them! You see, I have every confidence in your wisdom except where these sort of things are concerned, when you wrap your wisdom in a hood of optimism and only take it out when things are too far gone for mending.

Vita Sackville-West to Harold Nicholson

Long Barn
21 December 1926

My own, *nothing* is wrong. PADLOCK. What 'reservations' or 'half truths' have you detected in my letters? There have been none, I have told you everything day by day exactly as it has happened. I swear to tell you at the first sign of "muddle with Virginia." My dearest, how can you speak of reservations and half truths when I have told you all about that business? Even that I *did* sleep with her, which I need never have told you — but that I wanted you to know everything that happened to me while you were away. (If you had been at home I might not have told you.) There is nothing I will not tell you, that you want to know. I am absolutely devoted to her, but not in love. So there. Oh my darling, has all my wretchedness at being separated from you then failed to convince you of my absolute love for you? It can't, it can't; you *must* know. It was only that you had 'flu, wasn't it? Oh darling, I get frantic when I think of you having even a moment's anxiety.

Harold Nicholson to Vita Sackville-West

Long Barn
23 October 1927

Viti — I am sitting in my rabbit hutch and you are in reach of me. But when you read this I shall have no dear neighbour. Little one, be not angry with me for being so obstinate and selfish. It *is* Othello's occupation [diplomacy] — and however much it may depress and irritate me, I feel that without it I would become *not* a cup of tea but a large jug of tepid milk.

Darling, do you remember saying once that you had never established an absolutely satisfactory relation with anyone — not even with me? That was years ago. I don't think you would say that now. I feel that our love and confidence is absolute. I mean in the technical sense of absolute: it is relative to nothing but itself: it is untouched by circumstances, emotions: it is certainly untouched by age. Darling — isn't this a great comfort? *Cosa bella mortal passa: ma non d'arte.* I feel that our love is something as detached from circumstance as the beauty of a work of art. This gives one security in all this transience. If one of us died, this love would live, although in agony. Our love will only die with both of us.

Vita Sackville-West to Harold Nicholson

Sissinghurst
31 March 1941

My darling

I have just had the most awful shock: Virginia has killed herself. It is not in the papers, but I got letters from Leonard and also from Vanessa, telling me. It was last Friday. Leonard came home to find a note saying she was going to commit suicide and they think she has drowned herself as he found her stick floating on the river. He says she had not been well for the last few weeks and was terrified of going mad again. He says, "It was, I suppose, the strain of the war and finishing her book and she could not rest or eat."

Why, oh why, did he leave her alone knowing all this? He must be reproaching himself terribly, poor man. They had not yet found the body.

I simply can't take it in — that lovely mind, that lovely spirit. And she seemed so well when I last saw her, and I had a joky letter from her only a couple of weeks ago.

She must have been quite out of her mind or she would never have brought such sorrow and horror on Leonard and Vanessa.

Vanessa has seen him and says he was amazingly self-controlled and calm, but insisted on being left alone — I cannot help wondering if he will follow her example. I do not see him living without her.

Perhaps you better not say to anyone that it was suicide, though I suppose they can't keep it out of the papers. I suppose there will have to be an inquest.

What a nightmare for L. to have to go through. When they find her body, and all that.

Your *Mar*

Harold Nicholson to Vita Sackville-West

Ministry of Information
2 April 1941

I am glad I came down last night since I was so worried about you and it was a relief to see you taking the shock so well. I hope you can manage to dismiss the physical aspect from your mind and to concentrate only upon the great joy that friendship has been to you. But, my dearest, I know that Virginia meant something to you which nobody else can ever mean and that you will feel deprived of a particular sort of haven which was a background comfort and strength. I have felt sad about it every hour of the day.

Vita Sackville-West to Harold Nicholson

Sissinghurst
4 June 1941

My darling,

I write this after dinner. A big thunderstorm is circling round somewhere: a pale flash comes, and then a dim rumble some appreciable time later. I was up in the potting shed, getting out the dahlias from under the bench. (I have not dared to plant them out before now, because of the frosts.) I was thinking to myself, as one does think when one is alone and doing something mechanical like putting dahlias into a trug, I was thinking, "How queer. I suppose Hadji and I have been about as unfaithful to one another as one well could be from the conventional point of view, even worse than unfaithful if you add in homosexuality, and yet I swear no two people could love one another more than we do after all these years."

It *is* queer, isn't it? It does destroy all orthodox ideas of marriage?

Yet it is true, so true that I know our love to be like a great oak tree with lots of acorns, or like a tulip-tree with lots of flowers.

I do think we have managed things cleverly.

I was sorry I had said to Cyril that I wanted you to divorce me for the sake of economy; I thought he might misunderstand so I wrote to him and put it right. I don't think he would misunderstand, but I wasn't taking any chances.

Goodnight, my darling.

Your
Mar

Vita Sackville-West/Virginia Woolf

Spanning nearly two decades, the prolific correspondence of Virginia Woolf and Vita Sackville-West narrates an intense professional, social, literary and intimate relationship. The two authors enjoyed a romantic friendship based, in many ways, on the attraction of opposites — the almost purely intellectual Virginia and the vigorously social Vita. They met in 1922, when Virginia was forty and Vita thirty. Both were married, but three years after they met they became lovers. In 1928 Woolf published the novel *Orlando,* whose title character was modeled on Sackville-West. Later, their passion cooled and the women drifted apart. Vita took up with other lovers, but Vita and Virginia remained good friends and regular correspondents until Virginia's suicide in 1941.

Vita Sackville-West to Virginia Woolf

Long Barn, Weald,
Sevenoaks.
18th September [1925]

My dear Virginia

You are a very, very remarkable person. Of course I always knew that,
—it is an easy thing to know,—the Daily Xpress knows it,—the Dial
[New York] knows it,—organs so diverse,— the Daily Herald quotes
you as an authority on the vexed question as to whether one should cross
the road to dine with Wordsworth, — but I feel strongly that I have only
tonight thoroughly and completely realised how remarkable you really
are. You see, you accomplish so much. You are one perpetual Achievement; yet you give the impression of having infinite leisure. One comes
to see you: you are prepared to spend two hours of Time in talk. One
may not, for reasons of health, come to see you: you write divine letters,
four pages long. You read bulky manuscripts. You advise grocers. You
support mothers, vicariously. You produce books which occupy a permanent place on one's bedside shelf next to Gerald [sic] MANLY Hopkins
and the Bible. You cast a beam across the dingy landscape of the Times
Literary Supplement. You change people's lives. You set up type. You
offer to read and criticise one's poems, — criticise, (in the sense which
you have given to the word,) meaning illumination, not the complete
disheartenment which is the legacy of other critics. How is it done? I
can only suppose that you don't fritter. Now here am I, alone at midnight,
and I survey my day, (the first that I have spent in peace for some
weeks,) and I ask myself what I have done with it. I finished the hops
for Leonard, found an envelope and a stamp, and sent it off. I planted
perhaps a hundred bulbs. I played tennis with my son. I endeavoured to
amuse my other son, who has whooping-cough, and tries to crack jokes
between the bouts. I read a detective story in my bath. I talked to a
carpenter. I wrote five lines of poetry. Now what does all that amount
to? Nothing. Just fritter. And yet it represents a better day than I have
spent for a long time.

Do you do it by concentration? Do you do it by organisation? I
want a recipe so badly.

I assure you, it was misery to stop your anonymous little village boy
and turn him into the Mercury who would ultimately reach your cook,
who would ultimately reach you [with the saucer-garden]. It was unselfish, wasn't it? also, to be honest, I was frightened of Leonard. I knew

he would look disapproving if I appeared at the house. He would look the more disapproving because he wouldn't know how much *I* approved, —of his care of you, I mean. After leaving Rodmell I took a road that wasn't a road at all; that is to say, it started by being a road and then melted away into grass, so that the last five miles of my journey were accomplished over pure Down, —very bumpy, but full of larks. A shepherd whom I met stared incredulously at the appearance of a blue motor in the middle of miles of rolling turf.

Yes I will send you my georgics [*The Land*] when they are more consecutive; at present there is a spider here and a farrowing sow there, —not tied together by any intelligible link. I will take advantage, quite unscrupulously, of your offer; but I shall continue to wonder how you fit it all in.

I like the sense of one lighted room in the house while all the rest of the house, and the world outside, is in darkness. Just one lamp falling on my paper; it gives a concentration, an intimacy. What bad mediums letters are; you will read this in daylight, and everything will look different. I think I feel night as poignantly as you feel the separateness of human beings; one of those convictions which are so personal, so sharp, that they *hurt*. It seems to me that I only begin to live after the sun has gone down and the stars have come out.

Vita

Virginia Woolf to Vita Sackville-West

52 Tavistock Square, W.C.1
Tuesday, Dec. 22nd [1925]

My dear Mrs Nicolson —ah hah! —this is only to say what in the scramble I had not time to say yesterday, that my address is Charleston, Firle, Lewes, till Monday next, and hoe for a letter from you. Also that I woke trembling in the night —what at? At the thought that I had been grossly inhospitable about lunch on Sunday. There it was smoking on the table —chicken and apple tart, cream, and coffee: and you, after motoring, spoiling, caring cossetting the Wolf kind for 3 days, sent empty along the pavement. Good God —how the memory of these things bites like serpents in the night! But the bite was assuaged by the pleasures.

I am dashing off to buy, a pair of gloves. I am sitting up in bed: I am very very charming; and Vita is a dear old rough coated sheep dog:

or alternatively, hung with grapes, pink with pearls, lustrous, candle lit, in the door of a Sevenoaks draper. I'll ask Nessa whether Saturday or Sunday [at Charleston] and write to Knole. But do not snuff the stinking tallow out of your heart — poor Virginia to wit, and Dog Grizzle (who is scratching under my bed) Now for a Bus down Southampton Row.

Ah, but I like being with Vita.

VW

Vita Sackville-West to Virginia Woolf

Milan [mailed in Trieste]
Thursday 21st [January 1926]

I am reduced to a thing that wants Virginia. I composed a beautiful letter to you in the sleepless nightmare hours of the night, and it has all gone: I just miss you, in a quite simple desperate human way. You, with all your undumb letters, would never write so elementary a phrase as that; perhaps you wouldn't even feel it. And yet I believe you'll be sensible of a little gap. But you'd clothe it in so exquisite a phrase that it would lose a little of its reality. Whereas with me it is quite stark: I miss you even more than I could have believed; and I was prepared to miss you a good deal. So this letter is just really a squeal of pain. It is incredible how essential to me you have become. I suppose you are accustomed to people saying these things. Damn you, spoilt creature; I shan't make you love me any the more by giving myself away like this — But oh my dear, I *can't* be clever and standoffish with you: I love you too much for that. Too truly. You have no idea how stand-offish I can be with people I don't love. I have brought it to a fine art. But you have broken down my defences. And I don't really resent it.

However I won't bore you with any more.

We have re-started, and the train is shaky again. I shall have to write at the stations — which are fortunately many across the Lombard plain.

Venice.

The stations were many, but I didn't bargain for the Orient Express not stopping at them. And here we are at Venice for ten minutes only, — a wretched time in which to try and write. No time to buy an Italian stamp even, so this will have to go from Trieste.

The waterfalls in Switzerland were frozen into solid iridescent curtains of ice, hanging over the rock; so lovely. And Italy all blanketed in snow.

We're going to start again. I shall have to wait till Trieste tomorrow morning. Please forgive me for writing such a miserable letter.

V.

Vita Sackville-West to Virginia Woolf

Long Barn, Weald,
Sevenoaks.
Wednesday [December 1, 1926]

My darling, is this yours? It is a young cuckoo in my nest, anyway, and I think I borrowed it off you once.

Last night I went to bed very early and read Mrs Dalloway. It was a very curious sensation: I thought you were in the room — But there was only Pippin, trying to burrow under my quilt, and the night noises outside, which are so familiar in one's own room; and the house was all quiet. I was very unhappy because I had had a row with my mother and very happy because of you; so it was like being two different people at the same time, and then to complicate it there was a) the conviction that you were in the room, and b) the contact with all the many people that you had created. (What a queer thing fiction is.) I felt quite light, as though I were falling through my bed, like when one has a fever. Today I am quite solid again, and my boots are muddy; they weight me down. Yet I am not as solid as usual, — not *quite* such an oaf, — because there is at the back of my mind all the time (slightly lifting the top off my head,) a glow, a sort of nebula, which only when I examine it hardens into a shape; as soon as I think of something else it dissolves again, remaining there like the sun through a fog, and I have to reach out to it again, take it in my hands and feel its contours: then it hardens, "Virginia is coming on Saturday." I am going to dinner at Knole tonight, and I shall meet an oil magnate and his wife; but it will be there all the time, a will o' the wisp that lets itself be caught, "Virginia is coming on Saturday."

But she won't, she won't! something will happen. Of course something will happen. Something always does, when one wants a thing too passionately. You will have chicken pox, or I shall have mumps, or the house will fall down on Saturday morning. In the meantime there are three cows staring over the stile; they are waiting for cake. There is a nebula in their minds too, "At four o'clock we shall have cake." And for them, lucky brutes, nothing will happen. But for me there is the whole range of human possibility.

If ever you tried not to have chicken pox, try now. If ever you tried not to be given a headache by Sibyl Colefax, try now. (I remember, ominously, that you said you were going to tea with her on Friday.) Please try with all your might not to let anything happen. I will be responsible for you after you have arrived, — only, please arrive. (I will let you know the trains tomorrow.) Bring your work, I won't interrupt. I so want you to be happy here. I wish, in a way, that we could put the clock back a year. I should like to startle you again, — even though I didn't know then that you were startled.

V.

Virginia Woolf to Vita Sackville-West

52 T.[avistock] S.[quare, W.C.I]
[December 8, 1926]

Dearest Vita,

(Now why did I say that?) Yes, Monday, undern 2.30. Please come, and bathe me in serenity again. Yes, I was wholly and entirely happy. If you could have uncored me — you would have seen every nerve running fire — intense, but calm. Then how hard you worked, like a navvy, and I saying to myself all the time, Anyhow this is in Vita's line.

But why, darling Mrs N., honourable Mrs N. insist upon Knole? To see me ridiculous, the powder falling, the hairpins dropping, and not a word said in private between us? Is it one of your moonlight, romantic, stags barking, old man feeding them from a bucket in the snow, ideas? It shall be considered, anyhow. But Arnold Bennett has sold my books twice as fast as before: 6 sell instead of one. Please be rude to him and then Teheran will leap: it is doing very well: 6 sold to Smiths, one at the door to an old woman with long teeth. Cameron [*Victorian Photographs*] moving, not fast, but with the dignity of a battleship taking the water. Logan [Pearsall Smith] to tea, very American. Raymond — I eat all my words — very charming, very gay, very simple, very what one calls nice.

But its Vita I adore.

Yr
Virginia

We want puppy back on Jan 1st. I think. Can we?

Vita Sackville-West to Virginia Woolf

London-Dover
[January 28, 1927]

My darling, it's so shaky I can hardly write, we are tearing through my Weald — (see Passenger to Teheran, Chap. 2 passim.) So odd to have all the same emotions repeated after a year's interval — but oh *worse* where you are concerned. I really curse and damn at the pain of it — and yet I wouldn't be without it for anything — I shall remember you standing in your blue apron and waving. Oh damn it, Virginia, I wish I didn't love you so much. No I don't though; that's not true. I am glad I do. I don't know what to say to you except that it tore the heart out of my body saying goodbye to you I am thankful to have had yesterday, a real gift from the Gods — Oh my darling you *have* made me so happy, and I do bless you for it — and I oughtn't to grumble now — ought I? but I really do feel wretched — You won't be able to read this letter — I sent you a telegram from Victoria —

Your
V.

Vita Sackville-West to Virginia Woolf

Sherfield Court,
Sherfield Upon Loddon,
Basingstoke.
Sunday [Saturday, June 11, 1927]

So you are alone, in your Constable country of elms and meadows, with your blue tit nest ("a wild bird's nest in Helen's breast"?) and your Ouse, and your shingled church tower; and I am here among all these people, just a little bewildered and perplexed by all their talk, as is Harold too, from the fresher air of Asia. It seems to me all a little stale, careful, dead? Are we wrong? or are they?

Do you know what I should do, if you were not a person to be rather strict with? I should steal my own motor out of the garage at 10 p.m. tomorrow night, be at Rodmell by 11.5 (yes, darling: I did a record on Friday, getting from Lewes to Long Barn in an hour and 7 minutes,) throw gravel at your window, then you'd come down and let me in; I'd stay with you till 5. and be home by half past six. But, you being you, I can't; more's the pity. Have you read my book? Challenge, I mean? Perhaps I sowed all my wild oats then. Yet I don't feel that the impulse has left me; no, by God; and for a different Virginia I'd fly to Sussex in the night. Only, with age, soberness, and the increase of considerateness, I refrain. But the temptation is great.

A thin Clive; a haggard Clive.

Oh Lord! They've come to fetch the letters for the post.

Your
V.

Virginia Woolf to Vita Sackville-West

[52 Tavistock Square, W.C.1]
[1927(?)]

Look here Vita — throw over your man, and we'll go to Hampton Court and dine on the river together and walk in the garden in the moonlight and come home late and have a bottle of wine and get tipsy, and I'll tell you all the things I have in my head, millions, myriads — They won't stir by day, only by dark on the river. Think of that. Throw over your man, I say, and come.

Vita Sackville-West to Virginia Woolf

Long Barn
Monday [August 8, 1927]

I was going into Sevenoaks to pick up the boys, when I saw the postman's scarlet bicycle leaning against the village letter-box. That meant that the afternoon's post had arrived. I stopped; went in; and said Are there any letters for Long Barn? There were. Among them was a typewritten envelope which contained a letter from you. I felt myself flush with rage, as I read it, — I don't exaggerate. I didn't know I was so jealous of you. *Who* is your damned man with the acquiline nose? Look here, I really mind. But if it comes to that, I have on my table a letter of the same sort, — which I haven't answered. What sort of answer I send, depends on you. I really am not joking. If you are not careful, you will involve me in an affair which will bore me horribly. If you are nice, on the other hand, I'll send my correspondent packing. But I won't be trifled with. I really mean this.

For the rest:

(1) I'll bring my camera, only my charge is £1 per snapshot, not 2/6.

(2) I won't bring Pippin, I think, because she might be sick in the motor.

(3) I'll come at 4 Thursday.

(4) I'll stay till Friday.

(5) I'd like to lunch at Charleston if you will *promise* to leave directly after lunch so that I may have you alone again.

(6) I will certainly lay myself out to please you.

I do get so angry about you

V.

Virginia Woolf to Vita Sackville-West

52 Tavistock Sqre. [W.C.1]
9th Oct. [1927]

Look, dearest what a lovely page this is, and think how, were it not for the screen and the [Mary] Campbell, it might all be filled to the brim with lovemaking unbelievable: indiscretions incredible: instead of which, nothing shall be said but what a Campbell behind the screen might hear. Really, its worse than being bound in morocco by Lytton, and read by all the tarts of the moment. Which reminds me, do you know a man of that persuasion called Cecil Beaton — who wants to photograph me, and Osbert will comment upon the portrait in a catalogue; and shall I go and be done? I say no: I say I am living perpetually in Sussex. I say, judging from your style and manner (this is what I say to Cecil Beaton) you are a Mere Catamite. Clive who came in yesterday, dropping with sleep after what I understood was an orgy, confirmed this. Why was he dropping with sleep? Oh, he said, after they'd all gone, he got into bed, but couldn't shut his eyes. Being in a close costive contrary mood I did not egg him on. So he went to Paris, and will be back next week, and then I'm to dine with him. Aint it romantic — this visionary and aetherial presence brooding diaphanous over Gordon Square, like a silver spangled cloud? What are we to call her? Clive bursts into Nessa who's solidly carving mutton for the children and rambles about, romanticising about Life, London, Autumn fires being but a man of 46 at his prime. Only in August I was thinking he would string himself from a lamppost. But Vita, my dear, please not a word to anyone about Clive's money and Nessa: that would be fatal, and no doubt he has honourable intentions and will make a rich woman of her next quarter day. She seems perfectly serene.

Here occurs a terrific gulf. Millions of things I want to say can't be said. You know why. You know for what a price — walking the lanes with Campbell, you sold my love letters. Very well. So we will skip all that and move on to Mrs Wells, and death, and the funeral at Golder's Green, to which I'm going tomorrow, if I can scrape together a sufficiency of clothes. Wells wrote Leonard the oddest post card. I wont say that it was a picture post card, with a view of Easton Church, but practically that; and just a line to "say my wife died last night; or we had hoped to ask you and Mrs Woolf down for a week end." I'm going to the funeral to see whats done with the bodies of unbelievers. What fun! How I love ceremonies, and collocations (is that allowable?) of the human kind!

Yesterday morning I was in despair: You know that bloody book which Dadie and Leonard extort, drop by drop, from my breast? Fiction, or some title to that effect [*Phases of Fiction*]. I couldn't screw a word from me; and at last dropped my head in my hands: dipped my pen in the ink, and wrote these words, as if automatically, on a clean sheet: Orlando: A Biography. No sooner had I done this than my body was flooded with rapture and my brain with ideas. I wrote rapidly till 12. Then I did an hour to Romance. So every morning I am going to write fiction (my own fiction) till 12; and Romance till 1. But listen; suppose Orlando turns out to be Vita; and its all about you and the lusts of your flesh and the lure of your mind (heart you have none, who go gallivanting down the lanes with Campbell) — suppose there's the kind of shimmer of reality which sometimes attaches to my people, as the lustre on an oyster shell (and that recalls another Mary) suppose, I say, that Sibyl next October says "Theres Virginia gone and written a book about Vita" and Ozzie [Dickinson] chaws with his great chaps and Byard [of Heinemann] guffaws, Shall you mind? Say yes, or No: Your excellence as a subject arises largely from your noble birth. (But whats 400 years of nobility, all the same?) and the opportunity thus given for florid descriptive passages in great abundance. Also, I admit, I should like to untwine and twist again some very odd, incongruous strands in you: going at length into the question of Campbell; and also, as I told you, it sprung upon me how I could revolutionise biography in a night: and so if agreeable to you I would like to toss this up in the air and see what happens. Yet, of course, I may not write another line.

You will come on Wednesday undern? You will write, now, this instant, a nice humble letter of duty and devotion to me.

I am reading Knole and The Sackvilles. Dear me; you know a lot: you have a rich dusky attic of a mind. O yes, I want very much to see you.

Yr V.W. (thats because of Campbell)

Vita Sackville-West to Virginia Woolf

Long Barn.
Tuesday [October 11, 1927]

My God, Virginia, if ever I was thrilled and terrified it is at the prospect of being projected into the shape of Orlando. What fun for you; what fun for me. You see, any vengeance that you ever want to take will lie ready to your hand. Yes, go ahead, toss up your pancake, brown it nicely on both sides, pour brandy over it, and serve hot. You have my full permission. Only I think that having drawn and quartered me, unwound and retwisted me, or whatever it is that you intend to do, you ought to dedicate it to your victim.

And what a lovely letter you wrote me, [Mary] Campbell or no Campbell. (How flattered she'd be if she knew. But she doesn't, and shan't.) How right I was, — not that it needed much perspicacity, — when I realised at Clive's that here was the most . . . what shall I say? you want duty and devotion, but if I wrote what I really think you would only say that Vita was laying it on a bit too thick. So I better not expose myself to your jeers. But how right I was, all the same; and to force myself on you at Richmond [in January 1923], and so lay the train for the explosion which happened on the sofa in my room here when you behaved so disgracefully and acquired me for ever. Acquired me, that's what you did, like buying a puppy in a shop and leading it away on a string. Still trotting after you, and still on a string. For all the world like Pinker.

Last night was the most beautiful misty moonlight night I ever saw in my life. No, I did *not* go down the lanes. I hung out of my window and listened to the dead leaves twirling down in the stillness. I thought how lovely and lonely it must be at Laughton. I was sorry about Laughton, — a fairy-story place for Virginia to live in.

Moody is writing a novel. About spiritualism.

No, I have never heard of Mr Cecil Beaston [sic] but please do go and be photographed and give me one.

Darling, I can't come up tomorrow, and am sending you a telegram to that effect. I won't tell you why, — a squalid reason. I shall come up next week though, and probably stay a night in London. And what about you coming here one of these days? You said you would, and the advantages are obvious.

Not a word from that bloody Foreign Office. I fear they are plotting something very dark. Harold approaches his correspondence more and more gingerly. Oh, by the way, he finished his book today and it has gone to be typed. So you will have it soon.

I wish you were here. The days and nights are beautiful as only autumn can be. This sounds like Clive when his autumn fires are best, and ripe apples dropping on his head, but I assure you I am not in the same mood as Clive. No. My delight is purely aesthetic, and country bumpkin I am good, industrious, and loving; how long will it be, though, before I break out? I would never break out if I had you here, but you leave me unguarded. Now, none of that means anything at all, so don't imagine that it does. I am Virginia's good puppy, beating my tail on the floor, responsive to a kind pat.

V.

Vita Sackville-West to Virginia Woolf

Knole, Sevenoaks,
Kent
Thursday [December 29, 1927]

Will this ever reach you? are you completely snowed up? is it very beautiful among the Downs? does Pinker like it? have you perhaps gone back to London? have you anything to eat? Shall I ever get to Sherfield tomorrow? shall I ever see you again? shall I ever write another book? I feel that the answer to most of these questions is in the negative.

I cashed your cheque, not because I wanted the 12/6 but because I thought that would make you feel even more like other women — and I knew it would come back to you eventually with my endorsement on the back, quite as though you were a really grown-up person. Now tomorrow I shall be confronted with Ethel [Smyth] and her eagle eye; I must display, I feel, no enthusiasm about any of my friends; or I say, shall I drag a completely red herring across her path? That would be rather fun. I'll invent a new beauty, whom nobody has ever seen, I'll ask Ethel if I may bring her to dinner, a dinner which on one pretext or another will have to be permanently put off. What shall we call her? You think of a suitable name, something very romantic, like Gloria Throckmorton, or Lesbia Featherstonehaugh. She is only nineteen, has run away from her family in Merioneth, and taken a flat in London. She is more lovely than Valerie, more witty than Virginia, more wanton than Mary, and a better golfer than Miss Cecilia Leitch.

On Xmas day I went to Brighton, throwing up floods on either side, and in torrents of rain. I looked wistfully to the left as I passed through Lewes.

Knole is all soft and white, and the snow falls in great flumps as the men shovel it off the roof. We are quite cut off except by walking. No motors, no telephone. I wish you were here. You're coming to Long Barn, aren't you though? and in no Puritanical frame of mind?

Your
V.

Virginia Woolf to Vita Sackville-West

Monks House, Rodmell [Sussex]
30th Aug 1928

How do you live the life you do? Sixty people to dinner [in Berlin]. One for three days entirely dissipates my soul, and sends it floating, like duckweed, down a dirty river. I am very hot. I have been mowing the lawn. It looks now like a calm sea through which several large ships have passed leaving wakes behind them. Then I ate two plums which make my hands sticky. For many days I have been so disjected by society that writing has been only a dream — something another woman did once. What has caused this irruption I scarcely know — largely your friend Radclyffe Hall (she is now docked of her Miss owing to her proclivities) they banned her book; and so Leonard and Morgan Forster began to get up a protest, and soon we were telephoning and interviewing and collecting signatures — not yours, for *your* proclivities are too well known. In the midst of this, Morgan goes to see Radclyffe in her tower in Kensington, with her love [Lady Troubridge]: and Radclyffe scolds him like a fishwife, and says that she wont have any letter written about her book unless it mentions the fact that it is a work of artistic merit — even genius. And no one has read her book; or can read it: and now we have to explain this to all the great signed names — Arnold Bennett and so on. So our ardour in the cause of freedom of speech gradually cools, and instead of offering to reprint the masterpiece, we are already beginning to wish it unwritten.

I am observing with interest the fluctuations of my own feelings about France. Leonard says he can't come. Like an angel he says but of course go with Vita. Then he somehow conveys without a word the fact of his intolerable loneliness without me — upon which I give it all up; and then suddenly think, what an unwholesome sentimental state this is! I will go. And then visualise myself saying goodbye to him and cant face it; and then visualise a rock in a valley with Vita in an Inn: and *must* go. So it goes on. Meanwhile Ethel Sands advises us to go to Auxerre, Vezelay, Autun, Semur, Saulieu (Hotel de la Poste has wonderful food) and we are to stay at least two nights with her and Nan. I think I must manage to come. But it will be the greatest proof of devotion. And Leonard may make it impossible — Can you put up with these vacillations:? Anyhow I shall see you before anything need be done.

I am very happy and not very happy. Do you like these states of mind to take precedence of all else in letters? I am happy because it is the loveliest August; downs so brown and grey, and the meadows so — I forget what. On the other hand, I have to work all day — it seems — grinding out a few notes like those a blunt knife makes on a whetstone, at novels and novels. I read Proust, Henry James, Dostoevsky; my happiness is wedged like (but I am using too many metaphors) in between these granite blocks (and now that they are granite blocks I can compare my happiness to samphire, a small pink plant I picked as a child in Cornwall).

Why need you be so timid and pride-blown, both at once, over writing your novel? What does donkey West mean about her ambition and failure? Why should you fail at this prosy art, when you can please Jack Squire with poetry? (Thats a nasty one) I am entirely of your opinion that Heaven has made us and not we ourselves. I accept no responsibility for anything I write or do. I like your fecundity. And; surely, for the last ten years almost, you have cut back and pruned and root dug — What is it one should do to fig trees? — with the result that you write sometimes too much like a racehorse who has been trained till his tail is like a mouses tail and his ribs are like a raised map of the Alps. Please write your novel, and then you will enter into the unreal world, where Virginia lives — and poor woman, can't now live anywhere else.

I've not seen Dottie: but then I said very incautiously that I would like to buy some bricks off her, and that one mustn't say to a woman with ten thousand a year. For then she sighs to herself "Virginia only thinks of my possessions" Is this true psychology? At any rate it is true that Pinker is breeding. She has at least six inside her, and the lice and a bad paw, all of which occupy our time incessantly. "Are you sure lice don't travel — is this a louse — what are nits — " such is our talk; and we had a play by Bobo Mayor; made poor Lydia who acted in such despair that instead of spending the week end with Lloyd-George, she spent it with the Spinaches.

We didn't clap loud enough: but then we were sitting in the rain.

Yes, I think I must come to France, and I dont think Leonard will miss me one scrap.

Yr

Vita Sackville-West to Virginia Woolf

39 Manger-strasse II
Potsdam.
31st August [1928]

Henry (Pinker's younger brother,) the boys, and I went for a walk in Potsdam. We walked down long, tidy, cobbled streets, with trams squealing round the corners and the dust whirling in clouds before the incessant wind. I felt extremely depressed. Am I for ever, I thought, to spend my life walking the streets of Potsdam, Belgrade, Bucharest, Washington? Then I remembered that I had lost my cigarette case, with a £10 note in it, *and* my motor license, *and* a cheque from The Nation, *and* another cheque, *and* a photograph small but precious of Virginia, *and* a prescription belonging to somebody else. I remembered also that the Foreign Office had refused to pay for the dinner to the MP's, which had cost us something over £100. So my depression deepened. But then we came home and I found in the letter box a letter which I knew to be from you, even though the envelope was typewritten, and my spirits rose. I have now thrown the boys into the lake, and am at liberty for at least half an hour.

I feel very violently about The Well of Loneliness. Not on account of what you call my proclivities; not because I think it is a good book; but really on principle. (I think of writing to Jix suggesting that he should suppress Shakespeare's Sonnets.) Because, you see, even if the

W. of L. had been a good book, — even if it had been a great book, a real masterpiece, — the result would have been the same. And that is intolerable. I really have no words to say how indignant I am. Is Leonard really going to get up a protest? or is it fizzling out? (What a conceited ass the woman must be.) *Don't* let it fizzle out. If you got Arnold Bennett and suchlike, it would be bound to make an impression. (Avoid Shaw, though.) I nearly blew up over the various articles in The New Statesman. Personally, I should like to renounce my nationality, as a gesture; but I don't want to become a German, even though I did go to a revue last night in which two ravishing young women sing a frankly Lesbian song.

France. . . . Well, you can get a pale reflection of the matrimonial miseries which *I* undergo. You hesitate to leave Leonard for six days; I leave Harold several times a year for several months. I see him off to Persia. He sees me off to England. We are perpetually in a state of saying goodbye.

By the way, when you say "Ethel Sands advises us," etc, do you mean (by us) you and Leonard, or you and me?

I will leave you to your own fluctuations, which amuse me a good deal. I will only say, that you mustn't come if it's going to make you miserable all the time. But you wouldn't.

Don't tell me that it is a lovely August in England. It is so cold here that I sit with an eiderdown over my knees. It rains nearly every day. It is a foul climate. You mustn't say it is lovely in England, or that the Downs are golden or whatever it is — because then I rebel against my lot.

Yr. V.

Vita Sackville-West to Virginia Woolf

Long Barn, Weald,
Sevenoaks.
11th October 1928

My darling,

I am in no fit state to write to you — and as for cold and considered opinions, (as you said on the telephone) such things do not exist in such a connection. At least, not yet. Perhaps they will come later. For the

moment, I can't say anything except that I am completely dazzled, bewitched, enchanted, under a spell. It [*Orlando*] seems to me the loveliest,
wisest, *richest* book that I have ever read, — excelling even your own
Lighthouse. Virginia, I really don't know what to say, — am I right? am
I wrong? am I prejudiced? am I in my senses or not? It seems to me that
you have really shut up that "hard and rare thing" in a book; that you
have had a complete vision; and yet when you came down to the sober
labour of working it out, have never lost sight of it nor faltered in the
execution. Ideas come to me so fast that they trip over each other and I
lose them before I can put salt on their tails; there is so much I want to
say, yet I can only go back to my first cry that I am bewitched. You will
get letters, very reasoned and illuminating, from many people; I cannot
write you that sort of letter now, I can only tell you that I am really
shaken, which may seem to you useless and silly, but which is really a
greater tribute than pages of calm appreciation, — and then after all it
does touch me so personally, and I don't know what to say about that
either, only that I feel like one of those wax figures in a shop window, on
which you have hung a robe stitched with jewels. It is like being alone
in a dark room with a treasure chest full of rubies and nuggets and
brocades. Darling, I don't know and scarcely even like to write, so
overwhelmed am I, how you could have hung so splendid a garment on
so poor a peg. Really this isn't false humility; *really* it isn't. I can't write
about that part of it, though, much less ever tell you verbally.

By now you must be thinking me too confused and illiterate for
anything, so I'll just slip in that the book (in texture) seems to me to
have in it all the best of Sir Thomas Browne and Swift, — the richness of
the one, and the directness of the other.

There are a dozen details I should like to go into, — Queen Elizabeth's visit, Greene's visit, phrases scattered about, (particularly one on
p. 160 beginning "High battlements of thought, etc" which is just what
you did for *me*,) Johnson on the blind, and so on and so on, — but it is
too late today; I have been reading steadily all day, and it is now 5
o'clock, and I must catch the post, but I will try and write more sensibly
tomorrow. It is your fault, for having moved me so and dazzled me
completely, so that all my faculties have dropped from me and left me
stark.

One awful thought struck me this morning: you didn't, did you,
think for a second that it was out of indifference I didn't come to London
yesterday? You *couldn't* have thought that? I had got it so firmly fixed in
my head that Oct. 11th was the day I was to have it, that I was resigned
(after all these months) to wait till then. But when I saw it in its lovely
binding, with my initials, the idea rushed into my head and utterly

appalled me. But on second thoughts I reflected that you could not possibly so have misunderstood.

Yes, I *will* write again tomorrow, in a calmer frame of mind I hope — now I am really writing against time — and, as I tell you, shaken quite out of my wits.

Also, you have invented a new form of Narcissism, — I confess, — I am in love with Orlando — this is a complication I had not foreseen.

Virginia, my dearest, I can only thank you for pouring out such riches.

V.

You made me cry with your passages about Knole, you wretch.

Vita Sackville-West to Virginia Woolf

24 Brücken Allee
Berlin N.W. 23
Thursday [January 31, 1929]

Your little shaky pencil letters simply wring my heart — oh, how damnable space and time are — you see, all my pictures of you are at two days' remove. I know you were in bed still when you wrote, but what I don't know is whether you're still in bed *now* — or whether you've been promoted to the sofa — anyhow I gather that you have been rather bad — you always understate your ills — and that is quite disturbing enough for me. Berlin did that to you — the fiend — The coffin of Berlin is becoming absolutely studded with nails — nails with big brass heads — like the Lord Treasurer's [Thomas Sackville] chest at Knole — and the biggest nail of all, so far, is that it made Virginia (who is more precious to me than a whole Lord Treasurer's chest full of pearls and rubies) ill. Yes, I wish I could open your door suddenly — instead of your painted Mary [Hutchinson] — and talking of Mary I saw the most marvellous photographs of her. . . . but I'll go back to the beginning, because I had a funny day yesterday — the sort of day that amuses Virginia — beginning with low life and ending with high — beginning with a rakish little ghost from Teheran and ending with a Papal Nuncio and a red headed Lesbian in the middle.

The ghost from Teheran suddenly appeared, having come to Berlin to see me — *not* from Teheran but from Sweden — a squalid rather amusing Montmartre sort of person — always full of fantastic stories which may be true and on the other hand may not. I had been bored with her in Teheran but was pleased to see her here — and she wanted to see the Aquarium so we went — heavily haunted by memories of Virginia it was — and then I took her along to tea with the red headed Lesbian — where we found Pirandello and his two little tarts that he travels about with — and several other very shady-looking people.

Red-head is a photographer — and there on the walls amongst the photographs of every conceivable European celebrity from Hindenburg to André Gide was our Mary [Hutchinson] marvellously portrayed. Red-head manoeuvred me into a dark little room where she showed me photographs of Josephine Baker stripped to the waist, — very beautiful, — and other photographs of an indecency which I won't describe; leered at me; made me take my hat off; and finally pestered me into saying I would sit to her tomorrow morning. She fair gives me the creeps. I came home and had a bath. Then finished up the day by despatching my Teheran friend off to Paris, and going to a great huge dinner at the Embassy — footmen in knee breeches; a sort of Suisse holding a silver topped pole which he banged on the floor every time the door opened; stars and ribbons; a lady who has had 5 husbands, including a Persian prince, and a final husband who is the nephew of the first one, — she changes her wig, too, according to her mood, so that it is sometimes grey, sometimes black, sometimes red —; gold plate in rivers down the table; and the Papal Nuncio in rose-red silk with a great gold cross on his breast. (He'll probably be the next Pope.)

Potto *would* have wagged his tail.

And all the time I thought of Virginia lying upstairs in Tavistock Square, and wished I were there.

And Frau [Katie] Stresemann got hold of Harold and said "I know you think I'm a fool, because whenever you see me you ask me if I have been dancing much lately, but I'm not a fool, and I can tell you that you are wasting yourself *and* your wife on this idiotic profession." Which improved my opinion of the lecherous Katie.

Did I tell you we were going to Rapallo for a week on the 9th? Yes, I surely did.

Oh my darling do be good and look after yourself — Leonard sees to that, I know — but I simply can't bear you to be ill. I *wish* I were there —

Your
V.

Virginia Woolf to Vita Sackville-West

Monk's House, Rodmell, near Lewes, Sussex
Friday [August 30, 1940]

I've just stopped talking to you. It seems so strange. Its perfectly peaceful here — theyre playing bowls — I'd just put flowers in your room. And there you sit with the bombs falling round you.

What can one say — except that I love you and I've got to live through this strange quiet evening thinking of you sitting there alone.

Dearest — let me have a line — let us meet next week. But one can scarcely bear it. Only we must.

Yr loving
V.

You have given me such happiness.
385 Lewes. Ring me up anytime.

Vita Sackville-West to Virginia Woolf

Sissinghurst Castle,
Kent.
1st September 1940

Oh dear, how your letter touched me this morning. I nearly dropped a tear into my poached egg. Your rare expressions of affection have always had the power to move me greatly, and as I suppose one is a bit strung-up (mostly sub-consciously) they now come ping against my heart like a bullet dropping on the roof. I love you too; you know that.

I didn't like to go away last Friday because they had no other ambulance-driver for the village ambulance but me — and fights were going on all day and distant sinister thuds — not so very distant. But I have now secured the services of a lady who could drive the ambulance in my place if necessary. She has a most romantic life-history which you would enjoy — It includes a vine-yard in Corsica which she ran for 5 years until brigands made her life impossible. But that is nothing to her matrimonial tragedies.

Anyhow, it means that I can now get away. So may I telephone one morning and ask if it would be convenient for me to come?

Would you tell Leonard that I sent my Country Notes off to the Press? also my signed copy of our agreement.

Your loving, very and permanently loving

V.

Edith Sitwell

With her brothers, Osbert and Sacheverell (Sachie), Dame Edith Sitwell ruled one corner of the modern literary universe for a significant part of the twentieth century. From her English homes the poet and critic propounded her firm if sometimes peculiar opinions on writers living and dead, corresponding with many of the former. Sitwell never married, living instead with her brothers for most of her life and gathering about her a large coterie of friends. Her letters to notables such as Dylan Thomas, Stephen Spender and Benjamin Britten are peppered with references to writers like T. S. Eliot, Edmund Gosse, Federico García Lorca and Algernon Swinburne, a first edition of whose work she received from John Maynard Keynes. Elsewhere, Sitwell sent Hugh Walpole's mother heartfelt condolences on his death and described to James Purdy her encounter with the young Beat poets Allen Ginsberg and Gregory Corso.

Edith Sitwell to Dylan Thomas

[January 1936]

Dear Mr Thomas,

Though we have never met, I am unable to resist writing to you to tell you, however inadequately, with what deep admiration and delight I have read your very beautiful poem which begins with the line

'A Grief ago'

and the beautiful and strange poem in this quarter's *Life and Letters*. It is no exaggeration to say that I do not remember when I have been so moved, profoundly so excited, by the work of any poet of the younger generation, or when I have felt such a deep certainty that here is a poet with all the capabilities and potentialities of greatness. I am completely overcome with this certainty and this admiration. Only a young man who is going to be a great poet could have written the lovely, true, and poignant poem in the programme — (the first one also, has a fine quality) — I cannot recover from it. I think I am learning it by heart. — And as for the poem in *Life and Letters* only a poet with real greatness could have written those extraordinary second and third lines of the passage which begins:

> 'What is the metre of the dictionary?
> The size of genesis? The short spark's gender?
> Shade without shape? The shape of Pharaoh's echo.'

Or the wonderful two lines which begin the poem, — or the line

> 'Death is all metaphors, shape in one history'

I have just finished writing about 'A Grief ago' for the *London Mercury*. — My friend Mr Herring writes me that a new book of yours will be appearing soon. I have already told my agent that I wish to review it, but I would be most deeply grateful if you could tell me who is publishing it, and when it will appear so that I may make certain to have the delight and honour of writing about it. — I have a great admiration, too, for many of your 18 poems, but your two latest have excited and delighted me beyond measure. — I must confess that the first poem I read of yours I did not like, technically — and felt it my duty to say so though without mentioning your name, taking the former only as an example. I know now, without any possibility of doubting it, that in you we have a poet from whom real greatness may be expected.

This is a very inadequate letter. I hope we may meet one day. There are innumerable questions I want to ask you. Your work has, I can assure you, no more true admirer than Yours sincerely, Edith Sitwell.

Edith Sitwell to Dr. Dorothea Walpole

Renishaw Hall
1 July 1941

Dear Dr Walpole,

I did not write at first, because I knew you would be overwhelmed with letters, but I have felt for you so very deeply in your great sorrow and terrible loss.

How much we all shall miss him! — My brother Osbert and I talk of this every day. We are only three — (my two brothers and myself) — of the many, many people to whom he has shown endless kindness, practical sympathy and help, — and such a wide and generous under-standing of motives, of aims, pioneer work, of everything that came under his eyes. — There can never have been a more generous-minded man, or a man with a broader outlook, and all this in addition to his own fine work. — How did he ever find time to do *that* work, and all those kindnesses? — Osbert showed me your letter; I can understand what a brother he must have been, knowing the *person* he was.

I remember so well the time, many years ago, when Hugh and I were both on the committee that was going to choose a present for Thomas Hardy on his 80th birthday, — all the givers and signatories had to be under a certain age, — I forget now what age. But Hugh said, suddenly: 'We must ask May Sinclair,' 'Oh,' said somebody, 'she is *much* over the age limit.' 'I don't care,' said Hugh. 'She must be asked. It will hurt her dreadfully from every point of view if she is not.'

Only a small thing, perhaps, but so typical of that delicate feeling for others, that warm kindliness.

We have been more angry, — are more angry — than you can know, over the mean, petty, *envious* notice in *The Times*, and that letter from the man Pollock. He is disgraced for ever by having written such a letter. We feel terribly about this pain having been added to what you are bearing in grief, and the dreadful suddenness of that grief.

In what contrast is that mean, petty, cheative envy to Hugh's gener-ous warm recognition of qualities in every writer of worth.

And in what contrast is that meanness to the noble tributes of T. S. Eliot, Sir Kenneth Clark, and J. B. Priestley. Those will remain. The others will go where all dirty things go.

You must not dream, please, of answering this letter. — I just had to try and express how much I feel for you and for Hugh's brother in your grief, — and to tell you how much we shall miss him.

Believe me, the deepest sympathy, Yours sincerely, Edith Sitwell.

Edith Sitwell to Stephen Spender

Renishaw Hall
20 June 1943

Dear Stephen,

Thank you a thousand times for sending me the Lorca. What a *wonderful* poet, and what a wonderful thing for him that he had such a poet as translator.

I cannot bear to think that he is dead. It seems one of the most terrible things that has happened to us. How I hate the hate that killed him.

His poems have such an intoxication that when reading them, and for many, many hours after, days after, one feels like a bumble-bee that has been for a whole afternoon in the heart of a tiger-lily flower. (We once had a lily here that bore *108* flowers on one stalk: it was photographed naturally for all the gardening papers. The bees came from miles and miles, and there were the most disgraceful Bacchanalian scenes: bees hardly able to find their way home. That is what I feel like about Lorca: excepting that one does *not* fall asleep, but becomes, on the contrary, extremely awake.)

The poems have an incredible beauty. How wonderful is the girl gathering lilies

> *'with the grey arm of the wind*
> *encircling her waist'*

— that poem has haunted my mind ever since you first translated it.

I am so happy to have this book, given me by you. — Again, this book contradicts what Shelley said about translation. This has all the honey left to it, and all the heady flower scents, and all the human blood, too. What a terrific poem is the 'Lament for Mejías'.

The murder of Lorca seems symbolic. It is just one of the most terrible and significant things that has happened to us: I find myself repeating it over and over again.

I was so delighted by your letter. — Lady Crewe is beside herself with pleasure about the prospective reading. She telephoned and told Osbert. We long to know all the proposed details.

I have received from the gentleman who owns the Blue Book Press, South Croydon, a letter assuring me that he has 'noted' that I am 'interested in poetry'. He has, it seems, written a book of poems entitled *In my*

Garden. This work, 'although it has received quite a nice notice from the *Publishers Gazette,* has not received a notice from the bigger papers, such as *The Times Literary Supplement.'* If, on reading this work, I 'care to increase its sales by getting for it the right kind of publicity', its author will be 'glad to recognise your services'.

'Now, then, will you be tempted?' as an old lady wrote to me when she asked me to a tea party to meet the great-niece of a former editor of the *Wide World Magazine,* —will you come in with me on this? I suppose we shall have to hand over part of our rake-in to the Editor of the *T.L.S.* . . . Still, the author is evidently going to make it worth one's while. The only snag is, I see his business telephone has been cut off, which looks sinister. . . . He says his sister in New Zealand thinks it is a lovely book.

Oh, dear, it is so sad.

We long to hear all about your adventures at Dorothy Wellesley's reading. It takes place on Wednesday or Thursday, if I mistake not. I hope she will have a great success, poor woman. . . . Incidentally, Walter Turner is really exceeding himself. Stephen Tennant has written me a very nice letter, covered with a design of roses painted by himself. I am about to answer this. What an extraordinary book Einstein's is; thank you for telling me about it. I am looking forward with the greatest excitement to seeing the sonnets. I do hope they are nearly finished.

Osbert's best wishes. Love to Natasha. Affectionately, Edith.

Edith Sitwell to Lord Keynes

Renishaw Hall
1 August 1943

Dear Maynard,

I am at once almost too aghast and too touched at your kindness to know what to say. When Osbert showed me your letter my feelings entered into an all-in wrestling match which is still going on. He *told* me he had written to you — but I didn't believe him.

I do not know what I can say to show my gratitude to you. I think I have never heard of anything so kind and so generous in all my life. And I feel it is not fair to accept it, but at the same time it would be ungracious not to. I do indeed thank you.

I had wanted the book so wildly for this reason. I have a particular feeling for Swinburne partly because, when I was seventeen, I ran away from my grandmother in Bournemouth, in order to put roses and pour libations of milk (and put a honeycomb) on Swinburne's grave in the Isle of Wight. This, of course, was in the days when, at seventeen, one must be clamped to an older female, or one's name was mud. Now I have several Swinburne manuscripts.

Then, too, I have written a poem in which I have incorporated a line of Ben Jonson's: *Out danced the babioun.* I am going to look out that poem of mine, and the workings of it, have them bound, and send them to you. This will take some little time, I suppose, but I shall see to it at once. With the very greatest gratitude and appreciation of your quite extraordinary kindness, Yours very sincerely, Edith Sitwell.

Osbert says I am one of the Gold-Diggers of 1943!!

Edith Sitwell to Benjamin Britten

As from Castello di Montegufoni
26 April 1955

My dear Ben,

I am so haunted and so alone with that wonderful music and its wonderful performance that I was incapable of writing before now. I had no sleep at all on the night of the performance. And I can think of nothing else.

It was certainly one of the greatest experiences in all my life as an artist.

During the performance, I felt as if I were dead — killed in the raid — yet with all my powers of feeling still alive. Most terrible and most moving — the appalling loneliness, for all that it was a communal experience one was alone, each being was alone, with space and eternity and the terror of death, and then God.

What a very great composer you are! and what a very great singer Peter is.

I can never begin to thank you for the glory you have given my poem. . . .

Edith Sitwell to James Purdy

Renishaw Hall
25 July 1958

Dear James,

I dare not imagine what you must think of me for not having written before to thank you for that masterly short story, every sentence of which bears your signature, and for your letter.

The reason I was so slow in writing was *A* that I strained my eyes correcting the proofs of 14th century poems (which are the very devil to do), with the result that I got migraine in its worst form, and *B* that, not allowed to get on with this in peace, I have been dragged ceaselessly from pillar to post. I've had the oddest adventures. In one, Quentin was involved. Two very young men, Americans, and one having a great sweetness of expression, both poets, — you probably have read about them in the *New York Times*, — were introduced to me and came to lunch, accompanied by Quentin, who was looking *terrified*! (I may say at this point, that the episode was just as I was beginning the migraine attacks, and was not, as you might say, *curative* in its effects.) They behaved with great courtesy. The poor boy with the sweet expression had, he told me, been sent to prison *at the age of 17 for three years* for organising a bank robbery! If ever, in my life, I saw anyone who had obviously been sweetened and in a way re-formed, by such a terrible experience, it was that boy. I am sure he is a kind of haunted saint, — a saint who has lost his way. For he *has* lost it. The other looked like a famished wolf. The trouble is, I understand, that they are both addicted to a habit the result of which is that nobody can *ever* tell *what* they will do next. (But they can be relied on to do it!) In an interview given to the *N.Y.T.* the poor boy who had been in prison said that at a recital he gave of his poems in Paris, he had removed all his clothes, and recited as he was when he was born.

Next day I received a letter from a friend of mine, a Don at Oxford, giving me such really terrifying information, that I took to my bed, and lay there with my mouth open, pondering!

However, the luncheon party went off all right, with no untoward incidents. The young man did not recite, and the old ladies whose only experiences are going to dim churches and dimmer lectures, remained wrapped in their mental cotton wool! The young men returned to Paris, so I haven't seen them again.

How is your play growing? It is so exciting to think of it. I think with joy of your 'Coronation' at the hands of the Academy of Arts and Letters. My, there must have been some sour faces!! Affectionate best wishes, dear James, from Edith.

I wrote these two poems, just before being floored by Fate.

T. E. Lawrence

An archaeologist with a profound respect for Arabic culture, T. E. Lawrence became a hero of the British Empire during World War I, when he helped the Arabs oust their Turkish oppressors. To his disgust and despair, England added Mesopotamia to its empire rather than protecting Arab freedom. Lawrence of Arabia, as he was known, spent the rest of his life dodging publicity and the imperial honors he did not want, finally dying in a motorcycle accident in 1935. In this letter, written from a Royal Tank Corps camp seething with male energy, Lawrence reflected on human sexuality and morality.

T. E. Lawrence to Lionel Curtis

[Bovington Camp, March 27, 1923]

It seems to continue itself today, because I've been wondering about the other fellows in the hut. A main feeling they give me is of difference from the R.A.F. men. There we were excited about our coming service. We talked and wondered of the future, almost exclusively. There was a constant recourse to imagination, and a constant rewarding of ourselves therefore. The fellows were decent, but so wrought up by hope that they were carried out of themselves, and I could not see them mattly. There was a sparkle round the squad.

Here every man has joined because he was down and out: and no one talks of the Army or of promotion, or of trades and accomplishments. We are all here unavoidably, in a last resort, and we assume this world's failure in one-another, so that pretence would be not merely laughed at, but as near an impossibility as anything human. We are social bed-rock, those unfit for life-by-competition: and each of us values the rest as cheap as he knows himself to be.

I suspect that this low estimation is very much the truth. There cannot be classes in England much more raw, more free of all that the upbringing of a lifetime has plastered over you and me. Can there be profit, or truth, in all these modes and sciences and arts of ours? The leisured world for hundreds, or perhaps thousands of years has been jealously working and recording the advance of each generation for the starting-point of the next — and here these masses are as animal, as carnal as were their ancestors before Plato and Christ and Shelley and Dostoevsky taught and thought. In this crowd it's made startingly clear how short is the range of knowledge, and what poor conductors of it ordinary humans are. You and I know: you have tried (Round Tabling and by mouth) to tell all whom you can reach: and the end is here, a cimmerian darkness with bog-lights flitting wrongly through its gas.

The pity of it is, that you've got to take this black core of things in camp, this animality, on trust. It's a feeling, a spirit which colours every word and action, and I believe every thought, passing in Hut 12. Your mind is like a many-storied building, and you, its sole tenant, flit from floor to floor, from room to room, at the whim of your spirit's moment. (Not that the spirit has moments, but let it pass for the metaphor's sake.) At will you can be gross, and enjoy coffee or a sardine, or rarefy yourself till the diaphancité [*sic*] of pure mathematics, or of a fluent design in line, is enough to feed you. Here —

I can't write it, because in literature such things haven't ever been, and can't be. To record the acts of Hut 12 would produce a moral-medical case-book, not a work of art but a document. It isn't the filth of it which hurts me, because you can't call filthy the pursuit of a bitch by a dog, or the mating of birds in springtime; and it's man's misfortune that he hasn't a mating season, but spreads his emotions and excitements through the year . . . but I lie in bed night after night with this cat-calling carnality seething up and down the hut, fed by streams of fresh matter from twenty lecherous mouths . . . and my mind aches with the rawness of it, knowing that it will cease only when the slow bugle calls for 'lights out' an hour or so hence . . . and the waiting is so slow. . . .

However the call comes always in the end, and suddenly at last, like God's providence, a dewfall of peace upon the camp . . . but surely the world would be more clean if we were dead or mindless? We are all guilty alike, you know. You wouldn't exist, I wouldn't exist, without this carnality. Everything with flesh in its mixture is the achievement of a moment when the lusty thought of Hut 12 has passed to action and conceived: and isn't it true that the fault of birth rests somewhat on the child? I believe it's we who led our parents on to bear us, and it's our unborn children who make our flesh itch.

A filthy business all of it, and yet Hut 12 shows me the truth behind Freud. Sex is an integer in all of us, and the nearer nature we are, the more constantly, the more completely a product of that integer. These fellows are the reality, and you and I, the selves who used to meet in London and talk of fleshless things, are only the outward wrappings of a core like these fellows. They let light and air play always upon their selves, and consequently have grown very lustily, but have at the same time achieved health and strength in their growing. Whereas our wrappings and bandages have stunted and deformed ourselves, and hardened them to an apparent insensitiveness . . . but it's a callousness, a crippling, only to be yea-said by aesthetes who prefer clothes to bodies, surfaces to intentions.

These fellows have roots, which in us are rudimentary, or long cut off. Before I came I never visualised England except as an organism, an entity . . . but these fellows are local, territorial. They all use dialects, and could be placed by their dialects, if necessary. However it isn't necessary, because each talks of his district, praises it, boasts of it, lives in the memory of it. We call each other 'Brum' or 'Coventry' or 'Cambridge', and the man who hasn't a 'place' is an outsider. They wrangle and fight over the virtues of their homes. Of solidarity, of a nation, of something ideal comprehending their familiar streets in itself—they haven't a notion.

Well, the conclusion of the first letter was that man, being a civil war, could not be harmonised or made logically whole . . . and the end of this is that man, or mankind, being organic, a natural growth, is unteachable: cannot depart from his first grain and colour nor exceed flesh, nor put forth anything not mortal and fleshly.

I fear not even my absence would reconcile Ph.K. to this.

E. L.

F. O. Matthiessen

From 1924, when they met, until 1945, when Cheney died, F. O. Matthiessen and Russell Cheney shared a gratifying long-distance love affair. An Oxford graduate student and then a Harvard professor, Matthiessen lived for much of that time in the United States, while Cheney, an artist, spent most of his time in France. They met at least once a year and in the meantime exchanged more than three thousand letters, addressing each other as Rat (Cheney) and Devil (Matthiessen). Both feared their sexual relationship would be found out, and the necessity of secrecy plunged Matthiessen into periodic depressions. Five years after Cheney's death he committed suicide. The following letter, however, was written in happier times.

F. O. Matthiessen to Russell Cheney

Oxford, England
Wednesday
January 28, 1925

Dearest Rat,

It came this morning — your first letter — just as I had figured it would. I lay snuggled deliciously in bed while the chapel bells were ringing, saying to myself: I'll lie here until I know that by the time I'm up and dressed and down the postman will have been around and I will have a letter from Rat.

There were a few tears — inevitably — swift hot tears of supreme joy, no pain, no sorrow, only the sudden penetration of your complete tenderness and devotion and the desire to have my arms around you and hold you to me close.

It takes strong men — men, as Foster [a Yale classmate and close friend] would say, who are capable of shaping destiny to their own ends — to handle the situation of love and separation, and still maintain balance of life. We are complex — both of us — in that we are neither wholly man, woman, or child. We love each other, we have accepted each other, and now it requires great energy of creation to fashion our inner lives so that they can endure the many months that we are destined to be apart during the next fifty years.

Fortunately our work binds neither of us to any one place. Every summer when you are available I am free — to come and bring my books and writing. We can settle in France, or in America, or where you will for three month periods together. You say that I am building air castles? Well, what else do you suppose that I live by?

And in the meantime there is our sure antidote for loneliness: it is activity. These two days at Oxford have not been unhappy. I have plunged into new fields of reading, and my mind is sparking through new labyrinths. Hours slip by, slip into days, and I am energetic, keen, vigorous.

Of course, dear feller, it is harder for you: for you are the artist.

Then, too, Cassis is more solitary than Oxford—for here I feel the undergraduate life pulsing on every side of me although I form no part of it. During your long quiet evenings you must either read and write, or be miserable and drink! How about a letter to Piccolo instead of that tenth cognac, Mr. Cheney?

I'm going out now to buy a frame for San Giorgio, and also to meet Mrs. Allcroft—you remember, the English lady I spent last Christmas with. I look forward to a long sympathetic talk, since I have not seen her since June.

Am I eating off the mantelpiece? Not yet, for the Fellows of the College are now busy electing a new Warden, and not until tomorrow will they have time for me. Popular opinion seems to point to the following alternatives:

(1) A fine of 5 to 10 pounds.

(2) "gated" for the rest of the term—which means that I wouldn't be allowed to go out after 7 o'clock any night!

(3) "Sent down," which means I would return to Cassis and lose my degree—not very likely.

Goody-bye, dear Heart—

Federico García Lorca

In August 1936, the charismatic and gifted poet-playwright Federico García Lorca was executed by Spanish Nationalist followers of Francisco Franco. A victim of fascism and homophobia, he had by then gained international fame for his hotly sensual poetry, which conveyed gay desire in a straight guise. At home, García Lorca's populist convictions inspired his folk dramas and led him to produce classical Spanish plays for the peasants of the countryside. While working on one of these productions he met surrealist painter Salvador Dalí and fell in love. García Lorca wrote smoldering poems to Dalí, and Dalí painted numerous studies of García Lorca, but the painter's sexual conflicts made the relationship a painful one. Only fragments of their correspondence survive, but dozens of García Lorca's letters to other friends have been preserved. Warm and emotional, these shed light on his personal relationships and reveal his spirit as a poet, as a Spaniard and as a man.

Federico García Lorca to Adriano Del Valle

[May 1918]

[May today in time and October above my head]

PEACE

Friend:

I was very pleased to receive your letter and you can be sure that it gave me moments of great spiritual satisfaction. I come before you merely as a companion (a companion full of sadness) who has read some of your lovely poems.

I am a poor impassioned and silent fellow who, very nearly like the marvelous Verlaine, bears within a lily impossible to water, and to the foolish eyes of those who look upon me I seem to be a very red rose with the sexual tint of an April peony, which is not my heart's truth. I appear before people (those things that call themselves people as [illegible word] says) like an Oriental drunk on the full moon and I feel like a Chopinesque Gerineldo in an odious and despicable epoch of Kaisers and La Ciervas (down with them!). My image and my verses give the impression of something very passionate . . . and, yet, at the bottom of my soul there's an enormous desire to be very childlike, very poor, very hidden. I see before me many problems, many entrapping eyes, many conflicts in the battle between head and heart and all my sentimental flowering seeks to enter a golden garden and I try hard because I like paper dolls and the playthings of childhood, and at times I lie down on my back on the floor to play games with my kid sister (she's my delight) . . . , but the phantom that lives within us and hates us pushes me down the path. One must move along because we must grow old and die, but I don't want to pay attention to it . . . and, nevertheless, with each day that passes I have another doubt and another sadness. Sadness of the enigma of myself! There is within us, Adriano my friend, a desire not to suffer and an innate goodness, but the external force of temptation and the overwhelming tragedy of physiology insure our destruction. I believe that everything around us is full of the souls that passed on, that they are the ones who provoke our sorrows and that they are the ones who enter the kingdom inhabited by that white and blue virgin called Melancholy . . . , or in other words, the kingdom of Poetry (I have no conception of poetry other than the lyric). I entered it a long time ago . . . ; I was ten years old and I fell in love . . . ; and then I immersed myself completely, making my vows to the singular religion of Music and donning the vestments of passion that She lends to those who love her. After I entered the kingdom of Poetry, I ended by anointing myself with love for everything. To sum up, I'm a good boy, who opens his heart to the whole world. . . . Of course I'm a great admirer of France and I hate militarism with all my heart, and feel only an immense desire for Humanity. Why struggle with the flesh while the frightening problem of the spirit exists? I love Venus madly, but even more I love the question, Heart? And most of all, I keep to myself, like that rare and true Peer Gynt with the button moulder . . . ; I want me to be myself.

As for the things I'm doing, I can only tell you that I'm working hard; I write a lot and do a lot of music. I have written three books (two of them poetry) and expect to do more work. As for music, I am now busy taking down the splendid interior polyphony of Granadan folksongs.

As for my first book, I thank you for your praise. Let me tell you that in writing about it you don't have to say anything to me, because once the book hits the streets, it's no longer mine, it's everybody's. . . . In my book (which is very bad) there is only one great emotion that always flows from my sadness and the ache I feel before Nature. . . . I don't know if you can tell how sincere I am, impassioned and humble-hearted. It's enough for me to know that yours is the spirit of a poet. And even if you were unable to see the poor light of my soul that I shed in this letter or even if you should laugh, I would only feel the intimate bitterness of having shown something of my interior reliquary to a soul who closed his eyes and smiled skeptically. Of course I dismiss this. I am a great romantic, and that is my chief pride. In a century of zeppelins and stupid deaths, I sob at my piano dreaming of the Handelian mist and I create verses very much my own, singing the same to Christ as to Buddha, to Mohammed, and to Pan. For a lyre I have my piano and, instead of ink, the sweat of yearning, yellow pollen of my inner lily and my great love. One must kill the "little rich boys" and annul the laughter of those who love Harmony. We must love the moon over the lake of our soul and make our religious meditations over the magnificent abyss of full-blown sunsets . . . , because it colors the music of our eyes. . . . I leave my pen now to board the pious ship of Dreams. Now you know what I'm like in one aspect of my life.

If you wish to answer me, the address is Acera del Casino . . . , though I'm sure my uncle knows it. Give him my warmest greetings. He's very good and very affectionate . . . , but he doesn't know me in depth. For him I've always been a boy who has spoken little, has smiled and nothing more. Forgive me my horrible handwriting. I've been very sincere with you. . . . Read this sad letter, meditate on it, and afterwards I'm sure you'll say ". . . But what a fellow! So young! In short, a poet." And here's my left hand, which is the hand of the heart

Federico

A favor. . . . Don't ever sing the "Song of the Soldier" (it's the work of a musical barber!); even though they threaten to shoot you. Otherwise you can't be my friend.

Federico García Lorca to Melchor Fernández Almagro

[Granada, August 1924]

Dear Melchorito:

Your letter took so long! . . . But better late than never. Did you like Burgos? What a sweet memory, full of truth and tears, overcomes me when I think of Burgos. . . . Does this shock you? I am nourished by Burgos, because the cathedral's great towers of air and silver showed me the *narrow gate* through which I had to pass in order to know myself and know my soul. What green poplars! What an old wind! Oh, Tower of Gamonal and Sepulcher on San Amaro! And, oh, my child heart! . . . My heart never again will be as alive, as full of pain and eternal grace.

Your card from Burgos has exacerbated my old painful stigmata and has caused a resin of light and nostalgia to well from my body.

I piously remember [Martín Domínguez] Berrueta (who treated me in such a charming way) since it was through him that I lived unforgettable hours which made a profound impression on my life as a poet.

But I have no time now to ask him to forgive me . . . , although he smiles at me from afar. . . . God will have forgiven him his childish pedantry and his petty pride in exchange for his enthusiasm, which, even if it were (and this is not known) for *ulterior motives*, was, in the end, *enthusiasm*, the wing of the holy spirit.

I've had a bad time these past few days, because I wanted to dedicate to our friend [José de] Ciria [y Escalante] a tender and authentic memorial, but no matter how hard I struggled I couldn't get (and this is rare for me) my fountain, my fountain!, to flow for him. Yesterday afternoon I was in a cool and dark poplar grove and I told him: "Pepe, why don't you want me to evoke you?" And I felt my eyes fill with tears.

Then, after ten days of continuous effort, I was able to give birth in an instant to the sonnet I'm sending you.

But it seems to me that we should *commune* through Ciria and forget him in appearance. One must *make him a part of oneself* and smile without knowing his name. Do you always keep in mind that you have eyes? And, nevertheless, all of life enters us through them. Let us convert our dead into *our blood* and forget them.

Once in a while I'm seized by a strange happiness I have never felt before. The very sad happiness of being a poet! And nothing matters to me. Not even death!

If you answer me immediately, I will send you poems and drawings. In a few days, the angelic Falla will get to work on my little opera. I expect we'll have a good time, since the subject has wit and style, which is necessary in any theatrical poem.

Adiós. Write me soon. A hug for you and best regards to your family.

Federico

On the Death of José De Ciria y Escalante

Who can say that he saw you? And at what moment?
What sorrow of illuminated shadow!
Two voices resound: the clock and the wind.
While dawn floats off without you.
A delirium of ashen spikenards
invades your delicate brow.
Man! Passion! Sorrow of light! Memento.
Return turned into moon and heart of nothing!
Return turned into moon: With my own hand
I'll toss your apple over the turbid river
of red fish in summer.
And you, above, on high, green and cold,
forget yourself!, and forget the vain world,
delicate Giocondo. My friend!

This sonnet, naturally, contains a lot of restrained and static sentiment. I'm satisfied. Although I'll have to polish it a bit. Is it worthy of Ciria? Tell me the truth. I'd like to dedicate three or four to him and I want them to be sonnets, because the sonnet preserves an eternal sentiment, which doesn't fit in any other vessel better than this apparently cold one. Tell me what you think of this.

Adiós, and console yourself thinking how our friend is with God in the divine surroundings of air and endless sky. Death to cold science! Long live mystic science, and love, and friendship!

Federico García Lorca to
Melchor Fernández Almagro

[Granada, the end of September 1925]

Dear Melchorito:

You don't know how much we've grieved, I as well as my family, over the death of your poor Aunt Juana, so innocent and loving.

Just now I remember the day she made us hug each other in order for her to see the reality of our great friendship, blessed be her delicate and Christian soul a thousand times over!

And when are you visiting? We're all awaiting you with true affection and we're planning to dine together in your honor.

You don't have any idea of the enthusiasm your book aroused in Valdecasillas [Alfonso García Valdecasas] and [Antonio] Luna [García]. . . . And that's the way it ought to be, because the book is worthy of it!

I'm working a lot these days.

For the *first time in my life* I'm creating erotic poetry. A singular field has been opened to me, which is renewing me in an extraordinary way. I don't understand myself, Melchorito. My mother says: "You're still growing. . . ." And I, on the other hand, am *getting into problems* that I should have confronted long ago. . . . Am I backward? . . . What is this? It seems as though I've just attained my youth. That's why when I'll be sixty I won't be old . . . I'm never going to be *old*. *Adiós*. I feel like talking with you . . . and asking your advice.

Federico

Federico García Lorca to Sebastian Gasch

[1927 (?)]

Everyday I appreciate Dalí's talent even more. He seems to me unique and he possesses a serenity and a *clarity* of judgment about whatever he's planning to do that is truly moving. He makes mistakes and it doesn't matter. *He's alive*. His denigrating intelligence unites with his disconcerting childishness, in such an unusual combination that it is absolutely captivating and original. What moves me most about him now is his *fever* of constructions (that is to say, creation), in which he tries to create out of *nothing* with such strenuous efforts and throws himself into the gales of creativity with so much faith and so much intensity that it seems incredible. Nothing more dramatic than this objectivity and this search for happiness for happiness' sake. Remember that this has always been the Mediterranean canon. "I believe in the resurrection of the flesh," says Rome. Dalí is the man who struggles with a golden ax against phantoms. "Don't speak to me of supernatural things. How repulsive is Santa Catalina!" says Falla.

> *Oh straight line!*
> *Pure lance without a knight!*
> *How my twisted path*
> *dreams of your light!*

Say I. But Dalí doesn't let himself be led. Besides his faith in astral geometry, he needs to be at the helm. It moves me; Dalí inspires the same pure emotion (and may God Our Father forgive me) as that of the baby Jesus abandoned on the doorstep of Bethlehem, with the germ of the crucifixion already latent beneath the straws of the cradle.

Federico García Lorca to Salvador Dalí

Barcelona, July 1927

Cadaqués has the vitality and permanent neutral beauty of the place where Venus was born, *but where this has been forgotten.*

It aspires to pure beauty. The vines have disappeared and day by day are exalted the sharp edges which are like waves. One day the moon will move with the elasticity of a damp fish and the tower of the church oscillate like soft rubber over the hard or *sorrowful houses,* of lime or chewed bread. I get excited thinking about the discoveries you're going to make in Cadaqués and I remember Salvador Dalí the neophyte licking the twilight's shell without going in altogether, the pale pink shell of a crab lying on its back.

Today you're inside. From here I can hear (ay, my little boy, how sad!) the soft trickle of blood from the Sleeping Beauty of the Wood of Gadgets [in your painting of Saint Sebastian] and the crackling of two little beasties like the sounds of a pistachio nut cracked between one's fingers. The decapitated woman [in your painting *Honey Is Sweeter Than Blood*] is the finest imaginable "poem" on the theme of blood, and has more blood than all that spilt in the European war, which was *hot* blood and had no other purpose than to *irrigate* the earth and appease a symbolic thirst for eroticism and faith. Your pictorial blood and in general the whole tactile concept of your physiological aesthetic has such a concrete, well-balanced air, such a logical and true quality of pure poetry that it attains the category of *that which we need absolutely* in order to live.

One can say: "I was tired and I sat down in the shade and freshness of that blood," or: "I came down from the hill and ran all along the beach until I found the melancholy head in the spot where the delicious little crackling beasties, so useful for the digestion, gathered."

Now I realize how much I am losing by leaving you.

The impression I get in Barcelona is that everyone is playing and sweating in an effort to *forget*. Everything is confused and aggressive like the aesthetic of the flame, everything indecisive and out of joint. In Cadaqués the people feel on the ground all the sinuosities and pores of the soles of their feet. Now I realize how I felt my shoulders in Cadaqués. It's delicious for me to recall the slippery curves of my shoulders when for the first time I felt in them the circulation of my blood in four spongy tubes which trembled with the movements of a wounded swimmer.

Federico García Lorca to Jorge Zalamea

[1928]

I would be sorry
if
you
were
miffed
at

the letter I sent you. Can't a poet scold his wayward friends? Come now, I should hope so. It would be foolish. And you are no fool. What do you know about what I'm feeling? I wouldn't have been at ease without saying what I said.

But I showed you quite well that I wasn't angry.

Good-bye.

I'm working on a poem now called the "Academy of the Rose and the Jar of Ink" [unpublished]. The poem is cruel, but clean. Dalí is coming in September. In his last letter he told me: "You are a Christian tempest and have need of my paganism. This past season in Madrid you gave yourself to something you should never have given yourself to. I'll come to get you to give you a sea cure. It will be winter time and we will light a fire. The poor beasts will be nearly frozen. You will remember that you are an inventor of marvels and we'll live together with a camera."

He's like that, this marvelous friend.

Aren't you coming to Granada? Come!

Adiós. Another more heartfelt *adiós*.

Adiós.

And another from further off.

Fede
ri
co

Federico García Lorca to Jorge Zalamea

[Autumn 1928]

Dear Jorge:

I got your letter. I thought you were angry. I rejoice with all my poor heart (this unfortunate child of mine) to find you the same as before, as at first. You're suffering but you shouldn't. Sketch out a plan of your desire and live within it, always within a norm of beauty. That's what I do, dear friend . . . but how difficult it is for me! But I do it. I'm slightly out of sorts with the world, but the living beauty that my hands touch makes up for every displeasure. And being involved in serious emotional conflicts and nearly *overcome* by love, by society, by ugly things. I keep to my norm of happiness at all costs. I don't want them to defeat me. You shouldn't let yourself be defeated. I know very well what you're going through.

You're in a sad age of doubt and bear an artistic problem on your shoulders that you don't know how to solve. Don't worry. That problem will take care of itself. One morning you'll begin to see clearly. I know. It grieves me to know you're passing through bad times. But you should learn to overcome them one way or another. Anything is preferable to being eaten up, broken, crushed by them. By sheer will power, I've *resolved* these past few days, one of the most painful periods I've experienced in my life. You just can't imagine what it is to spend entire nights on the balcony looking at a nocturnal Granada, *empty* for me and without finding the least bit of consolation in anything.

And then . . . trying constantly to see to it that your state of mind does not filter into your poetry, because it will play you a bad trick by exposing the purest in you to the eyes of those who should *never* see it. That is why, for discipline, I'm doing these precise *academic* things now and opening my soul before the symbol of the Sacrament, and my eroticism in the "Ode to Sesostris," which I've halfway finished.

I speak of these things, because you ask me; I will speak no more of that which, external to me, wounds me from afar in the surest and most sapient way.

But I defend myself! I'm more valiant than the Cid (Campeador).

This "Ode to Sesostris" will please you, because it belongs to my *furious* genre. The "Ode to the [Most Holy] Sacrament" is almost finished. And it seems to me to contain great intensity. Probably the greatest poem I've done.

The part I'm working on now (it will have a total of three hundred verses) is "Devil, second enemy of the soul," and that's strong.

> *Deep blinding light of crackling matter,*
> *oblique light of swords and star's quicksilver,*
> *announced the loveless body coming*
> *through all the corners of open Sunday.*
>
> *Beauty's form without nostalgia nor dream.*
> *Murmur of liberated and mad surfaces.*
> *Marrow of the present. Feigned security*
> *of floating on the water with the marble torso.*
>
> *Body of beauty which throbs and escapes.*
> *A moment of veins and navel's tenderness.*
> *Love between walls and confined kisses,*
> *with the sure fear of the burning goal.*
>
> *Beautiful with light, orient of the feeling hand.*
> *Storm and youth of bristles and mollusks,*
> *fire for the sensitive flesh that burns,*
> *nickel for the sob that seeks God flying.*

It seems to me that this "Devil" is really a Devil. Each time this part gets more obscure, more metaphysical, until at the end there surges forth the extremely cruel beauty of the enemy, a wounding beauty, enemy of love.

Adiós. I gave you the whole boring account. A very warm embrace from

Federico

Write me.

Federico García Lorca to Carlos Morla Lynch

[Granada, latter half of August 1931]

Dear Carlos:

What grief! All day long I thought of you. In my house, the same. When I told my mother the enchanting words of Gitanillo about the Virgin, she cried, and a woman who was there sewing, very Andalusian, said: "God bless him, you can be sure he is now in the Virgin's arms!"

It has been a grievous pain, and I can imagine how you must have suffered, and I'm with you because I understand you and because I too am accustomed to suffer because of things which people don't understand or suspect.

Between one person and another there are spider threads that little by little turn into wires and even bars of steel. When death separates us there remains a bloody wound in the place of each thread.

You must know I don't forget you for a moment and I wish I could embrace you with the tenderness and lyric foolishness I feel for you. Tenderness because it comes from the blood and foolishness (oh, sweet silliness and divine blather of infants!) because it comes from the soul, which is the most foolish of our possessions.

But I want you to be strong, because it hurts me that you should add sufferings to the many you've had, although I know this is impossible in a heart so great and elevated as yours. God too has to be good to you, and the same with the Virgin, the Holy Virgin, full of swords like a bull, who shelters the *toreros* and who takes to herself those who are handsome and good as was Gitanillo.

Carlos, I embrace you with all my affection. Regards to Bebé and to Carlitos. And tell Rafael [Martínez Nadal] that his treatment of me is vile. I haven't done anything to him and he hasn't answered my last four letters. I'm really hurt. He's either bad or irresponsible. I'd gladly punch him. I'm fit to bust.

Adiós, Carlitos. A thousand embraces for you and write me a lot.

Federico

Marcel Proust

One of the first major modern novelists directly to address homosexuality in his work, Marcel Proust had an enormous impact on succeeding generations of writers. This perhaps had more to do with the extraordinary style and structure of his masterpiece, *À la Recherche du temps perdu*, than with its content, but the immense experimental work's comprehensive analysis of the human condition would not have been complete without mention of homosexuality. Just as important, it would have failed as a work of autobiography. A fan, in particular, of Colette, Proust started work on his series of linked novels in 1905, when his asthma became so severe that it confined him to his bedroom. The first installment appeared in 1913, with three more following before his death in 1922; the remaining three segments were published posthumously. Upon its publication in 1921 the fourth title, *Sodome et Gomorrhe*, caused a furor because of its gay theme. The response initiated a spirited exchange between Proust and his friend Comte Robert de Montesquiou.

Marcel Proust to Colette

102, boulevard Haussman.
[1914]

Madame,

I thank you profoundly for having sent me *Les Heures Longues*. My thanks will be briefer than I would have liked, because for two years my eyes have given me a great deal of trouble, and as my general state of health is not good enough to allow me to consult an oculist, during the normal hours, I have no sense of direction, and that makes everything difficult. Yet in spite of that, I read your book, almost the whole of it, at one sitting. I am not yet at the stage of the blind man whom you imagine listening to the presence and the sound of the day, in the tomb without stars. I can hardly read at all, but I cannot resist delightful things. This Venice in your book to which I have just referred appears to me one of the most astonishing things. This silting up, this sorbet eaten blindly have delighted me (and this is twilight carnival with its shadow-mask!). I have never been to Rome, but your Rome is nonetheless marvellous. These towers which walk carrying before them the future and the fortune of Italy, how truly 'roman' they are. You probably do not know that it is here that you meet (oh! even if you know it, in the shadow of plagiarism, it is so distant that it is absolutely different, there is really no connection) with Bossuet, who speaks of living towers which know how to repair the breaches made in them. He also was a Roman. Your cats, who are cats right up to their wanderings round the columns, have delighted me. And if my eyes did not hurt me so much, how much I would like to talk to you about Saint-Malo and Verdun, about everything, for your style, and your colour are full of such perpetual finds that if one noted everything one could write you a letter as long as your book.

Please accept my respectful admiration.

Marcel Proust.

Marcel Proust to Colette

[1919]

I have just found this letter which I wrote over six weeks ago. I am sending it to your publisher, as I cannot find your address. Again I send you my respectful admiration.

> 102, boulevard Haussman (provisionally), for the house has been bought by a banker, who wants to make it into a bank and give notice to all the tenants.

Madame,

I wept a little this evening, for the first time for a long time, and yet for some time I have been full of sorrow, suffering and worry. But the reason I wept was not due to that at all, but to reading Mitsou's letter. The two last letters are the chef-d'œuvre of the book (I mean of *Mitsou*, for I have not yet read *En camarades*, my eyes are very bad, I cannot read quickly).

Perhaps, if it was absolutely necessary in order to show you that I am sincere in my praise, to tell you that I would not allow myself to be called a critic, in connection with a Master as yourself, I would find that this letter from Mitsou is so beautiful, but also a little too pretty, because amongst so much that is admirable and profoundly natural there is just a touch of preciousness. Indeed, when, in the restaurant (in the amazing restaurant, to which I compare with a little humiliation my innumerable inferior restaurants, sodoms which you do not know yet, and which will appear gradually) (in the restaurant which makes me also think with a little melancholy of this dinner which we were to have together and which, like everything else in my life since that time — and for a long time before — could never happen), the blue lieutenant speaks of a nice wine which tastes of coffee and violets, this is so much in the character and language of the blue lieutenant. (In this restaurant, how I love the wine waiter, with his dreamy haughtiness, etc!) But for Mitsou, there are in her letter things which would have seemed to me far too 'pretty' if I had not found from the beginning (like you, is it not?) that Mitsou is much more intelligent than the blue lieutenant, that she is admirable, that her momentary bad taste in furnishing has no importance. (I wish that you could see my 'bronzes', it is true that I have simply kept them, and not chosen them), and that moreover the miraculous progress of her style, which is as rapid as hail, corresponds exactly with the title: How wit comes to young girls.

Madame, I wrote all that a fortnight ago, but there have been such ups and downs in my health, such serious ones, that I have not been able to finish my letter. Since things became better my first gesture is to beg you to accept my respectful admiration.

Marcel Proust.

Marcel Proust and Comte Robert de Montesquiou

[1921]

Proust to Montesquiou:
It has been an *idée fixe* with me, an obsession such as one sometimes gets for one particular flower on a piece of wallpaper, to find at least two copies of the first edition — if more were not obtainable — one for a poor

old friend of Mama's who has really been a second mother to me, the other for you. . . .

Montesquiou to Proust:
I am filled with admiration for the strategy of your art (which is probably a combination of natural instinct and deliberate planning, because, no matter how much one may scheme, one can never be quite sure of producing the effect at which one aims) with its succession of lightning blows, book following book so quickly that those who read them merely because it is "the thing to do" are given no breathing space, no time in which to realize that, in point of fact, they really like something else much better though it may not be nearly so good. . . .

Proust to Montesquiou:
If you still have a vague recollection of *A l'ombre des jeunes filles en fleurs* (forgive me for referring to my own forgotten works, it is you who lure me on to do so), you may recall a scene in which Monsieur de Charlus looks fixedly but absent-mindedly at me one day when we are both near the Casino. When I wrote that, I had in mind, for a moment, the late Baron Doazan, who was a familiar figure in the Aubernon salon, and shared the tastes of Monsieur de Charlus. But I soon forget all about him, and set myself to construct a Charlus, conceived on much larger lines, and entirely invented. . . . *My* Charlus has a terrible fall in the last volume, but does (to my mind) take on a certain amplitude. There are plenty of people who are convinced that Saint-Loup is d'Albuféra, though I never, even remotely, intended anything of the sort. I have an idea that he must think so himself; I can't otherwise understand why he should have quarreled with me, but he has, and I feel deeply hurt in consequence. . . .

Montesquiou to Proust:
To revert for a moment to the subject of "keys." Whether they be true or false, the work of Louis XVI or of Gamain, concerns only the author. For us the interest is merely secondary. . . . Why should we care? Does it really matter to us whether the cook has put vinegar or savory herbs into his sauce? I live retired from the world, but I was familiar with the men of the generations you are concerned to portray, though I never knew d'Albuféra. His mother was my sister's daughter-in-law, but we lost touch with the family after Elise's death. As you describe him he seems a pleasant enough creature, especially in the picture you give of him, sitting alone in the restaurant with his back to the wall, and fidgeting about for all the world like a dancer of the Russian Ballet. There is a shade of the obsequious, perhaps, in his friendship for you, but he is

not without a certain elegance in the high-kicking episode which you describe. But everything you say of him might apply equally well to Guiche, who, so it always seemed to me, must have been the model for Saint-Loup. . . . For the first time, someone has ventured, you have ventured, to deal openly, and on a big scale, with the vice associated with the names of Tiberius and the Shepherd Corydon. You have made it the subject of a novel, as Longus or Benjamin Constant made the emotion of love. . . . What the consequences may be we shall see, and I have little doubt that you are already feeling some of the effects. . . . You have made for yourself a name in the world; you are an influence among those who control decorations and literary prizes (though you are worth something better than such baubles), and it may be, therefore, that you will succeed in your tilting at hypocrisy, or, if you prefer it, at assumed decency of behavior. But will you? I wonder. The enemy is very powerful. . . .

Proust to Montesquiou:
For many long weeks now I have been at death's door, not as the result of a *cancer,* as you so kindly assume . . . but literally succumbing to fatigue. I must ask you to permit me, after so much bowing and scraping, to make, with due respect, my final adieux. In a note which might have been written by a man of twenty-five you convey sad news to your obedient, your more than centenarian friend. . . . Do you really believe that my feelings of admiration and gratitude have cooled? . . . Your charge is completely unfounded. It was *I* who wrote last, and you never deigned to reply to my letter. . . .

Gertrude Stein/Mabel Dodge/H. G. Wells

A pioneer of modern literature and a patron of modern art, Gertrude Stein stands, along with her lifetime companion, Alice B. Toklas, as an icon of lesbian history. In her youth she collaborated closely with her brother Leo to promote emerging artists; she continued these efforts after their estrangement. Her acquaintances ranged far and wide both in Europe, where she lived, and in the United States, where she was born, encompassing notables such as publisher John Lane, painter Roger Fry, essayist Logan Pearsall Smith, playwright and novelist Israel Zangwill and composer Virgil Thomson. These fragments of letters to and from her friend Mabel Weeks, socialite and art collector Mabel Dodge, H. G. Wells and Carl Van Vechten discuss Stein's singular work, including her acclaimed word portrait of Dodge.

Gertrude Stein to Mabel Weeks

[1904]

I am afraid that I can never write the great American novel. I don't know how to sell on a margin or to do anything with shorts and longs, so I have to content myself with niggers and servant girls and the foreign population generally. Leo he said there wasn't no art in Lovett's book and then he was bad and wouldn't tell me that there was in mine so I went to bed very miserable but I don't care there ain't any Tchaikovsky Pathetique or Omar Kayam or Wagner or Whistler or White Man's Burden or green burlap in mine at least not in the present ones. Dey is very simple and very vulgar and I don't think they will interest the great American public. . . . My book is finished now and the worst thing will be to get it published . . . it will certainly make your hair curl with the complications and tintinabulations of its style, but I'm very fond of it. I think it a noble combination of Swift and Matisse . . . just starting on a new one . . . it does not seem to matter much to me whether it gets published or not.

Mabel Dodge to Gertrude Stein

[1911]

To me it is one of the most remarkable things I have ever read. There are things hammered out of consciousness into black & white that have never been expressed before — so far as I know. States of being put into words the 'noumenon' captured — as few have done it. To name a thing is practically to create it & this is what your work is — real creation. It is almost frightening to come up against reality in language in this way. I always get — as I told you — the shivers when I read your things. And your palette is such a simple one — the primary colours in word painting & you express every shade known and unknown with them. It is as new & strange & big as the post-impressionists in their way &, I am perfectly convinced, it is the forerunner of a whole epoch of new form & expression. It is very morally constructive for I feel it will alter reality as we have known it, & help us get at Truth instead of away from it as 'literature' so sadly often does.

One cannot read you and still go on cherishing the consistent illusions one has built up about oneself and others.

H. G. Wells to Gertrude Stein

17, Church Row, Hampstead
[January 1913]

Dear Miss Stein

I have just read *Three Lives*. At first I was repelled by your extraordinary style, I was busy with a book of my own and I put yours away. It is only in the last week I have read it — I read it with a deepening pleasure and admiration. I'm very grateful indeed to you for sending it to me and I shall watch for your name again very curiously and eagerly.

Very sincerely yrs
H. G. Wells

Gertrude Stein to Mabel Dodge

[February 1913]

John Lane is an awfully funny man. He waits round and he asks a question and you think he has got you and then you find he hasn't. Roger Fry is going to try to help him land me . . . but the most unexpected interested person is Logan Pearsall Smith. He went quite off his head about your portrait and is reading it to everybody. Never goes anywhere without it and wants to do an article on it for the English Review. Among other things he read it to Zangwill and Zangwill was moved. He said 'And I always thought she was such a healthy minded young woman, what a terrible blow it must be for her poor dear brother.' And it seems he meant it. Then when L. would persist in reading it and rereading it Z. got angry and said to Logan 'How can you waste your time reading and rereading a thing like that and all these years you've refused to read Kipling.' And the wonderful part of it was that Z. was not fooling.

We have been seeing all kinds of people and last night we had an evening with Paul and Muriel [Draper]. We were there for dinner. [Robert de la] Condamine and the younger Rothenstein were there and Condamine and I got along beautifully . . .

Roger Fry is being awfully good about my work. It seems that he read 3 Lives long ago and was much impressed with it and so he is doing his best to get me published. His being a Quaker gives him more penetration in his sweetness than is usual with his type, it does not make him more interesting but it makes him purer.

Gertrude Stein to Carl Van Vechten

[January 1931]

My dearest Carl

Voilà pourquoi j'avais . . . well anyhow we have decided to publish ourselves, Alice is managing director I am author, and we hope there will be purchasers, and so to be so best to you both, and will you Carl if you can do a notice somewhere or get somebody else to of the edition and the book, perhaps that would help, anyway it's a try and I am very happy about it. We have been having a hectic one might almost say lurid winter so far, there is this and many other things and then we have quarrelled beginning with Bravig Imbs going on through Tonny and George Hugnet, ending with Virgil Thomson and now we don't see any of them any more, but we seem to be seeing almost everybody else such is life in a great capital, otherwise calm. Basket had distemper but he is now well, I am writing plays rather nice ones, Bernard Faÿ is translating me on Madame Récamier, that pleases me . . .

Edwina B. Kruse

Her relationship with Edwina B. Kruse was one of many thrice-married writer Alice Dunbar-Nelson would have within the black lesbian community that thrived in the 1920s, at the height of the Harlem Renaissance. The daughter of emancipated slaves, poet/journalist/essayist Dunbar-Nelson became a leading figure of that movement. She was twenty-five years old at the turn of the century, already married to Paul Laurence Dunbar and the author of two story collections. Two years later her marriage crumbled and she moved to Wilmington, Delaware, where she became close friends with Kruse. Three brief telegrams sent by Kruse during three days in October 1907 bespeak the warmth of their liaison.

Edwina B. Kruse to Alice Dunbar-Nelson

October 5, 1907

I want you to know dear, that every thought of my life is for you, every throb of my heart is yours and yours alone. I just can not ever let any one else have you.

October 6, 1907

I *wish*, oh! how I do wish you were here — Alice! I wish I had never let you go away at all. Gertrude and Etta send love and I can't send any because it is all there in Ithaca wound up in you.

October 7, 1907

I'll be more cheerful tomorrow. How I want you, my love.

Angelina Weld Grimké

Angelina Weld Grimké wrote poetry, plays, stories and essays that voiced a deep concern with the problems confronting the African-Americans of her era. A fixture of the Harlem Renaissance, she never married and had at least one "disastrous" lesbian affair. Some of her romantic poetry is transparently lesbian, expressing love for a woman in a voice identified neither as male nor as female. Her prose generally focused on racial issues, and she gained a reputation as an astute commentator on race relations in the United States. When asked to submit a story for publication in the *Atlantic Monthly*, she replied with this proposal.

Angelina Weld Grimké to Mary Knoblauch

[1920]

I am sending enclosed a story. It is not a pleasant one but is based on fact. Several years ago, in Georgia, a colored woman quite naturally it would seem became wrought up because her husband had been lynched. She threatened to bring some of the leaders to justice. The mob made up of "chivalrous" and brave white men determined to teach her a lesson. She was dragged out of town to a desolate part of the woods and the lesson began. First she was strung up by her feet to the limbs of a tree, next her clothes were saturated with kerosene oil, and then she was set afire. While the woman shrieked and writhed in agony, one man who had brought with him a knife used in the butchering of animals, ripped her abdomen wide open. Her unborn child fell to the ground at her feet. It emitted one or two little cries but was soon silenced by brutal heels that crushed out its head. Death came at last to the poor woman. The lesson ended.

Last fall, I think it was you printed an article entitled "Can These Things Be?" That was a very terrible arraignment of the Turks. It, of course, did not happen in America.

The fact of the lynching upon which I based my story happened in the civilized U.S.A. in the 20th Century. Was this woman, I wonder, lynched for the "usual crime?" "Can These Things Be?" Even the Turks have been astounded at the brutality and the ruthlessness of the lynchings in this country. Where are these lynchings leading the U.S.A.? In what will they end?

Alain Locke

Although centered in New York, the Harlem Renaissance took place on both sides of the Atlantic. Its European headquarters was Paris, which fell head over heels for jazz in the 1920s. Many leading African-American writers, musicians and artists spent some time there, forming a vibrant contingent of the American expatriate community. Among their numbers were the critic Alain Locke and the poet Langston Hughes, who became lovers. This letter fragment captures in a few words the highly charged sensations of new love.

Alain Locke to Langston Hughes

[1924]

Today, the atmosphere is like atomized gold — and last night you know how it was — two days the equal of which atmospherically I have never seen in a great city—days when every breath has the soothe of a kiss and every step the thrill of an embrace.

I needed one such day and one such night to tell you how much I love you, in which to see soul-deep and be satisfied—for after all with all my sensuality and sentimentality, I love sublimated things and today nature, the only great cleanser of life, would have distilled anything. God grant us one such day and night before America with her inhibitions closes down on us.

Carl Van Vechten

As author, critic and patron, Carl Van Vechten had the peculiar but influential role of a white man deeply involved in the Harlem Renaissance. He was unapologetically gay, a fact that defined his friendships and permeated his seven novels. Among those was *Nigger Heaven*, a work that troubled many African-Americans both for its title and for its portrayal of life in Harlem. But Van Vechten enthusiastically supported the work of young black writers, financially and critically; his remarkable photographs remain an invaluable record of African-American activity in the arts. It sometimes seems that Van Vechten knew everybody who was anybody among the glitterati, from Gertrude Stein and Langston Hughes to Zora Neale Hurston and Hugh Walpole. A small selection of his letters offers a glimpse of the lives of the beautiful (and often gay) people of his era.

Carl Van Vechten to Gertrude Stein

151 East 19th Street
New York City
[April 5, 1917]

Dear Gertrude Stein, Almost everything is happening here, besides our going to war. Sarah Bernhardt has been operated on at the age of seventy-three and had several kidneys removed. A day or two after she sits up in bed and eats spinach, a vegetable which had been denied her for two years previously. She plans to begin another farewell tour of America in August, and is really intending to put on the whole of *L'Aiglon* . . . The Romanoffs, I gather, are lucky if they get spinach. We are hoping that the Hohenzollerns will soon be in a similar predicament.

Isadora Duncan is dancing the Marseillaise and Tschaikowsky's Marche Slav, with a symbolic reference to the Russian revolution, to packed houses. People — this includes me — get on the chairs and yell. Then Isadora comes out slightly covered by an American flag of filmy silk and awakens still more enthusiasm. It is very exciting to see American patriotism thoroughly awakened — I tell you she drives 'em mad; the recruiting stations are full of her converts — by someone who previously has not been very much interested in awakening it.

Then there is the Salon des Independents (so to speak — at least), which has already had two scandals. The first concerned the rejection by the board (which is not supposed to have the power to reject anything) of an object labelled "Fountain" and signed R. J. Mutts. This porcelain tribute was bought cold in some plumber shop (where it awaited the call to join some bath room trinity) and sent in. When it was rejected Marcel Duchamp at once resigned from the board. Stieglitz is exhibiting the object at "291" and he has made some wonderful photographs of it. The photographs make it look like anything from a Madonna to a Buddha. The exhibition itself is pretty tiresome but there is one picture, The Claire Twins, which you may hear of again. It will probably be bought by the Prado. It belongs in Spain.

Fania has been appearing in [Frank] Wedekind's "The Awakening of Spring." At least she appeared in it once. Then the police stepped in and now all concerned are awaiting a decision from the bench of the Supreme Court.

I am writing. My new book is finished *[Interpreters and Interpretations]*, but it will not appear until fall. We do want to see Paris again soon. I have a feeling that the war will last a very long time; everybody is so anxious that it should stop, but it won't. I should like to see you run a FORD. Perhaps I will yet. all felicitations and salutations to you both from us,

Carlo V. V.

Oh yes, Valentine de Saint Point is here too. She gave an exhibition of métachorie (gratis) at the Metropolitan Opera House, about which people are still talking. She has two boys and a monkey with her . . .

Did you ever know Paulet Thévenaz? He is here too.

Ever so many are here . . . but few are chosen!

I never see Mabel [Dodge]. Does she write to you?

Mina Loy (Mrs. Haweis) has a wonderful primitive (sort of Cimabue) in the exhibition.

Do write me soon, and vibrantly!

Carl Van Vechten to Langston Hughes

150 *West* 55th *Street*
New York City
[Early August 1925]

Dear Langston, The histoire de ta vie was so remarkable both as regards manner and matter that I hesitated for some time before deciding what should be done with it. It seemed absurd for me to write a preface about you when you had written such a beautiful one yourself, but another idea has dawned which seems even better. I have discussed the matter with Mrs. Knopf and she agrees with me fully. As I wrote you before I think you are a topnotch writer of prose: in this biography you have an amazing subject. Treat it romantically if you will, be as formless as you please, disregard chronology if you desire, weaving your story backwards and forwards, but however you do it I am certain not only that you can write a beautiful book, but also one that will *sell*. There will be in it not only exciting incident, vivid description of character and people and places, but something more besides: the soul of a young Negro with a nostalgia for beauty and colour and warmth: that is what I see in all your work. Now this is why the book will have an enormous appeal, because hundreds of young people, nay thousands, have this same nostalgia but they do not know how to express it, but they react to it emotionally when it is expressed. What I want you to do, therefore, is to *write this book*. It may be as long or as short as you please. I know it is hard to write a book with all the other things you have to do, but *I am sure you can do it*. What I am going to suggest to you is that you *make yourself* write a little every day: say 300 words. You will find this method hard at first and very easy after a week or two. In fact, some days you will want to write 2,000 words, but however many words you have produced on a certain day make yourself write the stipulated 300 on the next. [. . .] I shall be very happy when you write me that you have begun this book. Be as digressive as you please — when anything reminds you of something else, another experience, another episode, put it down. Try to be as frank as possible, but when your material runs a little thin, don't be afraid to imagine better material or to put down someone else's experience as your own. [. . .]

I hope Vanity Fair will like your poems as much as I did; but if they don't, remember that that will not destroy their beauty. I can recall the time, not so very long ago, when a paper of mine would come wandering back refused by eight or ten magazines. Off I would shoot it to another and eventually it would usually be accepted. You have caught the jazz spirit and the jazz rhythm amazingly; some of them ought to be recited in stop-time!

Firecrackers is my new novel. In it appear characters from all the old ones. I hope soon to start work on my Negro novel, but I feel rather alarmed. It would have been comparatively easy for me to write it before I knew as much as I know now, enough to know that I am thoroughly ignorant! [. . .] pansies and marguerites to you!

Carl

Carl Van Vechten to Ellen Glasgow

150 West 55th Street
New York City
29 August 1932

Dear Ellen: There is a kind of "They couldn't help it" implication to every page of "The Sheltered Life" which makes it the most human and (hence) the most pathetic of your books. The characters lead their disordered (and sheltered) lives under the spell of their doom. I think never have divided natures been more skilfully & subtly presented. — Jenny Blair really loves Eva and in her passion for George there is no thought of hurting Eva. Of course George really loves Eva too — completely — and in his philandering he has no intentions of hurting her. And they suffer. And Eva who believes that nothing can be divided, that *feeling* must be *one* and steadfast, suffers still more, first because she is afraid she will lose the object of her steadfast feeling, and second because she is afraid she has lost it. I have seldom read a book that so mercilessly exposes the sadistic nature of God and you have never before written a book which is rooted so deeply in the inexplicable torments & impulses of earthly creatures.

Sheaves of cornflowers & poppies to you from your admiring

Carlo

Carl Van Vechten to Gertrude Stein

150 West 55th Street
New York City
[December 1, 1934]

Dearest Gertrude, Your letters about the Dance Marathon and the Squad Car are pretty cute and Thornton Wilder has got me down with jealousy. Don't go and like him BETTER, PLEASE! . . . What I mean by schedule is, how long can I write you at the Drake, and where do I write you after that? So please ask Alice to let me know. *All* your letters are here, including one from Alice addressed to 150 West 50th street, so the heart of the post-office is in the right place. Did Alice write Mrs. Walter Douglas, Wayzata, Minnesota? PLEASE DO NOT MISS THIS. Address Muriel Draper, care of the American Embassy, Moscow and it will reach her (in time for Christmas). Marie Harriman sent me a telegram (which I am looking for this minute and cannot find) asking me to ask you to be the guest of honor at the opening of the Rose Show (Sir Francis and not the "is a" kind) on Friday. I telephoned her and told her you wouldn't be back till the holidays. Beau Broadway in the N Y Telegraph says spies have discovered you call each other Lovey and Pussy. No one he says has yet reported on what you and Alice call C. V. V. (so Woojums is still inviolate! Don't you go calling T[hornton] W[ilder] a woojums! I will bite him!). Tell Alice I never got her letter from the Plane, so where was this sent? (Oh yes, I remember I did get two serial cards!) Did you get Arthur Griggs obituary?

I spend all my time in the darkroom crying for my beautiful pair of Woojums who are TRAVELLING in the WEST. LOVE, LOVE, to you BOTH! Fania and Pearl and EDITH send LOVE!

Carlo

Carl Van Vechten to Arthur Davison Ficke

101 Central Park West
New York City
23 December 1940

An attempt at a definition, Arthur: When one awakens to the fact that one knows nothing, that all knowledge is relative, that all events are liable to extremely opposed interpretations, that morality is as governed by chic and fashion as a woman's dress, that people are undependable, unreliable, and unreasonable, that Life itself is incomplete and insecure, he may be said to be comparatively mature. bloody thoughts to you!

Carlo!

It was very pleasant today. [. . .]

Carl Van Vechten to Alice B. Toklas

101 Central Park West
New York City
28 July 1946

Dearest Mama Woojums, Your telegram was heartbreaking. It came to me early this morning, brought in by a young girl. I hadn't had the slightest preparation for this. Only Montie Johnson told me a few days ago that some one just back from Paris reported Gertrude hadn't been well. But Baby Woojums' letters to me were full of health and cheer and I am so happy she received the preface to Selected Writings and approved. [. . .] It is wonderful to remember I have known you both since 1913 without a break . . . but it is horrible to realize that *her* part of the communication can no longer exist. Those who knew her only through the greatness of her work will never know how great she could also be in friendship! It seems as if Selected Works had been arranged for by Divinity to appear at the exact moment when they are most needed . . . but much more will eventually be revived. However, I always had it in mind to preserve as much as possible of the most important pieces in this one volume so that any reader might form his own conclusions of her work from a study of this book alone. I hope you will write us as soon as you can to tell us as much as you can. You have our very deepest sympathy and love and if you need assistance on any details of all the thousand and one things that will come up now and in the future you can always turn to Fania and

Papa Woojums!

Carl Van Vechten to Mark Lutz

101 Central Park West
New York City
[April 1952]

Dearest Bino, TWO Specials arrived from you today. One at dawn, the next at daybreak. [...]

Essbees see too much of each other and a party of them alone turns into a gossip fest. A few girls makes them more reasonable. The best Essbees know this and act accordingly, saving their exclusive parties for the bedroom. Occasionally I give an all-male affair, but it seldom works out well. I mean I get bored. [...]

I can't think of anything I want for my birthday so you can send me a carnation as usual.

I shop at Manganaro's later today. Hal [Bynner] dines here Monday. I lunched with Miss Ettie [Stettheimer] today. [...] Miss Ettie is regaining her health and strength and bad temper rapidly and even talks of giving me a birthday party. [...]

so love to you, sir and mister,

Carl Van Vechten to John Breon

101 Central Park West
New York City
28 April 1952

Dear John, Your letters are wonderful and I can see that you ARE in love, and it makes me very happy, because I've known for a long time you never have been in Love. It will do a lot for you and will make you quite different and the NEXT TIME you may be even more in love. For it is seldom that any one is in love only once (it DOES happen) and the *first* time is seldom permanent, and if you do get over this, don't get cynical about it. Realize that it was something that had to happen and how and why are unimportant, the sooner the better, and keep an open

mind and heart, and it will happen again. I am not PRAYING that you
will get over this time, but warning you that you MAY. But whatever
and however, you will become a better boy through this. [. . .] Your
letters, you know, are contradictory, full of passion and confusion, but I
am sure you will be all right NOW. You've never been so frank WITH
YOURSELF before. You have INDICATED A GOOD DEAL without
saying it. But you'll breeze through it all in the end and it's going to be
OKAY. [. . .] Love to you, John, whatever and however,

Carlo

Somehow I like you more now!

Carl Van Vechten to James Purdy

146 Central Park West
New York City
18 November 1956

Dear Jaime: Voltaire remarks so truly: Le Superflus est une chose neces-
saire, and my motto is A little too much is just enough for me!

63:Dream Palace is NOW My Dream Palace. The pranks of Fenton
Riddleway, the exasperating behaviour of the greatwoman, the huddled
belligerency of Claire, the unholy purposes of Parkhurst, all fascinate
and bewilder and repel me. Somehow I felt as tho I were watching
sexuality on TV or watching orchestral instruments enjoying orgasms
with each other. I pray that your books will never end and then they do
quite unexpectedly with the word "motherfucker." [. . .] I want to send
some of your wetdream palaces around and I find your publisher ridicu-
lously slow in shipping. We must think of a better plan. You should be
very happy and perhaps a very little mad. Wave your arms, Jaime, wave
your arms.

> *Said a morbid and dissolute youth*
> *I think Beauty is greater than Truth,*
> *But by Beauty I mean*
> *The obscure, the obscene,*
> *The diseased, the decayed, the uncouth.*

yours in threnody and wild roses,

Carlo

Carl Van Vechten to James Purdy

[146 Central Park West
New York City]
11 July [1957]

Dearest Jaime, [. . .] Obscenity is variable according to the personality. Perhaps the most obscene piece of music I know is also the most beautiful: The Prelude to Tristan und Isolde which accurately describes a FUCK. To me I cannot see how an audience can sit through it without a sexual thrill or at least a cockstand, but from the bland expressions on people's faces I think many of them take it as calmly as the Overture to William Tell. But to judge that 63 Dream Palace is obscene is to believe Water Cress is obscene because it has the same initials as Water Closet. [. . .]

As you so sensibly submit [Dwight] Eisenhower is a grinner. I do not recall a picture of Lincoln grinning altho he found himself in much the same situation that Eisenhower does. He did something about it, but Eisenhower grins through it. [. . .] Love, indeed,

Carlo

Carl Van Vechten to Fannie Hurst

146 Central Park West
New York City
5 February 1960

Dearest Fannie, Zora [Neale Hurston]'s death has affected me profoundly. I had not heard from her in perhaps fifteen years and had no idea where she was. But I discover, as sometimes happens too late, that I loved the girl. I have learned before through other deaths that I am inclined to miss Negroes more than white people: they are so much warmer (as a rule so much more intimate without being offensively so). My heart has been broken many times as a result of these endearing qualities. [. . .] It seems a dreadful trick of fate that we shall never see her again. She was a remarkable personality and a remarkable writer. Had I known where she was or that she was poor I would of course have sent her some money, almost a blank cheque for her to fill in.

Fortunately, Scribner was her last publisher, and the Times obit couldn't be more distinguished about anybody. I have asked the Yale Library to give a show of her work, etc. I am writing you, because somehow we always shared Zora, a common annoyance and a common love, something we will both remember with a great deal of pleasure.

I embrace you,
Carlo Patriarch

Carl Van Vechten to Fannie Hurst

146 Central Park West
New York City
5 July 1960

Dearest Fannie, I am certainly glad that I begged you to do the piece on Zora [Neale Hurston]. It is a chef d'oeuvre, a masterpiece and while I read it I cried. You make all the girl's faults seem to be her virtues. As a matter of fact, they were NOT faults, they were characteristics. There's quite a difference. What it comes down to is the fact that Zora was put together entirely differently from the rest of mankind. Her reactions were always original because they were her OWN. When she breezed into a room (she never merely entered), tossed a huge straw hat (as big as a cart wheel) on the floor and yelled "I am the queen of the Niggerati"* you knew you were in the presence of an individual of the greatest magnitude. You have certainly written the greatest obit I have ever read and perhaps cheered Zora in whatever department of oblivion she has CHOSEN to reside.

With love to you always,
Carlo, the happy octogenarian

Fania says that Zora's remark about me, quoted by you, is more extraordinary than anything else that has been said of me by any other member of the race.

*a term she herself invented

Richard Wright

In novels such as *Native Son*, short story collections such as *Uncle Tom's Children* and the autobiographical *Black Boy*, Richard Wright observed and commented upon the urban African-American condition. Sometimes best-selling and always provocative, his work earned the respect of fellow writers, black and white, and the ire of racists and conservatives. Eventually his politics—especially his affiliation with the Communist Party—forced him to move to Europe. Wright was deeply conflicted about his sexuality, terrified that he might be gay and vehemently homophobic. Yet his friends included numerous open gays, such as Gertrude Stein and Carl Van Vechten, not a surprising fact given the unfettered morality of the Harlem Renaissance and other contemporary literary movements. Stein was an especially enthusiastic fan of his work, and the two writers maintained a trans-Atlantic friendship via post.

Richard Wright to Gertrude Stein

89 Lefferts Place, Apartment C-23, Brooklyn, New York, May 27, 1945

Dear friend Gertrude Stein:

It was indeed pleasant to get a letter from you and from a country I have never visited but always wanted to visit. . . .

The things you said about Black Boy made me very glad. . . . I can well understand why the American soldiers are worried about Negroes. And why you wonder about them. America has made Negroes into a strange people. Negroes are free now, on their own, and they live in a land where everywhere they turn they see mean images of themselves. They live and move and walk through the white world with fear in their hearts, and many feel that they are not wanted anywhere, and others feel that it would be lowering themselves to speak to whites unless they are spoken to first. It is all like a nightmare. But for writing, it is great. Negro life as it relates to white life shimmers with a thousand little dramas and I've been able to get only a shadow of what I've seen and felt on paper. . . .

We have made for ourselves a very tragic thing in America, and we are afraid of it. I get many, many letters from white people; they ask me,

Tell me what to do. And I cannot tell them what to do, for I know that they know what to do about Negroes. They know what to do and they would rather die than do it. So, what can you say to people like that? They come to me and want to talk, want to hear what Negroes feel, and when I tell them, they are distressed and sad. They say, If I felt like that I'd kill myself. To most of them I say as your Melanctha said in your Three Lives, If I ever killed myself, it would be by accident, and if I ever killed myself by accident, I'd be awful sorry. I expect them to laugh with me when I say that, but they don't; not one has laughed so far. So guilt and fear stand staring at each other, each knowing that something is going to happen, each waiting for something to happen. . . .

Is it bad in France now? Is there enough food? Was there much destruction? What do the American boys think of the Nazi prison camps where so many people were killed? Over here most people refused to believe that such things were happening; but when they saw the pictures, they wanted every last German killed. I predicted that many of the leading Nazis would live to write their memoirs; also I told my friends that many of them would be photographed and interviewed. They were. I don't know what we can do with the Germans; I'll guess that we will help them to start all over again. Of course, everybody now is talking about the next war, that it will be against Russia. All day the radio talks of it. The death of Roosevelt simply knocked all the optimism out of people. The world looks so bleak they are scared. We want to get back to work and buy cars and radios. No doubt we will.

But books are selling like mad. I don't know why. . . . My own Black Boy has sold more than 450,000 copies since March first. And the weekly sales at present total more than 3,000. Frankly I don't know why people read my work; it upsets them terribly. . . . It may be that they like to be upset. Not knowing what to do in life about feeling and living, they can feel and live with a book.

Your Wars I Have Seen had some very very funny things in it; I've seen copies of it in the subway, people riding and reading it. . . .

Really next year I want to bring my wife and child to France, to Paris. I'm going to try my best to do that. . . .

As ever,
Dick Wright

P.S. Did you know that your book hit the best seller list? Well, it is there and I hope a great many folks read it.

R. W.

Edna St. Vincent Millay

One of the most popular poets of the twentieth century, Edna St. Vincent Millay rose to fame as an inhabitant of bohemian Greenwich Village in the 1920s. She arrived there from Maine via Vassar College, where she had cultivated a respect for Sappho and had lesbian relationships with more than one fellow student. After graduation Millay employed the mail to maintain passionate friendships with some of her Vassar comrades, particularly Charlotte (Charlie) Babcock, Edith Wynne Matthison, Isobel Simpson and Anne Gardner. At Chumley's speakeasy and the Liberal Club in the Village she met Eugene O'Neill, Elinor Wylie, Louise Bogan and many other novelists, poets and playwrights. Poet Arthur Davidson Ficke, initially of romantic interest, became a sort of mentor. Signing herself Vincent or Edna, Millay sent letters to her comrades from her childhood home in Camden, Maine, from her apartment in the Village and from various points on a trip to Europe, where she worked on a novel that was never published. Her later letters came from Steepletop, the home she shared with her husband, Eugen Boissevain, in upstate New York.

Edna St. Vincent Millay to Edith Wynne Matthison Kennedy

Camden, Maine,
July 28, 1917.

Dear Mrs. Kennedy:

Camden is about one hundred miles from Kennebunkport; I just asked "Information." Are you coming up to see me? — I wish you would; you would like it here; it is beautiful. Norma will let you pick the peas; we have the first ones tomorrow, and I am going out to pick them right after I finish this letter. Please come up here to see me. Then we can all come back — I mean go back — together. That means that I am inviting Mr. Kennedy, too. *I want so much to see you.*

I can come before August 13 — indeed, I *will* come whenever you want me — I will do whatever you want me to do — but it would be better, because of many things, if I could go back with you when you go back from Kennebunkport. One reason why it would be better later is that I am doing quite a bit of tutoring now and quite a bit of type-writing.

I will do whatever you tell me to do, however. I am beginning by writing you by return mail, — the first thing you have asked me to do. Love me, please; I love you; I can bear to be your friend. So ask of me anything, and hurt me whenever you must; but never be "tolerant", or "kind". And never say to me again, — don't dare to say to me again — "Anyway, you can make a trial" of being friends with you! Because I can't do things in that way; I am not a tentative person. Whatever I do, I give up my whole self to it; and it may be a trial — of course, most things are, I suppose — but I never am conscious of making a trial; I am conscious only of doing the thing that I love to do, — that I *have* to do — and I *have* to be your friend. It may seem to you that it is only a trial, but I can't think that you meant that. Didn't you just say that to frighten me into consciousness of the enormity of being friends with you? — But enormity does not frighten me; it is only among tremendous things that I feel happy and at ease; I would not say this, perhaps, except that, as I told you, I do not trouble to lie to you.

"So *that's* all right, Best Belovèd, — do you see?"

Yes, your typing *is* rather rotten, I am enchanted to be able to say. My own is rather admirable, don't you think?

No, I don't mind wearing other people's things, — I had five room-mates last year at Vassar — because if they are things I like I always feel myself into them until I forget that they actually "belong" to anybody at all, — a dangerous propensity, you will say, and one with an imminence toward kleptomania! But I shall try to bring a few quite nice things with me; I will get together all that I can, and then when you tell me to come, I will come, by the next train, just as I am. This is not meekness, be assured; I do not come naturally by meekness; know that it is a proud surrender to You; I don't talk like that to many people.

With love,
Vincent Millay.

Edna St. Vincent Millay to Isobel Simpson

139 Waverly Place
New York
[January 30, 1918]

Isobel, dear,

Someday I shall write a great poem to you, so great that I shall make you famous in history, or dedicate a book to you, or collect a fortune &

die & leave it to you, — or perhaps, more than all of these, I shall write you a letter, thanking you as nearly adequately as ever may be, for service done me or some lovely gift —, some whole garden of lovely gifts — sent me on no occasion whatever & for no reason at all. Meanwhile I shall probably go on as I have done, — thinking of you in the day-time & wondering where my pen is & did I bust the point in removing the stopper from the sulpho-napthol? — & at night dreaming suggestive dreams of telegraph-blanks & telephone-booths & corner letter-drops, — all respectable or accepted means of interborough communication.

The scarf did come, — thank you — so did the roses or orchids or other trifling flora. God forgive me my silence.

Vincent.

Edna St. Vincent Millay to Isobel Simpson

[January 9, 1920]

Dearest Little Sphinx, —

Edna never wrote her own true love at all to thank her for lovely Christmas gift — Edna is a Pig *who walks by Himself.*

It is such a lovely little lacquer chest, dear — quite beautiful — it looks charming on my desk — on my lacquer tray by the tea-things, & also on the dressing-table, to hold exquisite, exotic, poisonous perfumed jewelry which I aint got at all! —

This is not half as nice a letter, belovèd child, as I wish to write you, — but I am so tired these days — working terribly, terribly hard — & I write you stupidly, dear, do you see, rather than wait & not be writing you at all.

With how much love you know,
Vincent

Thursday night

Edna St. Vincent Millay to Anne Gardner Lynch

7 Floragasse,
Vienna, Austria.
Dec. 23, 1921

Anne, darling, —

I have just got your letter. Oh, if I could just get my arms about you! — And stay with you like that for hours, telling you so many things, & listening to all that you must have to say. — I love you very much, dear Anne, & I always shall. — Ours was a perfect friendship — I knew it at the time — and it is still just as true. I would do anything in the world for you, & I know that you would for me. — And it doesn't matter if we never write, and never see each other, it is just the same, — except that it would be so nice to see each other!

I have thought of you a thousand times, & wondered, wondered acutely, with anxiety & such deep well-wishing! — how you were getting on. A dozen times I have started to write you. The little card that came with your wedding announcement & had your New York address on it, has travelled about with me everywhere, because I was always on the point of writing & I wanted your street & number where I could lay my hands on them.

Dear, by the time you get this letter your baby will be very near to life. If you want to know how I am feeling about you, & all I am wishing for you, & how my heart will be with you from this time on until I hear from you again, you have only to imagine to yourself just how, in the same circumstances, you would be feeling about me.

Also, may its sex, temper, & general topography be what you prefer! Also, may it wait & be born on the 22nd of February, which is my birthday, & I will be its god-mother.

* * *

Dear, there's no room here for more than a word. All that you told me is in my heart & on my mind. And I shall go through it all with you as surely as if you were clinging to my hand.

— Your Vince.

Edna St. Vincent Millay to Isobel Simpson

Hôtel du Panorama
Cassis-sur-Mer
Bouches du Rhône, France.
Dec. 15, 1922.

Dearest Little Sphinx:

My instinct, of course, when you tell me to *come home,* is to *come home!* —
But I have a mother with me who *won't come home* until she has seen
Italy! — at any rate, we are leaving France very soon & going in to Italy.
We are going slowly along the Riviera, to Cannes & Nice & Monte
Carlo, & then on to Italy. In the spring we are going to spend a month
in Paris, then a month in London, & then we are going to *come home!!*

Dear, there *has* been something wrong with me, — I have been very
sick; but I am better now. I have been quite respectably, but very unro-
mantically ill, — trouble arising from an improper diet, unfamiliar queer
foods in Hungary & Albania, etc., which have played the devil with me.
— Thank heaven mother has been with me, & has been getting me
straightened out. — But I came within an ace of having peritonitis, which
is not a tidy thing to have.

Well, so much for that. — Only now I am really better, & you mustn't
worry about me any more, sweetheart. — I love you always, just as ever.
And someday, before very long, I shall see you again, — and you will
squeak such a silly little squeak, just as ever, & we shall both be so
happy. — So goodbye, little sphinx, and Merry Christmas, and a Very
Happy New Year.

From your most loving serpent,
Edna.

Edna St. Vincent Millay to Elinor Wylie

Steepletop, Austerlitz, N.Y.
Day after Easter [April 18, 1927]

My darling:

Enclosed you will find a letter from me to the League of American
Penwomen. If the address is wrong or insufficient, change it — (on your

typewriter!) — Please read the letter, then post it at once. — Be a good girl, & do as I tell you, & post it at once.

Vincent.

To the League of American Penwomen

[Steepletop, Austerlitz, N.Y.]

Ladies:

I have received from you recently several communications, inviting me to be your Guest of Honour at a function to take place in Washington some time this month. I replied, not only that I was unable to attend, but that I regretted this inability; I said that I was sensible to the honour you did me, and that I hoped you would invite me again.

Your recent gross and shocking insolence to one of the most distinguished writers of our time has changed all that.

It is not in the power of an organization which has insulted Elinor Wylie, to honour me.

And indeed I should feel it unbecoming on my part, to sit as Guest of Honour in a gathering of writers, where honour is tendered not so much for the excellence of one's literary accomplishment as for the circumspection of one's personal life.

Believe me, if the eminent object of your pusillanimous attack has not directed her movements in conformity with your timid philosophies, no more have I mine. I too am eligible for your disesteem. Strike me too from your lists, and permit me, I beg you, to share with Elinor Wylie a brilliant exile from your fusty province.

Very truly yours,
Edna St. Vincent Millay

Edna St. Vincent Millay to Arthur Davison Ficke

Steepletop, Austerlitz, N.Y.
May 25, 1938

Dear Arthur,

More dirt about the Pulitzer Prize!

After you had left the other day I kept on thinking about what you had said; that is, was it possible that this prize is being given or with-held more for moral than for aesthetic reasons? I decided finally that you were right about this: that it was not only possible but that it was the case. But I arrived at my conclusion in a rather round-about way. I thought first of Elinor Wylie. It seemed to me extraordinary that she had never received this prize; that even her posthumously published "Collected Poems" containing every line of poetry she had ever published, should be passed over by them, was puzzling. I thought they must have had something against her, but what could it be? Even a group of doddering octogenarians could not fail to be aware of the unusually high-class quality of her work. She was an aristocrat, a lady, and her grammar was faultless. The subject matter of her poetry was the furthest thing from erotic. What could they have had against her? Then it came to me. They knew, as everybody knew, that she had left her husband and her child to run off to Europe with a married man. That was why *she* never got a Pulitzer Prize. This suddenly was plain to me.

Then I thought of you. Why had you never received the Pulitzer Prize? Why did even your selected poems get no attention from this group? I thought as I had thought of Elinor: he is a gentleman and a graduate of Harvard, his grammar is faultless, the subject matter of his poetry has never been such as to cause either Professor Bliss Perry of Harvard or Governor Wilbur Cross of Connecticut to turn his face aside and take snuff out of embarrassment. I recalled that at one time you had been curator of Japanese Prints at Harvard; then suddenly I remembered something else. I remembered why you thought it advisable to resign from this position and all the circumstances attending the resignation. "Of course," I said to myself, "that's it, why certainly."

Then I thought of Robinson Jeffers. Why had he never received it? This was easy. In his case, it is the subject matter of his poetry. Rape, incest, homosexuality and other forms of plain and fancy fornication are the subject matter of all his books. No chance for him.

I wondered why I, having been once awarded this prize in 1923, never received it afterwards, although Robert Frost and E. A. Robinson seemed to be taking turns at receiving it year after year. I remembered that not so very long after "The Harp-Weaver" was published I went to Boston and walked up and down before the State House and carried a placard protesting against the execution of Sacco and Vanzetti, suggesting that President Lowell of Harvard was withholding evidence which might have freed these men; that I was arrested and taken to jail for this and that the whole country knew it. With how much affection following this action of mine would an aged professor of Harvard look upon my subsequently published volumes? With how much affection would any aged and conservative governor of a New England state look thence forward upon the published works of a person who had agitated as I had done against the governor of a neighboring New England state? That became at once pretty plain.

Now take Robinson and Frost. What a relief these two poets must have been to the harassed judges of the Pulitzer award. If their private lives, both sexual and political, were not thoroughly blameless, I have never heard about this. The judges must have felt entirely happy and at ease in their minds the moment either Robinson or Frost published a new collection of poems.

You hit it without any doubt when you said the prize was awarded, probably, or withheld for moral rather than other reasons.

Well, this is a long letter, but I thought my findings on the subject might amuse you.

By the way, did you know that the third member of the triumvirate was that poet whom I once met in your house in Sante Fe and a good poet, I thought, too — Leonard Bacon? What is he doing limping with that pack?

Love,
Vincie.

Edna St. Vincent Millay to Leonora Speyer

Steepletop, Austerlitz, N.Y.
March 18, 1943

Dearest Nora, — It was a shame! — I did so want to see you again! — But you were beautiful that night — radiant. I don't remember a word you said — I day [sic] say it was very wise, and I'm sure it was very witty. But sitting there beside you I didn't even try to listen, except to the sound of your voice, — and for the rest, just looked at your face. — *Nobody* has more beautiful eyes than you — although they are really and always blue; the color of the sea sometimes, they make me think of these two lines of Matthew Arnold's, whole poetry I love so much:

> *"Eyes too expressive to be blue*
> *Too lovely to be grey." —*

Since this is apparently a love letter, I sign myself

Yours with love,
Edna.

Thelma Wood/Djuna Barnes

The avant-garde American novelist Djuna Barnes, a habitué of New York and Paris, was openly gay and engaged in a long string of lesbian romances. Remarkable to the commanding Gertrude Stein only for her "beautiful legs," the author of *Ryder* captivated, among others, Carson McCullers, who suffered through a fierce and unrequited crush on the older writer. Barnes's novel *Nightwood* fictionalized her tortured relationship with the ravishing Thelma Wood, portraying Wood as the cold Robin Vote and herself as the vulnerable Nora; the character of Jenny Petherbridge represented the woman for whom Wood left Barnes. As Nora does in the novel, Barnes tried to exact revenge on the unfaithful Wood by seducing "Jenny." The incident elicited a regretful letter from Wood to Barnes, and Barnes later wrote of their alienation — and *Nightwood*'s role in it — to Natalie Barney.

Thelma Wood to Djuna Barnes

[June 1930(?)]

— I simply cannot understand what you mean by keeping ["Jenny"] in a state of such "bewildered hope." She seems to think so too — What in heavens name can I say more than I have — The morning you saw us, I had said such terrible things I hated myself — and because I would not go with you two you said I "shirked."

How could I feeling as I did towards her — and in front of you? I have asked her not to come here but have gotten letter after letter saying it would be alright — and that I loved her — I became frantic — then hypnotized and resigned — like the measles . . .

. . . I did not want such a thing to be known between us — something I did not care about — it seemed a shame for foolishness to spoil us — I wanted no acknowledged disloyalty and after you came back from N.Y. I loved you so terribly — and my one idea was to wipe out the fact I'd been stupid — I tryed desperately — with her I wheedled and raved, I was cruel and sweet — and no good — always if I did not see her or call she sent something or a note — and it made you unhappy — and I did see — till I thought I'd go mad. I spent one morning till six pleading and trying to keep her from doing anything foolish — yet insisting I wouldn't see her again — and then I got a note from Ros saying she was in a high

state of fever — and I was stupid enough to listen. I told her I was going
to you with it all — I saw I was losing you — and I felt I could save it if I
came to you — and again I listened to her — She swore it would be alright
she would meet you and become friends as I had always begged her to.

Then she played tricks and sent a note — and you were going out
and asked me to come with you and I wanted so to — and didn't dare —
and you were so beautiful — and we got you a flower — then I went to
her and cried and raved for two hours — and again she promised to be
good and friends — But she's mad — she gets things out of the balmy blue
— She tells me and writes me things I have never said or done — I have
lied to you, my precious — but I swear — never to her . . .

As for the rest of our eight years you seemed to have had a pretty
rotten time — with my brutishness and I'm sorry — sorry — you say you
know me now so terribly well. Something is undoubtedly wrong with me — I
lack perhaps a conscience or sensibility or memory or logic or all — when
I left France I felt as you say just unfit for human dignity . . .

. . . I did not mean to reject your friendship — that I took for granted
in the course of events — as we loved each other — But perhaps it's grown
so collosal in your mind you would not want that either — for after all
why an untrustworthy and unmannerly friend?

A kiss for Dilly,
Your Simon

Djuna Barnes to Natalie Barney

[1932]

She says the book proves I never understood her — & that she does not
much care to have it printed is clear — tho she does not directly ask me
to destroy it — I admit the writing game is "dirty" but I hoped the book
was good enough — I'm uncertain at the moment, as baby Charles has
torn it to pieces as a work as a whole — says it has no plot (which does
not so much matter) but has also no design — is written in different styles
— does not hold together, — & is not as good as "Ryder" in spite of
"splendid spots" about what John thought & Victor too. . . . Only you
Lloyd Morris & Solita (in parts) really seemed to be pleased with it. I
should not hesitate about it were I not uncertain in my own mind, which
is because I have seen so much of it, worked it over so often and heard
so many opinions, that I am confused. I should put it away for a year

(Charles says 100[?] years) & then see what I think of it. I am sure it will estrange T. even more than she now is, which I shall not like, but then what do I like just about now? . . . T[helma] is sailing about the 9th of June — no news here — one day like another — fine weather & sea & boats right under the window (am in Arab Quarter) hooting all day & night & I want to be on all of them!

Amelia Earhart

Amelia Earhart's sexuality may have been ambiguous, but her resolute feminism and androgynous style — not to mention her adventurous life — have made her a lesbian luminary. The aviator won fame in 1928 as the first woman to fly across the Atlantic Ocean (as a passenger) and a year later helped found the Ninety-Nines, America's first female flying organization. She flew the Atlantic solo in 1932, becoming the first woman to do so, and went on to set a variety of records before disappearing in 1937 while attempting a round-the-world flight. Earhart championed women's rights and refused to give in to sexist convention in her personal life. Even in her marriage to publisher G. P. Putnam, she laid down ground rules that preserved her independence.

Amelia Earhart to Virginia Park

[March 6, 1914]

Blessings on thee, Little Ginger —

. . . Of course I'm going to B.M. [Bryn Mawr] if I have to drive a grocery wagon to accumulate the cash. You see I'm practicing grocery boy language because if I use up all my money going to hear grand "Hopery" why — I'll be minus later that's all. I wish you were up here because Parsifal and I don't know what are coming here. I suppose they will be in K.C. [Kansas City] I'm all thrills. Did you hear Paderewski . . . I wonder if he played Chopin Funeral march down at St. Joe as he did here.

You miss much by not having Gym. Last Fri. we had a circus.

We played B.B. [basketball] just like you and I did once upon a time (remember) No boys tho. I don't know when I've been so tired.

All the girls are so nice it's a joy to be with them don't you know. I am doing my best to get some of them to go to B.M. with Ginger and Millie.

Your letter was scrummy. So long and joysome. I'll send you the translation of your Cicero. I'm a shark . . . Your letter was very funny. I lawffed ex'cessively.

Speaking of funny things, my dear freshman of a sister spoke very importantly of "forum" in their class meeting (All those lambs attend their meeting religiously) completely mystifying the family until mother had the happy thot she meant quorum . . .

It's so hot today I am just baked. I want this reading matter to go off on the next mail so I'll cease.

Love, Mill.

I'll write you a sensible letter someday. You needn't ans. this communication unless you have nothing else to do. All contributions, however, are thankfully received at this end.

Amelia Earhart to Amy Earhart

[1930]

Dear Mother,

. . . I shall not stay in New York very long I think as I am going west again to pick up my ship. There are several dates in Middle West I must keep too . . .

I am not marrying *anybody.*

A.E.

Amelia Earhart to George Putnam

[February 7, 1931]

Dear GP,

There are some things which should be writ before we are married. Things we have talked over before, — most of them.

You must know again my reluctance to marry, my feeling that I shatter thereby chances in work which means so much to me. I feel the move just now as foolish as anything I could do. I know there may be compensations, but have no heart to look ahead.

In our life together I shall not hold you to any medieval code of faithfulness to me, nor shall I consider myself bound to you similarly. If we can be honest I think the differences which arise may best be avoided.

Please let us not interfere with each other's work or play, nor let the world see private joys or disagreements. In this connection I may have to keep some place where I can go to be myself now and then, for I cannot guarantee to endure at all times the confinements of even an attractive cage.

I must exact a cruel promise, and this is that you will let me go in a year if we find no happiness together.

I will try to do my best in every way.

A.E.

Anaïs Nin/Henry Miller

In 1932, French writer Anaïs Nin plunged into heated affairs with both June Miller and her husband, struggling American author Henry Miller. Married at that time to Hugh Guiler, Anaïs was at first put off by Henry's advances and instead became infatuated with June. The two women carried on a brief, apparently unconsummated but feverish affair before Henry and Anaïs fell in love. Anaïs and Henry both remained obsessed with June, who remained faithful to neither. As deeply as they felt for each other, Anaïs and Henry kept June at the center of their relationship as a sort of mutual persona. In their letters, Nin and Miller returned again and again to the woman who had claimed both their hearts.

Anaïs Nin to June Miller

February 1932

I cannot believe that you will not come again towards me from the darkness of the garden. I wait sometimes where we used to meet, expecting to feel again the joy of seeing you walk towards me out of a crowd — you, so distinct and unique.

After you went away the house suffocated me. I wanted to be alone with my image of you. . . .

I have taken a studio in Paris, a small, shaky place, and attempt to run away only for a few hours a day, at least. But what is this other life I want to lead without you? I have to imagine that you are there, June, sometimes. I have a feeling that I want to be you. I have never wanted to be anyone but myself before. Now I want to melt into you, to be so terribly close to you that my own self disappears. I am happiest in my black velvet dress because it is old and is torn at the elbows.

When I look at your face, I want to let go and share your madness, which I carry inside of me like a secret and cannot conceal any more. I am full of an acute, awesome joy. It is the joy one feels when one has accepted death and disintegration, a joy more terrible and more profound than the joy of living, of creating.

Anaïs Nin to Henry Miller

[Louveciennes]
Feb. 13, 1932

Please understand, Henry, that I am in full rebellion against my own mind, that when I *live*, I live by impulse, by emotion, by white heat — June understood that. My mind didn't *exist* when we walked insanely through Paris, oblivious to people, to time, to place, to others. It didn't exist when I first read Dostoevsky in my hotel room, and laughed and cried together, and couldn't sleep, and didn't know where I was . . . *but afterwards*, understand me, when all basis, all awareness, all control has been knocked out of my being, *afterwards* I make the tremendous effort to *rise* again, not to wallow anymore, not to go on just suffering or burning, and I grasp all things, June and Dostoevsky, and *think*. You got the thinking. Why should I make such an effort? Because I have a *fear* of being like June *exactly* — I have a feeling against complete chaos. I want to be able to live with June in utter madness, but I also want to be able to understand afterwards, to grasp what I have lived through.

I may be wrong. You see I can give you a proof that the *living madness* is more precious to me than my thoughts: however much I think of you I couldn't *give* you what *feelings* I've lived through with June. I could give you explanations, general talk, etc., but not the *feelings* themselves. I can also give you the only criticism I could make of Dostoevsky, and there are in my journal four pages of my incoherent feelings about the reading of *The Possessed.* Can you understand that? Only thought comes to the surface, though very often, when your letter moves me, as I told you the very first time, I am almost ready to give everything, just as that day when I was so upset and beside myself — the first day you came — I was about to read you everything I had written in my journal — because your own despair aroused my confidence in you. Forgive me. Do you remember what was the first thing we did? We went out — I raved about the "healing" quality of the place. It was laughable. We weren't seeking to be healed, but I sought my mind again. I knew you were suffering torture — I evaded plunging, because it meant plunging into my own torture, too. I say again, I may be wrong. Yes, I am wrong. Today I exploded into fearful rebellion against analysis. Even if the second movement in all my sonatas is extricating myself from chaos, even if I have much of Gide in me, and that I may someday, like Lawrence, turn around and write my own explanations of my books (because other people's explanation of what is conceived in white heat by the artist sickens me), even if I do that, understand me, what comes first is the artist, the sensing through emotion, that *envahissement* by sensations which I feel and which breaks me to pieces.

You ask contradictory and impossible things. You want to know what dreams, what impulses, what desires June has? You'll never know it, not from *her.* No, she couldn't tell you. But do you realize what joy June took in my telling her what our feelings were — in that special language. How could I do that? Because, because I am not *junk* all the time, I am not always just living, just following all my fantasies. Because I come up for air, for understanding. I dazzled June because when we sat down together the wonder of the moment didn't just make me drunk — I lived it with the consciousness of the poet, mind you, not the consciousness the dead-formula-making psychoanalysts would like to put their clinical fingers on — oh, not that, no, a consciousness of acute *senses* (more acute than the drugged ones). We went to the edge, with our two imaginations. We died together. But — June continues to live and die —

and I — (oh, god, I hate my own work, I'd much rather just live) — I sit down and try *to tell you* — to tell you that I'd much rather go on living ecstatically and unknowing to you — to all — and you beat your head against the wall of our world, yes, and it is I because of my demoniac creative power of realization and coordinating mystery — I who will tear veils. But not yet. I don't want to. I love my mystery, I love the abstract, *fuyant* world I live in as long as I don't begin my *work*, the forcing out of delicate, profound, vague, obscure, voluptuously wordless sensations into something you can seize on — perhaps never. Perhaps I'll renounce my mind, my works, my effort, and merely live, suffer, wallow, elude your knowledge, your *seizure* of either June or me. Why do *you* want more clarity, more knowledge — you do not ask it of Dostoevsky — you thank god for the living chaos. Why then do you want to know more about June? Because you too are a writer, and mysteries inspire you but they must be dominated, conquered.

A little irony. It was you the writer who gave June the words with which she praised & described me. It was something about "her figure bore a faint resemblance to the beautiful Byzantine moths in silk and fur . . ." I found it in the first novel. For the painters I had always been "a Byzantine." I was amazed at June's uncanny description of the "splendor of subtle oriental sophistication" etc.

She had promised to write me a great deal. She has not written. Has she written you, and do you have an address you can give me? Yes I want to write her.

Don't worry about the effects of your correcting my English. Nothing could make me *conscious* — but you will not be *rewarded* because on days like today I would write you any way at all — and I don't really care, as long as you understand. I don't care about beautiful or perfect English. If it comes out perfect or beautiful — very well — and I'm willing to work, but you know, I don't *care enough* about just that — I'm so full, so excited, so feverish — language will always drag and lag behind. I don't even read over my letters to you. Your poor sensitive English ears! The kindness in your help, I realize that.

Please buy extra coal and wood.

I'll answer the rest of your letter tomorrow.

Anaïs

Anaïs Nin to Henry Miller

[Louveciennes]
February 25, 1932

Henry:

Perhaps you didn't realize it, but for the first time today you shook and startled me out of a dream. All your notes, your stories of June never hurt me. Nothing hurt me until you touched on the source of my terror: June and influences on June. What is June? *Is* there a June? When you talked about hating "Broadway," and that when you first met June she was just about to go Broadway—that without you she would have; when I realized that you met her and gave her most of what made her dazzle me, your influence—the terror I have when I remember her talk and sense through it how much loaded she is with the riches of others, all the others who love her beauty. Even "Count Bruga" was Jean's creation. When we were together June said: "You will *invent* what we will do together." I was ready to give her everything I have ever invented and created, from my house, my costumes, my jewelry to my writing—my imaginings, my life. I would have worked for her alone.

The words she used were yours, the fantasie belonged to Nastasia.

Understand me. I worship her. I accept everything she is, but she must *be.* I only revolt if there is no June (as I wrote the first night I met her). Don't tell me that there is no June except the physical June, don't tell me, because you must know: you have lived with her.

I never feared until today what our two minds would discover together. But what a poison you distilled—perhaps the very poison which is in you. Is that your terror too—do you feel haunted and yet deluded, as by a creation of your own brain? Is it a fear of an illusion you fight with crude words. Tell me she is not just a beautiful *image.* Sometimes when we talk I feel that we are trying to grasp her *reality.* She is unreal even to us—even to you who have possessed her, and to me whom she has kissed.

I didn't know why I couldn't write her. Now I know: I doubt what I mean to her except when she is *here,* by my side. I haven't written because I sensed Jean in the background—June showing Jean my letter—a *different* June, another June, not *mine.* And I want to let her move on, as you move on, I don't want to hold her. Pride perhaps.

These days I live only either in ecstasy or in maddening pain. To-night after our talk, it was pain.

Anaïs

Henry Miller to Anaïs Nin

Clichy
Friday [October 21, 1932]

Anaïs — this is my very first opportunity since June has arrived. She is now on her way to meet you. I can image that you had a splendid talk last night — June seemed to be very happy, very contented. I hear rumblings of change of mind about my book, and wonder whether you were really convinced by June or whether you capitulated for political reasons. In any case, it's all right. I want you to get the whole picture, for your sake as well as mine. June has said some profound, most profound things in the great welter of talk which has rolled over me like a steam roller these last few days. Our sessions have lasted until six in the morning — that's why I fell asleep, drugged and exhausted last night. There is a radical improvement in her physically and nervously. I think even the talk will abate as she gets over the idea of combatting me. We had some illuminating discussion on this subject only last night. And I think I can go on with the book, even in her presence, with perhaps some fantastic and even more sagacious or penetrating sidelights thrown on the whole work. You will see. At any rate, thanks to you I am not being crushed this time; the difference is so marked, now that we are living under a sheltered roof and can act like human beings. Had we to live outdoors again, from café to café, I would have been cracked, no doubt of it. June immediately wanted to "do things" — practical things (which sound rather impractical to me), but I am discouraging her for the time being, urging her to just take it easy, and I hope you won't think this selfish of me. I understand how much more difficult it must be for you now, but please realize that I, or we, are content with anything. June is deeply appreciative (and I suspect she would still be if she knew the whole truth). Don't lose faith in me, I beg you. I love you more than ever — truly, truly. I hate to put in writing what I wish to tell you about the first two nights with June, but when I see you and tell you you will realize the absolute sincerity of my words. At the same time, oddly, I am not quarreling with June. It is as though I had more patience, more understanding and sympathy than ever before. All this may mean a protraction beyond what I originally anticipated, but I think it for the best. I can't be mean or spiteful, or anything, but just what I am. June, it seems to me, is making heroic efforts to be what I should like her to be — and I can't help but to be touched by that. There is, too, a sort of tacit realization that another scene, such as last Christmas, would completely destroy us. Not a word about love has been mentioned, no cross-examinations, no prying curiosity — we're just taking each other for what we are as well as we can. For June's own sake I am very glad. She needed this sort of equilibrium, this new confidence in herself. Instead of criticizing her I am praising her when possible, and it affects her admirably.

As to a way out! The other night, in referring to the book which Bradley has, I mentioned that there was a possibility of it being printed privately, through you, and June immediately grasped for that in preference to the other. Said that she would like to go back to America with a number of copies and dispose of them for me — which it is quite possible she could do.

Of course, Anaïs, I don't know at all how you feel now about June, whether that first exultation is there and deepened or the reverse. I'll only say to you that you are free to do with her as you will — that's my gift to you, my love for you. I find it impossible to be jealous. I know that better than ever now. When I see June returning and smiling radiantly, and I hear little fragments of your words with her, I feel beautiful about it — and Hugo's attitude makes me sick and only more conscious of how wrong, how absurd, how futile it is. I am hurt that he should have treated you as he did — not because it may affect me adversely, believe me, but that it is so humiliating for you, so small, so lacking in human sympathy. But I too was that sort of man once, and I should forgive, only now it seems incredible that I ever was that. (At least, I had more grounds for my behavior — all that June tells you to the contrary notwithstanding.) June is perhaps not lying to you — nor I either; you are seeing, or going to see, how far apart two human beings can be even though they live together and love one another. I am listening to June attentively and seriously, when she speaks of the book and my lack of insight. Sometimes she is right, but often too she is wrong; I do know things that she doesn't know herself, about herself. And if I do not defend myself too strongly it is not because I am overwhelmed by her but that I want to spare her future pain. I can afford to be wrong, because I am more right — that's all.

I think it is quite possible for you to say to June that you want to make a rendezvous with me, at Louveciennes, and that ought to disarm her even more. I am not appearing too anxious to see you, because I am acting. But I have missed you greatly, and I have been thinking of you at moments when, God help me, no sane, normal man ought to. You can't imagine how terrible it was to get your letter, with all that it breathed, at that moment when it was impossible for me to do anything. And I had to destroy the letter, having merely been able to rush through it, which saddened me much. I suggest that you write me through Fred, either here or at the office, and allow a sufficient interval of time for me to respond because he cannot always hand it to me at once. If the letters come here I will probably get them first; don't put your address on the back (because June knows you haven't much in common with Fred) and address them on the typewriter. If you write to the *Tribune* (5 Rue Lamartine) they will be delivered to me next afternoon, you understand.

And please, dear, dear Anaïs, don't say cruel things to me as you did over the telephone — that "you are happy for me." What does that mean? I am not happy, nor am I greatly unhappy; I have a sad, wistful feeling which I can't quite explain. I want you. If you desert me now I am lost. You *must believe in me*, no matter how difficult it may seem sometimes. You ask about going to England. Anaïs, what shall I say? What would I like? To go there with you — to be with you always. I am telling you this now when June has come to me in her very best guise, when there should be more hope than ever, if I wanted hope. But like you with Hugo, I see it all coming too late. I have passed on. And now no doubt I must live some sad, beautiful lie with her for a while, and it causes me anguish, and that pains me terribly. And perhaps too you will be seeing more in June than ever, which would be right, and you may hate me or despise me, but what can I do? Take June for what she is — she may mean a great deal to you — but don't let it come between us. What you two have to give each other is none of my affair. I love you, just remember that. And please don't punish me by avoiding me. Why not occasionally come to Clichy? Do you think you can act it out here, or is it likely to prove too great a strain? Only do what you think best, what it is humanly possible for you to do. And tell me if you think I am asking too much of you?

I understand you are to meet again tomorrow night, but there is no mention of me. I feel badly. Not to deprive you of anything, but that I must be excluded. Please don't make of me another Hugo.

Henry

P.S. I stole the Elie Faure book *for you*. It is grand. It will make you delirious.

The diaries I am holding — the big one is in Fred's room and you are to ask him for it. I didn't want it to be here in my room because I don't remember what I wrote in the review of it. And I stopped working on your little diary, only because you insisted. But please let me have the other — I want to do them all for you. I want to do everything for you.

Anaïs Nin to Henry Miller

[Louveciennes]
[October 25, 1932]

You don't know the wild things I wrote the first day June was here, Henry. What I imagined I could *give* you — that I would make superhuman efforts to give you a more selfless June and to give June her Dostoevsky — you. And I was between you and June like between two torturers. When I told June I love you I felt I made you my greatest gift — I knew it would augment June's love! I was giving you to each other by *revealing* you to each other. And so yesterday I was again so dazed that things didn't turn out as I expected. It was so good that we laughed together, Henry. Anything that exists between June and me only brings out in relief my deep deep love of you. It is as if I were experiencing the very greatest test of my love for you — the greatest *test* of all life. And I find that I can be drunk, drugged, ensorcelled, everything that could make me lose myself, but that there is always always always *Henry* . . . that what I would fling away for you is every day more tremendous, yet I would fling it away for an hour like yesterday's. I need to see you again. I won't hurt you anymore with mention of others. You don't need to be jealous. I belong to you, Henry.

Anaïs

Can't you telephone me Friday morning before I leave . . . perhaps come Friday afternoon — I didn't know until June came *how much* I loved you!

I cannot write you as much or as freely as before — you understand why.

Your last pages are strange. There are some phrases which are terrible for June to see. Don't *show* them to her. The quotations are extraordinary and how they apply to you, describe you.

Have read a fecund book — *Gide* by Ramon Fernandez. Have marked it for you. Will bring it Thursday. It raises a big question about your work. Observe marks and what I wrote on last page. We must talk it over. It seems as if in the last book you were doing a Gideian multilateral trick — novelist, dramatist, critic, writer and analyst all in *one* — revealing all.

Fernandez says Gide failed because he sacrificed the art of the novel to his criticism, *and* because he lacked *passion*. Now as you are surcharged with passion it seems to me you can keep your book *moving dramatically, alive*, while yet being *critical* within the book and revealing the work in the novelist's head. To me a *unique* combination. Is that clear?

Theodore Dreiser

Author of *Sister Carrie, An American Tragedy* and other classics of modern literature, Theodore Dreiser ranked among the first completely American novelists. *Sister Carrie,* his first novel, provoked controversy for its frank treatment of sexual subject matter, but it earned Dreiser the support of influental literary figures such as H. G. Wells and Hugh Walpole. His membership in the Communist Party did little to endear him to the mainstream American public, although *An American Tragedy* proved popular enough to be made into a feature film. This letter, written late in his career, provides a snapshot of one of his intimate relationships with men.

Theodore Dreiser to George Douglas

> [Iroki
> Old Bedford Road
> R.F.D. 3]
> *Mt. Kisco, New York*
> *January 28, 1936*

George dear,

Thanks for the letter. I always read your words as I do pages from Plato or Huxley or Spencer or any of my favorite commentators on life and wish that we were in the rear garden in the swing, watching the birds at the pool or the stars in the sky. We were happiest alone, but I dislike thinking of you alone again. You are so appropriately and desireably the center of a Johnsonian table, and it should be prepared for you. Most naturally and affectionately my mind runs to the evenings — walking under the still trees, and saying over and over and over that life is what it is. To return as we did and open Swinburne or Shakespeare, or Keats, or Sterling, or Shelley! The tall bamboos are outside the window! a mocking bird begins at midnight! I can see the green electric words Gaylord over the roof-tops! And you read or present in your own words what is or was — the mutton birds of Australia, the one-time Bohemia of San Francisco.

Hail, George! Oh, ho! I am grateful. And I could cry.

T.D.

We plan to move back to L. A. — most surely. How I wish I could spend more days with you. I have almost enough material for all — all of the topics I want to deal with.

Hermann Hesse/Thomas Mann

Nobel Prize–winning German novelists Hermann Hesse (1946) and Thomas Mann (1929) exchanged letters from 1904 to 1955, a tumultuous period for their fatherland. Throughout, they maintained a formal tone and focused on literature and politics rather than personal matters. Both were fervent humanists disgusted with the emptiness of bourgeois German life, but where Mann was a highly social creature who traveled widely and met many celebrities of the day, Hesse lived an isolated life in self-imposed exile to Switzerland. The letters included here document the rise to power of Adolf Hitler and the Nazis in the 1930s.

Hermann Hesse to Thomas Mann

Mid-July, 1933

Dear Herr Mann,

Your son Michael has written me a nice letter. I enclose my answer. Our wives have also written to each other, and now it is my turn, although I have been kept very busy lately. But I think of you a good deal, and have often been reminded of you in the last few weeks. For one thing, by the Fiedler affair in Altenburg; of course you have heard about the trial. And then Bruno Frank came to see us once. He spoke of you so eloquently, knowledgeably, and admiringly that it was a real pleasure. I was reminded of my first meeting with Frank, in 1908 I think; even then you were his model and guiding star. As you see, I am reminded of you by one thing and another, and some of our conversations have left their echoes in my mind.

I am rather sorry I didn't overcome my diffidence when you were here and show you the introduction to the book I have been carrying in my head for the last two years. It was written more than a year ago and predicts the present spiritual state of Germany so accurately that I was almost frightened when I reread it the other day.

Right after you left, I decided to devote myself to your work for a while. I hadn't read *Buddenbrooks* and *Royal Highness* for years. What with the state of my eyes, reading plans are hard to carry out, but now we have made a beginning: For some days *Buddenbrooks* has been our evening reading. My wife reads it aloud with enthusiasm and then, for the length of a whole evening, you are very much a living presence in our midst.

My role in Germany and German literature is now, for the present at least, more pleasant than yours. Officially I have been spared. In appeals to the Hitler Youth to cultivate their German authors, I find myself neither among the recommended Kolbenheyers nor among the "big-city hacks" to be avoided. This time I have been forgotten, and that I appreciate, though I am well aware that it's an oversight and that the situation may change from one day to the next.

The letters that supporters of the regime write me from Germany are very strange; they are all written in high fever; in high-sounding words they glorify the unity and even the "freedom" that now prevail in the Reich, and then in the next line they fume about the stinking Catholics or Socialists, adding: Now we'll show them. It's a war-and-pogrom atmosphere, exuberant and dead drunk; the same tones as in 1914 without the naïveté that was then possible. All this will cost blood and more; the smell of evil is very strong. Yet now and then I am moved by the blue-eyed enthusiasm and spirit of self-sacrifice that are discernible in many of them.

I hope you are having a bearable time of it, and I hope we shall see each other again in the not too distant future.

Please give your wife and Mädi my very best regards.

Cordially yours,
H. Hesse

Thomas Mann to Hermann Hesse

Sanary s/Mer, July 31, 1933

Dear Herr Hesse,

What a kind and charming letter you've written me! It has given me great pleasure. Many thanks. I often think of you too, of your gentle wife, your lovely house, the countryside, and the comforting hours spent there with you. I was feeling rather low at the time, but now I am happier and easier in my mind, and going about my work as usual. I've had my struggle and now it's over. True, there are still times when I ask myself: Why? Other people manage to live in Germany — Hauptmann, Huch, Carossa, for instance. But the temptation is short-lived. I couldn't do it. I'd suffocate and waste away. And it is impossible for purely human reasons as well, because of my family. One of these days I shall have to say all this publicly, that is, when I am officially summoned to return. Day after day the news from Germany, the deceit, the violence, the ridiculous show of "historical grandeur," the sheer cruelty, fill me with horror, contempt, and revulsion. I am no longer moved by the "blue-eyed enthusiasm" you speak of. That kind of stupidity, it seems to me, is no longer permissible. I believe a terrible civil war to be inevitable, and, as our Matthias Claudius says, I don't want to "share the blame" for all that has happened, is happening, and will happen.

What a pity you didn't read me your introduction; it sounds fascinating. I'm very fond of such exchanges and I'd have been a receptive listener. Soon after my arrival here, I arranged for periodic evenings at which Schickele, my brother, Meier-Gräfe, Aldous Huxley, and I take turns at reading selections from our most recent work.

Fischer is going ahead with his plans for publishing the first volume of my biblical novel in the autumn, and the foreign publishers are going along. It is hardly possible to foresee how the distribution will be handled in Germany under present or foreseeable conditions. I imagine the book will soon be where its author is, that is, outside Germany.

But tell me, won't you send me that introduction? I should very much like to read it and should return it immediately.

We haven't made up our minds yet whether to spend the winter in Nice, where we have been offered a beautiful house for not much money, or go to Zurich directly and look for something permanent. I shall be losing my German citizenship and shall probably become Swiss. The only thing that makes us hesitate is the thought of Vienna which, if it succeeds again in resisting the Turks, would of course be ideal for us. But that is most uncertain, and it seems more likely that we shall soon be moving nearer to you.

Kind regards from us all to you and your wife.

Sincerely,
Thomas Mann

Thomas Mann to Hermann Hesse

Arosa, March 11, 1934

Dear Herr Hesse,

The news of Wiegand's death has moved me deeply. Grief and care made short shrift of him. One sacrificial victim among many. But a sacrifice to what? — I shall write to his widow.

Why did you send me those monstrosities from Munich and Leipzig? I cast only a half-hearted glance at them; my eyes fell on a motto in which that repulsive scarecrow Hitler compares himself effusively and intimately with Wagner. That was more than enough.

All the same I feel sorry about our beautiful, smiling Bavaria, and I envy you your detachment and freedom of movement. Here too, people who are well-disposed toward me advise me to go back to Germany; they tell me I belong there, that exile isn't right for me, that the new rulers would even be glad to have me back, etc. That's all very well, but how would I live and breathe there? I can't imagine. I should perish in that atmosphere of lies, mass hubbub, self-glorification, and concealed crimes. German history has always moved in waves, with high crests and deep troughs. This is one of the deepest depressions, perhaps the deepest of all. What is truly unbearable is that it should be regarded as a "rising."

We have been here for almost two weeks. Unfortunately the föhn has been blowing almost without interruption. Under the circumstances, I have not been able to work very much and should probably not even have tried. In my case the climate in itself calls for an athletic effort.

I have already heard from Bermann that the *Rundschau* is planning to publish something connected with your sublime and mysterious plan, and I am eagerly looking forward to it. In the present issue it has given me special pleasure to see the fine poem on man that you sent me when I was in Küsnacht.

I hope you will not be disappointed in my second volume. I hear at least that Walser's jacket design is even better than the first.

Kind regards to you and your wife from the two of us.

Yours sincerely,
Thomas Mann

Hermann Hesse to Thomas Mann

March, 1934

Dear Herr Thomas Mann,

Thank you for your letter from Arosa. Since then we too have been having strangely capricious weather here in the Ticino. The other day, for instance, there was a fine storm with magnificent thunder and at the same time it was snowing hard.

It was mostly by chance that I sent you the newspaper with the account of the Wagner orgy in Leipzig with my last letter. It had just come on the morning when I was writing to you, and since I myself seldom get to see German newspapers, I forgot for a moment that you have far more occasion than I to see such documents of our times. But now that I examine my motives more closely, I must own to an element of malice or *schadenfreude.* As you know, I heartily agree with your critical, disparaging remarks about Wagner's histrionics and swagger, but honorable and even touching as I find your attitude of loving him all the same, I can only half understand it. To be perfectly frank, I can't bear him. And at the sight of that paper, with Hitler's superlatives about Wagner, I suppose my feelings toward you were something on the order of: "There's your Wagner for you! That scheming, unscrupulous careerist is just the right idol for the new Germany, and the fact that he was probably a Jew makes him even righter."

I too am convinced that you can't live in Germany. Pleasant as it may be to see that everyone who is remotely intellectual is coming into conflict with the regime and being included in the persecution of Christians (even a perfectly harmless lecture by Kolbenheyer was banned by the police) the whole situation looks very serious, for there is no doubt that they are heavily rearming. I hardly know what I would want or decree if I were obliged for a minute to direct history — I almost think I would have the French march across the Rhine and make Germany lose a war which in a few years it may win.

As every year at Easter, we are expecting a mass invasion of foreigners in the region. It brings with it a few welcome visitors, but far too many at once, and usually the weather amuses itself by making a mockery of the visitors' dreams of the sunny south. March to May is traditionally a rainy season here. That you didn't run into it last year was a pure stroke of luck, which the heavens may well have granted for your sake. May they continue to favor you. The lonelier I get between the German Germans and the German refugees, the more I think of you.

Frau Wiegand is still with us. My wife sends her warm regards.

Cordially yours,
H. Hesse

Hermann Hesse to Thomas Mann

June 1950

To Thomas Mann on His Seventy-fifth Birthday

Dear Herr Thomas Mann,

It is quite a while since I made your acquaintance. It was in a hotel in Munich. We had both been invited there by S. Fischer, our publisher. Your first short stories and *Buddenbrooks* had been published, and my *Peter Camenzind;* we were both bachelors and great things were expected of us both. In other respects, to be sure, we were not much alike, as could be seen even by our clothing and shoes, and this first meeting, brought about by chance and purely literary curiosity — I asked you among other things whether you were related to the author of the three Duchess of Assy novels — hardly seemed to augur the beginning of a friendship.

Before this friendship, one of the most gratifying and harmonious of my later life, could nevertheless come into being, a good many things we didn't dream of in that pleasant hour in Munich had to happen and both of us had to travel a difficult and often dark path from the seeming security of our national ties through loneliness and ostracism to the clean and rather cold air of a world citizenship which in your case has very different features than in mine, but which nevertheless unites us far more firmly and reliably than anything we may have had in common at the time of our moral and political innocence.

In the meantime, we have come to be old folks; few of our companions of those days are still alive. And now you are celebrating your seventy-fifth birthday. I join you in celebrating it, thankful for everything you have written, thought, and suffered, thankful for your intelligent yet enchanting, uncompromising yet playful prose, thankful for the great store of love, warmth of heart, and devotion, so shamefully little appreciated by your former compatriots, that has been the source of your life-work, for your fidelity to your language, for your integrity and warmth of conviction which, I hope, will endure beyond our lifetime as elements of a new morality in world politics, of a world conscience, at whose first childlike steps we are now looking on with hope and solicitude.

Dear Thomas Mann, may you long remain among us. Speaking not as the representative of a nation, but as a solitary individual whose true fatherland, like yours, is still in the making, I greet you and thank you.

Cordially yours,
H. Hesse

Thomas Mann to Hermann Hesse

Pacific Palisades, California
June 14, 1952

My dear Hermann Hesse,

I absent on this occasion? Impossible! But neither can I participate in any significant way. I wrote on your sixtieth, I wrote on your seventieth birthday, and now I can think of nothing more to say. *J'ai vidé mon sac.* I know I love you and admire you with all my heart. But everyone knows that, and so do you. Let me then, on your seventy-fifth birthday, simply say it once again and sincerely congratulate you on the blessed, joy-giving life you have led, and wish you happiness and peace and serenity for the evening of this life that still bestows gifts and is still precious to us.

"The world is governed by confusing doctrines that make for confused actions," says Goethe in his last letter. That's how it is today, and still worse, it seems to me, more dangerous and more difficult for a thinking man to maintain an attitude of decency and to hold his own against the absurd, confused powers of the day — as you, esteemed friend, are endeavoring to do in your "fortress." And in this, as I see it, you — pure and free, intelligent, good, and steadfast as you are — succeed admirably: On this, too, on this exemplary attitude, on this most of all, I congratulate you. And don't die before me! In the first place, it would be an impertinence, for I am "next in line." And moreover, I should miss you terribly in all this turmoil. For in it you are a good companion, a consolation, prop, example, and encouragement, and without you I should feel very much alone.

I shall soon be with you in your "fortress" with the good ladies. We shall scold and sigh and despair of mankind a little, though at bottom that is not our way, but at the same time get some amusement out of its great, great stupidity. Flaubert managed to wax positively enthusiastic over it. "H-énorme!" he would say, filled with amazed admiration by its gigantic proportions.

Auf Wiedersehen, dear old companion of my travels through this vale of tears, in which both of us have been given the consolation of dreams, play, and form.

Yours ever,
Thomas Mann

T. H. White/Mary Potts/David Garnett

Author, teacher and avid sportsman, T. H. White suffered throughout his life from the self-loathing inspired by his attraction to S/M. Several attempts at love left him determined never to act on his feelings, but unlike many other closeted gays of his time he found it impossible to marry, even for convenience. As a result, the love of his life turned out to be his dog, a female Irish setter named Brownie. He did, however, sustain various human friendships, notably with David (Bunny) Garnett, a member of the Bloomsbury crowd, and the academic Potts family (L. J., Mary and son William). It is to these friends that White confided his passion for Brownie and his intense grief at her death.

T. H. White to William Potts
[December 28, 1943]

FROM TIM

DEAR WILLIAM,

THANK you very much for the handsome and cheering *CALENDAR* which you have sent to me for Christmas. I shall now be able, for the first time in my life, to put the proper date on all my letters for a year, and I have been very careful to put the right one on this letter, in red ink, as you see.

I do not know what kind of letters you generally like to get, and so I am going to write to you about my DOG. Her picture is on the outside of this letter, so that you will know what she looks like. Her name is BROWNIE, but that is only her pet name, for she was born of noble parents who christened her BROWN MAID OF TINGEWICK at the Kennel Club. As I was your godfather when you were christened, would you like to be hers? It is a bit late, but could still be done.

Now the house in which Brownie was born was a public house in which I used to live. It belonged to an innkeeper and his wife called Mr. and Mrs. Blaize, and Brownie's mother belonged to them too. The mother was very fond of having puppies, and her husband, Brownie's father, was a member of the Highest Canine Aristocracy. He had won so many prizes for the blueness of his blood, and other accomplishments, that he had the right to write the letters CH. before his name. It stands for CHAMPION, and is for dogs the same as being a Duke. Naturally all his puppies were of the utmost value, for this reason, and Mr. Blaize used to sell them to the Stately Homes of England, where they lived happily ever afterwards. Sometimes he kept one or two himself, to train them, or when he could not get a buyer, and therefore the public house generally had about half a dozen puppies in it, owing to the fondness which Brownie's mother had for having them. Sometimes Mr. Blaize used to take the puppies to dog shews, where they also won prizes for their aristocratic principles. They used to get brushed and combed twice a day for the month before they went, and CHAMPION BROWN MAID OF TINGEWICK won no less than ten prizes in her first year at dog shews which were as far apart as Bedford and Aberystwyth. Sometimes she won FIVE POUND at a time.

Now there was always a good deal of a scrum at bed-time in the kitchen of the public house where all these puppies lived. Naturally there were some beds which were more popular than others, and the brothers and sisters could never agree who was to have them. The Duke and his Duchess often went up to bed with Mr. and Mrs. Blaize, leaving their children to fight it out. I am sorry to say that some of the brothers were rather cads, in spite or perhaps because of their birth, and one of them was actually a drunkard. He once drank a whole pint of bitter which I had left on the floor beside my chair in the kitchen, and this made him feel so ill that he put his head into my coat pocket without my noticing, and sicked it all up again in the pocket. He felt very ashamed after that. All the puppies were always trying to sit on my lap, and, although I was kind to them in a thoughtless way, I never knew one from another.

Now, although Brownie was little, she used to think a good deal, and one day she thought that she was getting about fed up with drunken brothers and having to fight for beds. She also thought what a handsome and interesting man I was. I used to let Mr. Blaize bring her out when I had a shooting party, to train her for the gun, and she had been in my motor car, which she adored, and she knew quite well that these things belonged to me and not to Mr. Blaize. She also knew that I had a bedroom of my own, with no brothers or sisters in it.

In short, Brownie fell in love with me. She was modest at first, and did not like to mention it, but she tried to tell me as well as she could, with soft looks and so on, and I was such a fool that I did not notice. In the end, she had to declare herself. I had gone up to bed and was brushing my teeth, and the usual battle had started in the kitchen, when Brownie tapped rather shyly on my door and said: "Please, sir, can I sleep with you?" I didn't mind, one way or the other, so she came in, and there she was on the foot of the bed in the morning, looking as pleased as Punch. She thought she had got off.

Poor darling, she had only flattered my vanity. I still did not really think about her a bit. Mr. Blaize noticed it long before I did, and he insisted on giving her to me as a present. She went everywhere that I went, was very beautiful and famous, behaved most lovingly, and so I accepted her as a present — just as if she was a lampshade, or anything else without a soul.

I was kind, if you see what I mean, but I did not love her for herself alone, and, however much she tried to tell me about these things with her eyes, I was too stupid to listen.

Then, when we had been together for about two years, without my ever realising what a lovely person she was, I got interested in hawks and falcons, which I used to train to catch rabbits and grouse. They are very difficult to train, and you have to think about them constantly, and poor Brownie was always getting in the way as she asked me to love her, so it was always: "Oh, GO away, Brownie" or "Now DO leave me in peace for a MINUTE" or even "Oh, you NAUGHTY girl, now you've frightened the hawk." I hardly said a word to her except these, because I was so busy.

Brownie had tried to tell me about her love for two years in vain, and now she saw that she would never succeed. She saw that I did not love her, but only hawks, and it broke her poor heart. One day, she trod on a thorn, and I took it out for her and patted her for a few seconds, and after that she trod on thorns every day for a week, or pretended to if she could not find them, but all in vain. I just told her that she was shamming, and would not pat at all. She saw then that all her life and hopes were wrecked, and that there was nothing left but death.

There is a horrible disease which dogs have, which is called DIS-TEMPER. If they get it before they are a year old, they often get over it. If they get it when they are older, they nearly always die. It is terrible to see it. Brownie decided, on purpose, to have it, as she could not bear to live any longer without love. She decided to die.

She had had it for a day before I noticed, but, when I did notice, the miracle happened all at once in my heart. Something in her dying look at last penetrated my thick skull, and things began to happen. I shut up those ridiculous hawks in their barn, telling her that they could starve for all I cared; I wrapped her up in the best eiderdown; I bought bottles of brandy and port and stuff to make junket; I had a veterinary surgeon every day, and even a human doctor twice; and I sat up beside her, day and night, with hot-water-bottles, for a week. She got rennet every two hours, with a teaspoon of brandy, and I told her over and over again that if she would not die I would never keep hawks any more, or go to cinemas or to dances or to any place where she could not come as well. I promised that she should be my real wife, not a lampshade, and I told God that if he let her die I would kill him.

But I couldn't stop her. She got weaker and weaker, and it was awful to hear her breathe, and the doctors and the vet were useless, and you could hardly feel her heart. At last there came a minute when I said: "In a quarter of an hour she will be dead."

Then I said: "Well, there is nobody left in it but Me and Death. We will fight it out. I can't possibly make her any worse, so at least I will do something to see if I can make her better." So I went upstairs for the *Encyclopaedia Britannica,* and read the article on DISTEMPER. It was vague and cautious, which most of the articles in that book are, and the only ray of light I could get out of it was something like this: "It has been claimed by some writers on the subject that quinine is a specific of some merit . . ." Well, there was a bottle of quinine in my cottage. I gave her a half human dose, which burned her weak throat but she was too feeble to cough it up, and sat down to stroke her. When the quarter of an hour was up, she stood up on her shaky legs, and was sick. The next time the rennet came round (I mean WEY — the juice of the junket) she actually drank it, instead of having to have it poured down her throat. That night she suddenly ran out into the darkness, or rather tottered out, and vanished. It was pitch dark. I stayed for hours calling her and walking about in the wood with candles, but I could not find her and she did not come back. At last I knew that she had died in a ditch, so I went back and cried myself to sleep, but I got up again at dawn, and went to look for her body. I was calling and looking when she staggered out of the wood, not quite sure who she was or who I was, and I carried her home in floods of tears, but they were quite needless. She was cured. She soon got raw eggs and port wine, then she got fish; then she got rice puddings and soups; then she got roast beef, turkey, caviare, plum puddings, pate de foie gras and gallons of champagne.

If you think this is a sad story, WILLIAM, you must think again, for it has a happy ending. However wicked I had been before, I kept my promises after. I never went to cinemas or dances or libraries any more; I asked her advice whenever I went near a hawk, and soon dropped them altogether; I fed her on my own dinner every day; she slept, and still sleeps, not on my bed but in it, with our arms round each other's necks; she had every possible excitement that could be suitable to her rank, including going in trains, motors, aeroplanes and crossing the Irish Sea in a ship (when I slept in the boiler room with her, because they would not let her sleep in the cabin with me); she had a special grouse moor taken for her, of ten thousand acres, and on this she learned to exercise her own trade as a setter, which she did to perfection; she was never smacked for anything whatever; she had pets of her own, just like my hawks, which she used to carry up to bed with her in her mouth, and these included baby hares, baby rabbits, baby chickens and some moor hens (she never hurt any of them, carrying); she was endowed with property of her own, including a rubber ball, several daffodil bulbs, some bits of wood, and two collars, all of which she keeps under the dining room table (one of the collars, the sunday one, is of plaited silk with a real gold clasp); she goes shooting every day for two hours, because this is her favourite occupation, and she has become the most wonderful of all gun dogs, and the rarest (because it is so difficult to be it) that is to say A RETRIEVING SETTER.

Perhaps the best of all is that she is still alive, and fat, and healthy, with no bad consequences of her distemper, and, although she is about SEVENTY years old by human standards, she is as cheerful and merry as a baby. We have both agreed that she is to live to ONE HUNDRED AND FIFTY by human measure, and then we will both die together, so that neither of us can live to be sad for the other.

You have seen her yourself. Do you remember?

When you see her again, you must be very polite and gentle, because of her noble blood and impressive marriage. She is a LITTLE grand, on account of these qualities — not snobbish, but dignified, you understand, and it is no good taking liberties. If you pulled her tail, or hugged her without being asked, she would never dream of biting you, but she would think the worse of you in consequence. Nobody will be cross with you, however much you pull her tail, but it is only that a loving person like yourself would hardly like to do so. Besides, if you were her Godfather, it would scarcely be the thing.

WITH LOVE FROM
TIM

(CH. MRS. BROWNIE WHITE OF TINGEWICK)
(Her Paw)

ALL THE ABOVE IS ABSOLUTELY TRUE, TO WHICH WE GIVE OUR SIGN AND SEAL AT OUR CASTLE OF DOOLISTOWN, ON THE TWENTY-EIGHTH DAY OF DECEMBER 1943, ACCORDING TO WILLIAM'S CALENDAR.

T. H. White to Mary Potts

Doolistown, Trim
[November 25, 1944]

My dearest Mary,

I am so unutterably miserable and disconsolate, in fact howling like a baby, that I am sure you will forgive me if I try to howl on you. You know it's just sort of hysterical relief and are too generous not to help. The fact is that my darling of all darlings, my Brownie, died today. The awfulness of it, is that I was not here to help. In all of fourteen years of life I have only been away from her at night on three occasions: when I made a five day visit to England in desperate hurry; when I had my appendix out; when I had my tonsils out (two days). But I did go into Dublin and such places for a nine hour visit, about twice a year to buy books, and today was one of those unlucky days, it was not even a question of sleeping away from her, it only happened twice a year. I left her in perfect health in my bed where she always slept and was a splendid hot water bottle to me, when I got back they told me she was dead. I do not know what filthy witchery may have been practised upon her, even poison, or whether it was merely incompetence or whether nothing could have saved her in a sudden attack; I would not think about the worse of these things, but anyway she is dead now, without my having been able to help or save her as I have done three or four times before, and I am writing with her sweet dead face on my lap, as I am going to sit up with her tonight. When I had my tonsils out, I noticed that consciousness was liable to persist after apparent inertia and it is only for this that I want to sit up. To-morrow I must bury her. I don't know what I will do after that. She was absolutely well and in roaring form till the moment I left her. We slept comfortably tussling as usual for the best place in the bed. She was too lazy to get up and see me off as she had been in other occasions. I have come back to a dead wife who was mother, child and mistress to me for fourteen years, unprepared. I do not mind in the least bit about myself — for me it will even be a relief to be able to visit libraries; it is this cold Brownness on my lap, which I did not help to die that's breaking my heart into bits.

When I first got her, I was a very ignorant young sportsman; I often spanked her for matters which were no fault of hers. Setters are very sensitive dogs who take things to heart; I might have spoilt her entirely, making her a coward and a fool, but luckily I pulled up in time and at the end of her life she had implicit trust in me. I could have shook a whip at her and she would not have blinked — which is unusual in setters as they are timorous. She thought me the most superb of doctors as I had brought her through dreadful illnesses, but when she came to die, I was not on hand — a chance of one hundred and eighty to one. Brownie was the chief factor in my life, she was more to me than you are to Potts, because I had to look after her (fear of running over by motors and that sort of thing) which Potts does not have to do for you. She was the only perfection I have ever known, she was gentle and loving and trustful and afraid of cows, she was a superb gun-dog. I am writing all this, dry-eyed now, trying to convince myself, with the soft eyes on my lap that won't open. Don't tell Potts about it but don't either of you write about her to me for some time. It is like being in some other planet which I can't understand yet. I tried to cry on purpose and succeeded in a way, but that has nothing to do with it. Crying is only a self-indulgence and the awful feeling that it happened when I was not there to help, won't be lulled by this. She seemed to have ten years of life before her and lies as beautifully now as she ever did. All the happiness I have ever had was from her; if only I could have helped her to die. This morning before I left, she ate half my breakfast in bed. Now I am eating a cold sausage which she would have liked and stroking the cold silk head, and now again I am crying so much that it finishes the page very nicely.

From Brownie's Tim

T. H. White to David Garnett

[Doolistown]
[(?) November 25, 1944]

Dearest Bunny, Brownie died today. In all her 14 years of life I have only been away from her at night for 3 times, once to visit England for 5 days, once to have my appendix out and once for tonsils (2 days), but I did go in to Dublin about twice a year to buy books (9 hours away) and I thought she understood about this. To-day I went at 10, but the bloody devils had managed to kill her somehow when I got back at 7. She was in perfect health. I left her in my bed this morning, as it was an early start. Now I am writing with her dead head in my lap. I will sit up with her tonight, but tomorrow we must bury her. I dont know what to do after that. I am only sitting up because of that thing about perhaps consciousness persisting a bit. She has been to me more perfect than anything else in all my life, and I have failed her at the end, an 180–1 chance. If it had been any other day I might have known that I had done my best. These fools here did not poison her — I will not believe that. But I could have done more. They kept rubbing her, they say. She looks quite alive. She was wife, mother, mistress & child. Please forgive me for writing this distressing stuff, but it is helping me. Her little tired face cannot be helped. Please do not write to me at all about her, for very long time, but tell me if I ought to buy another bitch or not, as I do not know what to think about anything. I *might* live another 30 years, which would be 2 dog's lifetimes at this, but of course they hamper one very much when one loves them so desperately, and it is a problem. I am certain I am not going to kill myself about it, as I thought I might once. However, you will find this all very hysterical, so I may as well stop. I still expect to wake up and find it wasn't. She was all I had.

love from TIM

As a matter of fact, I believe they did poison her. But what does that matter? she was everything, everywhere, for ever, my Brown.

T. H. White to David Garnett

Doolistown, Trim, Co. Meath, Eire
November 28th, 1944

Dear Bunny, Please forgive me writing again, but I am so lonely and can't stop crying and it is the shock. I waked her for two nights and buried her this morning in a turf basket, all my eggs in one basket. Now I am to begin a new life and it is important to begin it right, but I find it difficult to think straight. It is about whether I ought to buy another dog or not. I am good to dogs, so from their point of view I suppose I ought. But I might not survive another bereavement like this in 12 years' time, and dread to put myself in the way of it. If your father & mother & both sons had died at the same moment as Ray, unexpectedly, in your absence, you would know what I am talking about. Unfortunately Brownie was barren, like myself, and as I have rather an overbearing character I had made her live through me, as I lived through her. If I got another bitch and the same thing happened I feel it might be the end of me when she died. I shall never be married, and have no friends except you. An alternative might be to bury myself in Museum Libraries for the rest of my life, and to grow dessicated in them, keeping my eggs to my own basket, which, when destroyed, will be unable to regret them. Or I could get two dogs and breed up vast families of puppies, but what would be the good of that? It would only be an occupation. Brownie was my life and I am lonely for just such another reservoir for my love — not for an occupation. But if I did get such a reservoir it would die in about 12 years and at present I feel I couldn't face that. Do people get used to being bereaved? This is my first time. If it was going to ache less when I got it again 12 years hence, I think I might chance it. Or I could get a bitch who wasn't barren, and keep one or two of her puppies about us to help tide over the next time. Perhaps this last is the best idea, unless the Museum Library one is. I would value the advice of somebody in his right mind who was accustomed to bereavements. I am feeling very lucky to have a friend like you that I can write to without being thought dotty to go on like that about mere dogs.

They did not poison her. It was one of her little heart attacks and they did not know how to treat it and killed her by the wrong kindnesses.

If I can learn to eat a little, I will go to Dublin for a week and try the Library dodge. But I will not buy a dog till I hear from you.

You must try to understand that I am and will remain entirely without wife or brother or sister or child and that Brownie supplied more than the place of these to me. We loved each other more and more every year. It actually grew. Even if I got another bitch, it would take 12 years to get back to where I was on saturday. It was because we were both childless that we loved each other so much. If I got one that had children, we would probably never rise to the same love. An unbearable 12 year future comes in again. So I will stop going round and round.

love from TIM

It seems to be insoluble.
The first advice that will spring to your lips will be 'Take a wife'.
That is quite impossible.

T. H. White to David Garnett

Doolistown, Trim, Co. Meath, Eire
November 29th, 1944

Dear Bunny, I hope this will be the last of these insane letters, and I do beg you to forgive me for writing them. I know I ought not. It helps to write and I believe you to be sterling enough to bear with me, just for these three times. I couldn't do it to anybody else, and without your help I would have died. I have found out how people 'die of a broken heart'. It just means that they lose interest in being alive. Also, it is not the deceased person that dies (for them) but it is themselves that die: all that they consisted of, for the last 12 years in my case, steps into the past, leaving them to start a new life all over again, for which, if old, they lack the power to re-organise and re-integrate, and consequently they give it up. Brownie has been quartering in front of me for 12 years, while I have plodded behind that dancing sprite, so now it is difficult not to follow her still, into the past.

I am afraid that you are going to advise me to get married. It is physically impossible. I can't go into all this in a letter, but I will explain if I ever see you again, and if you want to know.

Now the whole thing boils down to one conundrum. If you were an orphan and a widower without siblings, would you accept the offer of having an only daughter brought by the stork tomorrow, knowing that she herself was bound to die in 12 more years, probably in your own lifetime? The *pro*'s are that you would have those 12 happy years, that you could make her happy, and that she would have lived out her natural life. The *con*'s are, or is, that it would probably be your own death sentence, deferred. I dont think I can go through this again.

I have an affectionate disposition and as I could not take a wife I needed something to lavish it on, which was why, apart from Brownie, I was always fooling about with hawks and badgers and snakes and God knows what else. I know it is difficult to understand old maids like me, except with a kind of pitying contempt, but if anybody can it will be you. (I dont feel at all contemptible.) I loved Brownie more than any man I have ever met has loved his natural wife. We were like cats on hot bricks away from each other, and thought about each other all day, particularly in the last years. It is a queer difference between this kind of thing and getting married, that married people love each other most at first (I understand) and it fades by use & custom, but with dogs you love them most at last. They are meaningless to begin with, and if I bought a bitch puppy tomorrow she would not replace Brownie for a long time to come.

It is perhaps a matter of life or death to me to know whether to recommence the same long trail with a new puppy, which I feel morally certain would end in both our deaths, because I would be too old to make a fresh start in 12 years time, or whether to have nothing more to do with dogs. In the latter case I might not be able to keep it up (living) and I dont know where I would put my surplus affections.

The whole and single unnaturalness of the position is that dogs and men have incompatible longevities. Everything else is perfectly natural and I would not have it altered in any respect. I regret nothing about Brownie, except the bitter difference of age.

I always tried to hide how much I loved her, for fear of this silly reproach about old maids.

It was because we were both barren that it came to mean so much. If I got a fertile puppy, it would never rise to the same thing (which I want it to) but on the other hand I would probably not die of her death (which I dont want to).

So you see it is quite a nice little problem for you convalescent novelists, who write books about ladies who turn into foxes, and I am beginning to feel that I am really doing you quite a favour to explain it all so nicely, instead of using you as a weeping post for selfish ends. At least I have not hung on how I cry all day and most of the night, because there is nowhere I can go, neither on long walks nor to bed, where I was not accustomed to go with her. She slept with me, ate my food. The only escape is to write to you, and even that she once shared. I was her companion, master, valet, protector, upper servant and physician. She depended on me for everything, and I failed her in the end. Would it have been easier for both of us if she had died in my arms? Could I have saved her? Two things I will never know.

Anyway, there is the problem of the Vita Nuova. Please be tender with it.

love from TIM

T. H. White to David Garnett

Doolistown, Trim, Co. Meath, Eire
December 1944

Dear Bunny, I am over the worst, though there is still one thing I can hardly bear to think of. Brownie had immense confidence in me as a doctor and used to come to me for help when she felt an attack coming on. She used to come and look up at me and register being ill. Because I was away, she couldn't do it when she was dying, but she knew she was dying, and went to tell Mrs. McDonagh as a last resource, which failed her. When I think of this my heart is an empty funnel. There is a physical feeling in it. After she was buried I stayed with the grave for one week, so that I could go out twice a day and say 'Good girl: sleepy girl: go to sleep, Brownie.' It was a saying she understood. I said it steadily. I suppose the chance of consciousness persisting for a week is several million to one, but that was the kind of chance I had to provide against. She depended on me too much, and so I had to accept too much responsibility for her. Then I went to Dublin, against my will, and kept myself as drunk as possible for nine days, and came back feeling more alive than dead. She was the only wonderful thing that has happened to me, and presumably the last one. You are wrong that her infertility was due to our relationship. It was the other way round. She adopted me off her own bat, and I took her to the sire at 18 months and several times after, before I cared two straws about her. I also took her to vets, to find out why she flinched at the critical moment, and they said that the passage was malformed. After that, I just used to leave her loose when she was in season. I dont know what I told you before, but I have found out some things. One is that bereaved suicides commit it out of tidyness, not out of grand emotions. Their habits, customs and interests, which means their lives, were bound up with their loved one, so, when that dies, they realise that their own habits etc. are dead. So, as they see that they are dead already, they commit suicide in order to be consistent. Everything is dead except their bodies, so they kill these too, to be tidy, like washing up after a meal or throwing away the empties after a party, and I daresay they find it as tedious. The other thing I have found is that the people who consider too close an affection between men and animals to be 'unnatural' are basing their prejudice on something real. It is the incompatibility of ages. It is in Lucretius. He says that centaurs cannot exist because the horse part would die before the man part.

> *Sed neque Centauri fuerunt, neque tempore in ullo*
> *Esse queat duplici natura, et corpore bino*
> *Ex alienigenis membris compacta potestas, . . .*
> *Quae neque florescunt pariter, neque robora sumunt*
> *Corporibus, necque projiciunt aetate senecta.*

All I can do now is to remember her dead as I buried her, the cold grey jowl in the basket, and not as my heart's blood, which she was for the last eight years of our twelve. I shall never be more than half a centaur now.

I must thank you very, very much for your two letters, which have left me as amazed at your wisdom as I always was at your kindness and information. I have done what you said I was to do, or at any rate I have bought a puppy bitch. Brownie had taught me so much about setters that it seemed silly to waste the education, so I stuck to them. No setter could ever remind me of her, any more than one woman would remind you of another, except in general terms. The new arrangement looks like the foetus of a rat, but she has a pedigree rather longer than the Emperor of Japan's. She is called Cill Dara Something or-other of Palmerston, but prefers to be called Killie, for lucidity. She nibbles for fleas in my whiskers. We are to accept the plaudits of the people of Erin next St. Patrick's day at the Kennel Club Shew, where we intend to win the Puppy Class and the Novices: in the Autumn we go to watch the Field Trials, which we win the year after. When we have collected 15 points or green stars and can call ourselves CH. in the stud book we are coming to repeat the process in England. We are to have about 4 litters of puppies. Then it is to be America: the camera men & reporters, the drive up Broadway with typists showering us with tape, the reception at the White House, the spotlights at Hollywood. In short, we are determined to make good.

If you really want a Pointer and were not suggesting him in order to encourage me, I will gladly train one for you . . .

Do you think it would be wrong of me to write a book about Brownie, or that I ought to wait seven years before starting? I have a strong feeling that I want to write it now . . .

I have joined the Kennel Club as a life member, as I am going to have hundreds and hundreds of setters from now on, to prevent loving one of them too much. When I went to their office about half a dozen dog-like women attended to me so faithfully and gently, and one of them was so exactly like a bull-dog, that I celebrated my entry by crying all over my cheque book. She was solid gold and stood by and gave moral support without speaking. I can't remember whether she barked a bit.

I was very angry when I heard that you were still limping, but on second thoughts I suppose it is only fair to give you about 18 months before you get back to normal. I dont think it is a good idea that you should have gone back to the office.

love from TIM

Elizabeth Bowen

Irish novelist and short story writer Elizabeth Bowen grew up with a mentally ill father and no mother (she died young) at her ancestral family home, Bowen's Court. Perhaps as a result she took an unconventional view of morality in her life and work, mingling with many gay friends and creating a number of gay or arguably gay characters. Married to Alan Cameron at twenty-four, she lived at various times in New York and Brazil, with stops in Key West, San Francisco and many other cities throughout Europe and the United States. She came into contact with most of her prominent literary peers, engaging in a brief fling with May Sarton and establishing a pivotal friendship with poet Marianne Moore. And like so many significant writers of her generation, she corresponded with Virginia Woolf.

Elizabeth Bowen to Virginia Woolf

Bowen's Court
January 5th [1941]

Dear Virginia,

I found the letter I began to you here, but it seemed so faded that I tore
it up, and it was like a letter written by someone not me to someone not
you. And for months now I have been completely dumb: there seemed
to be nothing to add to anything, even in what I said to you. I think about
you so much, especially shredding those red currants in the evening up
in that top room. And were all those streets that were burnt the streets
we walked about? I have never seen them since. When your flat went
did that mean all the things in it too? All my life I have said, 'Whatever
happens there will always be tables and chairs' — and what a mistake.
Clarence Terrace is now perfectly empty, except for ourselves in No 2,
and one other, a house with a *reputation*, full of rather gaudy, silent young
men who come out in the mornings and walk about two and two, like
nuns.

Alan was here for Christmas, but went back two days ago. I am
going back to London at the end of this month. I was there in September
and part of October, but in a stupefied excited and I think rather vulgar
state. To be here is very nice, but I no longer like, as I used to, being
here alone. I can't write letters, I can't make plans. The house now is
very cold and empty, and very beautiful in a glassy sort of way. Every
night it freezes. There are some very early lambs, which at night get
through the wires and cry on the lawn under my windows. I am doing
the last chapter of the Bowen's Court book: I don't want you to see it
till it is done, because the last chapter seems to, or ought to re-write
retrospectively all the rest of the book. It is also rather painful and rather
difficult, because some of the people in it are still alive. A book of short
stories of mine is coming out this month or next: they are mostly rather
long ago ones, except one long one called *Summer Night* which I should
like very much to know what you think about. I wrote it since I saw you.
As soon as I have a copy of the book, may I send it? They made me
correct the proofs in a great hurry, but there's no sign of it's coming out
yet. I should like to know what you think of all the other stories, but
they seem such a long time ago.

Is all the Hogarth Press at Rodmell now? I try and imagine it, and
where everyone lives. I wonder if anyone is in the cottage we looked at,
with all those oak beams and brass blinkers. I also imagine the hills, and

the stretch of your lawn up, in this glass weather. I wonder if the lily pond froze. Have you ever been a whole winter at Rodmell before, I wonder? I would in ways like to be a whole winter here, only I get rather pent-up with no one to talk to. In winter this is a nice house for two. Now *all* the petrol has stopped and we are immobilised, at least immobilised until we get new ideas about time. No motor car ever lived here until ten years ago, so it really is artificial to fuss. I wish now I had a riding horse. I bought a bicycle a year ago but on it I can't think; I keep wanting to get off and sit on the bank to smoke and think and cheer up. I bicycled yesterday morning into the town, Mitchelstown, where one of my aunts lives: she has rooms in the square. It is a beautifully planned but sad little town up under the Galtee mountains: do you remember it — I expect you drove through. The eight miles of road along under the mountains was very raw with wind and I disappointingly hated every mile, except for the pleasure of getting off at my aunt's — having arrived, I mean. This week I am going to Dublin: I take a flat there, very small, the rooms looking on to Stephen's Green. In Dublin I get engaged in deep rather futile talks; it is hard to remember the drift afterwards, though I remember the words. I suppose that (smoke-screen use of words) is a trick of the Irish mind. They are very religious. It is the political people I see mostly: it seems a craggy dangerous miniature world. I can't write any more about that but would like to talk *very much*.

Ever since June I felt I couldn't bear to read French, then I thought I would begin again with someone I liked least, so I bought some collections of Maupassant I hadn't got already, and brought them here. Read in the middle of winter here they are extraordinary. I suppose he had sharp senses but really rather a boring mind. You soon get to know his formula but there is always the fascination; it is like watching someone doing the same card trick over and over again. I did feel the fascination so strongly that I wondered if I were getting rather brutalised myself. There is a particularly preposterous story called *Yvette*, about a young girl whose mother takes a summer villa on the Seine. Looking at the pictures, which are so good and open sort of windows in the writing, I wondered whether illustrations were such a bad thing. Nobody illustrates now, I wonder whether they could.

I wonder if you have snow. I have a card you sent me with Rodmell church with snow on it. This makes me feel very homesick. I feel a sort of despair about my own generation — the people the same age as the century, I mean — we don't really suffer much but we get all sealed up. This letter was interrupted by a telephone call: I got up and was cruel to a neighbour called Mr Gates. I said, 'How can you be so absolutely stupid when you have got an Austrian grandfather?' which is really an unforgivable thing to say to a country neighbour: if one is even a degree more imaginative than anyone else one ought to be nice to them, but how hard it is. And this is certainly no time to be querulous. In principle I feel very humble indeed. I have been cruel to Mr Gates because I made the mistake I so often make, of idealising at the outset a stupid person.

I do long to see you again. I shall be back in February and wish I were back now. Please give my love to Leonard.

Love from Elizabeth

Elizabeth Bowen to Leonard Woolf

Bowen's Court
April 8th [1941]

Dear Leonard,

It was very good of you to write to me, as and when you did. I do thank you. I have been in Ireland for the last three weeks, so your letter, sent on from Clarence Terrace, reached me here last Saturday. I had not heard anything at all till the Thursday before that, when someone told me what they had heard on the wireless. English papers take nearly a week to come. It meant a good deal, then, to get your letter. You and Virginia and Rodmell had, for those two days, hardly been out of my thoughts — not by day and not much by night. I had begun to imagine what I learned from you to be true — that she had feared her illness was coming back.

You said not to answer your letter, and above all I don't want to trouble you with words now. And it is no time to speak of my own feeling. As far as I am concerned, a great deal of the meaning seems to have gone out of the world. She illuminated everything, and one referred the most trivial things to her in one's thoughts. To have been allowed to know her and love her is a great thing.

I have been thinking so much about you. I hope it is not an intrusion to say this. If there is any practical thing I can do, in the next few months, I know you will be friendly enough to let me know. And if you ever had time to see me, and felt disposed to see me, it would be very kind of you. I am crossing back to London this week, and shall be at Clarence Terrace for some weeks after that.

Elizabeth

Elizabeth Bowen to William Plomer

Bowen's Court
6 May [1958]

Dearest William,

I only got back from America a week ago; one of the best things about home-coming was to find your *At Home.* It, I have been reading over these last days, with deliberate slowness, to make it last. Thank you for it twice over: I deeply appreciate having your name, and indeed my name in your hand, inside. This book is really magnificent; the best account of your and my times, and of having such times as one's own times, that I know. And I don't know how to tell you how I admire, and envy, the brilliance *and* depth, suppleness and yet no less precision, of the writing.

Best of all, the book is you, as we know and love you. (I don't know why I use the first person plural instead of the first person singular.) Again and again reading it I felt as though you were in the room: at the same time, I remained rightly in awe of that nonpersonal greatness one recognizes in a friend. On the whole, I haven't cared very much for most of my contemporaries' autobiographies (such as, though don't tell them) Stephen's and John Lehmann's. Most people do better to keep their traps shut; but you are an exception.

I was grateful, apart from many other things, for the return to life, for me, of Virginia and Tony: they are the only two of the dead whom I *truly* miss. (Alan never seems dead, in the sense that he never seems gone: I suppose that if one has lived the greater part of one's life with a person he continues to accompany one through every moment.)

Only you seem able to bring back Virginia's laughter — I get so *bored* and irked by that tragic fiction which has been manufactured about her, since 1941. As for Tony, I have so often tried (and so invariably felt, tried in vain) to give any idea of him to people who did not know him or barely knew him.

I *can't* believe — though I'd believe it if you say so — that I went to tea at Virginia's, and met you there, on the afternoon of George V's funeral. My cousin Noreen, who was staying with us, and Billy Buchan and I had got up at 4 a.m. to watch the procession in Edgware Road; and I remember nothing else about the afternoon except being anaesthetized by tiredness, plus in vain looking for food for that night's dinner (to which I do remember you and Tom Eliot came) with all shops shut: a condition I'd forgotten to foresee. I remember finally coaxing a large veal-and-ham pie, at black market price, out of [a] little restaurant in the understructure of Baker Street Station where I sometimes ate.

If I were a marker of books (out of sympathy; approbation) I should be drawing constant pencil-marks down your margins. You crystallise things I didn't know I had felt or thought. Also you say intransigent things with which I occasionally disagree; but I couldn't go into those unless I had both you and the book here at the same time, which I fear is unlikely.

What an agreeable life we all had, seeing each other *without* being 'a group'. Perhaps ours was, is, the only non-groupy generation: the younger ones now sound as though they'd started doing that again — or haven't they, really?

I wonder how you feel in the 1950s? Personally I am enjoying this epoch — it is really the first one, it seems to me, in which I've enjoyed being 'grown up' as much as I expected to do when I was a child. The only sad thing is that, owing to the necessity to work so hard, I have altogether ceased to be able to write letters — as I used to do, if you remember, copiously in the 1930s. Not that that's probably a great loss to anyone else; but it *is* a loss to me, because writing to anybody is one great way of making oneself feel one is in their presence. It's unnecessary for me to say, I wish I saw you; say that I greatly miss you. I somehow fatalistically know you'll never come here; yet against all hope I continue to imagine you someday again will. While there's life there's hope — which is the major distinction between one's relations with the living and one's relations with the dead. Here I *am* (I continue to state) with Eddy Sackville-West, who'd also love to see you, living nearby for the summer part of the year. Towards the end of October I'll be going back to New York for another two months.

My reasons for not more often coming to London are of the most banal kind: it's all so expensive. In New York I earn money as well as spend it. And the snag about going to London, but not living there is that it's harder to see those who don't live there either. How well we all do by living elsewhere, all the same.

> Dear William, my best love and, again, thanks.
> *Elizabeth.*

Tennessee Williams

The creator of such plays as *Cat on a Hot Tin Roof, A Streetcar Named Desire* and *The Glass Menagerie*, Tennessee Williams was a giant in American letters. He cut an eccentric, openly gay figure on the celebrity scene with notables such as Carson McCullers and Truman Capote, establishing himself in Key West from the 1950s onward. His letters delineate a life of adventure, lust and dissipation, shadowed by a persistent loneliness.

Tennessee Williams to Donald Windham

[Captain Jack's Wharf, Provincetown, Mass.]
[July 29 and 30, 1940] *Monday P. M.*

Dear Donnie:

Your letter came at a very opportune moment as I was feeling blue. My life is now full of emotional complications which make me write good verse — at least a lot of it — but make my mental chart a series of dizzy leaps up and down, ecstasy one moment — O dapple faun! — and consummate despair the next. Never thought I could go through something like this again. But never do you know!

Depression this morning occasioned by the fact the ballet dancer stayed out all night. So far no explanation, though I suspect a nymph at the other end of the wharf and am moving to a single bed downstairs till suspicions confirmed or dispelled.

Shades of Gilbert Maxwell. Isn't it hell?

But, oh, God, Stinkie, I wish you could see him in his blue tights! Well —

It looks like I may stay here a week or so longer. Aside from the emotional business, life here is delightful. I am being courted by a musician and a dancing instructor and a language professor, one of them has a big new Buick and drives us all over the Cape. They all want Kip but hope to English off me or something since he is so apparently less accessible than me — an unmistakable bitch. — I think love has made me young again, or maybe it's the blue dungarees.

Full of quaint and curious people, this town, and the sand-dunes, sea-gulls and the clear, cool tranquil bay water is "Il Paradiso" sung by Enrico Caruso!

I even have a little female on the wharf who wants to be an actress and washes my sweat-shirts for me.

They had another announcement of my play in Sunday *Times*. Said the play cast first would be the first produced. But I have heard no definite statement from Langner.

If everything fizzles out I'll come home very quickly. But please don't hope to see me that soon. — Has Beatty sent in? If she does keep the fifteen for rent. Otherwise I will send it. — Let me know. — You might write her personally — give her a goose in the conscience if she has one!

Love to you both, remember me in your orisons, sweet nymph —

Tennessee

Later: Everything is okay again and I didn't have to move downstairs after all. He slept alone on the beach because he needed some sleep. Doesn't get much with me. But that's his own fault for being so incredibly beautiful. We wake up two or three times in the night and start all over again like a pair of goats. The ceiling is very high like the loft of a barn and the tide is lapping under the wharf. The sky amazingly brilliant with stars. The wind blows the door wide open, the gulls are crying. Oh, Christ. I call him baby like you call Butch, though when I lie on top of him I feel like I was polishing the Statue of Liberty or something. He is so enormous. A great bronze statue of antique Greece come to life. But with a little boy's face. A funny up-turned nose, slanting eyes, and underlip that sticks out and hair that comes to a point in the middle of his forehead. I lean over him in the night and memorize the geography of his body with my hands — he arches his throat and makes a soft, purring sound. His skin is steaming hot like the hide of a horse that's been galloping. It has a warm, rich odor. The odor of life. He lies very still for a while, then his breath comes fast and his body begins to lunge. Great rhythmic plunging motion with panting breath and his hands working over my body. Then sudden release — and he moans like a little baby. I rest with my head on his stomach. Sometimes fall asleep that way. We doze for a while. And then I whisper "Turn over." He does. We use brilliantine. The first time I come in three seconds, as soon as I get inside. The next time is better, slower, the bed seems to be enormous. Pacific, Atlantic, the North American continent. — A wind has blown the door open, the sky's full of stars. High tide is in and water laps under the wharf. And now we're so tired we can't move. After a long while he whispers, "I like you, Tenny." — hoarse — embarrassed — ashamed of such intimate speech! — and I laugh for I know that he loves me! — That nobody ever loved me before so completely. I feel the truth in his body. I call him baby — and tell him to go to sleep. After a while he does, his breathing is deep and even, and his great deep chest is like a continent moving slowly, warmly beneath me. The world grows dim, the world grows warm and tremendous. Then everything's gone and when I wake up it is daylight, the bed is empty. — Kip is gone out. — He is dancing. — Or posing naked for artists. Nobody knows our secret but him and me. And now *you*, Donnie — because you can understand.

Please keep this letter and be very careful with it. It's only for people like us who have gone beyond shame!

10.

Tennessee Williams to Joe Hazan

[August 1940]

I am leaving in a couple of hours for Taxco and Acapulco. Mexico City is too big to take in one gulp so I am going away to the beach till my throat stops aching and then come back and try to swallow some more. At first I thought there was nothing here: mistaken: there is a tremendous lot but I am not strong enough for it right now. I go up and down, up and down the seesaw of moods, because my nerves are exhausted. . . . Last night, for instance, I was entertained at the home of Juanita, who is the queen of the male whores in Mexico City. They accosted me on the street and took me there. Such strangeness, such poetic "license"! We sat in a room with pale pink walls and an enormously high ceiling, covered with pictures of nudes and pictures of Saints and madonnas. The bed was very wide to accommodate several simultaneous parties and was covered with a pale lettuce-green satin spread. Above it hung a handsome black and silver crucifix and Jesus with great sorrowful eyes looking over the pitiful acts of lust that went on there. No doubt thanking his lucky stars that he remained a celibate on earth, because if he had not — it is quite likely he would have been a fairy. Some of the whores were very, very lovely with eyes dark and lustrous as those of the Christ and smooth olive skins. But I stayed out of bed with them because I suspected they were all rotten with disease. I could speak no Spanish but "Mana [*mañana*] es otro dia," they could speak no English, so there was none of that tiresome necessity for conversation which I despise so much. We laughed and drank together and three who had exquisite high voices and a feminine quality that was graceful and charming . . . sang a beautiful song called "Amor Perdida" — very haunting. They were like sad, wonderful flowers — *Fleurs de mal* — their price was two pesos, the equivalent of forty cents. And one was so lovely that when he kissed and embraced me, I had an orgasm, but I showed more than my usual discipline and kept out of any real mischief. . . . She seemed to understand intuitively the state that I was in and her whole manner was brimming with kindness. My nerves straightened out and my head became cool and quiet. It was like having a raw wound wrapped in a long white bandage. I feel now that it will be a woman I will finally go to for tenderness in life. The sexual part — if there has to be any — would probably adjust itself in a while, since I am so easily directed in that way.

The mood that you were in when you wrote [your] letter is so much like mine! We are both standing on the outside of reality, looking in, and it appears all fantastic and empty. We are clutching at hard, firm things that will hold us up, the few eternal values which we are able to grasp in this welter of broken pieces, wreckage, that floats on the surface of life. . . .

Read the collected letters of D. H. Lawrence, the journal and letters of Katharine Mansfield, of Vincent Van Gogh. How bitterly and relentlessly they fought their way through! Sensitive beyond endurance and yet *enduring!* Of course Van Gogh went mad in the end and Mansfield and Lawrence both fought a losing battle with degenerative disease — T.B. — but their work is a pure shaft rising out of that physical defeat. A permanent, pure, incorruptible thing, far more real, more valid than their physical entities ever were. They cry aloud to you in their work — no, *more* vividly, intimately, personally than they could have cried out to you in their living tongues. They *live*, they aren't dead. That is the one ineluctable gift of the artist, to project himself beyond time and space through grasp and communion with eternal values. . . . And so we come back to the word "beauty" — which I thank God is significant to us both. Let us have the courage to believe in it — though people a call us "esthetes," "romantics," "escapists" — let's cling tenaciously to our conviction that this is the only reality worth our devotion, and let that belief sustain us through our black "tunnels." . . .

Kip wrote me a nice letter. He is living behind a wall without even a grated window for you to look through, you have to peek through the cracks, through the broken mortar, but when you do, you count more flowers than weeds on the opposite side. . . . Give him my best. . . .

Devotedly your friend,

10.

Tennessee Williams to Maria St. Just

1431 Duncan
Key West, Fla.
April 27, 1955

Dearest Maria:

Choppers [Carson McCullers] just now hauled her freight out of here but the Froggies are still here sitting! Key West was not for Choppers. She was here sitting for about two weeks, in Havana sitting for about five days, all the time swilling my liquor and gobbling my pinkie tablets in such a way that I reeled with apprehension. I was about to run out of pinkies. Two a night for Choppers, content with no less! Fortunately I was able to buy some without prescription in Havana. I had hoped Chops would start bobbing with creative activity. After two days dictating a short play [*The Square Root of Wonderful*] to me, she scuttled up [to] her ivory tower and bolted the door! Said she could not be rushed into writing, had to think and dream a long time first. Since we pursue opposite methods, she thought she'd better go home and germinate there till she got the whole thing in her chops and then start writing. So off went Choppers this morning on the nine-forty-five plane to Miami. Marion [Vaccaro] is to meet her at the airport and put her on an afternoon plane to New York, where Johnny [Nicholson] is to meet her and put her on an evening bus to Nyack. I hope he will drive her all the way in his car. I am worried over Choppers. I feel that she is dreaming herself away. I was very unkind. Did not quit work to go to the airport with her but let the Horse put her on the plane to Miami, but I paid her expenses going and coming. It is much easier to give money than love. Choppers needs love but I am not the Baa-Baa Black Sheep with three bags full for Choppers. I don't even have any for the Master or the Dame or the Little Boy Down the Lane. I care only, very much, about the studio mornings at the Olivetti. Perhaps in this way I can give more love to more people, at least I sometimes hope so. Of course there is a chance, maybe a good one, that Choppers will continue to work on the play, which was a very, very good one (she started [it] here) and keep her promise about it. Will you call her in Nyack? She needs every little bit of attention or affection, real or make believe, that anybody can give or pretend to give her.

The trouble is that life makes many demands, and these decimal offerings of the heart are never sufficient, not, at any rate, to someone like Choppers who asks for all but expects to get nothing. I think that her poor mother is dying of cancer. Her sister has been at home with her for the past two days. The first day her mother was able to answer the phone, but yesterday when we called again, she didn't. Choppers has had so much tragedy in her life that it scares you almost into feeling indifferent to her, as if she were hopelessly damned and you couldn't afford to think about it: the way I feel for my sister.

I hope you are still playing Blanche as well as you can with your whole heart and complete understanding and no intrusive annoyances from the management, because when I think about her, Blanche seems like the youth of our hearts which has to be put away for worldly considerations: poetry, music, the early soft feelings that we can't afford to live with under a naked light bulb which is now.

I think we're returning in about ten days. I will call you when the date is set. Spieglie Wieglie [Sam Spiegel] has been on the blower a lot, but is leaving this week for Europe. He says that he and Martin Jurow can work out a work-permit for you if Audrey doesn't. Keep on Jurow about it. He can easily do it and Audrey is on the West Coast for several weeks now. I think you should be able to get steady work on TV.

Love, 10

Tennessee Williams to Maria St. Just

June 22, 1976

T.W. for Maria

"Who is there to care beside yourself?" I exclaimed silently last night as I lay sleepless, turning over and over in my mind various unsatisfactory solutions to some very difficult problems which had to be resolved in the next few days.

What a flat-sounding word [friendship] is for what becomes, later on in life, the most important element of it! To me the French word for this deep relationship, probably all the deeper because it exists outside and beyond the physical kind of devotion, is much more appealing. It covers a broader spectrum and surely its depth is greater. The word is *l'amitié*.

That which we call and think of as "love" is often a promiscuous word in more senses than one. In all but the rarest cases in my experience I am afraid that it has depleted more than replenished the reservoir of my emotions, and in quite a number of cases it has also polluted and debased — and never mind if I come on as what I am, a man who is still a child in the shadow of a Protestant rectory.

L'amitié never involves a material transaction. You don't see it in a shop-window with a price tag attached to it or close beside it, and it requires no exertion of will to animate it with the breath of spirit. It is a consecrated thing and it is devoutly to be wished for, because, if it is real as opposed to artificial or trivial, it can endure until death, and Miss Elizabeth Barrett Browning was convinced that it lasted after. I think she is right to the extent that it lasts afterwards in the heart of the survivor.

. . . It is a delicate feeling, of course, and of course it is frangible and most certainly of all it must not be neglected. And yet it is long-suffering. It survives many unavoidable separations without disrepair, since it does not depend on physical presence as much as carnal attachment. Extended absences are a material element and this feeling that I call *l'amitié* has so little concern with material things.

I have been told and have no reason to doubt that *l'amitié* can exist between two men as well as between a man and a woman, but in my case it has occurred always with someone of the opposite gender.

I have had many close friendships with men which were without any sexual connotations, God knows. But I have found them less deeply satisfying than those I have had with a few women.

Of these women, the most important has been with [my dearest friend] Maria, as both Maria Britneva or as the Lady Maria St. Just.

Margaret Wise Brown

Author of *Goodnight Moon* and dozens of other children's picture books, Margaret Wise Brown was difficult yet charming, flamboyant yet shy, mercurial yet exacting. She published her first book in 1937, five years after graduating from Hollins College, and died fifteen highly successful years later at the age of forty-two. Her sparse, erratic romantic life included only one major relationship, with Michael Strange, the ex-wife of actor John Barrymore. Brown moved out of Greenwich Village and into the older woman's apartment on the Upper East Side of Manhattan, but as intense as the relationship was, it began to disintegrate within a year. Until Strange died in 1950, Brown alternately enjoyed and endured her lover's on-again, off-again affections. These two letter fragments, one in poem form, capture Brown's longing.

Margaret Wise Brown to Michael Strange

[October 29, 1947]

I don't know that [you love me] Rab. You only told me once in the past year. . . .

And ten days later — Crash — you said you didn't anymore. . . . There was a time I felt well loved by you and it was the warmest happiest time in my life. And I remember it. And that is all I can honestly say. Since coming back to America I have felt lonlier [*sic*] than I have ever felt in my life and you might as well know the truth — terribly raw and exposed. That is why I stay alone more and more — And that is why I can't rest more in a relationship that has lost the certainty it once had. I can rest in my love for you sometime. And I do. It is the center I come back to and revolve about. But loving the unknown becomes lonely sometimes. . . . It is very simple. I do not know that you love me any more.

Margaret Wise Brown to Michael Strange

[Mid-November 1947]

And send me words
By little birds
To comfort me
And Oh my darling
Oh my pet
Whatever else you may forget
In yonder land
Beyond the sea
Don't forget
Oh don't forget
            You married me —

Isadora Duncan/Mercedes de Acosta

Of the film actress Mercedes de Acosta, Alice B. Toklas once reported, "A friend said to me one day—you can't dispose of Mercedes lightly—she has had the two most important women in the U.S. — Greta Garbo and Marlene Dietrich." Indeed, de Acosta boasted that a female lover accompanied her on her 1920 honeymoon with painter Abram Poole, and on several occasions asserted, "I can get any woman from any man." A Hollywood fixture during the golden years of moviemaking, de Acosta entertained a long series of notable lovers, including Isadora Duncan. The 1927 poem that Duncan sent to her attests to her many charms, while her own 1932 billet-doux to Dietrich captures her passion for women.

Isadora Duncan to Mercedes de Acosta

[1927]

A slender body, hands soft and white
for the service of my delight . . .

Two sprouting breasts
Round and sweet
invite my hungry mouth to eat.
From whence two nipples firm and pink
persuade my thirsty soul to drink
And lower still a secret place
Where I'd fain hide my loving face
My kisses like a swarm of bees
Would find their way
Between thy knees
And suck the honey of thy lips
Embracing thy two slender hips.

Mercedes de Acosta to Marlene Dietrich

[1932(?)]

For Marlene,
Your face is lit by moonlight
breaking through your skin
soft, pale, radiant.
No suntan for you glow
For you are the essence of
the stars and the moon and
the mystery of the night.

Cecil Beaton

Through the ages, one small but persistent and significant theme of gay and lesbian life has been the love affairs — often triangular — carried on between gay men and women. A vivid example of the phenomenon was the romance between photographer Cecil Beaton and film star Greta Garbo. In 1947 their long friendship flared briefly into desire, then flickered back down to platonic intimacy. Garbo was also lovers with Mercedes de Acosta, a friend of Beaton's, whom they nicknamed Black & White (she always wore either black or white, or a combination of the two). After the Beaton-Garbo affair, Beaton's letter to Garbo (hers are yet unpublished) remained warmly affectionate, often playing on the multifaceted genderbending of their relationship.

Cecil Beaton to Greta Garbo

[April 30, 1950]

My Darling Sugar plum,

I am ravished by the gay thought of you. I wish you were here so that we could have some good laughs — some girlish giggles & what not. The snapshot I took of you at our last luncheon (not last supper!) is so delightful that just having had a quiz at it I am now in a very good mood. Darling Mmumm! . . . Have you been to the desert? I would like to know what you've been cooking in your double boiler. Is the ulcer reacting to your strict regime? Please bung us a line.

Suddenly you seem so very far away. It is time I telephoned, or got a postcard or some sort of news from you. A friend wrote me an extraordinary account of how he had seen you walking with S. in the uptown streets of New York, & it brought you so vividly to my mind that I felt I was seeing the incident myself.

Has Black & White been in touch? Do get her to bring a "new American citizen" over with her sometime this summer. It would be so nice for me.

Cecil Beaton to Greta Garbo

[July 16, 1950]

Dear Youth,

Have you yet learnt how to use a razor? Do you strop the blade against a leather prong in the bathroom each morning? Have you got to the age when you wear long pants & a dinner jacket in the evening? Has your voice started to break yet? Have you reached the age of puberty?

I expect you are nearing the stage when you will be thinking quite a bit about lovemaking. If so, & you feel like it, let me know if I can give you any pointers.

Dear heart. I trust you are not too lonely in the alley. Oh dear . . .

Mercedes de Acosta/Cecil Beaton

Friends and lovers of Greta Garbo, Cecil Beaton and Mercedes de Acosta shared a genuine concern for the unhappy Garbo, who spent much of her energy escaping the unwanted attention of fans and who was plagued by recurrent bouts of depression. Temperamental and demanding, she was a difficult friend; she also tended to fall into destructive relationships (such as that with George Schlee) and seemed incapable of being satisfied with either a man or a woman. Garbo grew increasingly gloomy as the years advanced, a fact that became the focus of the correspondence between Beaton and de Acosta.

Mercedes de Acosta to Cecil Beaton

[October 5, 1953]

Greta is back but I have not seen her. The night before she left for Europe in July she made a remark about you which I defended (too complicated to tell you about in a letter). We got into a row and I told her one or two truths. She was angry and left without calling me the next morning or saying good-bye. So, now, on her return, she has not called me. She has taken a flat in the same building with George Schlee and will move into it soon. It is really so idiotic and unnatural that after years of friendship, one has to still go on handling her with absurd "kid gloves," or else suffer a falling out of some kind. Naturally I miss her and not seeing her makes me unhappy. Life is rushing by so quickly it is a pity to miss any moments with people one loves!

Cecil Beaton to Mercedes de Acosta

[October 11, 1953]

Dearest Mercedes,

Very pleased to hear from you though sad to think you have had a falling out with Greta especially as it was on my account. It is very sad when people who love one another should see less of each other than those on more casual terms, & I feel very sad for Greta who is far from happy, & making her life all the time much more difficult. I don't know why she should turn against either of us as we have always been honest & have wanted to do the right thing for her. I trust she will have got in touch with you, as I'm sure she needs you — & I've always thought that the two of you would end your days together. I wish I genuinely thought that Schlee was a good person for her, but apart from any feelings that might be personal, I don't consider he is able to give her any of the things she *needs,* & she sacrifices all to a comfortable "safety first" policy.

Cecil Beaton to Mercedes de Acosta

[April 21, 1954]

It's sad Greta wouldn't come over & get out of her rut — but I have no influence in the face of the Valentinas.

I'm really sad she hasn't come along to see you. It *will* happen sooner or later that she puts an end to this ridiculous situation but it's awful that she doesn't have the same feeling that others have that *time* is important. To her it hardly exists & it means that although she is never living for the minute, she doesn't realise how soon life passes by. In my last letter I certainly recommended that she should become friends with you again with the unaltruistic suggestion that she should come with you to Europe where I, selfishly, would like to share the pleasure of her companionship. Apropos the Crocker story, it makes me annoyed that he, who is such a good friend of Greta's, should have repeated the adventure to anybody. Greta told me that she had been out with him, that they had had a bottle of red wine on top of cocktails, & as a result — wasn't it awful!! — she'd gone to sleep at the play.

It is something that happens to all of us — & I can't think what with the heat of the theatre & the boredom of the plays — how any audience remains upright. It is a ridiculous exaggeration to use the story as an indication that she is seriously drinking so whoever told *you* should be contradicted. G. occasionally takes a nip to keep warm or to brighten her spirits, but she's not dependent on it as a regular habit though God knows with that Schlee as intellectual mentor one might have recourse to *anything!!* I have of course torn up yr. letter & wouldn't even dream of remembering yr. version of the story which in itself was harmless. To hell with the gossips — & Harry Crocker should know better!

Mercedes de Acosta to Cecil Beaton

[December 11, 1961]

I imagine you will be in the country for Christmas and how lovely that will be. Here you know what New York is like, and in this commercial panic I find each year it grows drearier and sadder. I envy you in the country. You, no doubt, know that Greta has gone to Sweden. I learned of this from John Gunther although it was in the newspapers but on reading it I did not believe it until he told me it was true. He said she has gone *just* for Christmas but the newspapers said she had left America "for good and intended selling her flat." I must say, this gave me a *terrific* heart stab because I cannot imagine New York without her. So it was a great relief to me when John said *this* was not true and that she would be back. I imagine she has gone to stay with the Wachtmeisters who have a *lovely* place in the country and are distinguished people. I have not seen them since Greta and I stayed with them in 1937 and I don't believe she has seen them since then either. It may do her good to go back to her roots and at least be in the country and good food.

I remember they had *wonderful* food! But it is strange how lonely I feel now that I know she is not in New York. Even though I do not see her there was always the possibility of running into her, of hearing some news of her or even of her calling up. I was trying to make up my mind about sending her a tree.

Do let me know if you have any news of her plans. She will probably write to you or may even go to England to see you . . .

Cecil Beaton to Mercedes de Acosta

[September 12, 1962]

I have had no news of Greta except a *typewritten* letter (!) dated July 17 when her plans were negative — as usual. I s'pose she went back to Schlee. We all got up at 9 o'clock in the A.M. to see a festival of *old* films on the Lido Beach. The *Anna Christie* was a great experience not a bit dated — & Greta's performance wonderfully touching. They also showed extracts of a ghastly film called *Inspiration* in which Greta had frizzy hair & vampire's clothing, but even in this she was so much more marvellous in taste, tact, wit & quality of beauty than that cow Dietrich whose *Morocco* etc. were shown *afterwards!*

Bad luck on Dietrich. She looked good in close up with overhead lighting but in all the other shots was a German fat hausfrau with a potato nose . . .

Jane Bowles

Jane Bowles completed her entire body of work — one novel, one play and six short stories — before her mid-thirties and spent the remaining twenty years of her life struggling to write more. Married to gay writer Paul Bowles, she lived variously in Greenwich Village, Mexico and Morocco, with and without him, engaging in her own gay affairs. In her travels she sent letters to many friends, sometimes composing epic "agonizers" like this one in which she confided her innermost frustrations about her work and her personal life.

Jane Bowles to Natasha von Hoershelman and Katharine Hamill

[Tangier, Morocco]
[June 1954]

Darling Natasha and Katharine,

I never stop thinking about you but too much happened. Please forgive me if this is not an amusing letter. I tried last night to write you in detail but I had filled two pages just with Ellie and some clothes that the ladies and babies were wearing down in M'sallah, the day you left. I think I had better simply write you a gross factual résumé of what has happened. Then if I have any sense I shall keep notes. Because what is happening is interesting and funny in itself. I am a fool to have lost two whole months of it. I have no memory — only a subconscious memory which I am afraid translates everything into something else, and so I shall have to take notes. I have a very pretty leather book for that purpose.

The day you left I was terribly sad. I still miss you — in the sense that I keep thinking through it all that you should be here and how sorry I am that you left before I could truly take you into some of the life that I love. I turned sour on Ellie about half way up the pier. I could still see the boat. I worried about having exposed Katharine to all those tedious stories — touching in a way but tedious. Ice cream, herring, and the Chico Tax scandal with the brother. Of course it could only happen here on a trip for *Fortune*. I went down that long street, way down in, and landed in a room filled with eighteen women and a dozen or two little babies wearing knitted capes and hoods. One lady had on a peach satin evening dress and over it the jacket of a man's business suit. [A Spanish business suit.] I had been searching for Cherifa, and having been to about three houses all belonging to her family, I finally landed there. I thought I was in a bordello. The room was very plush, filled with hideous blue and white chenille cushions made in Manchester, England. Cherifa wore a pale blue sateen skirt down to the ground and a grayish Spanish sweater, a kind of school sweater but not sporty. She seemed to be constantly flirting with a woman in a pale blue kaftan (our hostess), and finally she sat next to her and encircled her waist. C. looked like a child. The woman weighed about 160 pounds and was loaded with rouge and eye makeup. Now I know her. An alcoholic named Fat Zohra, and one of two wives. She is married to a kind of criminal who I believe knifed his own brother over a card game and spent five years in jail. The other wife lives in a different house and does all the child bearing. Fat Zohra is barren. There was one pale-looking girl (very light green), who I thought was surely the richest and the most distinguished of the lot. She wore a wonderful embroidered kaftan, a rich spinach green with a leaf design. Her face was rather sour: thin compressed lips and a long mean-looking nose. I was sad while they played drums and did their lewd belly dances because I thought: My God if you had only stayed a day longer. But of course if you had, perhaps they wouldn't have asked you in (Cherifa I mean); they are so leery of strangers. In any case at the end of the afternoon (and part of my sadness was an aching jealousy of the woman in the blue kaftan), Cherifa took me to the doorway and into the blue courtyard where two boring pigeons were squatting, and asked me whether or not I was going to live in my house. The drums were still beating and I had sticky cakes in my hand — those I couldn't eat. (I stuffed down as many as I could. I loathe them.) But I was really too jealous and also sad because you had left to get down very many. I said I would of course but not before I found a maid. She told me to wait and a minute later came out with the distinguished pale green one. "Here's your maid," she said. "A very poor girl."

Anyway, a month and a half later she became my maid. I call her Sour Pickle, and she has stolen roughly about one thousand four hundred pesetas from me. I told C. about it who advised me not to keep any money in the house. She is a wonderful maid, an excellent cook, and sleeps with me here. I will go on about this later but I cannot remotely begin to get everything into this letter. You will want to know what happened about Paul, Ellie, Xauen.

Paul went to Xauen for one night, having sworn that he would not spend more than one or two nights at the Massilia. He came back disgusted with Xauen and then started a hopeless series of plans — plans for three of us in one house, and, as I wrote Lyn, I even planned to live in the bottom half of a policeman's house in Tangier Balia (the place with the corrugated tin roofs) while Paul and Ahmed lived in the little house in the Casbah. I felt Cherifa was a hopeless proposition, and had no particular desire to be in my house unless there was some hope of luring her into it. (Maid or no maid.) In the hotel I did try to work a little. But it is always impossible the first month and the wind and the rain continued. The rooms were very damp and cold and one could scarcely sit down in them. I became very attached to the French family who ran the hotel. We stayed on and on in an unsettled way. In the beginning Ellie would come by every day with her loud insensitive battering on the door, and her poor breezy efficient manner and I would try desperately not to smack her. I felt I could not simply drop her and so would make some half-hearted date with her always before lunch so that we could go to Georgette's. Ellie filled me with such a feeling of revulsion that I almost fell in love with Georgette. I never allowed Ellie within a foot of my bed from the moment you stepped on the boat. I have never in my life had such an experience. Nor will I quite understand what possessed me. Some devil but not my usual one. Someone else's devil. In any case she started taking trips. The first time she came back, when I heard the rapping, I said, "Who?" and she said, "The family!" That was it. From then on I could barely stand to be in the same room with her and I hated myself for it. All this revulsion and violence was on a far greater scale than the incident deserved but it must have touched something inside me — something in my childhood. I have never been quite such a horror. Some of it showed outwardly but thank God only a bit of what I was really feeling. She always asked after you. Every time I saw her, "Any letter today?" Also madly irritating for some reason. Finally she got the message and in any case she was away so much that I managed to sneak up here into the Casbah — and I don't believe she knows where I live, though surely she could find out. I hope by now that she is off on a new adventure. Sonie (a pal who takes in the cash at a whorehouse behind the Socco Chico), sees her occasionally and reported that she had left Chico Tax and was driving her own car.

   Paul had typhoid in the hotel and that was a frightening mess for two weeks. We were both about to move into our houses. He had found one on a street called Sidi Bouknadel (overlooking the sea) and I was coming here. Then he had typhoid, and then Tennessee came for two whole weeks. I moved in here while Paul was still in the hotel. For a while Ahmed and I were living together while Paul lingered on at the hotel in a weakish state. He is all right now. Ahmed stayed here during the whole month of Ramadan (the month when they eat at night) and I was with him during the last two weeks. Not very interesting except that every night I woke up choking with charcoal smoke, and then he would insist that I eat with him. Liver or steak or whatever the hell it was. At first I minded terribly. Then I began to expect it, and one night he didn't buy really enough for the two of us, and I was grieved. Meanwhile in the daytime I was in the hotel preparing special food for Paul, to bring his appetite back. There were always four or five of us cooking at once in the long narrow hotel kitchen, the only room that looked out on the sea. Meeting Tennessee for dinner and Frankie (they were at the Rembrandt) was complicated too. Synchronizing took up most of the time. We were all in different places.

I have kept out of the David life very successfully except on occasion. I could not possibly manage from here nor do I want to very much though I love him and would hate never to see him. I couldn't go it. The ex-Marchioness of Bath is here for the moment (married her lover, Mister Fielding, a charming man). I went to a dinner party for her in slacks — a thing that I did not do on purpose. They gave a party on the beach which I wiggled out of but Tuesday I must go to a big ball. However if one only turns up once every two weeks or so it's nice. Or occasionally one goes out twice in a row. They are all constantly at it. David suggested a pool of money so that I might have a telephone. Only Jaime seemed to understand that I didn't want one. The Fieldings are enchanting people and are off to write about pirates in the old days. They have some kind of little car they are going to live in. They will be gone six or eight months. By then Enid Bagnold should be back. Her play was the end or wasn't it? Please write me what you think, now that some time has passed. I scarcely ever go to the Parade. Too depressing. Then came the ghastly Indo-China Oppenheimer period which dovetailed with Tennessee's last days here and also a pitch black boy called George Broadfield who called himself "The New American Negro," and attached himself to me and Paul. I liked him but almost went mad because he was determined to stay in Tangier, and thought nothing of talking for seven or eight hours in a row. I told him he should go and live where there were other artists because there were so few of them here. (He himself is a young writer, or is going to be??) He said that Paul and I were enough for him and I was horrified. It was all my fault. The night I got *Vogue* in the mail, which quoted the remark you might have since seen about writing for one's five hundred goony friends etc., I went out and got drunk. I was terribly upset about it. Though I knew what I had meant I had certainly not made the remark expecting it to be quoted or I would have elaborated. I hate being interviewed and some-

thing wrong always does pop out everytime. I meant "intellectual" which
Walter Kerr in the Trib seems to have understood, but at the time I
was worried about my friends — the real supporters of the play and the
contributors to whatever chance it had financial and otherwise. Anyway
I was sick at my stomach. I did go to the Parade and did get very drunk.
This pitch black boy seemed charming so I latched on to him as one does
occasionally. He was a kind of God-sent antidote to the quotation which
I was ashamed of. Paul tried to console me saying that nobody much
read *Vogue* and that it would be forgotten. Of course later Walter Kerr
devoted a column to it in New York and it appeared in Paris as well
where there is no other paper for Americans, so if anyone missed it in
New York they have seen it in Paris or Rome. I now think of it as a kind
of joke. Every letter I receive has the article (Kerr's article) enclosed,
with its title "Writing Plays for Goons." They come in from all over
Europe and the United States. I keep teasing Paul about the scarcely
read copy of Vogue lying on the floor of the beauty parlor. So much for
that. But I did inherit George Broadfield for a while and because it was
my doing had to see him constantly for a week. I was a wreck — nervously, because he talked so much. Then he shifted on to Paul, finally
ran out of money and moved on to Casablanca.

One day before Ramadan and before Paul had paratyphoid, I went
to the market and sat in a gloom about Indo-China and the Moroccan
situation and every other thing in the world that was a situation outside
my own. Soon I cheered up a little. I was in the part where Tetum sits in
among the coal and the mules and the chickens. Two little boy musicians
came by. I gave them some money and Tetum ordered songs. Soon we
had a big crowd around us, one of those Marrakech circles. Everybody
stopped working (working?) and we had one half hour of music, myself
and everybody else, in that part of the market (you know). And people
gathered from round about. Just like Tiflis. Tetum was in good spirits.
She told me that Cherifa had a girl friend who was fat and white. I
recognized Fat Zohra, though I shall never know whether I put the fat
white picture in her mind or not. I might have said "Is she fat and
white?" I don't know. Then she asked me if I wouldn't drive her out to
Sidi Menari, one of the sacred groves around here where Sidi Menari (a
saint) is buried. They like to visit as many saints as possible, of course,
because it gives them extra gold stars for heaven. I thought: "Natasha
and Katharine will be angry. They told me to stick to Cherifa but then,
they didn't know about fat Zohra." After saying this in my head I felt
free to offer Tetum a trip to the grove without making you angry.

Of course it turned out that she wanted to take not only one, but
two neighbors and their children. We were to leave at eight thirty A.M.,
she insisted. The next day when I got to Tetum's house on the Marshan

with Temsamany (nearly an hour late) Tetum came to the door in a grey bathrobe. I was very surprised. Underneath she was dressed in a long Zigdoun and under that she wore other things. I can't describe a Zigdoun but it is quite enough to wear without adding on a bathrobe. But when they wear our night clothes they wear them over or under their own (which are simply the underpeelings or first three layers of their day clothes. Like in Tiflis.) She yanked me into her house, tickled my palm, shouted to her neighbor (asleep on the other side of a thin curtain) and in general pranced about the room. She dressed me up in a hideous half-Arab, half-Spanish cotton dress which came to my ankles and had no shape at all. Just a little round neck. She belted it and said "Now go back to the hotel and show your husband how pretty you look." I said I would some other day, and what about our trip to the saint's tomb. She said yes, yes, but she had to go and fetch the other two women who both lived in a different part of the town. I said would they be ready, and she said something like: "Bacai shouay." Which means just nothing. Finally I arranged to come back for her at three. Rather infuriated because I had gotten Temsamany up at the crack. But I was not surprised, nor was he. Tetum took me to her gate. "If you are not here at three," she said in sudden anger, "I shall walk to the grove myself on my own legs." (Five hours, roughly.) We went back at three and the laundry bags were ready, and the children, and Tetum.

"We are going to two saints," Tetum said. "First Sidi Menari and then we'll stop at the other saint's on the way back. He's buried on the edge of town and we've got to take the children to him and cut their throats because they have whopping cough." She poked one of the laundry bundles, who showed me a knife. I was getting rather nervous because Paul of course was expecting us back roughly around seven, and I know how long those things can take. We drove along the awful road (the one that frightened you) toward the grove, only we went on and on, much further out, and the road began to bother me a little after a while. You would have hated it. The knife of course served for the symbolic cutting of the children's throat, though at first I had thought they were going to draw some blood, if not a great deal. I didn't think they were actually going to kill the children or I wouldn't have taken them on the ride.

We reached the sacred grove which is not far from the lighthouse one can see coming into the harbor. Unfortunately they have built some ugly restaurants around and about the lighthouse, and not far from the sacred grove so that sedans are now constantly passing on the highway. The grove itself is very beautiful, and if one goes far enough inside it, far away from the road, one does not see the cars passing. We didn't penetrate very far into the grove because being a Christian (Oy!) I can't sit within the vicinity of the saint's tomb. Temsamany spread the tarpaulin on the ground and the endless tea equipment they had brought with them, and they were off to the saint's leaving Temsamany and myself behind. He said: "I shall make a fire, and then when they come back the water will be boiling." They came back. God knows when. The water was boiling. We had used up a lot of dead olive branches. They sat down and lowered their veils so that they hung under their chins like ugly bibs. They had bought an excellent sponge cake. As usual something sweet. I thought: "Romance here is impossible." Tetum's neighbors were ugly. One in particular. "Like a turtle," Temsamany said. She kept looking down into her lap. Tetum, the captain of the group, said to the turtle: "Look at the world, look at the world." "I am looking at the world," the other woman said, but she kept looking down into her lap. They cut up all the sponge cake. I said: "Stop! Leave it. We'll never eat it all." Temsamany said: "I'm going to roller skate." He went off and we could see him through the trees. After a while the conversation stopped. Even Tetum was at a loss. There was a little excitement when they spotted the woman who runs the toilets under the grain market, seated not far off with a group, somewhat larger than ours but nothing else happened.

I went to look for Temsamany on the highway. He had roller skated out of sight. I felt that all my pursuits here were hopeless. I looked back over my shoulder into the grove. Tetum was swinging upside down from an olive tree her knees hooked over a branch, and she is, after all, forty-five and veiled and a miser.

There is more to this day but I see now that I have done exactly what I did not want to do. I have gone into great detail about one incident, which is probably of no interest.

But as a result of that day Cherifa and I have been much closer. In fact she spends two or three nights here a week in dungarees and Haymaker shirts. She asked for five thousand pesetas (about one hundred and fifteen dollars) so that she could fill her grain stall to the brim. I have given her, so far, fifteen hundred pesetas. She sleeps in dungarees and several things underneath. I shall have to write you a whole other letter about this. In fact I waited and waited before writing because foolishly I hoped that I could write you: "I have or have not — Cherifa." The awful thing is that I don't even know. I don't know what they do. I don't know how much they feel. Sometimes I think that I am just up against that awful hard to get virgin block. Sometimes I think they just don't know. I — it is difficult to explain. So hard to know what is clever manoeuvering on her part, what is a lack of passion, and what is fear — just plain fear of losing all her marketable value and that I won't care once I've had her. She is terribly affectionate at times and kissing is heaven. However I don't know quite how soon or if I should clamp down. I simply don't know. All the rules for the playing the game are given me by Paul or else Temsamany. Both are men. T. says if you don't get them the first two times you never will. A frightening thought. But then he is a man. I told Paul one couldn't buy desire, and he said desire can come but only with habit. And never does it mean what it means to us — rather less than holding hands supposedly. Everything is very preliminary and pleasant like the beginning of a love affair between a virgin and her boy friend in some automobile. Then when we are finally in bed she says: "Now sleep." Then comes either "Goodbye" or a little Arabic blessing which I repeat after her. There we lie like two logs — one log with open eyes. I take sleeping pill after sleeping pill. Yet I'm afraid to strike the bargain. "If you do this, I will give you all of the money, if not — " It is very difficult for me. Particularly as her affection and tenderness seem so terribly real. I'm not even sure that this isn't the most romantic experience in a sense that I have ever had — and it is all so miraculous compared to what little went on before. I hesitate to rush it, to be brutal in my own eyes, even if she would understand it perfectly. I think love and *sex*, that is tenderness and sex, beyond kissing and less caresses, may be forever separate in their minds, so that one might be going toward something less rather than more than what one had in the beginning. According to the few people I have spoken to — among them P.M. (the Englishman who wrote the book) — I hate mentioning names — they have absolutely no aftermath. Lying back, relaxing, all that which is more pleasant than the thing itself, if one is in love (and only then) is non-existent. Just quickly "O.K. Now we sleep," or a rush for six water bowls to wash the sin away. I'm not even sure I haven't in a way slept with C. Because I did get "Safi-naasu." ("O.K. Now we sleep.") But it does not mean always the same thing. I am up too many trees and cannot write you all obviously. Since I cannot seem to bring myself to the point of striking a verbal bargain (cowardice? delicacy? love?) I don't know — but I simply can't — not yet. I shall have to wait until I find the situation more impossible than pleasant, until my nerves are shot and I am screaming with exasperation. It will come. But I don't believe I can say anything before I feel that way. It would only sound fake. My hunch is she would go away saying "Never." Then eventually come back. At the moment, no matter what, I am so much happier than I was. She seems to be getting a habit of the house. Last night she said, "It's strange that I can't eat eggs in my own house. But here I eat them." Later she said that her bed at home was not as good as mine. Mine by the way is *something*. Lumpy with no springs. Just on straw. A thin wool mattress, on straw. At home she sleeps in a room with her great aunt. The great aunt on the floor, Cherifa on the bed, natch. She's that kind. I find her completely beautiful. A little smaller than myself but with strong shoulders, strong legs with a good deal of hair on them. At the same time soft soft skin—and twenty-eight years old. Last night we went up on the topmost terrace and looked at all of Tangier. The boats and the stars and the long curved line of lights along the beach. There was a cold wind blowing and Cherifa was shivering. I kissed her just a little. Later downstairs she said the roof was very beautiful, and she wondered whether or not God had seen us. I wonder. I could go on about this, dear Katharine and Natasha, and I will some other time. I wish to Christ you were here. I can talk to Paul and he is interested but not that interested because we are all women. We see each other almost daily. His house is not far from here. And it is a lovely walk. Outside the walls of the Casbah, overlooking the beach and the ocean. Most of my time is taken up with him or Cherifa or the house and now work. I am beginning again to work. Before she came I was such a nervous wreck I couldn't do anything. Also I was in despair about all the world news and as I told you Paul's illness. Everything was a mess. Now I am in a panic about money and though I will write a play, I must write other things too for immediate cash. Not that I don't have any for a while but I must not use it all up before I have completed at least enough of a play for an advance. Thank God I am in a house and not in a hotel. Although the house has cost me a good deal until now, it won't henceforth because I've bought most everything I needed except a new bed for upstairs. I shall fill the house with beds—traps for a virgin. I feel happier now that I've written you. All the time I have been saying: I should write about *this* to N. and K. But it seemed impossible, utterly impossible to make a résumé of all that happened before. And as you see, it was impossible. I have not even found it possible to write in this letter why Tetum swinging from an olive tree in her cloak and hood should have precipitated all this but it did. I think Cherifa got worried about losing me to Tetum. She was so worried she asked me for a kaftan right off. Then started a conversation, a bargaining conversation, which resulted in her coming here after Ramadan to spend the night. But I can't go into that now. I always let Fatima (Sour Pickle) decide what we are to eat. It is all so terribly simple—all in one dish. Either lamb with olives or with raisins, and onions, or chicken with the same or ground meat on skewers or beef or lamb on skewers. (You remember how wonderful they taste). Or a fried potato omelet with onions, or boiled noodles with butter or eggs fried in oil, and always lots of black bread and wine at five pesetas a quart (excellent). I've had guests once, Tennessee in fact. White beans in oil and with salt pork like the ones I cooked for you. Lots of salad: cucumber, tomato and onion, all chopped up, almost daily. Fresh figs, bananas, cherries. Whatever fruit is in season. Wonderful bowls of Turkish coffee in the morning which are brought to our bed (when she is here as she happens to be now for a kind of weekend) or to me alone and piles of toast soaked in butter. At noon we eat very little. Usually, if Cherifa isn't here (she supposedly comes twice a week but that can include two afternoons) I go over to Paul's for lunch. Except that he never eats until three thirty — sometimes four. I get up at seven and by then I am so hungry I don't even care. But I like seeing him. We eat soup and bread and butter and cheese and tuna fish. For me tuna fish is the main diet.

I love this life and I'm terrified of the day when my money runs out. The sex thing aside, it is as if I had dreamed this life before I was born. Perhaps I will work hard to keep it. I cannot keep Cherifa without money, or even myself, after all. Paul told Cherifa that without working I would never have any money so she is constantly sending me up into my little work room. A good thing. Naturally I think of her in terms of a long long time. How one can do this and at the same time fully realize the fact that money is of paramount importance to one's friend and etc., etc. — that if there is to be much sleeping it will most likely be against their will or something they will do to please one, I simply don't know. Possibly, if it came to that, I might lose interest in the sleeping part, possibly why I keep putting off the bargaining — but the money I know is paramount. Yet they are not like we are. Someone behaving in the same way who was not an Arab I couldn't bear. All this will have to wait for some other letter. Perhaps it is all a bore; if so tell me. But I thought since you have seen her and Tangier that it would interest you. Please do me a great favor and save this letter. I cannot write more than one letter on this subject. If you think Lyn would be interested in bits and snatches of the letter read them to her because I can't, as I said write about it more than once. Not having seen Tangier or Cherifa, perhaps it would mean nothing to her. But we are on an intimate enough basis — she and Polly and myself — and they went through Marty with me a bit. I shall simply write her about my work and my health and I will tell her that you have a letter about "more stuff," if she wants to see it. And I shall tell her to call you, at the office. Perhaps you can meet some day for a drink if you all want to. I long to know Oliver's address. Lyn wrote me that he was in Calif. That's all. No address. Please write. I shall worry now about this messy letter.

All my love, always,
J. Bowles

P.S. This letter I shall now correct. I am sure it is unreadable but I'll do the best I can. Received your copy of "Confessions of an Honest Play-wright" today. Thank you. In Paris it has the other title, "Writing Plays for Goons." It's the end.

Jack Kerouac

Staunchly nonconformist, the members of the Beat Generation experimented with new literary forms, illegal drugs and freewheeling sex. A thoroughly male movement, Beat culture was pervaded with homosexuality. Gays such as William Burroughs and Allen Ginsberg found the openness liberating, but for Jack Kerouac sexual intimacy with men remained problematic. The author of *On the Road* enjoyed women and deeply feared being labeled gay. Some of his concerns, as well as a vivid image of Beat life, come through in his letters to good friend and fellow Beat Neal Cassady.

Jack Kerouac to Neal Cassady

[Rocky Mount, N.C.]
Oct. 3 '48

(SECOND LETTER — FAT & SATISFIED)

Dear Neal —

Okay — we'll wait and see about your R.R. job in Nov. and if you lose it, I'll come out to go on Standard Oil with you. I don't think my bookwork will hold me back once I get an agent. (But don't be *positive* it might not hold me up?) We'll *both* see in November.

The ranch information I will file away for future use. My brother-in-law's all hip on idea. No doubt, 'tho, that none of us have enough money for such an idea yet. But later . . . yes! (Wait!) (My book! my book! — it's great!).

Neal, I feel real good. As Lucien said to me the other week, on Washington Square, "And you know, boy, it gets more & more joyous all the time." Yessir! Not without grounds, either. When you knew me I was so locked up in a rigid "picture" of life that I refused, I absolutely refused to participate or believe in anything that did not fit in that picture. That picture was of all life not rooted to earth (actual farms, mind you) as being corrupt. Naturally, of course, beyond the *blithest* doubts, my mind was mad then — tho not my heart, for I continued loving. But I was insane. What you did was respect my heart, my "dignity." Well, I really like you, Neal, and even when I had the insane ideas which served as an artificial incubator for the novel, I liked you — especially when I saw you sitting in my father's chair one night puffing on a big cigar, with your "Western" vest, reading the papers, smiling. I said to myself, "Not only is Neal a mad character (as categorized in my "picture of life") but he is also a man with a sense of enjoyment (joyousness) and satisfaction and he knows how to work and make his way, and all those Chases and Temkos don't like him only because they don't feel it necessary to consider him their social & cultural equal (AND I DO? PITY POOR NEAL), which is a vanity in them I cannot understand yet. (No, I cannot buy it, either.) I said to myself, "Neal is a real good kid at heart, he's had a tough time and he has to fight, and he fights a sly fight the others consider obvious because it is nowhere as sly as theirs."

Tell me I'm wrong, put up your dukes, Neal. I *know* this is true. It is also true that I must learn indefatigable ways of fighting from you, and you must learn sadness from me. I think I'm almost ready to say I no longer "care" what you think about me, now all that concerns me is what I think about you — it's *you* that counts. I want to be normal, dammit. Normal people are not self-conscious so much as I've been. [. . . .] Forgive me, I'm *green*. I try to please and therefore I am all wrapped in my picture of myself as a clever pleaser — No? Pride prevents me from continuing enough to say, "Help me learn to be natural." (This suggests queerness . . . it is too "sissy . . . and it ends there on a note of social hysteria.) He-he! But listen . . . do you realize (this is apropos) that a new literary age is beginning in America? Sinclair Lewis et al sum up people by their social & cultural "positions." This is American Lit. in general . . . especially Lewis & magazines, and leftist writing, all. But, with the advent of Dostoevsky the Russian Christ, we young Americans are turning to a new evaluation of the individual: his *"position" itself*, personal and psychic. Great new age, truly, much further advanced than Sovietism. The Prophets were right! Nature Boy is only an American beginning of the last human preoccupation — the position of the soul among all the souls in the Forest Arden of the world, *the* crux of life.

Right?

Moreover [. . . .] I consider queerness a hostility, not a love. Woman exists because there was man — the penis exists because first there was void — (cunt) — therefore, "I have one of my own" (a void, or a penis) — "You have one of your own — you do not *really* wish mine without envy, hostility, aggression, and inverted desire." These are my views. . . . (SILLY) (SELF-CONSCIOUS TOO) . . . and I'm not saying them for *your* benefit (don't have to) so much as for "posterity" which might someday read this letter, all my letters (as Kerouac). Posterity will laugh at me if it *thinks* I was queer . . . little students will be disillusioned. By that time science & feelings intuitive will have shown it is VICE,

VICIOUS, not love, gentle . . . and Kerouac will be a goat, pitied. I fight that. I am *not* a fool! a queer! I am *not!* He-he! Understand? And forgive me for dramatizing the idiotic thoughts I have at moments. They're of no use to you. I am the Sly Idiot, I refuse to be accused of concealing anything. I am sad, and mad, and I wish I could be sensible like you & Paul & my sister & my mother & Ann etc.

Jack

P.S. — Neal, all your doubts about the semi-fertilized intelligence of my mind must be confirmed by this letter. Are they?

Jack Kerouac to Neal Cassady

[September or October 1957]

Dear Neal —

Come on you ole sonumbitch and get on that typewriter and write me your first letter in 5 years, if not to me, who? — Tell me what happened after I left, Louanne, etc. — My mother and I rode 4 days and 4 nights on the bus to Florida and got a $45 a month pad a week later then I went to NY for publication of my book & everything exploded — To the point where, for instance, Warner Bros. wanted to buy On the Road for 110,000 dollars with me playing part of Sal Paradise and my agent turned it down because it wasnt enuf money or something — Everybody asking me "WHO will play Dean Moriarty?" and I say "He will himself if he wants to" so boy maybe truly you can become movie star with luck (tho my girl Joyce says not to wish that fate on you) — Allen in Amsterdam with Gregory and Peter writes that you should play the part yourself, and him Carlo, and me Sal — But meanwhile I was asked to write 3-act play for BWay, which I did, just sent it in the other day, big shot producers reading it, again a part in there for you, for me, Allen, Peter, etc. it's the story of ACT ONE You and Al Hinkle walk in Al Sublette's kitchen play chess while Al and I toast Khayyam tokay and Charley Mew figures horses, Connie standing around, finally you and Charley and me play flute solos straight off that Visions of Neal tape of 1952 . . . crazy scene. Second ACT: You and me alone at races, playing third choice, Pulido, dreams, talk, Cayce, girls, beer in cartons, etc. including the horse that spilled in the backstretch and nobody cared — ACT THREE the night of the Bishop with Donovan, Bev, Carolyn, Allen, Peter, you, me, Bishop, Bishop's mother and aunt but all of it changed to

Lynbrook L.I. to New York Scene and the Bishop is "of the New Ara-
mean church" — Nothing incriminating — I mean only grayfaces won't
like it — Meanwhile magazines demanded shorts, so sold Baseball tale to
Esquire for 500, article on Beatness to Pageant for 300, blues tale to
Playboy for 500, and sold book to German and Italian publishers —
Appeared on TV, John Wingate's NIGHTBEAT before 40 million view-
ers and talked about God monstrously had Wingate fluttering thru his
prepared questions sweating I sprung God on him and he sprung dope
on me — went out got drunk with him after show — Little Jack Melody
phoned me at TV studio — Had hotel room with publishers drunk rolling
out my roll-Road-ms. on carpet for screaming interviewers, — BWay
producers bring beautiful models sit on edge of my (girl's) bed, ugh,
wanted to make it so much with so many — Went on 2 wild weekends
with Lucien and wife and two kids to upstate cold nippy Fall red-apple
country, drunk — Everything happened and I was wondering. what has
all this done to you, are people bugging you & chasing you in Frisco?
Man, that Mercedes Benz ride of ours to Mexico City on El Paso Hiway
not far off, I already (come next year) got enuf money to buy one! —
Main thing, is, movie sale. Marl Brando definitely interested, soon's he
crawls outa bed and reads ROAD he buy it, meanwhile Paramount and
Warners bickering — gossip columnists report that Slim Gaillard will
play himself in movie version! (we gets to get hi with Slim!) — This time
I no make faggot scene, but girls, girls, girls, — only a few feelers from a
few faggots in mail — Went out drank ate with Henri Cru, Bob Donlin
(who was snapped by Playboy magazine 150 color photos with me. I
feed him bit of spaghetti, he kiss me, we fall down in Bowery, talk to
bums) (later Stanley Gould shown with me in front of San Remo) —
everything happened — I was drunk all the time, no more wine, just
whiskey, which by the way is much easier than wine — All the time
wondering "What is Neal thinking?" and if I sell movie this Christmas,
as likely, as I pray for, will convert 150,000 into monthly trustfund
checks like Burroughs, not squander, will shoot right out to Frisco go
stay with you at Los Gatos pad with money to burn on groceries, kicks,
etc. — Promised Buddah would go meditate whole month in mountain
solitude, eat no meat if sell movie spend whole month praying for all
living creatures — Fathers of St. Francis of Assissi church 34th st. New
York saw me on TV talk about God and Francis and are giving mass for
my spiritual and temporal welfare — I also correspond now with mad
nuns at a monastery who love me — Write! I tell you more! Buddy as
ever.

　　　　　　　　　　　　　　　　　　　　　　　　　　　　Jack

p.s. After brot mother to Florida I took foolish trip to Mexico City, just in time for earthquake. Went to find Esperanza, couldnt, she must be dead, went to find Garver, he dead, died in July, alone. . . . Finally old Garver dead — I cried in Mexico, alone. . . . got drunk in Mexico, alone, stayed only 10 days and rode that bus again and again thru nightmare New Orleans again and again — Saw Dick Hittleman in NY and he says "Come on man go down to Mexico and make it with Diane, she needs somebody like you" I said "You tryna kill me man?" — wow — Had for awhile swollen balls and no sex, suddenly got letter from Gary Snyder in Japan, saying "I pray to Avalokitesvara Buddha and you be well quick" and suddenly as I read letter my balls went down and I been straight ever since and went to NY and balled with chicks and am straight again — ??? — The chick I really need is Gary's sister Thea — question marks mean: How come Buddha answers all prayer? Man on TV (Wingate) said: "Can you tell us to whom you pray?" and I said "To my brother Gerard, my father Leo, Jesus Christ, Avalokitesvara Buddha, and Our Mother in Heaven." Meanwhile, man, here's what: when I get check for $300 every month trustfund I travel and ball all over world, to India, Japan, racetracks, Mexico, Europe, Paris, all over, I move fast and when I make a million my monthly check will be $8,000 and that's when you and I make time in your old plan that Lazy Charley was gonna bring you, no Lazy Jack is the system.

Please give my love to Charley Mew, Al Hinkle, and Al Sublette, hey? — if you see them — I saw Jane Belson at a mad party in NY too — she was scared of me, I was drunk — My exwife Joan got divorce in Juarez and now wants me to sign adoption papers so her new Arab husband Aly adopt. I will move me and my Maw back to Richmond Hill Long Island next spring and then build me a logcabin on Lucien's land upstate and them will be my headquarters.

Now come on, Neal, reason I didn't see much of you in Frisco this last time was shortness of money. . . . no other reason — so write and let's get on the ball here, HIBALL

Rachel Carson/Dorothy Freeman

Meeting relatively late in life, naturalist Rachel Carson and her lover, Dorothy Freeman, shared a tender devotion that lasted eleven years, until Carson's death in 1964. At forty-six, Carson was already the renowned author of *Under the Sea Wind* and *The Sea Around Us* (her last book, *Silent Spring*, would be her most famous); the fifty-five-year-old Freeman was a wife and mother. Their mutual love of nature drew them together, though family and professional duties frequently kept them apart; Carson dedicated her third book, *Edge of the Sea,* to Freeman. Given Carson's fame, the women knew their correspondence would be published someday, so they destroyed some of their more intimate epistles — a practice they code-named the Strong Box. Nevertheless, thanks to their prolific correspondence a rich narrative of their relationship, their daily lives and Carson's creative process survived.

Rachel Carson to Dorothy Freeman

January 1, 1954

My Darling,

Now we have talked, but I shall write this anyway, as I'd planned to do, on this first day of a year from which we hope so much. Besides wanting to write to you on this particular day, I wanted to say a few of the things I've been thinking, before your letter comes, as perhaps it may tomorrow. But I won't mail this till it does.

    As I told you, you were always with me when I wakened in the night — and I did often, not being a very good train sleeper — and always the sense of your presence, and of your sweet tenderness, and love was very real to me. And I wondered if perhaps, in the same sense, I stayed in West Bridgewater that night. You don't need to answer that, for I think I know.

    And let me say again how truly perfect it all was. Reality can so easily fall short of hopes and expectations, especially where they have been high. I do hope that for you, as they truly are for me, the memories of Wednesday are completely unclouded by any sense of disappointment, or of hopes unrealized. And as for you, my dear one, there is not a single thing about you that I would change if I could! Once written, that seems an odd thing to say; I am trying to express my complete and overflowing happiness in the whole thing!

    I have always loved these lines of Keats' and now they keep coming into my mind as describing the feeling that exists between us:

> *A thing of beauty is a joy forever:*
> *Its loveliness increases; it will never*
> *Pass into nothingness; but still will keep*
> *A bower quiet for us, and a sleep*
> *Full of sweet dreams.*

I am certain, my dearest, that it will be forever a joy, of increasing loveliness with the years, and that in the intervals when being separated, we cannot have all the happiness of Wednesday, there will be, in each of our hearts, a little oasis of peace and "sweet dreams" where the other is.

I can see your eyes this minute — bless your dear heart!

My dearest love, always and always,
Rachel

Rachel Carson to Dorothy Freeman

Saturday night, February 6 [1953]

Darling —

Now — I saved this till last — the other letter is done, and I can just relax and say the things that are only for *you*. I really didn't plan to make it so long, and know you wouldn't expect me to — but it was all things I really wanted to tell you. Probably next week *that* part will be very short — just a report that I'm working hard and not much more. But really, dear, this is the part that means so much to me, as I'm sure you do understand, and I couldn't stop writing to you!

Your letter that came yesterday was one of the sweetest and most satisfying ones you have written me, which is saying a good deal. It, and the phone calls, and other letters, bring up so much that I wish I could say to you, but I suppose most of it *must* wait, until the happy day when we can talk about it instead.

Do you remember what someone said to the effect that (I'm quoting very inexactly) if he had two pennies he would use one to buy bread and the other to buy "a white hyacinth for his soul"? You, dearest, are the "white hyacinth" in which I invest part of my time — and I couldn't invest all of my time pennies in the "bread" of the book, even for two months, if it meant giving up all that you do for me.

Probably, just for the sake of disposing once and forever of the doubts in your mind, I should have tried to explain to you, when we were together, just why I need the "particular combination of qualities" that is you. It seemed too time-consuming a thing to bring into that short day — as it is for a letter — and besides I think I had the feeling that since you don't know most of my friends and family, anything I'd say in explanation might seem to imply quite unfair criticism of them. So, my darling, except for the little I say now, just try to accept in your heart and mind that the lovely companionship of your letters has become a necessity to me, and that, just by being you, you are helping me more than you can imagine. Surely you know I wouldn't say this if I didn't mean it! We can talk about it this summer, to our heart's content!

I don't suppose anyone really knows how a creative writer works (he or she least of all, perhaps!) or what sort of nourishment his spirit must have. All I am certain of is this; that it is quite necessary for me to know that there is someone who is deeply devoted to me as a person, and who also has the capacity and the depth of understanding to share, vicariously, the sometimes crushing burden of creative effort, recognizing the heartache, the great weariness of mind and body, the occasional black despair it may involve — someone who cherishes me and what I am trying to create, as well. Last summer I was feeling, as never before, that there was no one who combined all of that. I had always known such understanding of these things from my mother, but that was becoming so dim as you know, and for what reason. The few who understood the creative problem were not people to whom I felt emotionally close; those who loved the nonwriter part of me did not, by some strange paradox, understand the writer at all! And then, my dear one, you came into my life! Are you beginning to understand a little better? I knew when first I saw you that I wanted to see much more of you — I loved you before you left Southport — and very early in our correspondence last fall I began to sense that capacity to enter so fully into the intellectual and creative parts of my life as well as to be a dearly loved friend. And day by day all that I sensed in you has been fulfilled, but even more wonderfully than I could have dreamed.

So, my dear when you say, "Don't you ever wonder at it?" — of course the answer is yes — I feel such a joyous surge of wonder every time I stop to think how in such a dark time and when I least expected it, something so lovely and richly satisfying came into my life.

Darling, if you could only tell me now that you do understand and accept this — you, who understand so much, but have found it so hard to believe all this — because it concerns you! I would feel so much more at peace if I could feel that at last you do understand what you have done for me.

Of course — there is another side to all this. I know so well what this experience means to me — but I can't see that *I* can possibly be giving *you* anything comparable in return! But darling — before you begin to protest — let me say that I, unlike you, simply accept the fact that evidently — in a way I don't understand — I have filled some need in your life. What it is doesn't matter — unless or until you want to tell me.

Perhaps you don't even know. That part isn't important — I'm just deeply grateful that I can mean so much to you. There — I was only going to say "a little" about it, wasn't I — and I've gone on for pages! But if I have convinced you it is well worth it.

You will have this Tuesday, I suppose. I wanted to mail it tonight, but couldn't get to it in time. So you will have not only this "double feature" but my letter written last Wednesday to anwer. (And I imagine you *wanted* to reply to it sooner!) I'll anticipate a little by saying that I *was* a bit worried over the effect of my call on Monday — but that after talking to you Wednesday and particularly after your letter (of Tuesday-Wednesday-Thursday!) stopped worrying. But this time I'm really sincere in saying I won't call again for a good while. I think we both have ourselves under better control — we don't need to call for a while — and let's not.

I've laughed many times about my poor reception of your telepathy. Before my first reply to your question, "What do you usually do Wednesday evenings?" the thought of a call flitted quickly across my mind — yes, really — but was as quickly dismissed because after all you hadn't said any particular Wednesday — just Wednesday in general! (See how logic can lead you astray.) Then on my retake, I was so sure I knew what you meant! And if you needed proof that neither my senses nor my extra sense were working — you had it in the fact I allowed the line to be tied up so long. If I'd dreamed you'd be calling I would have been having fits about that — and what a strain the busy signals must have been on you! Goodnight dear — but I hope you were asleep a long time ago.

Sunday morning

Realizing that this Tuesday is one on which you say you are away all day — I'm going to try to get this into an earlier mail than our late-afternoon collection, and hope you may have it tomorrow. I know you are wanting to hear something after that wonderful Wednesday evening call, and perhaps to have a "postscript" to my recent letter.

Although this is growing into quite a volume, I haven't touched several of the things I wanted to talk about but will save them for another time. The chief subject of this letter is something I had to say — I hope you can tell me you do understand.

One thing more — that was a wonderful quotation from Toynbee. (And it is one illustration of your beautifully satisfying responses — I say something, and you reply in a way that shows you understand but also adds a new depth of meaning by your own comment!) But let me quote a line of this back to you — "when he (the creator) has *the good fortune* to enjoy the companionship of a few kindred spirits." So, darling, Mr. Toynbee is expressing what I have tried to tell you — that it is my good fortune — that my wonder is that something so lovely could have come into *my* life. Now this must be all. The next letter will be much shorter I promise you — both parts. And I do think we should give the one-a-week schedule a fair trial — it may be a very good thing for both of us once we get used to it. May I (please) look for yours maybe Thursday or Friday? Then mine will be mailed sometime over the week-end and perhaps usually reach you Tuesdays. Dear, I am so glad your mind is relieved after Stan's clinic check-up. And are you resting a lot for me — and May 11th?

> Darling, I do love you so dearly —
> *Rachel*

Dorothy Freeman to Rachel Carson

Monday morning, early, January 31 [1955]

Darling, my dearest,

Last night I spent with you from one to two o'clock. Reasons enough for lack of sleep: a rather stimulating day, the disconcerting news from Norwood, plus 9 cups of coffee which is a record for me — if not for you.

While I struggled for sleep I finally arrived at our Maytime, and particularly did my mind wander through your home as I first knew it. Oh, darling, live over those days to-gether sometime. Such happiness as those days brought to me. I remember the morning I got up before you did, to stand at the window for a long while looking down on your own special world. Darling, the tears came that morning — the whole situation was so lovely — so far lovelier than anything my wildest imagination could conjure up. Do you remember?

After a while with no suggestion of sleep I thought of the February letters. So to them I went. Do you know it took me a whole hour to read all you wrote me in that month? So how many valuable hours did you consume in the construction of them!?

What wouldn't the world give to have them? For, my darling, they are the most beautiful expressions of love I have ever read. So tender and loving and beautifully said. They began with the hyacinth letter — the Revelation.

If I could save only one letter from my mighty collection that would be the one. It is so precious. Of course, I practically can say it by heart for I must have read it literally a thousand times. You shall read it over when you come up for I want you to remember it all. I couldn't help thinking as I read "Just suppose I hadn't asked 'Why' so many times — you might never have written it" and how awful if you had felt as you did and I hadn't known it. And then the letters that followed as the result of that one.

There were smiles for me as I remembered all we experienced in that month. But what amazed me was the depth to which our love had gone in that time for after all we had been together exactly the 6½ hours at Southport in the summer previous plus the 13 hours here in December. What magic letters can work!

And in one letter there was an exclamation from you about such depths — as though we had already been to the bottom! Oh, darling, how little we knew then.

How much we have discovered in this past year. I cam remember thinking in the midst of those exchanges "How long can this last?"

Darling, I'm sure now that with me it will last as long as I shall live — the year has not dulled my love and devotion to you by one little neutron — in fact my love is as infinite as that beautiful morning star which is my first ritual of each day — to look out at it and speak to you, to reach you in your subconscious for I always hope you are asleep. This morning I thought what a lovely experience it would be if we could watch that star rise together. Did you ever set yourself to watch for the rising of a star? I did once — I think I told you — on Mt. Holyoke — only that was in the evening.

My darling, reading your letters last night was so warming I could almost feel your arms about me — and afterwards I went back to bed and dropped into a lovely sleep.

Oh, darling, can I ever make you know how much you mean to me? That was the burden of those letters — how much and why we need each other.

And you must know that I continue to need you and the year has taught me that you do belong to me.

Now, darling, the world calls. It has been so lovely to talk to you this morning to revive the year's memories.

The letters have been so precious always — but never more so than last night.

My darling, do you know how very very much I love and adore you? — I do.

Dorothy

Dorothy Freeman to Rachel Carson

[October 24, 1955]

Beloved,

What can I say on this day when I am so proud and so humble? My heart is full of so much that you know. I told you I wished I might have a gift for you for to-day that was just for Us! You said that my gift to you is the intangibles. And so, darling, it will be that way.

In your precious letter written after I left you (I found this in *The Open Heart* about a collection of letters: "They reflect the affectionate, high-spirited, often passionate individualism of men and women *reaching across the silence of space for the sympathy of that other heart.*" (I love that last phrase.) You said "I wish I could tell you in some way all that you meant to me, and the sense of peace, I feel when I am with you." Darling, if I could give no other gift, you have told me the one I would most wish to give you. And because I want you to remember it now because it belongs with that idea, I'm going to quote again the little poem that seemed made for us as long ago as the first time you came here for an over-night visit. Do you remember? Its title is

Peace

Peace flows into me
As the tide to the pool by the shore;

It is mine forevermore,
It will not ebb like the sea.

I am the pool of blue
That worships the vivid sky;
My hopes were heaven-high,
They are all fulfilled in you.

I am the pool of gold
When sunset burns and dies —
You are my deepening skies;
Give me your stars to hold.

Darling, I think that says everything, for I know you can read into it all that I do. Dearest, for all the moments that I have destroyed that Peace you find with me, I beg your forgiveness. And I know, because you understand me, I have it.

The list of other intangibles I would give you is long — happiness and health and laughter and beauty and music and friendships and now success for *The Edge of the Sea*.

For it, and for its dedication and for the experiences I have shared with you in your toil over it, for its poetry and for all that it evokes in me I give you my deepest gratitude. Darling, you never had a book dedicated to you (and such a book!) did you? So you can't quite know all that it means to me to see my name on the page of an important piece of writing — to Dorothy — with all that I know it means.

Last night I read in *The Open Heart* what Mr. Weeks had to say about a particular dedication of a book, which made me realize vividly how much meaning is read into a dedication by people like him, who know authors well.

And I know you must have been fully conscious of that when you made your decision. That, darling, is why I am so proud and so humble — that you were willing for the whole world to know. Can you understand how I feel?

Beloved, may *The Edge of the Sea* bring you joy as deep and enduring as the very sea itself — allways!

> Oh, my darling, I love you,
> *Dorothy*

Dorothy Freeman to Rachel Carson

[Late January, 1961]

. . . This is the bed where years ago you lay for a rest — a rest I thought you needed, so left you alone — and as I started downstairs that sweet little voice made my heart leap — "Hurry back." That was all I needed. I did.

Now in this setting where you always are, I have read again the Hyacinth Letter. How very, very precious it is. I shall always remember the warmth that flowed through me as I read the words, so exquisitely expressed, which told me that you needed "the particular combination of qualities that is you," and why you couldn't stop writing even for the "bread" of the book. No wonder you didn't need to read the card that accompanied the pot of "white hyacinths" yesterday. As I said recently I wish so much I had taken this letter for us to read together during my visit. It is so full of lovely, expressive phrases — "the lovely companion-

ship of your letters has become a necessity to me," "what sort of nourishment a writer's spirit must have," "someone who is deeply devoted to me
as a person, and who also has the capacity and the depth of understanding to share, vicariously, the sometimes crushing burden, of creative
effort, recognizing the heartache, the great weariness of mind and body,
the occasional black despair — someone who cherishes me and what I am
trying to create." "And then, my dear one, you came into my life!"

Dearest, can you *now*, did you *ever* understand what all that meant
to me? Remember that then you were the Famous Author, on a pedestal,
with that gulf between us. In that letter the gulf was bridged even altho'
it took a long time to destroy the pedestal. Its destruction came when I
grew to know you as a person who had worldly cares and burdens and
heartaches as I had. It is paradoxical that I could bring you down off the
pedestal and yet continue to worship you as I do, isn't it?

There are five long pages of this letter. I used to read them every
night for months, I do believe.

You go on to say — "there is another side to all this — but I can't see
that *I* can possibly be giving you anything comparable in return." "I,
unlike you, simply accept the fact that evidently I have filled some need
in your life. What it is doesn't matter. Perhaps you don't even know."

But I did know and I think that I answered that question. If you
could go back I think you'd find that my answer was that I felt in you I
had found a kindred spirit — someone who loved and enjoyed the things
of the inner being — which I so much needed, for at that time I had no
one with whom I could share my deep feelings for music, night, moonlight, sunsets, The Sea (remember) and all the other intangibles which
are food for that inner self.

Now 7 years have spun themselves out. And during them you have
not only been that kindred spirit in a thousand ways, but you have
enriched my life beyond measure. I wonder if you realize in what ways.
I could list so many — but I shan't try to think of them all.

Probably the fact that knowing you caused my reading to take a
new direction — you introduced me to authors I might never have known
if you hadn't entered my life — Jefferies, Williamson, Cloos, and oh,
especially Tomlinson. The natural world began to have so much more
meaning with you to share it — the joy of the interest in birds — and out
of that, dear, has developed Stan's great hobby. Oh, darling, as I look
back I think of all the ramifications that have resulted from some little
beginning.

I scarcely need to mention the opening of the door to the edge of
the sea with all the lovely experiences which grew out of that — there
again you were able to bring Stan into our interests.

Do you understand that if it hadn't been for you, darling, his retirement might be an empty existence!? And of course, all the exciting and lovely events that stemmed from your dedication of *The Edge of the Sea*. And all the sharing. The delight of discovering that you were a fan of E. B. White — and Robert Frost, bringing the fun of sharing anything new that E. B. produces. Not in the same category dear, but to find that you and I could understand each other so well when the subject is Cats. Who else (except Stan) in all this world could appreciate how we feel? Oh, Lois — of course. Which brings me to another category of the way you have enriched my life. In no other way would I have ever known people like the Teales and the Bestons — and this rare relationship with Lois.

Even if I never write at all, it has been enlightening to know people who have — and above all are You! I suppose you have no conception of how much I have learned from you about the profession — in small ways and in large ways I've been admitted to the secret order. Just that afternoon last spring with your files was worth a 4-year college course. And again Stan has shared that — another common ground for him and me.

Of course, darling, all that we have shared in the field of music I'm sure I could never expect to share with anyone else. Stan will always be an outsider. Recorded music — Our Symphony, Our Concerto, Our Leonard Bernstein — I suppose that is one area that perhaps does not need a sharer to be happy, but oh, how sweet to have one. Just to look in someone's eyes to find a response which tells you the feeling is the same.

And then there are so many tangible reminders of you. Here in my room, darling, there is your picture in which I've always thought you were listening for veeries — it's always there waiting when I come up here. In my jewel case the dear golden wreath lies on the velvet speaking to me of eternal friendship. The two dear lamps shed light and warmth and on the walls the woodland portraits — my white violets and my trilliums. Downstairs in the living room more woodland portraits and did I tell you that now the pewter candelabra holds the central place over the fireplace? And records — lovely records — including one we have not yet listened to together — Bach's *St. Matthew's Passion*. I shall have to take it the next time I go to Silver Spring. It will be so glorious on the Capehart!

Even the pen I write with speaks of you as well as to you.

But of all the tangibles, darling, of course the gifts of fine books you have showered upon us are the most enriching. I can't name them all — someday I think I shall make a list of them. But I must mention the Bent volumes—not easy to come by—and to accompany them the Bird Song Record! Oh, Darling, one of the first books was *The Wind in the Willows* —remember—how I loved that. Need I say that your own creations, your brain children are everything to me.

Besides all I have mentioned, I suppose the memories of the moments, the days, the nights, the weeks, we have spent together are most to be cherished. Someday I'm going through my diaries & make a list of them.

You spoke of the moonlight shining in your room—how many happy memories that evokes. If we had only moonlight, shared, to remember, our storehouse would be unusually rich. But there are the Sea, the Shore, the Woods, the Gardens, the Marshes, Phosphorescence, Wind, Sun, Sand, Scents—oh, my Darling.

And then there is the Sadness and the Unhappiness we've shared. I wonder how I could have stood all I did in those 1½ miserable years without your sustaining and continuing love and understanding. I have tried to imagine what it would have been like if there hadn't been your letters to take to bed with me, or your dear voice on the phone so frequently. To-day I remembered one little incident—do you remember the day at Southport when I threw my back out—my children were coming and I needed to see Mother. You drove me up to Edgecomb. And I think that was the day Mother had had another shock and was so disturbed. Oh, darling, it was so good to have you along. Little either of us dreamed when you wrote in the Hyacinth letter of heartache, great weariness of mind and body, the black despair in relation to creative writing that both of us were to meet those very things in other realms. How good we couldn't know the future. How lovely, how beautiful, how comparatively free from care was that first Maytime.

For me it has meant more than I can ever tell you to have your love to enfold me—love that was your arms about me in my dark hours.

My skies are brighter. Would, my dearest, that yours were. In your dark hours now, please know that my love, like enfolding arms, is about you as yours was about me.

Your skies will be brighter, too. The time for them to reach you seems long, but how shining they will be when you are well again.

Now I've read this over. Between the lines I hope you can read what I've never been able to say, adequately—that in the going-on-eight years in which I've known you, my life has been enriched, broadened, sweetened, smoothed, softened, and enlarged beyond expressing—all because of you. You have had fame and fortune and I'm glad. But I hope my love which you've had and continue to have has made you as happy as the fame and fortune.

And I believe it has. You have shown me in so many ways.

Are you glad we met? I know even if we could have met without the introduction by your wonderful *The Sea Around Us*, I should have found in you exactly as I have, the same qualities that have endeared you to me — so that the Fame would make no difference. There is no Pedestal. You are You, my Beloved One.

Wednesday morning

Darling, in reading this over I find I have not told you one half the thoughts I could or would. But I know you know. On the other hand, it is good to remember. I wish we could live all the lovely moments over again, together.

We are off to Norwood on a morning when it is still just zero!

This letter seems to be to serve as an anniversary remembrance of the Hyacinth letter — and that is what I wanted it to be.

With it goes the boundless love which has grown and grown over the years between.

I love you.
Dorothy

Dorothy Freeman to Rachel Carson

Monday Evening, October 14 [1963]

Dear Heart,

Late this afternoon you and I strolled about your beloved spot for a last look for 1963. As I drove in, the maple tree directly ahead as you start down the little rise on your road was yellow gold — the leaves still intact, with a westering sun gleaming through them. The earlier coloring maples have dropped all their leaves. As I started down the steps beside the garden a Monarch butterfly gave a lingering kiss to this clover. I wonder if he is on his way to California, too. Moppet's little grave is still green — some brave yellow Marigolds are blooming nearby. The masses of scarlet huckleberry never fail to amaze me and your ledges from shore to house are all afire — juniper and bayberry mingled their greens with it. The sun was warm so I lingered in it on the porch for a while but then decided I wanted to see that banking from the shore, with my back to the sun. The shutters on the door and window hurt me as I went down the path, and a thousand memories rose up to clutch my heart — memories of you and me happily moving through the bushes.

And of course, I never go over those rocks from the spruce to the beach without that remembrance of that dark night of phosphorescence. What delight. I went out to the second ridge of dry rocks to lean against them for a long while drinking in the beauty. The white birches with their yellow dresses shone brightly but of course the huckleberry dominated the scene. And can you imagine the thoughts that possessed me as I looked — all the lovely, sweet times together?

Then, later, as the tide was low enough I skirted the waxy sloping rocks on the seaweed to go over to the salt pond, stopping to pick a few garnets out of the old boulder, quite crumbly now.

The maples around the pond still have their leaves in many variegated colors so that seems to be the last of the glory. Roger's raft is high so I doubt that any storms will move it. I broke into your woods from the road, to cut up across the wooded area to the look-out spot above Steeveses'. I think that is one of my favorites — to look down on that sea of spruces, so lush, so green. And remembrances of warm afternoons when we sat there watching the blue sky with whatever creatures passed over us. And the dear little warblers in the spruces. Today only one chick-a-dee was about but he sang a lively song. Reindeer moss is dry and crisp underfoot while the checkerberry leaves have turned a dark, dark shiny green with red berries peaking from beneath. And thus I said good-bye, and I'll confess I couldn't see too well as I walked back to the car.

To-day has been warm with less wind so that the stillness is almost audible. In this lovely hush a noise of a human is almost unbearable. I sat on the Head when I came back & was startled to hear a door shut. I couldn't imagine — then I realized someone was at Cutlers'. But it wasn't right to intrude on the peace. Without the wind I am even conscious of the stillness of the trees and I realize that we have had an unusual amount of wind.

About a half hour before sundown we wandered up to Waneceks' where we had a broad view. It was warm enough so we sat on the rocks capturing all we can against the winter. Even before the sun set, streamers of ducks began crossing the western sky. They seem to take a course over the Kennebec now so they are barely discernible with the naked eye. But what fun with the glasses. As the flocks wavered and changed position Stan talked to them —"Come on, don't hang behind," "Get together fellows," etc. How wonderful that on the 14th of Oct. on the coast of Maine we were perfectly comfortable out on the rocks until it grew too dark to see the birds.

This is going to meet you in California. I do hope all goes well and right with you. Again let me say how glad I am that you are there. Please be awfully careful, dear. I think back to those early days when, if you went away, I had to know where you were every hour. This will be quite different — but I'm hoping that whatever you are doing you will find wonderful new experiences.

Stan says you must try to find the shop in the Fairmont that specializes in the most scrumptious sundaes. At least there was such a one in 1952 for we'd walk over from the Mark Hopkins to have one.

I wonder what 11 years have done to San Francisco — many changes, I'm sure but I trust it has retained its special flavor.

Darling, please know that although my body is separated from you by far too many miles, my thoughts are there — thinking of this really momentous occasion — are you sure such a famous celebrity is the same dear person I folded in my arms a month ago? It is hard to believe. Oh, — the bunchberry leaves have all turned the color of dogwood leaves in the fall — can't you picture what a gorgeous ground cover they make? If all goes well, we shall be in West Bridgewater when you return. Please read between these lines!

> I love you so,
> *Dorothy*

Rachel Carson to Dorothy Freeman

January 2 [1964]

Dear One,

I want to leave a little note behind for you to have under your pillow tonight — but it must be brief for I don't want to be away from you long enough to write it!

No visit could ever be long enough, but it has been wonderful to have the sense of leisure created by four days and nights unbroken by diversions. It has been a precious oasis in time, darling, to be cherished and returned to in memory always. As you, with your great gifts, always do, you have adorned the hours with love and tenderness, and with fun and laughter, too. It was especially precious to share the music with you, another thing you have given me.

I hope I have not spoken too much of the lurking shadows, especially since they may after all prove to be nothing — but it seemed better to speak of them rather than to have to write.

Now it is 6 P.M., and since I wrote this morning we have had our precious afternoon, which seems to leave nothing that needs to be said. I am so glad we had these hours, for wonderful as all the rest of the visit has been, I think we were closest this afternoon.

You reminded me of my letter after the 13 hours, and I think it was in that letter that I quoted: "A thing of beauty is a joy forever — its loveliness increases . . ." That has proved to be supremely true, darling, through all the ten years since I quoted it. And as long as either of us lives, I know our love "will never pass into nothingness" but will keep a quiet bower stored with peace and with precious memories of all that we have shared.

I need not say it again but I shall — I love you, now and always.

Rachel

Rachel Carson to Dorothy Freeman

January 24, 1963

Darling,

I have been coming to the realization that suddenly there might be no chance to speak to you again and it seems I must leave a word of goodbye. Perhaps you will never read this, for in time — if there is time — I may destroy it. But last night the pains were bad and came so often that I was frightened. No, that isn't quite the word, but I realized there might come a time when I wouldn't rouse from sleep in time to reach for the pills. And it seemed it might be a little easier for you if there were some message.

Perhaps I shall write this letter a little at a time, as I can and I shall leave it in an envelope addressed to you.

When I think back to the many farewells that have marked the decade (almost) of our friendship, I realize they have almost been inarticulate. I remember chiefly the great welling up of thoughts that somehow didn't get put into words — the silences heavy with things unsaid. But then, we knew or hoped, there was always to be another chance — and always the letters to fill the gaps.

I have felt, darling, that it is better for you that in this past year, the tempo of our correspondence has slowed down so greatly — to the point where I'm sure you no longer watch for the mailman. When there can be no more letters the wrench won't be quite so great.

What do I most want to say? I think that you must have no regrets in my behalf. I have had a rich life, full of rewards and satisfactions that come to few, and if it must end now, I can feel that I have achieved most of what I wished to do. That wouldn't have been true two years ago, when I first realized my time was short, and I am so grateful to have had this extra time.

My regrets, darling, are for your sadness, for leaving Roger, when I so wanted to see him through to manhood, for dear Jeffie whose life is linked to mine.

Perhaps there is more time than I think. But for the past year I have been able to feel much less optimism. And now this new development! But as to the angina, in a way it is almost like a secret weapon against the grimmer foe — so if it should take me quickly, darling, remember this is the easier way for me.

But enough of that. What I want to write of is the joy and fun and gladness we have shared — for these are the things I want you to remember — I want to live on in your memories of happiness. I shall write more of those things. But tonight I'm weary and must put out the light. Meanwhile, there is this word — and my love that will always live.

Rachel

April 11, 1963

My darling, For all these weeks I have written no more, but I have said so much in the letters that went to you that there has seemed to be no need. And now you know of the existence of this last little message to be left for you.

My sadness for you increases, darling. One by one, those you love are being taken from you, for now dear Willow is gone, and you must know I haven't long. And I know that both Willow and I, in our different ways, represented comfort for you in time of trouble, as well as companionship in happy moments! May there be new sources of strength, dear one.

April 30, 1963

My darling, You are starting on your way to me in the morning, but I have such a strange feeling that I may not be here when you come — so this is just an extra little note of farewell, should that happen. There have been many pains (heart) in the past few days, and I'm weary in every bone. And tonight there is something strange about my vision, which may mean nothing. But of course I thought, what if I can't write — can't *see* to write — tomorrow? So, a word before I turn out the light.

I have wanted so terribly to have you here. I've been afraid you wouldn't come if you knew how ill I feel, for you seem to think your being here would make it harder for me, while of course it is just the reverse. And of course I've felt this might be the last time I'd see you.

Darling — if the heart does take me off suddenly, just know how much easier it would be for me that way. But I do grieve to leave my dear ones. As for me, however, it is quite all right. Not long ago I sat late in my study and played Beethoven, and achieved a feeling of real peace and even happiness.

Never forget, dear one, how deeply I have loved you all these years.

Rachel

May Sarton/Louise Bogan

May Sarton and Louise Bogan met when Bogan was already an established poet and Sarton was an emerging writer. They exchanged a flurry of letters in 1954, followed by a slow, steady stream until Bogan's 1970 death. Ranging in subject matter from the social whirl of the literary world to the lonely toil of the writer, the correspondence sheds light on Bogan's battle with mental illness and on Sarton's retreat from the world. Fragments of Sarton's letters read alongside Bogan's short but complete missives describe a deep comradeship and sympathy between the two women.

May Sarton to Louise Bogan

[November 13, 1953]

It was a shock about Dylan Thomas. I shall always remember the flood of relief I felt when I first read "October Morning" and "Fern Hill" and "Do not go gentle into that good night," as if a long starvation were at an end. It is cruel that he should go, but it is, I suspect, the Dionysian fate, the exalted feverish climb that cannot make a natural end. How mysterious — these angels and self-destroyers who appear now and then.

But something has gone out of our world now forever and it does chill one to the bone. Also I get scared because such deaths make one feel responsible, I mean responsible for one's own future — to have more time in such a responsibilty. To use it well, to keep on is growing, to be implacably self-demanding and self-critical. Given less to begin with, we must become more (but I am talking of myself, not of you, of course) — What if Yeats had died at forty? Or Marianne Moore? I like best to think of poetry as a long life with the best at the end.

Louise Bogan to May Sarton

January 28, 1954

Dear May:

It was delightful to hear your voice, and to feel that you are working. Your letter this morning said many true things (and the poems, too). But what has never been explained thoroughly, by me to you, is the really dreadful emotional state I was trapped in for many years — a state which Raymond struggled manfully against, I will say, for a long time. In those days, my devotion came out all counter-clockwise, as it were. I was a *demon* of jealousy, for example; and a sort of *demon* of fidelity, too: "morbid fidelity," Dr. Wall came to call it. A slave-maker, really, while remaining a sort of slave. Dreadful! Thank God v. little of it got into the poems; but the general warp showed up in every detail of my life. Except for a certain saving *humor*, I should have indeed been a full *monster.* — During my illness, all this had to be relinquished, step by step. A new personality (that had been kept from coming into light and growth), slowly emerged; and it is this person that you now know. The successful love-affair which began when I was 39 and lasted for 8 years was utterly different from anything that had gone before: perfect freedom, perfect detachment, *no jealousy* at all — an emphasis on *joy*, that is. This is the only kind of relationship that is possible for me now: something *given by me* and received in an almost childish way.

What you say about my own development is perfectly true. I am trying to break through certain blocks in the "long prose thing": that will be "memory," if not "desire." So far as desire is concerned, I must wait. If it comes again, with a strength which I cannot withstand, and a *benevolence* (that is not the word, but then) I can recognize: good! But if not, not. — As I said to you the other night, quoting (I think!) St. Paul: With a great price bought I this freedom. — You understand.

Bless you. Keep feeling and working. For the work is really, for us, the important thing. The channels must be kept open so that it may live and grow.

Love, dear May,
Louise

May Sarton to Louise Bogan

[January 30, 1954]

The *New Yorker* stuff I am doing is easy because I am making no attempt to come to grips with *any* conflict (it would not be for them if I did, and it is not for me at this time. I have to wait for that until I am much older than you because it is all so rather *queer*, you know. I do not wish to be known as a queer person until I am firmly established for central reasons, not a periphery person) and I saw how it wrecked Le Gallienne to have people know too much about her private life. They could no longer *see* her as she really is. Instead of being true in its effect, or an effect of truth, it just makes people unable to hear what you have to say. At the root of this, no doubt, is Willa Cather's denial of the right to publish any letters in her will.

Louise Bogan to May Sarton

February 4, 1954

Dear May:

The matter of a more regular appearance of my "blurbs," in the magazine, has been troubling me. I spend an entire morning on *one* of those horrid little notices; and there are about twenty of them, at present, piled up in corrected proof. The women poet piece may be out today: I haven't see this week's copy yet, having spent the morning writing two more short notices: one on Padriac [Colum] and one on Sir Osbert Sitwell's *Wrack at Tidesend.* — It is silly to worry about this sort of thing, but I do take the *New Yorker* job seriously. If anything should go wrong with it I should have to go job-hunting, in truth, and that is a baffling prospect, at the moment. . . . I am sure that nothing will go wrong; but you see I have my worrying and fussing moments.

As for my eight-sided heart, which you question, dear May, I can only say that the octagonal here is somehow symbolic of freedom. Love of things, I suppose, understood, more than love of human beings. . . . The delight in objects, both natural and artifacts, which has grown in me ever since the *obsessive* person was left behind (or buried, if you like, in the lowest layer of the dream). The delight of the collector, which you sensed in my room; the delight of the naturalist (which I never had, when young, except in flashes, but which makes me scrutinize everything, from flowers to rocks on the shore, in these later years); the delight of the amateur in the arts (the piano and embroidery); the delight of the cook and the housewife. . . . All these are substitutes, I know; but they keep me alive and not only happy but occasionally full of joy. I do not speak of the delight of the maker, for writing has never been anything (except v. rarely) but tough and artisan to me.

Love, dear May,
Louise

May Sarton to Louise Bogan

[March 8, 1954]

There is nothing wrong for a man in picking up a sailor, but a woman who would do the equivalent would be violating herself (in either a heterosexual or homosexual relationship, *bien entendu*). The drive which is back of two women who unite in passionate love is therefore, as in any love relationship for a woman, first of all and primarily emotional rather than sexual. Emotion overflows and tries to find a medium of expression. If the medium is physical, as it may be, but does not have to be, what the woman discovers is herself *in* someone else. You break out of yourself through someone else, to find yourself. The excitement — and it is very great in its way — comes from the fact that you give the *same* pleasure which you receive. This is where it is hard to pin down in words (I am not writing a handbook). It is metaphysical because the caress contains *in itself* the love and is not a pure drive towards release as it is in a man. In other words, it is exceedingly pure and intense, an exchange of souls. I don't know about homosexual men but my guess is that it's quite a different thing because there the *primal* drive remains and sex must play a more obsessive part. The chances of a complete and happy mutual response are very much greater with two women and this is why I have always felt it dangerous (and in fact I would not myself do it) to initiate a woman who might be shifted out of her center.

One never reaches the deepest place of feeling part of the almost unconscious universe, of being *lost*. Instead one reaches a place of extreme consciousness; one is *found* as an individual. Greater subtlety, less depth, a greater sense of oneself and the other as a person different from others.

Louise Bogan to May Sarton

April 21, 1954

Dear May:

No, I'm not ahead of you, in the *Karmic* sense, I'm sure. I'm just *older!* At least twice in my present existence I have been forced to lose my life in order to find it. . . . This means losing people, for a time — and losing oneself — getting to the point where one gives up *completely* and merely keeps breathing, hoping that the power and the will to live will come back. The power of *persons* is lessened, after such experiences. It is a sort of amputation, I am sure; but one can manage, if one's heart and brain haven't been cut off. And one's hands — spiritual *and* corporeal. . . .

You should have the book by now. It is a *neat* book, I think, although it will never get a prize for the 50 Best.

Love,
Louise

May Sarton to Louise Bogan

Last night was a continuation of my birthday as Le Gallienne was here and we had a bang-up supper in her room at the Ritz and a long very good talk, looking down on the public gardens, a red umbrella, empty benches, the round soft umbrella shapes of the trees just in leaf, the little formal parterres of pansies, and rain. I was happy to see her this time at her very best, the true glory and greatness. This is something absolutely *pure* which she possesses and which I have never seen in another theatre person. The tragic thing is that it is not being used — though she has made a good life without the theatre now. She had just designed and added a guest wing to her house and wants me to come in June so maybe I could drive you back (though maybe the train is more restful, I don't know) — we talked about the possibility of a novel on the subject of women or should I say "Extraordinary Women"? — a project for my extreme old age I think. And about Virginia Woolf. And about various things Le G. is writing herself. Today I went to hear her read Shakespearian scenes and really play the whole of the Happy Prince at Simmons — a performance of the most subtle and perfect *control*. I wish you had been there. She looked very tired and — alas — very old the night before, and then it was exciting to see the stage presence, so radiantly alive, beauty put on from the inside, so to speak, and the amazing sapphire eyes, a *different* person.

Louise Bogan to May Sarton

October 15, 1954

Dear May:

The separation between *life* and *things* — O dear, I can't command the vocabulary to bring out what I meant! — Briefly (and awkwardly) — are not trees and skies and water and earth, nature; to which man is added: *Homo additus naturae?* To which human life is added, and from which it is not wholly (certainly) derived. And with human life we get all the significant blood and the tears. And the gift of the intellect. And the common law. And art. The same current runs through the whole set-up — natural and human: true. But in man the power is transformed; and it is this transformation with which we must deal. The trees and the stones and the sea serve us as symbols, and stand around us like brothers and sisters — but they are inhuman siblings. . . . It is from life we must draw art; and philosophy must get mixed up in the horrors, as well as the joys, of existence. . . . Now I stop!

The third class [at New York University] went off well. I gave them *texture* in a large dose: the silver cord, golden bowl passage from Ecclesiastes, really analysed down to the last vowel and consonant (I get this out of a book by a learned Oxonian); and a fragment from Keats'

"Ode to Autumn" (beginning with the hazel kernels, and ending with the bees' clammy cells) brings out the *m* and *z* sounds complete, with the undertones of *l* and *ɔ*. They seemed to enjoy all this. Next week: speed and tempo! I do think that modern poets write far too much at one speed. So I shall read a part of "Reynard the Fox," and perhaps the slowest poem in English: Collins' "Ode to Evening." — I find that the stuff they hand in is rather ingrown. I want to get them to look around and use material outside themselves. — Have you see, by the way, the new James Kirkup volume — *A Spring Journey?* I think he is shaping into something really interesting. He is now 32.

I hope that you're keeping a note-book. Dear May, I wish you all richness and deepness; and you are on the margin, I should think, of a new page.

Love,
Louise

May Sarton to Louise Bogan

[October 30, 1954]

It has been a week of good work and much inner stress, which is why I haven't written. I was consoled by a letter from Janet Flanner saying that it worries her that she is so violent "without warning," as that has been my state, to the point that I decided that in future I really had better go into a burrow and never see another human soul. It had been hard going to get through into the poems, but that is no excuse and I wonder how in Hell I shall ever learn both to be vulnerable enough, yet controlled. It seems to be one or the other. It does not help (yes, it does — what a lie) that people here are so understanding — I am never blamed, which makes me feel even more like a crminal. Well, enough of this. I have written 8 poems in the last 10 days or so and maybe one or two of them are good, better anyway than those you have seen. But I shall not know of course till much later.

Louise Bogan to May Sarton

November 13, 1959

Dear May:

It is wonderful to know that my poems *spoke* to you: "The Daemon" especially, which was written *(given!)* one afternoon almost between one curb of a street and another. *Why not?* is always a great help. God presses us so hard, often, that we rebel — and we should. Auden once told me that we should *talk back* to God; that this is a kind of prayer.

Love,
Louise

Louise Bogan to May Sarton

August 9, 1962

Dear May:

Bryher's book [*The Heart to Artemis*] set me off on Dorothy Richardson, the full run of whom I can get at the Mercantile Library. D. R. was *certainly* a forerunner; *Pointed Roofs* came out in 1915; and both V. Woolf and J. Joyce learned from her. She *is* quite tiresome when she gets off on *cosmic* themes, but she does that *v.* seldom. Wonderful on sight, sound, smell, the tactile sense (washing her hands with good soap becomes a shining moment!) And wonderful on men *versus* women. Men she dismisses as hopeless (spiritual) bunglers: creatures shut out from *the center.* She's not feminist *or* Bohemian at all. And O, those 1890 London streets and parks and interiors!

You want me to be frank, my dear:

I think you are still writing *around* your travel experience. I want to *hear* you and *see* you *right in* the gardens; right *beside* the river; right *next to* the stone god! I feel that you have *distilled* the moments too much — enveloped them with too much *calm.* "O God, how tired and miserable I was in this place or that"; or "How hot it was"; or "How restless and mortal I feel," or "How perfectly wonderful" . . . , etc., etc. "The great god sleeping" stanza is *v.* good indeed. But again, I feel that you are doing too much in *one poem.* Make three poems! And don't keep the question and answer form (which slows and dilutes). Just let's have *you* — right in the midst of one experience after another.

Breathe in! Breathe out!

Love,
Louise

May Sarton to Louise Bogan

[November 14, 1965]

It was so good to get your frail page in the mail. It is splendid that you trust your doctor there, and he does sound as if he were "getting at" things. I am consoled to hear that "anger" is a problem, for it is surely mine. But I could not read the second world — was it "reviewing"? For me depression is *always* suppressed anger I have discovered — and if the anger has not been suppressed, then guilt and shame because it is such a bad thing, except an occasional, very occasional "holy anger" I suppose. In order to keep an even keel, no doubt you have buried a lot of stress and strain in these last years — and maybe later on some of it can find its way into poems. Give your genius into the paws of the tiger he will not rend. . . .

Last night I saw Le Gallienne in *The Madwoman of Chaillot* (next week I'll see their production of *The Trojan Women*) and that is such an exhilarating play in a good childish-sophisticated way. Giraudoux has so much tenderness and so much wit — it is a charming combination. Do you remember all the Madwoman's widsom about how to *manage?* It reminded me of you and of myself. How fine to be mad enough to be sane. I laughed so much when the young man she rescues from suicide asks what he can do for her and she answers, "Lots of things. You can take the mouse out of the trap. I am tired of feeding it." The whole play is full of these tender paradoxes. Also when the wonderful King of the Sewers says, "They say we have orgies down here and the rats dance — it's ridiculous. The rats are not *allowed* to dance" etc.

May Sarton to Louise Bogan

[March 31, 1968]

You started a long train of thought about Virginia Woolf when you called. I do understand the reaction now to an overestimate in some ways. But can you name a novelist today for whose next book one waits with such excitement *because* you will have no idea what it will be like? The daring of her experiments, *Orlando, The Waves, To the Lighthouse,* the fact that she never lets the mold stay to be used again . . . this is already a sign of genius. Some of these experiments were failures, but all were extremely interesting. People blame her for *not* being Joyce . . . why should she be? She was not experimenting with *language* so much as *form,* and there is a real distinction here. That is all what *critics* look for. But what about the common reader? I have yet to find a woman writer who can illuminate in just this way "ordinary life" or any one who has stated what women's lives are, the complexity they have to weave together, the harmony they have to make out of the emotional chaos and physical disorder of "family life," the *art* this takes. She has done far more in a real, unblinking coming to terms with the woman than all the Betty somethingorothers and then "feminine mystique." (It is *not* a sentimental view or a "feminist" view of the novels. But for the common reader, perhaps her greatest gift comparable to Emily Dickinson) was to make the ordinary things of life, a woman knitting a sock, a certain light on the grass, marvelously new and touching.

In one of the fan letters I have had recently, a woman writes, "I've found through the years as my family responsibilities have increased that I must put a ban on my reading or I become too restless to stick to duties. But two people I can always read. Virginia Woolf, because of all her awareness of small things, which is contagious and I then notice all the *small glories of my daily life.* And you" etc. (underlining mine). It is easy to be patronizing to this gift as it is easy to sneer at the saints, but I do not believe it is nothing to give back courage and to illuminate *daily life* for those (most of us) close to despair all the time. The word is "life-enhancing."

Lorraine Hansberry

Best known for her play *A Raisin in the Sun* Lorraine Hansberry devoted her career to advancing the rights of African-Americans. Her plays, speeches, essays and articles addressed racial oppression directly and resolutely, making her one of the more important writers — black or white — of her generation. As literature and as social document, her work reflected and helped spur the emergence of the civil rights movement. One of her plays, *The Sign in Sidney Brustein's Window,* features a tormented gay character, David Ragin, through whom Hansberry advocates the acceptance of homosexuality. But race was always her primary concern, a concern that emerges in her letters.

Lorraine Hansberry to Nannie Perry Hansberry

Hotel Taft
New Haven, Conn.
January 19, 1959

Dear Mother,

Well — here we are. I am sitting alone in a nice hotel room in New Haven, Conn. Downstairs, next door in the Shubert Theatre, technicians are putting the finishing touches on a living room that is supposed to be a Chicago living room. Wednesday the curtain goes up at 8 P.M The next day the New Haven papers will say what they think about our efforts. A great deal of money has been spent and a lot of people have done some hard, hard work, and it may be the beginning of many different careers.

The actors are very good and the director is a very talented man — so if it is a poor show I won't be able to blame a soul but your youngest daughter.

Mama, it is a play that tells the truth about people, Negroes and life and I think it will help a lot of people to understand how we are just as complicated as they are — and just as mixed up — but above all, that we have among our miserable and downtrodden ranks — people who are the very essence of human dignity. That is what, after all the laughter and tears, the play is supposed to say. I hope it will make you very proud. See you soon. Love to all.

Lorraine Hansberry to Kenneth Merryman

April 27, 1962

Dear Kenneth Merryman:

I have received a great many letters from students but, I confess, not too many from "a white farm boy living on a rich, fertile farm on the Mason-Dixie Line" and so I was particularly pleased to hear from you.

You ask for my views of the "Negro Question" in the United States, with particular regard to Martin Luther King and the seemingly diametrically opposite techniques of the various freedom movements . . .

I look upon Dr. King's movement as a reflection of the sense of tactical reality which a desperate people constantly demonstrate. I mean that I doubt very much that there is any vast quantity of "love" being generated in the South by the barbarity of racist tactic and ideology. Rather, I imagine that leaders like Dr. King, with their insights into the mentality and traditions of this Republic, have tried to create instruments of struggle which do not lead head-on to the mass murder of our people.

Please understand that I do not mean that Dr. King or any of his associates are less than sincere in lifting the banner of love and non-violence into the winds of the struggle; I am sure that they are. But I am imposing on that my own thought that, given their assessment of the situation, they feel there is hardly another approach. I support them and applaud them.

At the same time, like most of my generation and, in particular, those behind my generation (I am thirty-two), I have no illusion that it is enough. We believe that the world is political and that political power, in one form or another, will be the ultimate key to the liberation of American Negroes and, indeed, black folk throughout the world. It is the political reality of the world without our own shores which even makes the King movement possible, in my opinion.

I think this is what the nation has to face; and, being black and a dedicated American patriot, I am glad. I think that Dr. King increasingly will have to face a forthcoming generation of Negroes who question even the restraints of his militant and, currently, progressive ideas and concepts. The pressure rears up everywhere: I think the daily press lulls the white community falsely in dismissing the rising temper of the ghetto and what will come of it.

In the twentieth century men everywhere like to *breathe;* and the Negro citizen still cannot, you see, *breathe.* And, thus far, the intensity of our resentment has not yet permeated white society which remains, in spite of the headlines, convinced it is *our* problem.

In fine, the nation *presumes* upon the citizenship of the Negro but is oblivious to the fact that it must *confer* citizenship before it can expect reciprocity. Until twenty million people are completely interwoven into the fabric of our society they are under no obligation to behave as if they were.

What I am saying is that whether we like the word or not, the condition of our people dictates what can only be called revolutionary attitudes. It is no longer acceptable to allow racists to define Negro manhood — and it will have to come to pass that they can no longer define his weaponry.

I think, then, that Negroes must concern themselves with every single means of struggle: legal, illegal, passive, active, violent and non-violent. That they must harass, debate, petition, give money to court struggles, sit-in, lie-down, strike, boycott, sing hymns, pray on steps — and shoot from their windows when the racists come cruising through their communities.

And, in the process, they must have no regard whatsoever for labels and pursed lips in the light of their efforts.

The acceptance of our present condition is the only form of extremism which discredits us before our children.

This has been a conversation not an essay and I hope of some meaning to you. If you should care to reply and argue or comment about any of it I would be delighted to hear from you again.

If not, may I wish you a happy and rewarding college experience for the next four years. I don't know what field you are going into — but whatever it is, bask in the opportunity for education, won't you? Mankind has labored a long time to accumulate all that goes into the books which are awaiting you and there is so much that is beautiful and stirring and inspiring in the achievements of the human race that one ought to go through the years of formal education in a state of perpetual exhilaration. And — neglect not the arts!

Warm wishes,

Lorraine Hansberry to the Editor of The New York Times

April 23, 1964

To the Editor,
The New York Times:

With reference to civil disobedience and the Congress of Racial Equality stall-in:

. . . My father was typical of a generation of Negroes who believed that the "American way" could successfully be made to work to democratize the United States. Thus, twenty-five years ago, he spent a small personal fortune, his considerable talents, and many years of his life fighting, in association with NAACP attorneys, Chicago's "restrictive covenants" in one of this nation's ugliest ghettoes.

That fight also required that our family occupy the disputed property in a hellishly hostile "white neighborhood" in which, literally, howling mobs surrounded our house. One of their missiles almost took the life of the then eight-year-old signer of this letter. My momories of this "correct" way of fighting white supremacy in America include being spat at, cursed and pummeled in the daily trek to and from school. And I also remember my desperate and courageous mother, patrolling our house all night with a loaded German luger, doggedly guarding her four children, while my father fought the respectable part of the battle in the Washington court.

The fact that my father and the NAACP "won" a Supreme Court decision, in a now famous case which bears his name in the lawbooks, is — ironically — the sort of "progress" our satisfied friends allude to when they presume to deride the more radical means of struggle. The cost, in emotional turmoil, time and money, which led to my father's early death as a permenantly embittered exile in a foreign country when he saw that after such sacrificial efforts the Negroes of Chicago were as ghetto-locked as ever, does not seem to figure in their calculations.

That is the reality that I am faced with when I now read that some Negroes my own age and younger say that we must now lie down in the streets, tie up traffic, do whatever we can — take to the hills with guns if necessary — and fight back. Fatuous people remark these days on our "bitterness." Why, of course we are bitter. The entire situation suggests that the nation be reminded of the too little noted final lines of Langston Hughes' mighty poem:

What happens to a dream deferred?
Does it dry up
Like a raisin in the sun?
Or fester like a sore —
And then run?
Does it stink like rotten meat?
Or crust and sugar over —
Like a syrupy sweet?

Maybe it just sags
Like a heavy load.

Or does it explode?

Sincerely,
Lorraine Hansberry

Anne Sexton

A gifted poet and anguished woman, Anne Sexton lost her battle with madness in 1974, when she took her own life. By then she had published six collections of her work, winning the 1966 Pulitzer Prize for *Live or Die* (two more books would appear posthumously). Her emotional, personal poems, dubbed "confessional" by critics, served much the same purpose as did the psychotherapy on which she relied so heavily. Sexton also turned to a psycho-therapist friend, Anne Clarke, for support, and it was with Clarke that she had her single lesbian affair. Although the affair was brief it was potent, eliciting from the troubled Sexton letters of an almost overpowering intensity.

Anne Sexton to Anne Clarke

[40 Clearwater Road]
jan what the hell is the
date . . . I guess it's prob the 21st or
something . . . no 22nd . . .
1964

Sweet Anne,

I love you. Do you know how I look for the mail and it is your letter that I hunt for, that I spring from the desk for when I hear the mailman slip his letters thru the lock. Yep! It's your envelope I hunt for. Yep! It's your voice. Your cadence!

Okay? [. . .]

Anne, the thing that really is bugging me, putting me, mouth at the wall [I *mean* wall] is that Dr. Martin is leaving . . . Christ. I can't. I *mean* I can't. That's all. I just can't. Christ's sake! How can I explain . . . it would take too many pages . . . hours . . . get the picture, Anne . . . eight years of therapy . . . At start me nothing . . . *really* nothing . . . for two years me still nothing . . . and then I start to be something and then my mother dies, and then father . . . a large storm . . . then recovery and that slow and trying to both Martin and me . . . I mean "hell" not just "trying" (and, for him too) . . . (I'm a very difficult, acting out patient) . . . and I'd come quite far, , , , but now . . . now . . . if he goes next Sept. and he thinks he will . . . I have had it. I can't make it (the intense trust, *the* transference all over AGAIN) . . . Anne! Please! Help me! Don't be my doctor . . . but for God's sake be my friend who is also a doctor. I could use that. I mean, I not only could use it . . . but it might be essential for me for a time . . . I HAVE GOT TO HAVE SOMEONE. (Am I too dramatic . . . after all, I know I'm not dying . . . not really . . . but it [is] so close . . . as you said, just as you said. When you die you are really alone. I mean no one is going along with you and you'd like to do it without losing control, to maintain a little pride, a little respect . . .) . . . Anne, I feel so alone. I think, between you and me, that I'm half so well and half so sick . . . and I don't want the sick to win . . . to lose all control . . . but . . .

but . . .

alone . . .

I was thinking more about facts of death (real death) after I read your letter and I thought, after your words, that this was, Indeed, the awfulness of dying . . . that you must do it alone. I remember well being right beside my mother as she died, and trying to help her, to stay there, *right there* so she wouldn't have to walk the barrier alone . . . to go as far as I could into that dumb country . . . I wanted to hold her hand, as one holds a child's hand, to take her across, to say "It's all right. I'm here. Don't be afraid." . . . And I did. And then she was gone. She was in the nothingness . . . Without me. Without *herself!* . . . Thus she made the transition from something-ness to nothingness . . . but what good was I? With all that love [longing] I couldn't stop the hours or the pain . . . I couldn't matter. No. Pain mattered more and it was, dear God, pain that rocked her out. Not me. For all my longing and my wanting, not me. And now she is a nothing. Except for me . . . for me she is a big something . . . a something I love and hate and still react and talk to. That is what keeps us alive. That living thing we leave behind. That['s] the flame. But that the body should be gone, a piece of furniture only , , , that dear body . . .

Oh anne.

Oh hell.

I feel awful. I tempered any suffering about "them" because I had "him" — good and bad and as doctory as he is . . . he was the first to believe in me . . . the first to care . . . the only . . . (it seems) and for him to leave is . . . is to leave myself. Do you know?

If I could run. If I could only. If I could put it out of mind . . .

Oh nevermind, Anne, what good will it do to talk about.

. . . Blah. Blah . . .

By the way, when I said, "what is death for you, something angry" I meant for *Me* (the you talk meant another voice asked it of me . . .) . . . but you and I are close enuf to mix up. Only in that little "drawing" it was a dialogue between me and me. Ya know?

For god's sake don't let Doc Martin mind his own store. He is about to leave it. I'll still be standing in it, looking around, wondering where in hell "this is" . . . Talk to me serious as much as you feel like it . . . it's half way like death . . . I need someone, aside from pain, to rock me out, away, alone. (Sorry this letter so sad. But it's real Sexton and thus, as always, real stuff . . . which means real LOVE

Anne Sexton to Anne Clarke

[40 Clearwater Road]
SUNDAY feb 9 1964

Dearly Anne,

A few words on a Sunday. One I note that my anxiety about us is quieter. I think it was the aftermath of worrying about the letter from you . . . I am much calmer today.

I'm writing to share a couple of ideas. Not to write about them but just to say them to you.

From Camus' notebooks . . . "an intellectual is someone whose mind watches itself. I like this because I am happy to be both halves."

And from something I read a few months ago and the source is forgotten . . . "the uncommitted life is not worth living."

. . . That's really all I have to say of any import.

My therapy is degenerating to SEX. Boy, there *are* some things that I do avoid, avoid, avoid! But we got to it by the back door, starting with the poem "Wanting to Die" [LD] . . . and the discussion of the sex of death. When (to me) death takes you and puts you thru the wringer, it's a man. But when you kill yourself it's a woman. And it goes on from there to his discovery that 1. I don't really think the dead are dead 2. that I certainly don't think I'll die even tho I'm dead 3. that suicides go to a special place . . . asleep for instance. 4. that suicide is a form of masturbation!!!

Well, my rationalization for today is that if "an intellecutal is some-one whose mind watches itself" the same could be said for masturbation or even better for suicide. Bow wow! How's that! I look at it this way (magically) that there are those that are killed and the few who kill and then the other kind, those that do both at once . . . I do think that killing people for any reason is perfectly terrible. I don't care what they did, even Hitler for instance. And I think that being killed is perfectly terri-ble, even dying softly in your sleep. But (I rationalize) when you take both things at once, then you have a certain power . . . power over what? Well, life for instance . . . and death too. I guess I see it as a way of cheating death. Doc Martin says (Christ I forgot what I was going to say??? INSTANT REPRESSION. For god's sake! Damn me. I was interested in what I was about to say . . . thinking . . . trying to remember . . . I KNOW). He sez it's a way of "staying alive" . . . and also (now I really remember!) a way of cheating pain. Killing yourself is merely a way to avoid pain despite all my interesting ideas about it.

It is a blue sky! A white snow. A yellow sun. Pretty nice out my window, rolling off into the distant pine trees . . . Sandy and Les are about to come over for a drink.

I shall now go out to new kitchen and prepare shrimp and cocktail sauce.

Anne Anne

Anne Sexton to Anne Clarke

[40 Clearwater Road]
thursday feb 27th, 1964

Anne!

[. . .] So, you're obsessional about stamps and stuff like that. I'm just a slob, myself . . . obsessional only when confronted with terror and then I make up little magical acts to save me . . . as how does one get on a J-bar lift when sking (that word!) (how spell it?) without being smashed on the rear, tumbledover, cracked on head, and left unconscious. How does one keep a plane in the air when everyone knows the engines could fail? How does a plane take off when everyone knows it is too heavy to be dragging up like a bird? how does one walk down the street and not look conspicuous and strange? how does one function at a party when you forget everyone's name and want to hide in a corner? how does one ask directions in a strange city and then remember them if one has dared ask? how does one keep a car in control when this one has known a steering wheel to break off in your hand, or the brakes to fail? how does one prevent shaking while speaking in public? how does one walk over a high bridge when it might break in two? how does one swim in rough surf without being pulled under and drowned by panic? how does one go to sleep without pills? how does one live with the knowledge that death, their special death, is waiting silently in their body to overtake them at some undetermined time? how can this be done if there is no God? how does one not get struck by lightning when everyone knows it could and just might strike YOU? or tornados that suck you right up into a cloud?

And of course I could go on. That's about all that I can think of that really terrify me and thus I try useless little obsessional ways of handling terror. I.e., on J-bar lifts I had about five things: let one go by empty, get skis in line, look a J-bar straight ON, have Kayo follow directly behind to pick me up or push me out of the way if I fall; hang on tight, etc. in airplane pray when it takes off; drink while in flight, in fact drink before taking off, hang on hard to person beside me as if their arm were trunk, good solid trunk, of grounded tree. . . . On street, go fast, look like you knew what you were doing, count the steps, watch your feet . . . at party, don't go or drink before going or look very pretty or only talk with your husband or drink more. With asking directions there is only one answer, take someone intelligent along with you. With car, forget it or drive faster or stop the car and talk to yourself . . . when not driving but riding, count the telephone poles . . . speaking in public, have a lectern, be quite drunk, be manic, be very well prepared. High bridge? run across it. Rough surf? almost drowned the last time I tried that. now stick to calm water . . . Sleep without pills? impossible. take pills! death? have fantasies of killing myself and thus being the powerful one not the powerless one. God? spend half time wooing R. Catholics who will pray *for* you in case it's true. Spend other half knowing there is certainly no God. Spend fantasy time thinking that there is a life after death, because surely my parents, for instance, are not dead, they are, good god!, just buried. Lightning? wear sneakers, stay off phone. Tornado? retire to cellar to look at washing machine and interesting junk in cellar.

How's that? Neurotic? You bet. I don't even know if it is obsessional, really. All, I know, very common fears anyhow. [. . .]

Love from me on this kind of sad sky-blue sun-struck snow day . . .

The Boston Groundhog
Anne

Anne Sexton to Anne Clarke

[14 Black Oak Road]
day after valentines.
65

Anne dear, your Jet plane letter today, full of your exhaustions of the literary life and your mentions of the yellow note I wrote that you carried with you to class.

I'm glad you liked my little note. It meant I love you.

It still does.

The music (Scott! [the Sextons' new stereo]) is playing strong. I was just lying on the ouch (couch) in my room looking out casually and I saw with shock the roof, snow lined, shining in the moonlight. When I saw that it hurt. I felt this awful pain. Does that make sense. A winter roof in the snow.??? There it was, beautiful and terrible. I thought I'd tell you.

It made me cry.

I don't dare walk outside where the sky must hurt even
extra with its full load of stars. The sky outside must ring.
I thought of sending you a valentine. I started and then I
never did. There are no valentines good enough, I said.

The winter has had little snow. Out here, where I live, there
are Black Oak trees but since so much new building has been
going on in this neighborhood there are no birds. When I
hear a bird at someone else's house I want to go out and
kiss its throat. There is a fireplace in my writing
room and lots of wood to burn. No view at all. No
water. The kitchen is very sunny and I sit at the
kitchen table often in the sun and muse. I haven't

written a poem since this summer, since M.G.H. . . . .
(have I been, unwittingly, lobotomized?)
Please miss us. You are always here,
in everyone's heart.
I'll return Hannah's letter when
I can put down her compliments.

Your valentine

John Cheever

.John Cheever's fictional portrayals of midcentury suburban America won him numerous accolades and earned him a prominent place in American letters before his death in 1982. His novels and short stories probed beneath the surface of middle-class life to explore its workings and expose its secrets. Cheever's insight into his neighbors' hidden lives corresponds to his own need to camouflage the gay feelings and experiences of which he was so ashamed. In his letters, however, Cheever did confide in friends, and his published correspondence includes one series of missives to an anonymous male lover.

John Cheever to ———

Cedar Lane
March 31st [1977]

Dear ———,

To scrutinize and examine my feelings for you is idle but there is nothing much else I can do with you in _____ All of my speculations may be no more than the thinking of a lecherous old man who hankers after the skin of someone younger but I will throw this out. Any dizzy analyst would declare that you are the ghost of my dead brother come back from the grave to solace the ghost of my long-gone youth. He would also declare that I am the spectre of your father, gotten richer and more literary. I think this shit. All I seem to know is that on that morning at ___ when we waited for ___, you seemed to lift from my shoulders, an aloneness that I was happy to lose. I can't imagine what your feeling was. My happiness continued through the plane trip and made Palo Alto seem charming. I wanted only that you be there; that if I woke in the night and asked for you I would hear your voice. That it may be my destiny to carry this aloness forever is a possibility and it is surely not your destiny, as a young man to carry my bags.

That is about it for this morning. The singular heat goes on and the botanicals, having no memory-bank, are all coming into bloom. We have all the flowers of spring. The old wander around, lamenting the fact that the hyacinths will soon be withered and buried in snow but they overlook the fact that the hyacinths are very resiliant. So are you and I.

Love,
John

John Cheever to ———

Cedar Lane,
May 12th

Dear ———,

Brooding, as I must, about homosexuality, I stepped out of the post-office yesterday morning and saw Them. This was in the parking-lot that serves the post-office, the super market, the cut-rate drugstore, liquor store and dry-cleaner. They arrived in a Mercedes 300, beautifully washed and polished. "You wash the car, Michael, I'll wash the sweaters." They were young & old, a very distinguished couple, distinguished in my eyes by their utter distaste for the merriment in the parking lot. They sneered at the old lady, looping towards the liquor store with her stolen four dollars, they sneered at the abandoned shopping carts, they sneered in fact at me. The old one was very skinny with a few strands of hair, dyed a marvelous yellow. The youth had all his hair and everything else, I guess, and he might have seemed quite beautiful if he didn't have a mouth like an asshole. The old one would be seen to walk as if his asshole were a mouth. In the back seat was an obligatory Mastaff, a massive, ornamental, brainless dog named after some international cocksucker. "He'll keep me company when I am abandoned by Michael," the old fairy will tell his guests. Having judged their environment to be loathsome they removed themselves from the Mercedez. Then they took from the back seat a large, beautifully wrapped box containing, I'll bet, a lamp base, thrown by the old one (a potter) on his favorite wheel to be mailed on consignment to a former Golden Gloves runner-up who had just opened an antique shop in Savannah Georgia. The message seemed to be that if you take it up the ass once too often you lose the blessedness of locomotion.

I'm delighted to think of you shuffling Falconer around and buying both Apples and a cook book. Apples did very well because (the publisher thought) people mistook it for a cook book. I'll go north tomorrow and spend much time on the telephone trying to straighten out the plane tickets. I have to deal with the embassy, Lufthansa, KLM and Sofia and in the end I'll fly Bulgar Wingski. I seem already to be somewhere between Yaddo, Sofia and Amsterdam and you. I'll write as soon as I get to Yaddo.

Much Love,
John

John Cheever to ——

Yaddo
February 9th

Dear ——,

I will call you tonight or tomorrow and ask you to return for the weekend and when you refuse, as I think you will, I will understand. This seems to be very much a part of my love for you. It all seems quite simple. Neither of us is homosexual and yet neither of us are foolish enough to worry about the matter. If I want your cock or your mouth I know I have only to ask and yet I know there is so much better for you in life than my love that I can think of parting from you without pain. This, of course drives my cock up the wall. It thinks you can hear it in ——. What I want is that which is courageous, intelligent and truthful for us both. One cannot work out a system of true and false in the space of one's life but I can find nothing false in my love for you. Of course it didn't matter that you didn't have an orgasim It wouldn't have mattered had you come seven times. It's terribly simple. I love you and I love to be near you.

It is late in the afternoon and I will go skiing before the light goes.

... Goodnight, my love, I would say if we were in bed together and —
lumped or unlumped — it would be for me a very good night.

Love,
John

John Cheever to ——

Wednesday

Dear ——,

I woke this morning with a hard wet cock and it's wet now after talking
with you but this isn't all of it; it's talking about the impossibility of
teaching and writing and happily eating a New York Steak at a place
called the firehouse where the lavish salad bar consists of iceberg heels
and pickled chickpeas and laughing and throwing snowballs and you
complaining about my tobacco cough and the size of my cock and you
driving back to —— with me in the back seat disguised as laundry. I
have thought for a year that such love must be perverse, cruel and inverted but I can find no trace of this in my love for you. It seems as
natural and easy as passing a football on a fine October day and if the
game bores you you can toss me the ball and walk off the grass and there
will be no forlorness. Both your short life and my long life have been, it
seems to me, singular adventures and to hold your nice ass in my hands
and feel your cock against mine seems to be a part of this astonishing
pilgrimage.

I want your soft balls, I want to take off your glasses, I want your ass,
your laughter and your loving mouth.

Love,
John

INDEX

Authorship of letters is indicated by page numbers in **boldface**.

ABOUT THE EDITOR

CONSTANCE JONES is the author of twelve books on a wide range of topics, from American history to sexual harassment. She has a degree from Yale University and has studied history at the doctoral level at City University of New York. A resident of New York City, she works as a book packager, editor and writer.

VAL CLARK is a poet, playwright and photographer. She lives intermittently in Washington, D.C., New York City and Amherst, Massachusetts, and is currently working on an anthology, *The Cafe-Goer's Literary Companion,* and a collection of short stories, *Extreme States of Emergency.*